Daytrips, Getaway Weekends, and Vacations in the Mid-Atlantic States

NEW YORK, NEW JERSEY, PENNSYLVANIA, DELAWARE, MARYLAND, WASHINGTON, D.C., AND VIRGINIA

"This book is chock full of suggestions. . . . Even if you travel vicariously from your armchair, there's fascinating information in this nicely written book."
—*Times Union,* Albany (NY)

"You don't have to travel far, spend a fortune, or take a lot of time. Patricia and Robert Foulke have just the thing to help you plan your getaway—**Daytrips, Getaway Weekends, and Vacations in the Mid-Atlantic States.**"
—*Glens Falls* (NY) *Post Star*

"Couples a melange of historical facts and anecdotes with eleven itineraries."
—*Mid-Atlantic Country*

"This easy-to-use guidebook gives the essential descriptions and simple directions while whetting your traveling appetite with poetic explanations of local history."
—J. Charles Lehmann, Director,
Maryland Office of Tourist Development

"If you're planning a vacation to the mid-Atlantic states this year, consider perusing eleven special itineraries suggested in this tempting new travel guide."
—Copley News Service

"Practical and easy to use. Many maps, photos, sketches, helpful marginal notes. Well worth it."
—*Travelwriter Marketletter*

D0182292

Daytrips,
Getaway Weekends,
and Vacations
in the Mid-Atlantic States

NEW YORK, NEW JERSEY, PENNSYLVANIA, DELAWARE, MARYLAND, WASHINGTON, D.C., AND VIRGINIA

Third Edition

by
Patricia & Robert Foulke

A Voyager Book

The Globe Pequot Press

Old Saybrook, Connecticut

For providing photographs used in this book, the publisher acknowledges the help of the state and local tourism boards, and specifically the New York State Department of Commerce, the Pennsylvania Bureau of Travel Development, the Gettysburg Travel Council, the Chester County (Pennsylvania) Tourist Bureau, the Pennsylvania Dutch Tourist Bureau, the Pocono Mountains Vacation Bureau, the Ocean City (Maryland) Department of Public Relations, the Virginia Division of Tourism, and the Washington Convention & Visitors Association, as well as Gordon Mahan and the Chesapeake Bay Maritime Museum.

"To Brooklyn Bridge" is reprinted from *The Complete Poems and Selected Letters and Prose of Hart Crane*, edited by Brom Weber, by permission of Liveright Publishing Corporation. Copyright © 1933, 1958, 1966 by Liveright Publishing Corporation.

Library of Congress Cataloging-in-Publication Data

Foulke, Patricia.
    Daytrips, getaway weekends, and vacations in the mid-Atlantic states : New York, New Jersey, Pennsylvania, Delaware, Maryland, Washington, D.C., and Virginia / by Patricia & Robert Foulke. — 3rd ed.
    p. cm.
    "A Voyager book."
  Includes index.
    ISBN 1-56440-144-8
    1. Middle-Atlantic States—Tours. 2. Family recreation—Middle Atlantic States—Guidebooks. I. Foulke, Robert, 1930-
II. Title.
F168.F68 1993
917.404'43—dc20   92-34320
                                         CIP

Manufactured in the United States of America
Third Edition/First Printing

About the Authors

Patricia and Robert Foulke have traveled together for thirty-nine years, including four fellowship and sabbatical years in Europe, a three-month voyage in the Mediterranean, and numerous trips in the United States to research articles and update their guidebooks. They have written books on New England, the Middle Atlantic states, and Europe within the last fifteen years. Their travel articles have appeared in the *Rotarian,* the *Christian Science Monitor,* the *Hartford Courant, Oceans Magazine, Greek Accent,* the *Detroit Free Press Magazine,* the *San Francisco Examiner,* the *Boston Globe, St. Petersburg Times, Off Duty Magazine, British Heritage,* the *Boston Herald, SAIL, Walking Magazine, International Living,* the *Glens Falls Post Star, Hawaii Magazine, Camping & Walking,* and *Vista, USA.*

Robert completed his undergraduate work at Princeton University and received a Ph.D. from the University of Minnesota. He is a professor emeritus of English at Skidmore College in Saratoga Springs, New York. Patricia earned her master's degree at Trinity College in Hartford, Connecticut, and taught elementary school, remedial reading, and special education classes until her retirement. The Foulkes live in Lake George, New York.

Contents

The information listed in this guidebook was confirmed at press time. We recommend, however, that you call establishments before traveling to obtain current information.

An additional note: All selections of lodgings and restaurants have been made by the author. *No one can pay or be paid to be included in this book.*

Introduction

We hope that this book will arouse your historical imagination, inspire you to explore a variety of interesting places, and provide you with details about what to see and do at the sites you choose to visit. Some people want to hit only the highlights; others prefer to poke around in places off the beaten track. In either case, once you are on your way, you will want to strike a nice balance between knowing what you are looking for and having the fun of discovering something unknown to most travelers. This book provides much of what you need to know, and the people you meet and circumstances of the day will often lead to the most surprising and memorable finds.

Travelers notoriously display the urge to collect things on trips. We would like to suggest a different kind of collection—not things, but the sights and sounds of places or man-made objects. How many rushing waterfalls can you find in the western part of New York state? How many lighthouses can you spot along the Hudson River? Look at the different kinds of construction of the bridges all around Manhattan, from the pioneering Brooklyn to the soaring Verrazano. Pennsylvania is famous for covered bridges; how do they vary from the Pennsylvania Dutch country to the Bucks County region? How many atria can you visit in New York City? How do the barns in Maryland differ from those in Pennsylvania? Make a study of the beaches along the Maryland, Delaware, and New Jersey coasts. Let your imagination refine your observation and put some focus into your travel.

This book suggests a variety of activities while you travel. If you have a strong interest in history, we have tried to provide just the right amount of information, letting you know what to look for when you are at a historic site. We have interviewed people with expertise in the museums and houses listed in each itinerary, and they have often given us more information than we can use in a book of this size. We try to include enough of it to whet your appetite and give you background for your visit.

For those of you who want to build a trip around doing more than seeing, we have suggested recreational areas that can provide both exercise and fun during your trip. This six-state region provides almost any setting that one could wish for active sports—mountain, lake, river, seashore—and each has its own character and ambience. In New York alone, for example, you can surf on the ocean beaches of Long Island; hike or ski in the Catskills or the high peaks of the Adirondacks; ramble through estate gardens in the mid-Hudson or run white water on the upper Hudson; cycle along the shores of the Finger Lakes or the towpaths of the old Erie Canal; or fish, swim, water-ski, and sail almost everywhere, from Peconic Bay at the tip of Long Island to the shores of Lake Erie.

TRIP PLANNING

Within a city or region, we have tried to cluster or group sites of interest so that you will know what is available nearby. We don't like to drive or walk back and forth randomly looking for something and know you won't want to either. Whenever possible we have also suggested, for your convenience, a pleasant place for lunch or dinner in the area.

Our planned itineraries will save you the time and trouble of gathering information and deciding on a route. You can choose to travel all of any itinerary, or part of one, or combine parts of several. We have moved around the mid-Atlantic states in a way that makes geographic sense, so you can connect easily from one itinerary to another. Some of the longer itineraries are not meant to be traveled in one chunk of time—unless you have a lot of it or are visiting from another part of the country or world. For example, from New York City you might choose to travel to the end of Long Island at one time and explore the Hudson River Valley and Catskills on another trip. From Philadelphia you may want to head west toward the Pennsylvania Dutch region or north to the Delaware Water Gap and the Poconos, or, nearer home, into Bucks County or the Brandywine Valley for day or weekend trips. The map accompanying each itinerary shows the route from place to place so that you can quickly visualize the possibilities.

Each itinerary contains sightseeing tips and

a good bit of detail about places of special interest. The description is not meant to be comprehensive but represents a selection of the highlights of each site, plus some little-noticed details that may give you the feel of the place. At times our enthusiasm runs away with us and we write a great deal; perhaps you will feel as inspired as we were.

A: New York City, Long Island, and the Hudson River Valley. The old cliché is right: Even if you might not want to live there, the Big Apple is fun to visit. Long Island is a microcosm containing great variety for you to enjoy, including those gorgeous beaches. The Hudson River Valley, caught between mountain ranges, has castles on the cliffs and legends galore.

B: Upstate New York. From Saratoga Springs with its horse racing and summer ballet or symphony to the Adirondacks—cool, green, with pure water and the peace of stream, lake, and mountain—you can have it all on a single circuit. The Thousand Islands have the special charm of diamond fragments filling a massive river from shore to shore, and the Mohawk Valley has rolling hills and villages with "Leatherstocking" charm.

C: Western and Central New York. Cities such as Syracuse, Rochester, and Buffalo are being revitalized and have much of historic interest to recommend them. The Finger Lakes, lined with vineyards and stretching into rolling hills, also have strong connections with American cultural and political history. Chautauqua has a special ambience that gets into your blood, and it represents a unique development in nineteenth-century thought. Niagara Falls is not only for honeymooners—the escarpment has geologic and practical dimensions that must be seen to be appreciated.

ITINERARIES

D: Northern Pennsylvania. Erie and Presque Isle have both the lure of lake recreation and a history ranging from the War of 1812 through rum-running during Prohibition. This itinerary continues across the northern section of Pennsylvania from Erie to Kinzau Dam, Coudersport, the Grand Canyon, Williamsport, and Lewisburg.

E: Western Pennsylvannia. Pittsburgh is no longer a smoky city but a beautiful one—go and see for yourself! After seeing Pittsburgh you can visit Fort Necessity, Ohiopyle, Fort Ligonier, Bushy Run Battlefield, Johnstown, and Huntingdon.

F: South-Central Pennsylvania. The Revolutionary and Civil wars ravaged much of this beautiful rolling area, but you can relive the events without the misery. Pennsylvania Dutch country lures visitors with its special foods and living history of one of the country's most interesting religious groups. The Brandywine Valley developed one of the first industries in the country and provided the setting for flourishing architecture, gardening, and art.

G: Eastern Pennsylvania. The streets and buildings of Philadelphia are a living museum of our independence, and they offer the visitor a full range of cultural opportunities. Bucks County, with its horses, inns, and canal, provides rural peace within easy reach of the city. The Delaware Water Gap and the Poconos go hand in hand, joining the natural beauty of mountain and river and furnishing the visitor with a full range of recreational opportunities.

H: Delaware. The shore has impeccable beaches and interesting remnants of nineteenth-century Americana, as well as all forms of water sports. The coast has tales of shipwrecks to tell, as well as nature preserves; and inland areas have fine colonial homes for you to visit.

I: New Jersey. This diverse state is not all megalopolis. The Pine Barrens, beaches, and harbors are treasures waiting to be discovered. Princeton is a college town, full of charm.

J: Maryland. Although small in size, this state is rich in contrasts between cities and almost untouched rural areas, and it surrounds a bay with two distinctive shores and a maritime life all its own.

K: Washington, D.C. Our nation's capital is one of the world's most carefully planned cities and contains a wealth of art and culture in addition to its public monuments and government buildings.

We have added two historic sites in Virginia—Mount Vernon and Williamsburg. Both fit in with Washington and the development of our country, and both are within easy reach of the city.

THE ARMCHAIR TRAVELER

As we traveled for this book, we became increasingly excited by the rare opportunity we have—to learn more about the rich historical heritage of these states and then have the fun of writing about it. As children we were taught a smattering of historical background about this part of the country, but now, with the chance to visit places and delve into details of local history by our own choice, we find the research for this book continually fascinating. Whether you will be taking a trip or traveling vicariously from your armchair, we hope to intrigue you with historical tales of real people who lived long ago.

ACCOMMODATIONS

For the past thirty-nine years, we have traveled in many parts of the United States and have lived in Europe while on sabbatical leave from teaching. In our younger years we camped most of the time in Europe, stayed in bed-and-breakfast establishments, and enjoyed occasional splurges, such as a castle in France with our children one New Year's Eve. We were able to stretch our budget and build up memories at the same time.

Now that B&Bs have become popular in this country, inexpensive accommodations can be combined with the pleasure of meeting people who live where you want to travel. B&B hosts are notable for offering specific local knowledge that you would never hear about in any other way. Inns, with their appealing dining, decorating and warm hospitality, offer another dimension for travelers. Some travelers "collect" inns, spurred on by yet another one to investigate, and most look forward to a chance to splurge on a special one now and then. Check our appendix for the inn and B&B list. We offer a selection along the itineraries; this list does not pretend to be comprehensive for each region but simply ones we have enjoyed.

INFORMATION

Your local library is a good source of books as you begin to plan a trip. Later you may want to buy some of them to take along on your trip. State tourism offices offer maps, information about historic sites, lists of accommodations and restaurants, and sightseeing suggestions. It's a good idea to write before you go.

Delaware: Delaware State Travel Service, 99 Kings Highway, P.O. Box 1401, Dover 19903. Phone: 800–282–8667 in Delaware or 800–441–8846 outside of Delaware.

Maryland: Maryland Tourism, Redwood Tower, 217 East Redwood Street, Baltimore 21202. Phone: 410–333–6611.

New Jersey: Division of Travel and Tourism, One West State Street, CN 826, Trenton 08625. Phone: 800–JERSEY–7.

New York: New York Department of Commerce, Division of Tourism, One Commerce Plaza, Albany 12245. Phone: 800–CALL–NYS.

Pennsylvania: Bureau of Travel Development, Department of Commerce, 416 Forum Building, Harrisburg 17120. Phone: 800–847–4872.

Virginia: Virginia Department of Economic Development, Division of Tourism, 1021 East Cary Street, Tower II, Richmond 23219. Phone: 804–786–2051.

Washington, D.C.: Washington, D.C., Convention and Visitors Association, 1212 New York Avenue, N.W., Washington, D.C. 20005. Phone: 800–368–9000.

If you would like information on a specific city or town, write: Name of city, Convention and Visitors Bureau or Chamber of Commerce, City, State, ZIP code.

BEFORE YOU GO

When you have considered where you want to go, weather and road conditions, crowds in high season, ferry schedules (if applicable), and any other contingencies, you're ready to get organized. We find it useful to make a list of the areas we want to cover, the activities we would like to enjoy, and possible side trips. A destination for each night with estimated mileage and driving time is the next step. Addresses and phone numbers we'll need along the route are added to the list. Then we put lists, brochures, travel articles, books, and other information we've collected into a large envelope for easy reference along the way.

FOOD

You will want to try the local cuisine as you travel. Be alert to special foods that are featured locally. Is there an unusual restaurant you've heard wonderful things about? It doesn't hurt to write or phone ahead for a reservation. (We have listed phone numbers for each of our suggestions.) Or, once you get into town, ask a native for a good place to eat. If you want to try regional foods and sample some terrific home cooking, look in the local papers or on bulletin boards around town for notices of church, grange, or special-event suppers. Craft fairs and bazaars often sell homemade baked goods as well.

ACTIVITIES

Enjoy! Remember that you are not working and not following a rigid schedule. Let the ages and interests of your family set the focus on your trip. Leave some time free for relaxation (defined as time to do nothing) and flexibility (the freedom to change your mind according to weather and mood).

When our children were little, we chose activities to appeal to their interests and levels of understanding. We visited zoos, country fairs, beaches, whaling museums, aquariums, restored villages, dinosaur traces, amusement parks, and planetariums; we took train rides and steamboat trips; we saw theater and puppet shows, baseball games and historical reenactments; and we canoed and sailed and swam and rowed. Whenever we could we prepared them for an activity—showing them pictures and talking about the historic sites we intended to visit. They especially loved hearing stories about the children who once lived in these old houses.

We let them guide us through museums, picking out displays that intrigued them, rather than stopping them (shifting from one foot to the other) in front of every exhibit. Then we would head for the museum shop and select postcards for our collections.

Children love nature trails with buttons to push and signs to read. They also love hikes, especially when they're well supplied with goodies for energy. Ours carried hard candies, raisins, fruit, gorp, and a jacket in a child-size rucksack and as we went along, we'd decorate the rucksack with souvenir patches from places we visited.

Whether you're traveling alone or with family, try something new on each trip. For starters, think about lake or white-water canoeing, kayaking, saltwater fishing, soaring, snorkeling, downhill or cross-country skiing, snowshoeing, or something else that appeals to you.

Most of us have a strong impulse to return with some booty from our adventures. You may want to collect postcards, decals, demitasse spoons, T-shirts, local books, cookbooks, state emblems, shells, rocks, or things for a special hobby.

We've added something new to this book as we did on the last edition of our *Daytrips, Getaway Weekends, and Vacations in New England*. Combining business with pleasure, we skied a number of ski areas and wrote for those of us who fall into the intermediate range a first run plus a day's worth of reasonable slopes for intermediates. This personal exploration on our part sets you off with confidence. After all, experts know where the black diamonds are, and beginners will want to try slopes groomed for them.

ACKNOWLEDGMENTS

We wish to thank those who have contributed expertise, time, enthusiasm, and encouragement to enhance this book:

Anne Ackerson, Janet Adams, Hollie Ainbinder, Jo Alexanderson, Linda and Rik Alexanderson, Linus Amorsingh, Andrew Anspach, Steven Apesos, Jackie Arvintinos, Ann Aubertine, Robin Austin, Vicki Aversa, Sue Bain, Irene Baker, Susan Barber, Ann and William Barclay, Lynn Barger, H. Grey Barr, Joe Barrick, Mary Lou Bartolotto-Connolly, Bruce Barton,

Michael Bassett, Jopie Been, Marilyn Behan, Sandy Belan, Louise Bem, Scott Bender, Eliza Benington, Betty and Stuart Berelson, Layne Bergin, Jo Betz, Bunny and Bill Bitner, Robert Black, Edward Bleecker, Betty Jean Bolton, Vicki and Vance Booker, Betsy Boyd, Lee Boyle, Dana Brancato, Susan Breen, Gretchen Broderick, Michael Broderick, Deborah Brown, Mary Ann Bungery, Brent Burkhardt, Paul Butchness, Donna Carlson, Pam Carter, Roger Cawley, Beulah Chabal, Errin Cecil, Robert Chandler, Lori Chrismer, Stan Clark, Gail Cleveland, Susan Cohen, Pamela Collins, Lucinda Costin, Andi Coyle, Bud Cramer, Jean-Marie and Denton Crocker, John Crowley, Marion Cushing, Virginia Daring, Thomas Darro, Michael Davidson, Barbara Davis, Linda Davis, Phyllis and Harvey Dearstyne, Vivian Degani, Justine Delaney, Louis DePalma, Joanne DeVoe, Maria DiBattista, Eugene Dilbeck, Philip DiOrio, Vince Diorio, Patricia Dolan, Nancy Doutt, Beth Dowling, Ellie and Bernie Dronenberg, Marge Dunham, Dale Dunshie, Mary Ann Dwyer, Sylvia Ebeling, Marion and Bill Eberhardt, Carolyn Eckert, Sylvia Eisenhart, Nan Eliot, Robert Ervien, Cindy Estes, Susan Everett, Louis Faccola, Donald Fangboner, Lisa Feinstein, Victoria Feldman, Robert Fenneger, George Finckenor, Ola and Robert Flick, Ann Flynn, Jan Foley, Renee Frank, Stuart Frank, John Frazier, Eileen Frear, Claude Frelke, Elaine Frieder, Myra and Stephen Fuguet, Gerald Gallagher, William Gallagher, Peggie Gaul, Sharon Gibbons, Thomas Giffen, Barbara Gilbert, Alice Gilbourn, Ann Gill, Nancy Gold, Kathy Golden, Susan and Robert Gorton, Judge and Mrs. John Gray, Bernard Groff, Betty Groff, Norma Groverman, William Guilfoile, Debbe Hagen, Wilma and James Hall, Al Halstrunk, Lucinda Hampton, Dot Harrington, Faire Hart, Susan Haswell, Ruth and William Heidgerd, Donald Heilemann, Sandra Henne, Karen

Hensel, Doris Herwig, Elizabeth Hibbard, Deborah Hickok, Helen Hoffmann, Elsie and Donald Hogan, Robert Holiday, Rosemary Holl, Mark Hoy, Adele Hudson, Carol Hudson, Evan Hume, Dorothy and William Huus, Barbara Ianuzi, Ken Jefferis, Dana Johnson, Maria Johnson, Marilyn Jones, Walter Jones, Diana Kaiser, John Kam, Marilyn Kane, Francis Kelly, John Kidd, Sandy Kleintop, Ruth Knoblock, Patricia Kohlhepp, John Kraft, Melanie Kuebel, Tom Kugle, Mark Kulkowitz, Corinne LaBoon, Charles LaForge, Lucinda Laird, Melanie Landis, Peggy Langrall, Barbara and Harold Lawson, Susan Lazarus, Jerry Ledges, Charles Lehman, Patricia Leiphart, Jean Louise LePage, Carol and Neil Levitt, George Lewis, Deborah Libster, Polly and Chuck Longsworth, Jean Lloyd, Mary Kay and Ron Logan, Robin Lynch, John MacBean, Juanita MacCarl, Kathleen Madden, Philip Magaldi, Betsy Magley, Mary Malloy, Debbie Maltrotti, Frank Mares, Sandie Marriner, Patrick Marsh, Mary Jane Martin, Doris Mashewski, Francine Mason, Betty Maxcy, Peggy McCabe, Vivian McCarty, Mary and Alan McGill, Donna McCole, Donald McHenry, Jill McKenzie, Gwen McLeod, James Mead, Michelle Micka, Stanley Mickus, Diane Miller-Hatcher, Patrick Milliman, Randy Mintz, Teresa Mitchell, Jan and Paul Morrill, Linda Morlacci, Betsy Morrow, Kay Morrow, Mary Mulcahy, Dorothy Mullen, Nicole Muller, Alice Mund, Thomas Murphy, Adrianna Naizby, Sharon Neratko, Lynn Neuman, Frankie Nevins, Doris Nicholson, Marilyn Oberg, Patricia and Robert Ochsner, Robert O'Connor, Robert Odenheimer, Karolyn O'Keefe, Cheryl Orlick, Melanie Ortel, Deborah Padgett, Karen Pailler, Kim Pheobus, Dan Porter, Carolyn Powell, Audrey and Robert Pratt, Jon Ramsey, Brian Rasmus, Patricia Redmond, Richard Renaud, Jean Richards, George Richardson, Kitty Ricotta, Bill Risse, Jane and Sally Rodman, H. Merrill

Roenke, Sam Rogers, Nancy Rooney, Sherry and Charles Roseman, Melissa Rosenberry, Bern Rotman, Margie Rumsey, Dawn Rusko, John Russell, Robert Rust, Leigh Sands, August Schiava, William Schickel, Marilyn Schoenherr, Roderick Seabrook, Ruth Seegrist, Susan Seifried, Frances Severn, Millie Seward, James Shaw, Michael Shaw, Barbara Shedd, Kathleen Sheehan, Arnold Sheer, Kitty Shriver, Cheryl Slavinsky, Ed Smalling, Arline Smith, James Smith, Shirley Smith, Marjorie Smuts, Peggy and Ray Spencer, Susan Spinzia, Chris Stamp, Karen Stanford, Florence Stedman, Eileen and Elwood Stitzel, Nancy Stone, Frederick Stynyer, Mary Summers, Charles Swain, George Taylor, Sharon and Greg Taylor, Stephanie and George Templeton, Harrison Terk, David Thomas, Joanne Thompson, Thomas Thompson, Eileen Thornton, Susan Trien, Michael Turback, Kitty Turgeon, Lorraine Turner, Lynn Tyson, Alice Urband, John Vanco, Carol and Peter Van Dyck, Ken Volk, Jane Wait, Herbert Ward, Ann Weidman, Shelly Weinraub, Catherine Wheeler, Edward Wheeler, Charlotte Whitcomb, Lenore and Buddy Whitcomb, Peter Wiles, Larry Williams, Thelma Williams, Shirley Wisenburg, Russell Wolf, Diane Wolfe, Kathleen Wolkowicz, Becky Woods, Karen Woods, Sheryl Woods, Anne Woodward, Clem and Robert Young, Ronald Young, Arline Zatz, Robert Zimmer, Michael Zuckerman, and John Zwierzyna.

ITINERARY A:

New York City, Long Island, and the Hudson River Valley

ROCKEFELLER CENTER

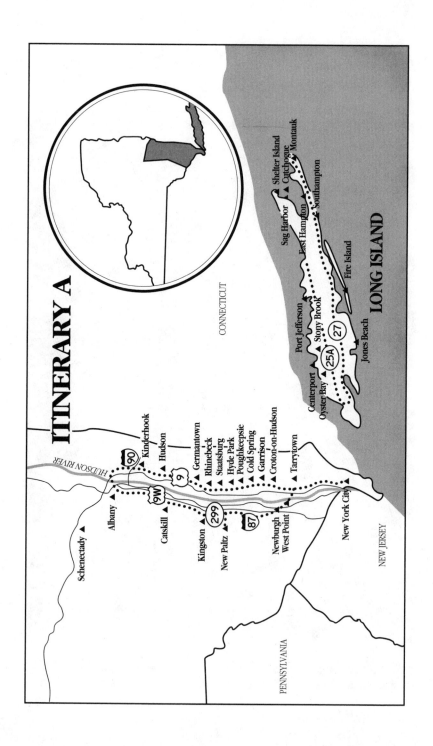

New York City, Long Island, and the Hudson River Valley

*This itinerary can begin in the New York City area, or it can contin-
ue from Itineraries B, G, or H. Like all of the itineraries, it can also be
traveled in reverse.*

⇝ *New York City* ⇝

New York, a city of eight million people that overwhelms visitors
who often don't know where to begin, contains 303 square miles, 578
miles of waterfront, 6,400 miles of streets, 3,500 churches and synagogues,
100 skyscrapers, 65 bridges, 230 miles of subway lines, 999 miles of bus
routes, 25,000 restaurants, 150 museums, 400 art galleries, 90 institutions of
higher learning, and much, much more. The sheer magnitude of the statis-
tics is staggering in itself, and visitors often find that the noise of honking
horns and squealing brakes, the motion of cars and taxis speeding along
the streets, and the confusion of dodging so many people while walking
further add to their uncertainty. The trick is to become oriented to the various sections of the city and then select a manageable area to enjoy, perhaps on a walking tour. If you want to preplan your visit, free information
will be sent to you from the **New York Convention and Visitors Bureau**
(Two Columbus Circle, New York, New York 10019; 212–397–8222). You
can also call the New York Sate tourist office in Albany for New York City
information (800–CALL–NYS) or the New York City office (212–827–6255).

For an overview of the city, visitors can choose from among a bus
tour, helicopter ride, cruise ship, and a skyscraper observation deck. We
tend to climb the tallest tower for a bird's-eye view of a strange city when
traveling in Europe, but in New York the sea of other buildings viewed
from above may be fascinating to the eye but hardly helpful for orienting
yourself. For arranging an initial tour, useful addresses include **Circle Line
Statue of Liberty Ferry** (Battery Park, South Ferry, New York, New York
10004; 212–269–5755); **Circle Line Sightseeing Yachts, Inc.** (Pier 83, foot
of West 42nd Street, New York, New York 10036; (212–563–3200); **Gray
Line of New York** (254 West 54th Street, New York, New York 10019;
212–397–2620); **Island Helicopter** (East 34th Street at East River, New
York, New York 10016; 212–683–4575); and **World Yacht Enterprises**
(Pier 62, foot of West 23rd Street and Hudson River, New York, New York
10019; 212–929–8540).

We managed an overview of the city by land, sea, and air. The helicopter trip swung around the Statue of Liberty, ran along the riverfront,
and hovered above the peaks and pinnacles of skyscrapers. The experi-

ence is both breathtaking and suggestive of the power that many see in the irregular pattern of buildings thrusting upward. For those who want to stay closer to the ground, bus tours are available in several sections of the city; the guide's narration will give you lots of anecdotes about the sites you are passing. Cruising by ferry or ship gives yet another dimension to your orientation. We took World Yacht's dinner cruise, where we went gliding by the lights of towering buildings and under the span of the Brooklyn Bridge.

Interested in collecting? As you tour New York, you will find a variety of sites pertaining to almost any special interest. If you like bridges, you can see one after another ringing the island and linking the boroughs, each with a tale or two to tell. In recent years hotels and corporate buildings have upgraded their interior space by the use of atria—peaceful havens of greenery, splashing water, and courtyards removed from outer confusion and noise; see how many you can "collect." Some atria are ringed with restaurants, galleries, and shops. Our favorites include **Trump Tower,** 56th Street at 5th Avenue, with an 80-foot waterfall; **IBM Atrium,** 56th Street at Madison Avenue, with tall bamboo trees; **Crystal Pavilion,** 50th Street at Third Avenue, with two water walls; **Citicorp Center,** 53rd Street between Third and Lexington avenues, under a slant-roofed silver tower; **Whitney Museum** in the Philip Morris Building, 42nd Street at Park Avenue, with lots of sculpture in a garden setting; **Park Avenue Plaza,** 52nd to 53rd Street off Park Avenue, with a waterfall; **Equitable Center,** 52nd to 51st Street at Seventh Avenue, with American art from the Whitney Museum; and **AT&T,** Madison Avenue between 55th and 56th streets, which includes the new InfoQuest Center on technology information. Parks, churches, museums, galleries, and theaters are found all over New York. A historical theme can be traced through the many sites that have been restored. More than forty islands lie within the New York City boundaries, bearing names like City Island, Roosevelt Island, Broad Channel Island, Governors Island, Staten Island, Ellis Island, Rat Island, The Raunt, Shooter's Island, Cuban Ledge, and Liberty Island. They make a fine addition to anyone's collection of interesting islands in the world.

MANHATTAN

Manhattan, named by the Algonquin Indians, "island of the hills," is the smallest of the five boroughs of New York City. It is 13.4 miles long and 2.3 miles across at the widest point. Moving from north to south with map in hand, you can visit the Upper East Side and Upper West Side, which bracket Central Park from 110th Street to 59th Street; Midtown, the Theater District, and the Garment District from 59th Street to 34th Street; what we call the Neighborhoods, an area of five neighborhoods from 34th Street to Houston Street; and Lower Manhattan. We will group sights within each of these areas for your convenience. Our selections are not meant to be comprehensive; it would take a lifetime to see them all.

CENTRAL PARK

Central Park contains 840 acres from 110th Street to 59th Street devoted to landscaped recreational areas designed by Frederick Law Olmsted and Calvert Vaux. Ponds, lakes, woods, and flowers fill this area in the middle of the largest city in the United States. At the northern end is **The Ramble** with its twisted, hidden paths leading up to **Belvedere Castle,** designed in 1867 by Calvert Vaux. The name Belvedere was derived from "bellevedere," or "beautiful view," which is available from the Gothic tower. The U.S. Weather Bureau moved into the building in 1919, and in 1930 an automatic weather recording system was installed. Restoration of the building took place in the 1970s, and now, as the Central Park Learning Center, the place provides educational programs for children and for the public.

Belvedere Castle
Central Park West &
 79th Street
New York 10024
212–772–0210

The geologic history of **Vista Rock,** with Belvedere Castle perched on the summit, stretches back 450 million years. Black mud lay on the floor of an ancient ocean, built up layer upon layer of sediment, and then was squeezed, heated, and crystallized as Africa and North America moved closer together. Mountains formed, eroded, and crowded up again and again. The two continents split apart, and the Atlantic Ocean rose to submerge the entire eastern part of the United States. During the Ice Age Vista Rock was covered with 1,000 feet of ice. As the glacier moved, boulders scraped and striated the rock; look at the twisted layers of this schist rock to see the record of its erosion.

The Lake contains an iron bridge with a graceful curve that makes a fine photographic frame; boats may be rented at the east end of it. To the north are the **New Lake, Shakespeare Garden,** and **Delacorte Theater,** which presents free "Shakespeare in the Park" performances during the summer. The Metropolitan Museum of Art is just beyond the New Lake. **The Mall** juts through the middle of the park and is lined with two rows of busts of famous persons, leading to a bandshell at one end. The southern part of the park contains playing fields and **The Central Park Zoo. Tavern on the Green,** on Central Park West (212–873–3200), has Baccarat chandeliers and provides a glassed-in view of the park during lunch or dinner.

Sadly, the pleasures of this beautiful park are no longer free of peril. The general caution given to visitors is simple: Never enter the park at night; some people feel that its more remote sections are not fully safe at any time. On the other hand, many New Yorkers continue to use and enjoy their magnificent park, and you will probably want to join them during daylight hours.

UPPER EAST SIDE

Museum Mile is the name given to an extraordinary string of major museums along Fifth Avenue from 103rd Street down to 53rd Street. If you find museums compelling, this mile can be the centerpiece of your visit to the city. We will list them from north to south.

The **Museum of the City of New York** traces the history of the city from its days as a Dutch trading post to the present. Exhibits include models of the *Half Moon* and *Dauphine,* a scale model of Nieuw Amsterdam in 1660, a collection of silver, a ship's figurehead of Andrew Jackson from the USS *Constitution,* life-size rooms of a Dutch nine-

Museum of the City of New York
Fifth Avenue & 103rd Street
New York 10029
212–534–1672

**Cooper-Hewitt
Museum
2 East 91st Street
New York 10128
212–860–6868**

**Solomon R.
Guggenheim
Museum
Fifth Avenue & 89th
Street
New York 10128
212–360–3500**

**Metropolitan Museum
of Art
Fifth Avenue & 82nd
Street
New York 10028
212–535–7710**

teenth-century home, nineteenth- and twentieth-century dollhouses, and the bedroom and dressing room from the house of John D. Rockefeller. The **Conservatory Garden** is across the street, in Central Park.

The **Cooper-Hewitt Museum,** the Smithsonian Institution's National Museum of Design, is in the renovated Andrew Carnegie mansion. The museum functions as a design reference center—a working museum with changing exhibits. The collection includes original drawings dating back to the fifteenth century; embroidered, woven and printed fabrics; silver, bronze, and metal pieces; and jewelry, wallpaper, porcelain, furniture, and clocks.

The **Solomon R. Guggenheim Museum** is housed in a building that Frank Lloyd Wright designed in 1943. This cream-colored concrete building looks like a corkscrew. Inside, the spiral ramp ascends for a quarter mile up to a 92-foot-high glass dome. We suggest you take the elevator to the top and then proceed down on foot. The collection includes paintings by Chagall, Picasso, Mondrian, Klee, Pissarro, Renoir, Monet, Cézanne, Van Gogh, Gauguin, Toulouse-Lautrec, and Degas. The museum was renovated in early 1992.

The Metropolitan Museum of Art contains collections dating from prehistory to the present. You will need a map in this immense structure that, with its wings, covers over thirty-two acres. Only one-fourth of the total collection is on display at a single time, and the volume is mind-boggling. Its departments include American, Ancient, Medieval, European Sculpture and Decorative Arts, European Paintings and Sculpture, Primitive Art, the Lehman Pavilion, Arms and Armor, Musical Instruments, Islamic, Far Eastern, Costume, Drawings, Prints and Photographs, and the Uris Center for Education.

The **Whitney Museum of American Art** owns the largest collection of American art in the country. Begun in the Greenwich Village studio of sculptress Gertrude Vanderbilt Whitney, the museum was founded in 1930. A sunken sculpture court in the center is the focal point for three cantilevered gallery floors. The collection includes works by Benton, Bellows, Prendergast, Hopper, Sloan, Calder, Nevelson, O'Keeffe, Rauschenberg, Reinhardt, and David Smith.

**Whitney Museum of American Art
Madison Avenue & 75th Street
New York 10021
212-570-3676**

The **Frick Collection** comprises works by European artists from the fourteenth through nineteenth centuries. The house was designed in 1913 for Henry Clay Frick and contains his personal furnishings and art collection. After his death his wife lived there until she died in 1935, when the house became a museum. The collection includes works by Boucher, Hogarth, Romney, Reynolds, Gainsborough, Fragonard, Vermeer, Bellini, Titian, and El Greco.

**Frick Collection
Fifth Avenue & 70th Street
New York 10021
212-288-0700**

The **American Museum of Natural History** is one of the largest natural history museums in the world. Among the more than thirty-four million species and substances exhibited are dinosaurs, elephants, a blue whale, minerals and gems, reptiles, primates, and birds. Other displays portray Eskimos, Indians, Africans, Mexicans, and Central Americans. The museum has a rare books section, and free lectures, concerts, films, and plays are offered during the year.

UPPER WEST SIDE

**American Museum of Natural History
Central Park West & 79th Street
New York 10024
212-769-5000**

The **Hayden Planetarium**, which is part of the Museum of Natural History, offers a sky show, the Guggenheim Space Theater, and the Hall of the Sun. Adjoining galleries contain exhibits on astronomy.

**Hayden Planetarium
Central Park West & 81st Street
New York 10024
212-769-5900**

The New York Historical Society is both a museum and a library. The collection contains decorative arts, watercolors by John James

The New York Historical Society
Central Park West & 77th Street
New York 10024
212-873-3400

Lincoln Center
Broadway & 65th Street
New York 10023
212-875-5000

MIDTOWN
Carnegie Hall
Seventh Avenue & 57th Street
New York 10019
212-903-9600

Museum of Modern Art
11 West 53rd Street
New York 10019
212-708-9480

Audubon, folk art, toys from the eighteenth century, furniture, and paintings by Stuart, West, Peale, Durand, Cole, and Church.

Lincoln Center was constructed between 1962 and 1968 to promote music, theater, and dance. The complex can seat 13,747 persons at one time. It consists of the Avery Fisher Hall, the New York State Theater, the Metropolitan Opera House, the Library and Museum of the Performing Arts, the Vivian Beaumont Theater, and the Juilliard School of Music. Tours of Lincoln Center are offered daily. Free concerts are given outside during the summer.

Carnegie Hall seats 2,804 persons in a building with perfect acoustics. Dating from 1891, with Tchaikovsky conducting at the first performance, this building has witnessed concerts by the finest musicians in the world. Faced with possible destruction, the building was saved by Isaac Stern and a group of New York patrons. The **Weill Recital Hall** (212–903–9600), seating 297 persons, features performances by contemporary music ensembles.

The **Museum of Modern Art,** although founded during an inauspicious time just after the stock market crash in 1929, has amassed a major collection devoted to the twentieth century. Disciplines include painting, sculpture, architecture, film, prints and illustrated books, photography, and drawings. The museum has been in its present location since 1939, and considerable expansion took place during the early 1980s. The expansion has doubled the space of the collection and provided an intriguing new structure with glass domes on a series of levels. Visitors can stop for a meal at the Garden Cafe and look out at the Sculpture Garden. Among the famous paintings hanging in the Museum are *Water Lilies* by Claude Monet, *The Bather* by Paul Cézanne, *Monument to Balzac* by Auguste

Rodin, *Dance* and *Memory of Oceania* by Henri Matisse, and *Starry Night* by Vincent Van Gogh.

Also on 53rd Street is the **American Craft Museum,** which exhibits contemporary craft making. Galleries are reached via a curving 40-foot-high "stairatrium" that flows up and down. The permanent collection includes work from World War II to the present in clay, glass, metal, wood, and fiber. Artists demonstrate their work in the "Meet the Artist" program.

Nearby, one of our favorite places for lunch is **La Fondue,** at 43 West 55th Street between Fifth and Sixth avenues (212–581–0820). The European ambience and French cuisine call for return visits. For Italian fare try **Mamma Leone's,** on 44th Street and 8th Avenue (212–827–6253), for a variety of special dishes. For a meal in a brownstone with a waterfall in the garden room, try the **Courtyard Cafe,** at 130 East 39th Street (212–685–1100).

Rockefeller Center is one of those places some visitors want to see every time they return to New York. Romantic images of the "real New York" from earlier decades seem to flow around Rockefeller Center. One of our favorite diversions is having a drink in the **Rainbow Room** (30 Rockefeller Plaza; 212–632–5100), sixty-five floors up, watching the city turn on its lights at dusk; then we feel we have really arrived. Renovated in 1930s Art Deco style, the Rainbow complex offers a view, with artwork including a Norman Bel Geddes ocean liner over the bar. Rockefeller Center is a collection of nineteen office buildings covering twenty-two acres and employing 65,000 persons. The **Channel Gardens** were so named because they are situated between the French and British buildings. Their blooming plants are changed seasonally, and benches provide respite from walking. **Rockefeller Plaza,** on the lower level, is filled with ice skaters in the winter, and flags of the

American Craft Museum
40 West 53rd Street
New York 10019
212–956–3535;
212–956–6047

Rockefeller Center
Fifth to Sixth Avenues
and 47th to 52nd
Streets
New York 10020

United Nations countries flutter in the breeze all around it. Shops and restaurants line the concourse area, and underground passages connect the buildings. The **GE Building,** at 30 Rockefeller Plaza, soars seventy stories into the air. José Maria Sert's painting *American Progress* hangs in the lobby.

Radio City Music Hall
Sixth Avenue & 50th
Street
New York 10020
212-247-4777

Radio City Music Hall is the place to go for a Christmas "spectacular" if you are in New York after mid-November. Other shows, movies, and pop concerts fill the hall throughout the year. The Rockettes have been dancing at Radio City since 1932. In 1979 the hall's elegant Art Deco architecture was completely restored. The chandeliers in the Grand Foyer can be lowered mechanically for cleaning—two tons of crystal and steel notwithstanding. Gold mirrors and gold-leaf ceilings make the mezzanine floors dazzle.

St. Patrick's Cathedral
Fifth Avenue & 50th
Street
New York 10022
212-753-2261

St. Patrick's Cathedral, dating from 1858 (although it did not open until 1879), was once thought to be too far out of town, if you can imagine that. Spires rise 330 feet, and the bronze doors open into the nave adorned with seventy stained-glass windows from Chartres and Nantes, France.

Grand Central
Terminal
Lexington Avenue &
42nd Street
New York 10017
212-935-3960

Grand Central Terminal is a Beaux Arts building with a gigantic concourse area leading up to a 125-foot-high vaulted ceiling decorated with constellations of the zodiac. Stop in **The Cafe,** at the top of the marble steps on the Vanderbilt Avenue side of the building, for a little something while you crane your neck to enjoy the constellations above. If you are so inclined, the scene is continually changing at a fast pace. For years the **Grand Central Oyster Bar** (212-490-6650) has been touted as the best place around for seafood; its popularity is quite evident during the lunch hour.

The **United Nations** consists of a narrow glass building (the Secretariat) adjacent to the

General Assembly, begun in 1947 by a committee of international architects. The dramatic complex is adorned by flags of the member nations
arranged in alphabetical order. To your right as
you enter is the Meditation Room with a Chagall
window, dedicated to Dag Hammarskjold. The
oval Assembly Room is fascinating to visit, and
you may wish to take a tour or sit in on a session. The Delegates Dining Room is open to the
public for lunch by reservation.

The **New York Public Library** was built
in 1911 to house the Astor, Tilden, and Lenox
libraries. The Beaux Arts building is guarded by
two friendly marble lions named Patience and
Fortitude. An architectural tour of the structure
is free. It has been newly renovated. Beautiful
Bryant Park is just behind.

South of the theater district is one building
few tourists miss. The **Empire State Building,**
once the tallest building in the world, has now
been topped by many others. The observation
level on the 102nd floor will provide an 80-mile
view if the visibility is good. The top of the
Empire State Building is brilliantly lit at night—a
treat to spot when you are on an evening
cruise. Runners might like to get in shape for
the annual Empire State Building Run—that's
right—up all 1,575 steps. In an internationally
popular contest, runners tend to make it up to
the top in twelve to fourteen minutes (the winners, that is!).

The **Guinness World of Records** is located on the concourse level of the Empire State
Building, next to the Observatory Ticket Office.
Look for Vincent Van Gogh's *Irises,* which sold
for a record $53.9 million in 1987; statistics on
volcanoes, the universe, and space; the longest
soft toy (250 feet), which looks like a pink-
plush centipede; a model of the world's tallest
man at 8 feet 11.1 inches; a display on crazy
eating; and much more.

**United Nations
First Avenue & 46th
 Street
New York 10017
212–963–7713**

**New York Public
 Library
Fifth Avenue & 42nd
 Street
New York 10036
212–340–0849**

**Empire State Building
Fifth Avenue & 34th
 Street
New York 10018
212–736–3100**

**Guinness World of
 Records
350 Fifth Avenue
New York 10018
212–947–2335**

THEATER DISTRICT

Most of the theaters lie between 40th and 57th streets on a north-south axis, bounded by Eighth Avenue to the west and Avenue of the Americas to the east, but 45th Street is noted for its cluster of legitimate theaters. **Shubert Alley,** between 44th and 45th streets, is the heart of the theater district and used only by pedestrians.

Dating back to 1753, when the Hallam Company arrived from London to produce drama in New York City, the public flocked to be entertained. In the 1830s Walt Whitman and Washington Irving encouraged serious theater as well as pure entertainment. Between 1850 and 1900 melodramas, plays with a message such as *Uncle Tom's Cabin,* and operettas were popular. Later the classics returned, as well as plays depicting themes of World War I. Euguene O'Neill was instrumental in presenting satire, expressionism, and realism. Plays presented real problems faced by people during that time. The theater of the absurd played with features of a world that didn't make sense. During the 1960s and 1970s, current social problems, political assassinations, and war played dominant roles in drama. If you're interested in half-price tickets for Broadway, Off-Broadway, Lincoln Center, and other performances, go to **TKTS** in Times Square or at the World Trade Center. Tickets for matinees are sold on Wednesdays and Saturdays from 10:00 a.m. until 2:00 p.m. Tickets for evening performances are sold Mondays through Saturdays from 3:00 to 8:00 p.m. On Sundays the hours for ticket sales are from noon to 8:00 p.m.

TKTS
Broadway & 47th
Street
New York

In addition to drama, New York City has fostered a rich literary heritage from its beginning. Washington Irving poked fun at the first Dutch settlers in his *History of New York.* Edgar Allan Poe, who lived in and out of New York during his lifetime, was a literary critic for the

New York Mirror. He caused an uproar when he accused Longfellow of plagiarism. **Poe Cottage** in the Bronx is open to visitors; there Poe lived a life of poverty—his wife died of tuberculosis with Poe's cloak around her, hugging the family cat for warmth. Herman Melville was born at 6 Pearl Street, near State Street, in 1819. After his marriage in 1847, he lived at 103 Fourth Avenue in Greenwich Village. He worked for a time as a deputy inspector at the New York Custom House and reflected the life of the city in stories like "Bartleby the Scrivener, A Story of Wall Street." Walt Whitman lived in Brooklyn in 1839 and in Manhattan in 1841. His New York works include "Mannahaata" and "Crossing Brooklyn Ferry."

Many novelists have found their material in both the high and the low life of the city. Henry James, born in 1843, lived at 21 Washington Place in Greenwich Village and later at 58 West 14th Street. He was very fond of his childhood neighborhood and wrote about it in *Washington Square.* Even after he moved to England, New York society provided one of the touchstones of value in his later, more complex novels. Edith Wharton was born to wealth, and her novels about old New York society include *The Age of Innocence, False Dawn,* and *New Year's Day.* Stephen Crane was born into a family of writers; as a young man he lived on New York's Lower East Side, where he wrote his first book, *Maggie: A Girl of the Streets.* He wanted to experience life in the Bowery for his writing and once slept in a Bowery shelter to observe the men who lived there; *Midnight Sketches* was developed from these experiences. Theodore Dreiser came to New York in 1894 as a newspaper reporter and wrote *Sister Carrie.* John Dos Passos lived in Greenwich Village in the 1920s, producing *Manhattan Transfer* during that time. Thus many of the traditions of

Poe Cottage
Grand Concourse &
Kingsbridge Road
Bronx 10467
212–881–8900

realism in nineteenth-century American fiction are inextricably linked to the life of New York, not to mention poetry—Hart Crane and the Brooklyn Bridge—or drama—Eugene O'Neill and the life of the waterfront. And because New York remains a mecca for writers, that close relationship between experience in the city and literature continues in the twentieth century.

Algonquin Hotel
59 West 44th Street
New York 10036
212–840–6800

The Algonquin Hotel has been a gathering place for literary wits and critics since the 1920s. For almost fifteen years the original group met every day and was known as the Algonquin Round Table or the Algonquin Wits, or, to those on the inside, as the Vicious Circle. Alexander Woollcott was the instigator of this group, which included writers, artists, musicians, and socialites. Their focus was to shape cultural and literary taste and to further their own careers; in some ways they were not unlike the Bloomsbury group in London, though more self-conscious and perhaps less talented.

Since those early days the management at the Algonquin has gone to immeasurable lengths to refurbish and renovate the hotel without changing its original character and ambience; rooms are just as comfortable now as they were in the 1920s. (See Inns appendix.) Even Hamlet, the cat, who lives under a sofa by the newsstand, fits into the decor. You can read about Hamlet in *The Algonquin Cat,* illustrated by Hilary Knight (remember *Eloise of the Plaza?*). People stream into the Algonquin for morning coffee or drinks in the main lobby—you never know what celebrity might be seated on the next couch. You can have lunch, dinner, or an after-theater supper in the Rose Room, elegant with crystal chandeliers and white-and-red decor, or enjoy a cabaret evening, with or without dinner, in the Oak Room.

Another restaurant to try after the theater is **Sardi's** (234 West 44th Street between

Broadway and 8th Avenue; 212–221–8440).
Caricatures of Broadway stars line the walls, and
the flavor is definitely theatrical.

West of the theater district is the *Intrepid
Sea-Air-Space Museum,* a technology museum
housed in the famous aircraft carrier that saw
action in World War II and the Vietnam War.
Exhibits explain air, sea, and space technology
within five theme halls: Navy, Intrepid,
Pioneers, Space Technology, and the Hall of
Honor. You can climb into the control bridge
and command centers of the carrier and see a
variety of aircraft close at hand. A wide-screen
film simulates what it is like to be on the flight
deck as jets scream off.

Intrepid **Sea-Air-Space
Museum
Pier 86, foot of West
46th Street at
Hudson River
New York 10036
212–245–2533**

Visit **Madison Square Garden,** a sports,
entertainment, convention, and office complex.
Over six million spectators pass through its
doors every year. The building is the third
Madison Square Garden in the city; it opened in
1968. The New York Knicks—professional basketball team—and the New York Rangers—professional hockey team—call Madison Square
Garden home. A wide variety of performances
and exhibitions are given there, including
rodeos, circuses, dance productions, tennis
matches, gymnastics exhibitions, and horse
shows.

**Madison Square
Garden
4 Pennsylvania Plaza
Seventh Avenue
between 31st
& 33rd Streets
New York 10001
212–563–8300**

This section of New York runs from 34th
Street south to Houston Street. The neighbor-
hoods include Chelsea, Gramercy Park,
Stuyvesant, Greenwich Village, and East Village.
Each has its own character and history.

NEIGHBORHOODS

Chelsea (from 14th Street to 25th Street,
from Eighth Avenue to the Hudson River) was
the name of the estate of Captain Thomas
Clarke, who bought the land in 1750. Clement
Clark Moore inherited his grandfather's land and
gave a sizable chunk to the General Theological
Seminary. Moore is perhaps best known for his

poem "A Visit from St. Nicholas." The motion picture industry got its start in Chelsea in 1905 but eventually moved to Hollywood. Chelsea is known for its many antiques shops on Ninth Avenue between 20th and 22nd streets.

Gramercy Park, a former marshland, was later converted into a London square surrounded by town houses. The park remains private; only residents have keys. In the center of the park stands a statue of Edwin Booth in his *Hamlet* costume. As you walk around the square, note the ornate street lamps and ironwork on some of the houses. A number of actors are memorialized in the windows of the **Little Church around the Corner,** which is also a popular place for weddings.

Stuyvesant (from Second Avenue to Third Avenue and 15th Street to 18th Street and Rutherford Place) was an elegant residential district during the nineteenth century. The square was a gift from Peter Stuyvesant, and his statue, complete with his peg leg, stands in the square in front of **St. George's Episcopal Church.** The **Friends' Meeting House and Seminary** was a stop on the Underground Railroad.

Greenwich Village has a flair all its own. The people who live there gravitate to **Washington Square** for soapbox orations and a parade of the most amazing outfits and hairdos anywhere. They really go all out for special events, such as the Halloween parade, which attracts a crowd standing six deep along the streets to ogle costumes that are more elaborate each year. Greenwich Village was settled by British colonists in 1690; they named the area for their village in England. During the early part of the eighteenth century, a number of large estates were built; the maze of winding roads evolved as the boundaries of those estates. Lavish town houses were built around Washington Square and along Fifth Avenue. You may want to walk along Washington Square North, where there are two rows of red-brick townhouses (numbers 1–13 and 21–26) dating from the 1830s. Look for both Doric and Ionic columns beside the entrances and note the cast-iron fences. Walk around behind Washington Square into Washington Mews and MacDougal Alley for a glimpse of renovated stables and servants' quarters of the old town houses. Gertrude Vanderbilt Whitney once had a sculpture gallery in one of the stables—leading eventually into the development of the Whitney Museum. One of the pleasures of Greenwich Village is spending time looking at the menus posted in front of the many restaurants before making a choice. These posted menus remind us of evenings spent strolling the streets in European cities and villages.

East Village was once the residence of wealthy New York families, but when they moved out it became an industrial area. **St. Mark's-in-the-Bouwerie,** dating from 1799, was once a country church. It stands on the site of Peter Stuyvesant's chapel. "Little Ukraine" is a grouping of Byzantine churches with rounded onion domes, and Ukrainian restaurants and shops. Artists and writers have been moving into lofts in the area. The area's boundaries are Broadway and First Avenue and Houston and 14th streets.

LOWER MANHATTAN

Lower Manhattan includes SoHo, the Bowery, Little Italy, TriBeCa, Chinatown, Wall Street, and the Battery. The original Dutch settlement of Nieuw Amsterdam flourished for forty years on what we now call Lower Manhattan. All traces of this village have disappeared, as well as buildings from Revolutionary War days.

SoHo, which means "south of Houston," was occupied by Indians during the seventeenth century. More recently the area's outdated industrial buildings have suddenly sprung to life with avant-garde galleries, boutiques, and restaurants. Sunday brunches are popular there. SoHo's boundaries are Houston and Canal streets, the Bowery, and Sixth Avenue.

The Bowery, located north of Canal Street to Houston, was once a farm, then an entertainment mecca, and eventually known as a skid row, inhabited by the poverty-stricken, drifters, and alcoholics. Recently revitalized, it is now home to many wholesale and retail shops.

Little Italy is the place to go for Italian cuisine or to buy special Italian foods not readily available elsewhere. **The Feast of San Gennaro** is held during September. **SPQR Ristorante** (133 Mulberry Street between Hester and Grand; 212–925–3120) is recommended for Italian cuisine and atmosphere, complete with a strolling musician. Their pasta is homemade. Little Italy covers Mulberry Street from Houston to Canal streets, and Lafayette Street to the Bowery.

TriBeCa, which means "Triangle Below Canal," has a group of Federal homes on Harrison Street. The area is seeing new life, as SoHo did, with the renovation of outdated industrial buildings into studios. TriBeCa is a trapezoid in shape, south of Canal Street, bounded by Broadway on the east and Chambers on the south.

Chinatown celebrates the Chinese New Year over a fifteen-day period with a parade featuring lions, dragons, and firecrackers. The lions go from door to door receiving red envelopes containing money in return for banishing evil spirits from homes and shops. Chinese legend says that Buddha invited all of the animals of the world to visit, but only twelve came, so he rewarded them by giving each in turn the honor of being animal of the year. The motif appears in Chinese celebrations as well as on gift items sold that year. You can spend time wandering along Mott, Bayard, and Pell streets past grocery stores displaying ducks, bean curd, and dried fungi and mushrooms. Make a list before you go of special herbs and condiments you may need to create your own Chinese meals at home.

Shops offer a variety of goods, including china tea sets and bowls, brocade jackets and dresses, ivory carvings, jade jewelry, lanterns, fans, and wall hangings. Look for the unusual telephone booths, which resemble pagodas.

Wall Street needs no introduction as the financial center of the city and the nation, but visitors are often surprised to find it shrouded in shadows created by the many skyscrapers soaring up from extremely narrow streets. The origin of the name is even less well known: In 1653 Dutch Governor Peter Stuyvesant had a wall built to protect the village from the Indians who lived on the other side. For a nineteenth-century response to being enclosed in Wall Street, read Melville's "Bartleby the Scrivener."

The **New York Stock Exchange** was designed by George B. Post with Corinthian columns and sculpture reminiscent of a Greek temple. Fortunes are made and lost on the trading floor. You can view the chaos from a visitors' gallery above and hear narration on the procedures in process. Exhibits show the history of the stock exchange and the financial organization of member companies.

**New York Stock Exchange
20 Broad Street
New York 10004
212-656-5167**

The **World Trade Center,** known as the "United Nations of Commerce," provides a center for international banks, custom house brokers, exporters, importers, trade associations, manufacturers, freight forwarders, trade development agencies, and transportation lines. The six-building complex was designed by Minoru Yamasaki and completed in 1970. The twin towers that soar 110 stories into the atmosphere are second in height only to the Sears Tower in Chicago. Construction of these massive towers without disturbing adjacent buildings was engineered by building a concrete wall entirely around the foundation area; then work could proceed inside the wall without worrying about water seeping in. The 1.2 million cubic yards of earth removed from the excavation area were deposited as fill in Battery Park.

The five-acre plaza within the World Trade Center is the site of concerts at noon, surrounded by people having lunch. The large bronze globe revolving in the pool was designed by Fritz Koenig, and the granite pyramid on the Plaza by Masayuki Nagare. The **Observation Deck** on the 107th floor and the open-air deck on the 110th floor provide a view you won't forget. You can also have lunch or dinner at **Windows on the World** (call 212–938–1111 for reservations), which is on the 107th floor of 1 World Trade Center.

Observation Deck
2 World Trade Center
New York 10048
212–435–7397

The **Battery** (the southern tip of Manhattan between State and Battery streets) was the spot where Giovanni da Verrazano, Estaban Gomes, and Henry Hudson came ashore. Twenty-one acres reach from the junction of the Hudson and East rivers to Bowling Green. In 1693 the British built a fort on an off-shore island, and in 1870 the island and mainland were joined by filling in the gap. Castle Clinton, built in 1807, was developed into Castle Garden in 1824 and used for entertainment. Lafayette attended Castle Garden in 1824, and in 1850 Jenny Lind was the star performer in a concert there. **Castle Clinton National Monument** (212–344–7220) is open and features exhibits on the original fort.

Battery Park City is a ninety-two–acre landfill recently completed with a new esplanade. Don't miss the Winter Garden.

The **Staten Island Ferry** is one of the bargains of New York City. For twenty-five cents you can board at the foot of Whitehall Street in Battery Park, chug out into the harbor, past the Statue of Liberty and Ellis Island to Staten Island, and return past that unmistakable skyline.

You can also take a ferry (Circle Line; 212–269–5755) from the Battery for a fifteen-minute crossing to **Ellis Island National Monument.** Take another ferry to the Statue of Liberty.

Imagine what it must have been like to leave friends, family, and home and step onto a ship with a piece or two of luggage. Passages across the Atlantic were miserable in steerage, with abominable living conditions and the real chance of storms to face. The sight of the Statue of Liberty extending her welcome must have lifted spirits with visions of a better life in the New World. But as the shop neared Ellis Island, people were full of apprehension, wondering if they would be accepted—or turned back. Everyone had to undergo a medical examination, some were detained, and 2 percent (12 million) were separated from their families and returned to their homeland. It must have been devastating. Ellis Island was called "the island of hopes and the island of tears."

Ellis Island has now been restored to the tune of $160 million. With about half of all American families remembering someone who came through, the urge to visit is real. The first wave of about 5,000 immigrants arrived just after the Revolution, then 150,000 during the 1820s, 1.7 million in the 1840s, and 2.5 million in the 1850s.

Begin your tour with a film, commencing with poignant photos of families leaving their homes in Europe, traveling steerage across the ocean, and arriving at Ellis Island. Scenes of the derelict Ellis buildings give way to the restoration that has now been completed. Museum dis-

Ellis Island National Monument
New York
212–269–5755;
212–363–3200;
212–363–3201;
212–269–5755
(ferry info)

plays trace the first moments of the peak immigration years, from 1880 to 1924, when people tried to adapt to their new life in America. Often their children were "go-betweens," and they had to walk a fine line between two opposing cultures—that of their parents, ingrained with ethnic mores, and that of their new friends and teachers, who often frowned on foreign ways. The children learned English and served as translators and envoys to the New World. Photographs throughout the museum bring visual impression to a new life. And voices of those immigrants who are still living can be heard describing their feelings at various stages in their adjustment.

We were especially touched by the Treasures from Home room. You'll see a lamb sugar dish brought from Russia in 1911; a copper coffee pot from Finland in 1923; a samovar from Germany in 1910; a copper cauldron from Italy in 1919; a green wooden ale bowl from Norway in 1900; a spinning wheel from Norway in 1894; a mangle board with carved pattern and "horse" handle, also from Norway, in 1890; a wedding dress from Armenia in 1890; a Black Madonna painting from Poland in 1909; a black Aragonese dress and fan from Spain in 1890; a regional dress from Moravia in 1920; and more. We recommend taking the first boat in the morning, before crowds appear. You can spend a number of hours on Ellis Island and then take a boat to the **Statue of Liberty.**

Statue of Liberty
New York 10004
212–363–3200
or
National Park Service
212–326–3200

She was refurbished in time for an extravagant 200th birthday in 1986, including complete reconstruction of her torch, by French craftsmen. Gold leaf was applied to the torch, and sunlight makes it glimmer. This favorite monument of every American was built by the sculptor Frédéric Auguste Bartholdi in 1886. She stands 151 feet high as she welcomes people to our shores. Many of us find tears streaming down our faces as we glide by her when returning by ship. The same thing happened to us more than thirty years ago when we saw a smaller replica of her on the shore of the Seine in Paris.

As you enter the museum, you'll come face to face with a copy of a lady's face—the Statue of Liberty herself. Her giant toes are on display a little farther on. A nearby plaque certifies that France gave her to America as a gift in 1886 as a token of friendship and liberty to enlighten the world. The idea had been proposed in 1865 by Edouard Réne Lefebvre de Laboulaye in his Paris home. Displays chronicle the development of the idea with sculptor Auguste Bartholdi, who was influenced by the Colossus of Rhodes from 300 B.C. Gustave Eiffel used his engineering skills to devise the support system and exclaimed, "It will hold!" During the 1980s restoration stainless steel replaced the rusted iron inside the statue. Wafer-thin sheets of copper were used with the "repousse" method, and you can see a movie showing workmen hammering the copper into shape.

The museum displays a collection of medals, programs, and books, as well as the sword of Captain of the Lafayette Guard, which led the land parade on October 28, 1886. Don't miss the display of "popular culture" items sold for the celebrations—plates, spoons, a Tiffany-style lamp, clock, quilt, whirligig (wind-up toy), and more.

You can walk partway up the pedestal for views all around or climb twenty-two stories up inside the lady into the crown.

Fraunces Tavern Museum is located upstairs in a historic building. This museum of early American history and culture was the site of George Washington's farewell to his officers on December 4, 1783, when forty-four officers attended a dinner in his honor. Washington toasted them, walked to Whitehall where he

**Fraunces Tavern Museum
Broad & Pearl Streets
New York 10004
212-269-0144**

took a boat to New Jersey, went to Annapolis, Maryland, and resigned his commission at a ceremony in the State House there. You can see the Long Room, now renovated and set for a dinner as it would have been that night. The Clinton Dining Room, across the hall, features wallpaper printed by Jean Zuber in 1834. This "historic" wallpaper depicts a number of important events against a background taken from various scenic spots in America. The furnishings are of the nineteenth century, mostly in Duncan Phyfe design. The room is named after Governor George Clinton, who used to entertain guests in Fraunces Tavern.

The museum houses a permanent collection that includes Chinese export porcelain, silver, documents, prints, paintings, maps, clocks, weapons, and sculpture. Special exhibitions are held, as well as a full roster of educational programs on topics such as science and witchcraft in colonial times, native American fare, reviving eighteenth-century etiquette, New York City folklore, and medicinal plants in colonial America. You can also have lunch or dinner downstairs in **Fraunces Tavern Restaurant** (212–269–0144), a favorite spot for those working on Wall Street.

South Street Seaport
Fulton & Water
 Streets at East River
New York 10038
212–SEA–PORT,
212–669–9400

South Street Seaport is a new restoration of a nineteenth-century port district. In 1625 the Dutch West India Company established a trading post called Nieuw Amsterdam, and the British took possession of it in 1664. After the Revolution, in 1784, the *Empress of China* sailed to Canton, providing a link between the Orient and New York. In 1793 Peter Schermerhorn consolidated his waterfront lots on Fulton Street, and the Schermerhorn Row landfill began to reclaim land from the sea. In 1811 he built a row of counting houses. Robert Fulton's ferry docked on Fulton Street in 1814, and soon a packet line began service between New York and Liverpool. In 1822 the first Fulton Market opened, and the Erie Canal was completed in 1825 to extend the linkage by water from the Hudson to the Great Lakes. As the waterfront developed, **Sweet's Restaurant** (2 Fulton Street; 212–825–9786) opened in 1842, and you can still have a meal there today. The Brooklyn Bridge construction began in 1870. Thomas Edison lit up South Street, the first commercial district in the world to have electric light, in 1882. A tin structure was built for the Fulton Fish Market in 1907. During all of this time, the area was alive with commercial enterprise— sailors in port from long voyages eager for activity and people who lived there going about their daily business.

In 1968 the Friends of South Street Seaport began planning for a new seaport, one that would depict the life of that area one hundred years ago. As you stroll through this walking village, away from traffic, you can feel some sensations from a century past.

Restored buildings house a gallery, stationer, book and chart store, boat building shop, and a children's center. During special programs children can learn how to furl a sail and sleep in a hammock and observe other aspects of going to sea.

Head for the waterfront to see a fine collection of historic ships on display. The *Peking* is a four-masted bark built in 1911 in Hamburg, Germany; exhibits below decks depict life aboard this square-rigger. The *Ambrose Lightship* marked Ambrose Channel in New York harbor beginning in 1907. The *W.O. Decker* is a wooden tugboat that reminds us of "Little Toot." The *Lettie G. Howard* was built in 1893 in Essex, Massachusetts, as a Gloucester fishing schooner, typical of those bringing fish into the Fulton Fish Market. The *Pioneer* started life as a sloop in 1885, then changed into a gaff-rigged schooner in 1968. You can go for a sail on her during the summer. The *Wavertree* sailed from Liverpool during the 1880s on the jute trade between Europe and India. The *Major General William H. Hart* was built in 1925 as a New York City ferryboat.

Fulton Fish Market
200 Front Street
New York 10038

The **Fulton Fish Market** is not easy to miss; if you like smells of the sea, you'll love it there. This market is the oldest continuously operating wholesale market in the United States, housed in the "Tin" building and "New Market." If you can arrive around 4:00 a.m., you will see lots of activity as fish are sold. A Fulton Fish Market tour is offered by reservation (212–669–9416). **Schermerhorn Row,** dating back to 1810, has reconstructed buildings housing restaurants and antiques, clothing, and gift shops. **Pier 17 Pavilion** is a steel and glass complex housing many more restaurants and shops. For a harbor cruise, try **Seaport Line** (19 Fulton Street; 212–608–9840).

The **Brooklyn Bridge** celebrated its centennial in 1983. It can be reached from Frankfort Street and Park Row. As the first suspension bridge and second-oldest bridge in New York, it has been called the "Eighth Wonder of the World." John Augustus Roebling was commissioned to draw up plans for the bridge in 1869. Unfortunately, he suffered a crushed foot before the bridge was completed, but his son, Washington Roebling, finished the bridge. Construction workers built caissons containing compressed air so that water would not disturb the work. The men went through a process of compression as they went down and decompression on the way back up, yet Washington Roebling suffered an attack of "the bends" and was partially paralyzed for the rest of his life. He continued to direct construction from a window overlooking the bridge. The bridge is 3,455 feet in length and the central span is 1,595 feet. It cost

$25 million and was completed in 1883. A series of legends, stories, jokes, and poems has arisen from this symbolic and beautiful bridge. Don't let anyone sell you the Brooklyn Bridge!—but if you could buy it, it would be worth a fortune.

To Brooklyn Bridge
Hart Crane

How many dawns, chill from his rippling rest
The seagull's wings shall dip and pivot him,
Shedding white rings of tumult, building high
Over the chained bay waters Liberty—

Then, with inviolate curve, forsake our eyes
As apparitional as sails that cross
Some page of figures to be filed away;
—Till elevators drop us from our day . . .

I think of cinemas, panoramic sleights
With multitudes bent toward some flashing scene
Never disclosed, but hastened to again,
Foretold to other eyes on the same screen;

And Thee, across the harbor, silver-paced
As though the sun took step of thee, yet left
Some motion ever unspent in thy stride,—
Implicitly thy freedom staying thee!

Out of some subway scuttle, cell or loft,
A bedlamite speeds to thy parapets,
Tilting there momently, shrill shirt ballooning,
A jest falls from the speechless caravan.

Down Wall, from girder into street noon leaks,
A rip-tooth of the sky's acetylene;
All afternoon the cloud-flown derricks turn
Thy cables breathe the North Atlantic still.

And obscure as that heaven of the Jews,
Thy guerdon . . . Accolade thou dost bestow
Of anonymity time cannot raise;
Vibrant reprieve and pardon thou dost show.

O harp and altar, of the fury fused,
(How could mere toil align thy choiring strings!)
Terrific threshold of the prophet's pledge,
Prayer of Pariah, and the lover's cry,—

Again the traffic lights that skim thy swift
Unfractioned idiom, immaculate sigh of stars,
Beading thy path—condense eternity:
And we have seen night lifted in thine arms.

Under thy shadow by the piers I waited;
Only in darkeness is thy shadow clear.
The City's fiery parcels all undone,
Already snow submerges an iron year . . .

O Sleepless as the river under thee,
Vaulting the sea, the prairies' dreaming sod,
Unto us lowliest sometime sweep, descend
And of the curveship lend a myth to God.

UPPER MANHATTAN

Cloisters
Fort Tryon Park
New York 10040
212–923–3700

The New York City area has many other sights to see. Although we have concentrated on middle and lower Manhattan, we will suggest further possibilities for you to explore in upper Manhattan and the other boroughs.

The **Cloisters,** a branch of the Metropolitan Museum of Art devoted to medieval art, was built in 1934 through the generosity of John D. Rockefeller, Jr. The name comes from the open, rectangular courtyards with covered arcaded walks around the sides, or cloisters, found in medieval monasteries in Europe. European art dating from the twelfth century is exhibited in the gardens, arcades, cloisters, and galleries. The collections include wood carvings, furniture, religious statuary of alabaster and ivory, gems, stained-glass windows, and marble capitals. Don't miss the set of seven tapestries known as "Hunt of the Unicorn." The rich colors of the tapestries give vibrancy to life in the fifteenth century. Fort Tryon Park is between Broadway and Riverside Drive, from 192nd Street to Dyckman Street.

Riverside Church is interdenominational. The Laura Spelman Rockefeller Carillon is the largest in the world, with seventy-four bells housed in a 400-foot tower. The church is especially known for its fine Gothic detail.

**Riverside Church
Riverside Drive &
122nd Street
New York 10027
212-222-5900**

The **Ulysses S. Grant National Memorial** is between 120th and 124th streets on Riverside Drive. Both Grant and his wife are interred there. Colorful mosaic work around the tomb was created by schoolchildren.

Nieuw Haarlem was settled in 1658 as a trading post and became a fashionable suburb after the railroad opened in 1837 and rapid transit lines emerged in 1880. The Harlem Renaissance of the 1920s produced a cultural center for black artists, writers, and performers. Now Harlem is undergoing a transition from abandoned buildings to luxury condominiums.

HARLEM

Visitors can take a Gray Line tour of Harlem (900 Fifth Avenue between 53rd and 54th streets; 212-397-2600) and leave the driving to someone else.

The **Cathedral of St. John the Divine** is the largest Gothic cathedral in the country. Stop by the fountain outside to see children's sculpture all around the edge of the fountain. Don't miss *Noah's Ark*. On the way to the cathedral, you'll pass Columbia University, Barnard College, Teacher's College/Columbia, Union Theological Seminary, City College of New York, and the Jewish Theological Seminary.

**Cathedral of St. John
the Divine
Amsterdam Avenue at
West 112th Street
New York 10026**

The Apollo Theater (253 West 125th Street; 212–749–5838) was where many black performers got their start, including Nat King Cole, Ella Fitzgerald, Pearl Bailey, Sarah Vaughn, Aretha Franklin, Sammy Davis, Jr., and Harry Belafonte.

BRONX
Bronx Zoo
Bronx Park
185th Street &
 Southern Boulevard
Bronx 10467
212–367–1010

New York Botanical
 Garden
Southern Boulevard
Bronx 10458
212–220–8700

The **Bronx Zoo** is believed to be the largest zoo in the world. The animals are housed in environments that include the African Plains, Wild Asia, Aquatic Bird House, World of Darkness, and a special Children's Zoo. You can take the Sky Ferry Aerial Tramway or the Safari Train for an overview of the zoo.

The **New York Botanical Garden** in the Bronx Park grows a changing display of plants and trees on 250 acres. The Lorillard Snuff Mill, dating from 1840, produced snuff during the nineteenth century, and fields of roses growing nearby contributed petals to blend with the snuff for a pleasant fragrance. Crystal Palace, an 1851 building constructed in Hyde Park, London, for the international exposition, was the inspiration for the Enid Haupt Conservatory building. The 90-foot-high glass dome shields a variety of palms, ferns, and tropical plants inside.

BROOKLYN
Brooklyn Museum
200 Eastern Parkway
Brooklyn 11238
718–638–5000

The **Brooklyn Museum** contains collections of Egyptian art, primitive artifacts from Africa, collections from the Middle East and the Orient, and Greek and Roman artifacts. Reconstructed rooms of a seventeenth-century Brooklyn house are on display, as well as paintings by both European and American artists. Don't miss the sculpture garden that displays articles from "lost New York," including a column base from the old Penn Station and a lion's head from Steeplechase Park at Coney Island.

The **Brooklyn Botanic Garden** is well known for its Japanese meditation gardens. The

Cranford Rose Garden contains many varieties of roses, and a special "fragrance" garden has been developed for the blind.

The **Brooklyn Children's Museum** began in 1899. Today it is a participatory museum where you can explore ethnology, natural history, and technology. Children can see a windmill and learn how it works, study fossils, or take a field trip. Workshops, demonstrations, storytellers, and concerts are available.

These suggestions are only a few of the sightseeing possibilities in the New York City area. It would take a lifetime to make a dent in all New York has to offer.

Brooklyn Botanic Garden
1000 Washington Avenue
Brooklyn 11225
718–622–4433

Brooklyn Children's Museum
145 Brooklyn Avenue
Brooklyn 11213
212–735–4400;
212–735–4432

⧟ *Long Island* ⧟

Call **Long Island Convention and Visitors Bureau** (800) 441–4601. There are a number of ways to reach your destinations on Long Island from New York City, including the Long Island Expressway, Route 495, down the center; to the north, the Northern State Parkway connecting with Route 25; or to the south, the Southern State Parkway connecting with Route 27. The **Long Island Railroad** runs down the island all the way to Montauk (718–739–4200, 212–526–0900, or 516–369–1666). **Long Island Airlines** services Long Island from New York, as well as Boston and Newark (516–752–8300). If you are coming from Connecticut, you can take one of two ferries: **Cross Sound Ferry** from New London to Orient Point (203–443–5281, 443–5035, 444–0783, or 444–0482) or the **Bridgeport and Port Jefferson Steamboat Company** (516–473–0631 or 203–334–5993).

Long Island has a fascinating geologic history. Thirty thousand years ago the glacier ground through New England, loosening rock, pulverizing it, and embedding it within glacial ice. When the glacier reached the coast, it was met by warm air, making it drop accumulated rocks and debris as it melted. These piles of rocks were pushed into ridges sometimes hundreds of feet high—glacial moraines that stretch the whole length of Long Island from New York City to the tips of Orient Point and Montauk. The extension of the moraine from Orient Point surfaces on Cape Cod; the one from Montauk reappears on Block Island, Martha's Vineyard, and Nantucket. Residents can attest to the rocks and pebbles under the surface of their land. Large boulders, swept along without being ground up, were also left along the north shore by the glacier. As the glacier melted, many streams flowed, carrying rock and pebbles to build up extensive plains; potatoes and vegetables now grow on the plains of Long Island.

Another specific glacial remain is the "kettle-hole" pond; Lake Success and Lake Ronkonkoma were formed this way. The original shape was outlined by a hard ice deposit that stayed put while water flowed around it. As the ice melted, round holes were left, some deep enough to fill with water and become lakes. Along the south shore the barrier beaches were formed by wave action working on rocks over the years to produce fine sand. That sand was moved by waves from the shore onto bars that grew into spits and peninsulas. The barrier beach along most of the south shore of Long Island protects the coast proper from the worst ravages of wind and wave erosion, but the sea is still working at reclaiming the land, as those who build too close to it discover to their dismay after a fierce winter northeaster.

Long Island offers a microcosm of a much larger region with distinct areas ranging from the mansions of the "Gold Coast," old whaling and fishing ports, and farms growing those famous "spuds" to the natural beauty of coastal spits of land, dunes, beaches, and small villages. Musical entertainment encompasses rock concerts and classical concerts. You can go to thoroughbred races, harness races, or auto races. There are many wineries for touring and tasting and a variety of seafood and ethnic restaurants. You can fish, sail, swim, or just relax on a summer holiday. Long Island, just 125 miles long and no more than 23 miles wide, packs in a lot of variety for visitors to enjoy.

We suggest beginning your tour on the north shore, heading for Orient and Montauk points at the forked end, and then continuing west along the beaches of the south shore. The Gold Coast stretches along almost one-third of the Long Island Sound shore. East of the Gold Coast is a historic triangle from Centerport to Stony Brook. Farmlands make up another third of the island, leading to the small villages, ports, and wineries of the North Fork. As you continue this circuit, take the ferries across to Shelter Island and Sag Harbor and then head out to Montauk Point. The South Fork, also known as "the Hamptons," is another, newer Gold Coast of exurban villas and mansions that serve as a retreat from the city. Its beautiful ocean beaches merge with the barrier beaches that line the remaining two-thirds of the Atlantic shore of the island, creating sheltered bays, all the way to Brooklyn.

PORT WASHINGTON   If you are driving out from New York City, you may want to take one of the faster highways to reach your first destination on the north shore. Take exit 36N from the Long Island Expressway for Port Washington and head north on Route 101 to **Sands Point Park and Preserve.** Captain Harry F. Guggenheim's **Falaise,** a twenty-six-room, Normandy-style manor house, is located on the property. The collection includes sixteenth- and seventeenth-century Spanish and French furnishings and Guggenheim's silver racing trophies. Outside, a panoramic view of Long Island Sound awaits you.

Sands Point Park and Preserve
Port Washington
516–883–1612

Retrace your way down Route 101 and take Route 25A east to Roslyn, once the home of William Cullen Bryant, who was an editor of the *New York Evening Post.* He lived there from 1843 to 1878, helping to name the town Roslyn because it looked like Roslyn Castle in Scotland. Christopher Morley also lived there on Searington Road, now in Christopher Morley Park. If you tour the house, look for the "dymaxion bathroom," which has all bathroom plumbing formed into one unit.

ROSLYN

Follow signs to Glen Cove to **Garvies Point Museum and Nature Preserve,** which has prehistoric archaeological displays. There are five miles of nature trails within this sixty-two-acre park.

Picture yourself dining in a restaurant that houses a fine collection of marine exhibits, prepares memorable seafood, and has a view of Long Island Sound stretching beyond the graceful crescent of the beach. **Steve's Pier I** (33 Bayville Avenue, Bayville; 516–628–2153) is nautical throughout—from the decor outside of the massive front doors to the bridge that crosses over a pool filled with milling lobsters, and into the spacious dining rooms filled with marine exhibits. Don't miss the collection of scrimshaw,

GLEN COVE

Garvies Point Museum and Nature Preserve
Barry Drive
Glen Cove 11542
516–671–0300

ship models, a 200-pound bell from an Onassis ship, harpoons, a sponge-diver's suit, and a model of the USS *Constitution*. Ask about the forty-four-pound lobster, Charlie, who lived in the lobby pool for a year.

OYSTER BAY

Sagamore Hill
Cove Neck Road
Oyster Bay 11771
516–922–4447

Continue on around Oyster Bay, which separates "West Egg" from "East Egg" in F. Scott Fitzgerald's *The Great Gatsby,* to **Sagamore Hill,** the home of President Theodore Roosevelt. Built in 1885, this house was named after Sagamore Mohanned, an Indian chief who lived in the area until the early eighteenth century. Outside, the house is painted red with green and yellow contrast. It has a front porch, where the Roosevelts used to sit and rock, watching the sunset as well as the lights from passing vessels on the Sound. On this porch Roosevelt was notified of his nomination for governor of New York in 1898, for vice-president of the United States in 1900, and president in 1904. Walk around to the side to see "Speaker Cannon," playfully named for Speaker of the House Joe Cannon; it was fired every Fourth of July, with Roosevelt on hand to see that the children "produced maximum noise with minimum risk of injury."

Inside the house most of the rooms are furnished as they were when Mrs. Roosevelt lived there, following her husband's death, until her own death in 1948. You can't miss all of the stuffed heads hanging in most of the rooms in the house, which, as a whole, resembles a hunting lodge more than an Oyster Bay mansion. The floors also display skins with heads from a white polar bear and several mountain lions. In the downstairs hall hangs a framed buffalo robe given to Teddy after Custer's Last Stand. As a deputy sheriff he once found and returned two stolen horses to an Indian; the man took them and left without a word but later returned and gave this pictorial robe, which depicts the Battle of Little Big Horn in 1876, to Roosevelt.

The North Room has an eclectic collection of gifts received by Roosevelt—including a Samurai sword from the emperor of Japan, elephant tusks from the emperor of Abyssinia, an oriental rug from the sultan of Turkey, and books from the kaiser of Germany. The table in the family room is set for dinner; note the silver candelabra and exquisite silver platter.

The library was also Roosevelt's study and office during his presidency. This comfortable room has a fireplace with a wooden mantel, leather chairs, a collection of bronzes, a portrait of a moose, books, and, of course, lots of animal heads. Upstairs, the master bedroom contains massive furniture designed by Frank Furness and Daniel Pabst of Philadelphia. Both the armoire and the bed have burled and carved floral or patterned designs.

The Gate Room replaced the nursery when the children became too old for the nursery and needed a giant playroom. With southern exposure this room was warmer than most in the winter; it was chosen by Roosevelt during his last illness, and he died there in 1919.

You can also visit **Old Orchard,** which Theodore Roosevelt, Jr., built in 1937 because he and his wife wanted a home of their own after years of living in rented houses. He lived there for three years before he was killed following the D-Day Battle on Utah Beach, in Normandy; his widow lived there for the rest of her life, until 1960. The house has three permanent exhibits: one is based on Theodore Roosevelt's public life, another depicts the family life at Sagamore Hill, and the third contains memorabilia from the six children: Alice, Theodore Jr., Kermit, Ethel, Archibald, and Quentin. Old Orchard is located on the Sagamore Hill property, on the side opposite the parking lot.

Old Orchard
Cove Neck Road
Oyster Bay 11771
516–922–4447

COLD SPRING HARBOR

Cold Spring Harbor Fish Hatchery and Aquarium
Route 25A
Cold Spring Harbor
11724
516–692–6768

From Sagamore Hill head south to Route 25A and east to Cold Spring Harbor, an active whaling port during the middle of the eighteenth century. The **Cold Spring Harbor Fish Hatchery and Aquarium** is housed in what was a water-powered woolen mill more than a hundred years ago. The hatchery raises over forty thousand brook trout, rainbow trout, and brown trout; you can see them in stages from eggs to fingerlings to eight-pounders. The aquarium has both photographs and live fish to watch eyeball to eyeball through the glass. Don't miss the Turtle Room.

Whaling Museum
Main Street
Cold Spring Harbor
11724
516–367–3418

A little farther east along Route 25A is the **Whaling Museum.** The museum was developed around the gift of a whaleboat from the American Museum of Natural History. This whaleboat came from the brig *Daisy,* built just a few miles east of Cold Spring Harbor, in Setauket, in 1872. Many local residents gave or loaned whaling artifacts, which had been kept in their families, to the museum. The collection includes figureheads, ship models, scrimshaw, harpoons, maps, and tools; there also is a diorama depicting life in the village in the 1840s. Look for the skull of the killer whale. The museum holds workshops, such as a "Ship in a Bottle" session and a whaling-log session; shows films; and conducts walking tours of the village.

HUNTINGTON

Huntington is located just a few miles east along Route 25A. Did you know that Nathan Hale was betrayed by his cousin and captured in Huntington? Apparently he was fully aware of the risk involved when he was sent behind enemy lines; he was executed as an American spy on September 22, 1776. There is a monument to him on Huntington Bay.

Nathan Hale
Francis Miles Finch

To drum-beat and heart-beat,
A soldier marches by;
There is color in his cheek,
There is courage in his eye,
Yet to the drum-beat and heart-beat
In a moment he must die.

By starlight and moonlight,
He seeks the Briton's camp;
He hears the rustling flag
And the armed sentry's tramp;
And the starlight and moonlight
His silent wandering's lamp.

With slow tread and still tread,
He scans the tented line;
And he counts the battery guns,
By the gaunt and shadowy pine;
And his slow tread and still tread
Gives no warning sign.

The dark wave, the plumed wave,
It meets his eager glance;
And it sparkles 'neath the stars,
Like the glimmer of a lance—
A dark wave, a plumed wave,
On an emerald expanse.

A sharp clang, a still clang,
And terror in the sound!
For the sentry, falcon-eyed,
In the camp a spy hath found;
With a sharp clang, a steel clang,
The patriot is bound.

With calm brow, and steady brow,
He listens to his doom;
In his look there is no fear,

Nor a shadow-trace of gloom;
But with calm brow and steady brow,
He robes him for the tomb.

In the long night, the still night,
He kneels upon the sod;
And the brutal guards withhold
E'en the solemn word of God!
In the long night, the still night,
He walks where Christ hath trod.

'Neath the blue morn, the sunny morn,
He dies upon the tree;
And he mourns that he can lose
But one life for Liberty;
And in the blue morn, the sunny morn,
His spirit wings are free.

But his last words, his message-words,
They burn, lest friendly eye
Should read how proud and calm
A patriot could die,
With his last words, his dying words,
A soldier's battle-cry.

From Fame-leaf and Angel-leaf,
From monument and urn,
The sad of earth, the glad of heaven,
His tragic fate shall learn;
But on Fame-leaf and Angel-leaf
The name of HALE shall burn!

**Heckscher Museum
Route 25A & Prime
  Avenue
Huntington 11743
516–351–3250**

**Walt Whitman House
Huntington Station
516–427–5240**

Back in town the **Heckscher Museum** houses collections of American and European sculpture and painting from the sixteenth to the twentieth centuries. Walt Whitman was born in this town, and you can visit his home. His desk, secretary, and some of his manuscripts and personal items are displayed.

Just beyond Huntington, the **Vanderbilt Museum and Planetarium** is located a short distance north of Route 25A on Little Neck Road. William K. Vanderbilt II built the original structure as a Japanese-style, six-room home in 1907 and later expanded it into the mansion you see today; he lived there until 1944. As you approach the estate, you can't miss the white-stucco, Spanish-style wall surrounding the property; the twenty-four–room mansion also represents Spanish Revival architecture and interior decor. Wrought-iron windows and heavy carved doors and furniture accent the style. The dining room contains an 11-foot-long, seventeenth-century refectory table made of carved walnut. Don't miss the "Organ Room" on the second floor, where the chairs are covered with French petit point and needlepoint.

Outside, concerts are given in the mansion courtyard. Walk down the path to the planetarium, which offers a program of shows throughout the year; it is considered among the dozen largest and best equipped in the country. The grounds overlook Northport Bay; take a stroll down to the boathouse for another view. Retrace your steps back to the main house and head to the right to reach the Hall of Fishes, once known as the Vanderbilt Marine Museum. Mr. Vanderbilt made a number of scientific explorations in the early 1930s, and many of the animal and marine life specimens in the museum are a result of these trips. On the second floor you will see both vertebrates and invertebrates, and the habitat wing contains dioramas of animals in their natural surroundings. Don't miss the whale shark hanging from the ceiling. The Bird, Moth, and Butterfly rooms display more collections.

Follow signs to **Sunken Meadow State Park,** which offers picnicking, three nine-hole golf courses, a driving range, swimming, athletic

CENTERPORT

**Vanderbilt Museum
and Planetarium
180 Little Neck Road
Centerport 11721
516–757–7500**

**Sunken Meadow State
Park
Sunken Meadow State
Parkway
Kings Park 11754
516–269–4333**

A•41

fields, hiking, nature trails, fishing, bike path, beach, bridle paths, and cross-country skiing in the winter. Here you will find the first total relief from the influence of the city and its outskirts in a landscape unaffected by economic development in any form. As you approach the park, you drive down off the ridges left from glacial moraine and move closer to the Sound, first through woods and then along an extensive salt marsh before you reach the beach. The approach itself provides half the pleasure of the park. This is truly a perfect spot to escape from frenetic city life.

East of the park on Route 25A, as you pass through **Smithtown,** look for the large bronze statue of a bull. It was apparently found on the coat of arms of Richard Smith.

STONY BROOK

The Museums
1208 Route 25A
Stony Brook
516–751–0066

Continue east on Route 25A to Stony Brook, where you will see several museums, including a village rebuilt in the 1940s using eighteenth- and nineteenth-century Federal architecture. The **Art Museum** contains paintings by William Sidney Mount, a nineteenth-century genre painter who caught the essence of rural life on Long Island. The **History Museum** houses collections of toys, dolls, costumes, decoys, and fifteen furnished miniature rooms. The **Carriage Museum** exhibits sporting rigs, pleasure vehicles, farm and trade wagons, sleighs, children's vehicles, coaches, and fire-fighting equipment.

The State University of New York at Stony Brook maintains a **Fine Arts Library** (516–246–5000), which sponsors a variety of cultural programs and gallery exhibitions.

PORT JEFFERSON

Port Jefferson is the landing for the ferry from Bridgeport, Connecticut. (Check page A•33 for information.) Also in Port Jefferson you will find **Brookhaven National Laboratory.**

This atomic research center offers films, computer games, and other exhibits.

Stay on Route 25A and Route 25 to **Riverhead,** the town at the junction of the North Fork and the South Fork that serves as a center for the surrounding potato-farming country. If you want to bypass the town and head out the North Fork, take Route 58 until Route 25 rejoins it and keep going east toward Cutchogue.

NORTH FORK

Cutchogue, meaning "principal place," is the site of **Old House,** built in 1649 on the Village Green. It is the oldest English house still standing in New York State. Look at the English Tudor construction that is made visible through exposed sections inside the house. The furniture was all handmade by the early settlers who lived in the area. The **Wickham Farmhouse** on the Village Green, built in 1700, contains period furnishings. The **Old Schoolhouse** was built in 1840 and now houses a collection of antiques donated by families whose ancestors lived in the area. The **Cutchogue Free Library** is now in the church built in 1862 by the Independent Congregational Church and Society in Cutchogue.

Cutchogue Free Library
Main Road
Cutchogue 11935
516–734–5537;
516–734–6532

A **Guild House** for artists and craftsmen is another building you can visit in Cutchogue. During the summer the town hosts a variety of events, including the Antiques Flea Market, Antique Car Show, Firemen's Parade and Drill, Village Square Dance, and the Outdoor Art Show of the Old Town Arts and Crafts Guild.

If you enjoy vineyards, don't miss **Hargrave Vineyard,** the first vineyard producing estate-grown and -bottled wines on Long Island since colonial times. Alexander and Louise Hargrave began their research for a good site in 1972 after first looking at the Finger Lakes area. The tasting room has an 8-foot

Hargrave Vineyard
Chutchogue 11935
516–734–5111

stained-glass window entitled "The Sower" (adapted from the François Millet painting) by Louis Comfort Tiffany.

Other wineries on the North Fork include Bedell Cellars (Main Road, Cutchogue; 516–734–7537), Bidwell Vineyards (Route 48, Cutchogue; 516–734–5200), Gristina Vineyards (Main Road, Cutchogue; 516–734–7089), Jamesport Vineyards (Main Road, Cutchogue; 516–364–3633), Lenz Winery (Main Road, Peconic; 516–734–6010), Mattituck Hills Winery (4250 Bergen Avenue, Mattituck; 516–298–9150), Palmer Vineyards (Sound Avenue, Aquebogue; 516–722–WINE), Paumanok Vineyards (Main Road, Aquebogue; 516–722–8800), Peconic Bay Vineyards (Main Road, Cutchogue; 516–734–7361), Pindar Vineyards (Main Road, Peconic; 516–734–6200), and Pugliese Vineyards (Main Road, Cutchogue; 516–734–4057). Some of them require an appointment; others welcome visitors anytime during opening hours.

Farther east on Route 25 is **Greenport,** a yachting center for the North Fork; the terminus for the Shelter Island Ferry is located here. Greenport had a somewhat notorious past during Prohibition days, when fast boats were in and out bringing liquor to their customers. Stop for a meal at **Chowder Pot Pub** adjacent to the ferry for Shelter Island (516–477–9821).

Orient Point State Park
Orient Point 11957
516–323–2440

Beyond Greenport at the tip of the North Fork is **Orient Point.** This is the terminus for the ferry from New London, Connecticut. **Orient Point State Park** is a 357-acre park on Gardiners Bay that is a favorite stop for migratory birds.

SHELTER ISLAND

From Greenport take the ferry to Shelter Island. Once the site of a Quaker settlement, Shelter Island is now a popular resort located between the North Fork and the South Fork. Shelter Island is popular with yachtsmen because it has three good harbors: Dering on the north, West Neck Harbor on the southwest, and Coecles Inlet on the east. Most of them have saltwater ponds with marshes and the attendant wildlife you might expect. The island is a great place for biking and walking.

During colonial days Quakers fled persecution in New England and found peaceful lives on Shelter Island. Determined to learn more about this heritage, we followed a map that was compiled by the **Shelter Island Chamber of Commerce** (Box 598, Shelter Island, New York 11964; 516–749–0399) and lists historic sites. The **Shelter Island Historical Society's Havens House Museum** and **Manhanset Chapel Museum** is open during the summer from Thursday through Sunday (as of this writing). The Havens House, on South Ferry Road, was the home of James Havens, a member of the provincial congress, who lived there from 1743. The pleasant white house, located on a curve in the road, was kept in the family until 1925. Turn left onto North Ferry Road to the 1890 Manhanset Chapel. A little farther along the road, you'll come to the site of the first meetinghouse, dating from 1743, next to the present Presbyterian church.

Continue north on North Ferry, and look carefully on the right for the little road leading to the **Quaker Cemetery.** A memorial sign at that point states that Nathaniel Sylvester and other Quakers came there to escape persecution. You can drive into the woods to the cemetery, which has a large stone table in the center and a number of grave markers surrounded by a fence. It was a poignant moment for us as we stood there remembering my husband's Quaker heritage, as his ancestors, Eleanor and Edward Foulke, had left Wales in 1698 to find freedom.

Stop for a meal at **The Cook Restaurant** (15 Grand Avenue; 516–749–2005), which was lively the night we were there with a film crew for a magazine. Also try the **Ram's Head Inn** (Ram Island Drive; 516–749–0811). (See the Inn appendix.) When you have finished exploring the island, take Route 114 to the ferry for North Haven and Sag Harbor.

SAG HARBOR

Sag Harbor's first inhabitants, the Indians, settled on a site that is now the center of town. They called it "Wegwagonock," or "Foot of the Hill." Later, as the place became a port, there was opportunity to take advantage of commodities going in or out, and by 1707 the British Crown was concerned enough about rum-running to appoint an officer to monitor this illegal activity.

Sag Harbor became a major whaling center during the eighteenth and early nineteenth centuries. She was second only to New Bedford in the whaling business. In 1871 the last whaler, the *Myra,* left the harbor.

The call "Ship in the Bay!" almost rings in your ears as you reminisce about the old days of whaling in town. And you can take a walking tour beginning at the Whaling Museum to see the homes built by whale oil. Don't miss the variety of picket fences and also doorways, each with different detail.

**Sag Harbor Whaling
Museum
Main & Garden
Streets
Sag Harbor 11963
516–725–0770**

The **Sag Harbor Whaling Museum** is the place to go to reminisce and to learn more about whaling and the people who spent their lives in that profession. The Greek Revival home was built by Minard Lafever for Benjamin Huntting II in 1846. Today a modernistic sculpture of a whaling ship with crew pulling on the oars stands on the front lawn. Inside you'll see rooms chock-full of cases of displays of items brought back, made by whalers, or enjoyed by their families. Two portraits of little girls are hung in the parlor—in those days itinerant painters brought along canvases with the body finished so only the head had to be added. Here also are collections of doll furniture, bottles, silver, sewing boxes, a wedding dress with tiny waist, paisley shawl, Japanese marriage shoes on stilts, Japanese shoes for bound feet, a peacock fan, gold luster-ware, daguerreotypes, and samples of crewel work done by a paralyzed Fannie Tunnison, who painted with her lips and tongue. Move along to a room of 1800s toys, including a wooden train on a circular track, circus equipment, a fire wagon, steamer, and mechanical banks. Look under the table for several sleds that were once pulled by goats. A globe of the heavens stands on the floor. Documents certify that Henry P. Dering was appointed customs inspector. A large anchor knot board was made by John Hensel, who wrote the definitive book on knots. Several clocks include one made from the wreckage of ships. Look for the barber pole dating from 1900, when haircuts were 15 cents. The barber, Mr. Battle, used to tell outrageous stories, such as the one about watermelon seeds (giant-size watermelons are grown locally) being used to roof a barn. Don't miss the unusual washing machine and also the "Mammy Rocker" in the kitchen.

Both Sag Harbor and Nantucket inhabitants tried beach whaling taught to them by Native Americans before they ventured with their equipment onto ships. You'll see a collection of harpoons, samples of whale oil (the darker the color, the cooler the climate where the whale lived), ships' logs, and lots of scrimshaw. Mr. and Mrs. Walter Pharr donated a Narwhal tusk that is second in size to one in the Smithsonian. We heard the story about the pilot who collected it in Alaska, flew it sticking out of his plane, then brought it on the train and finally the subway to Bayside Queens—such a journey.

The **Custom House** was the home of Henry Packer Dering, who was a U.S. custom

**Custom House
Garden Street
Sag Harbor
516–941–9444**

**First Presbyterian
  Church
Union Street
Sag Harbor**

master, in addition to raising nine children in his home. The lean-to section on Church Street was also the post office, dating from 1794. The first law passed in the United States occurred here in 1789. The office contains a history of Sag Harbor as one of two ports of entry—the other was New York. The kitchen must have been warm, with a huge fireplace and an oven for baking bread; don't miss the "baby minder" to keep little ones safe from the fireplace. Upstairs the master bedroom has a stenciled border. Many of the pieces were original in the Dering family. Look in the child's room for a squirrel cage.

An early version of the First Presbyterian Church, built after 1766, was called "a wooden building of uncouth shape" or "Old Barn Church." By 1816 parishioners had begun to build, and the place was dedicated in 1818, later becoming a community hall and theater; the building burned in 1924. The present church dates from 1844, was built by Minard Lafever, and is listed on the National Register of Historic Places. The style is Egyptian Revival, and inside Lafever decorated with Greek volutes, rosettes, and anthemia. The tower was requested by whalers to be tall enough to be seen easily by returning mariners. But in the 1938 hurricane, the steeple was lifted thirty feet into the air, landed on the ground, and then toppled into the cemetery, with its bell tolling once. You can see the original bell in the church entry. Look for the silver nameplates on the pews. Fluted Corinthian columns soar to the ceiling and the trompe l'oeil panel behind gives an impression of majesty. Don't miss the replicas of the original whale oil lamps in between lavender windows.

James Fenimore Cooper began writing one of his first sea stories in Sag Harbor in 1824. More recently the town was the scene for the filming of *Sweet Liberty* (with Alan Alda) at the American Hotel. Stop for a meal at the

American Hotel (516–725–3535), **Spinnakers** (Main Street; 516–725–9353), or **J. W. Ryersons** (516–725–3530).

Head south on Route 114 to Route 27, where you can turn east to **Montauk Point.** One of the most productive fishing spots anywhere is the "cod ledge" off Montauk. Go to the very end to enjoy the view of the ocean full of boats and to see the **Montauk Point Lighthouse,** which George Washington ordered built in 1795. Very wisely, he insisted that it be set almost three hundred feet back from the coast to allow for erosion. In November 1797 Jacob Hand lit the thirteen whale oil lamps for the first time; he was up all night making sure they were all burning. By 1987 the vigil was over as three Coast Guard seamen left their post to the automated areobeacon.

Part of the history of Montauk includes the visit by Theodore Roosevelt and his troops after the port of New York denied them landing (because of the possibility of disease) following the Spanish-American War. Rudolph Valentino filmed *The Sheik* here in the twenties, and during Prohibition the waters around the point were used for drops by rum-running boats.

During the 1880s it became popular to walk from New York City to the Montauk Lighthouse and back. New York newspapers played up each successful venture. Some of the walkers even stayed overnight with the lighthouse keeper. In 1890 J. O. Whittemore rode his cycle back and forth. (When we were there, hundreds of cyclists were going to the lighthouse on a bike-a-thon.)

In 1908 William K. Remsen of Brooklyn led a group of friends, each in his own car, on a wild ride to the lighthouse. The noise and smoke from those belching machines must have been something to witness. After they reached

MONTAUK

Montauk Chamber of Commerce
Montauk 11954
516–668–2428

Montauk Point Lighthouse
516–668–2544

East Hampton, the road deteriorated and several of the autos had problems: One rode off into the sea, another exploded, and others had a plethora of minor problems. Twenty-eight autos finally arrived, carrying all of the original forty drivers; they roared around the lighthouse three times. While they were climbing out of their cars, the lighthouse keeper approached them to express regret that he did not have enough food. But they did! From the cars came hampers of food for a great feast.

Second House Museum Montauk 11954 516–668–5440

On February 20, 1858, a second lighthouse was completed farther along on the Long Island shore. Mariners had for years trusted the only lighthouse on Montauk Point, but because the two lights looked the same, the Montauk light was changed into a flashing light. Since this was long before the era of radioed notices to mariners, captains who had been away for some time did not have any news of this change. The *John Milton,* a clipper ship of 1,445 tons, was on her way to New York from Peru when her captain saw the light during a storm. Thinking his landfall was the Montauk light, he continued on course, with the crew in fine spirits to be so near port. The cliffs were there to meet them head-on, crunching the hull, breaking spars, and scattering cargo. The lighthouse keeper and his assistant plowed through the snow to find the source of the ship's bell they had heard, only to find the wreck with timbers, cargo, sails, and bodies swathed in ice.

When we were there in May 1992, the lighthouse museum area was in the throes of final renovation and painting in order to be open for Memorial Day weekend of that year. We climbed up the 137 steps to the top of the tower. Views outside extend along the coast to crashing waves on the beach. Inside visitors can climb up six steps to see the continuously rotating giant beacon, which is lit twenty-four hours a day with a 1,000-watt bulb. Downstairs you can see the Fresnel lens that was up there from 1904 until 1987. A TV monitor presents a twenty-minute tape on the history of the lighthouse.

When you're ready for lunch, stop in **The Boathouse,** on South Emery Street (516–668–5574), or **Gosman's,** on West Lake Drive (516–668–5330).

In the town of Montauk, **Second House Museum** was built in 1746 and rebuilt in 1797. The "First House," built in 1744, burned in 1909. The Montauk Historical Association maintains the existing house, which includes an eighteenth-century kitchen.

From Montauk head west on Route 27 to **Hither Hills State Park,** which offers nature trails, hiking trails, picnicking, swimming, fishing, and camping, all in a beautiful setting.

Hither Hills State Park
Route 27
Montauk
516–668–2554

The next town, Amagansett, is the site of the landing of German saboteurs during World War II, in June 1942. They disembarked from a submarine, fooled a coastguardsman with their fluent English, then buried some incendiary bombs in the sand. These were uncovered, and the four Germans were captured after a fifteen-day chase.

AMAGANSETT

As you head west along the south shore of the Island, East Hampton is the first of the "Hamptons" you will come to. It is an attractive village with a number of historic buildings on its shady streets. In 1648 settlers purchased East Hampton for "20 coats, 24 hatchets, 24 hoes, 24 looking glasses and 100 muxes [an early tool used for making wampum]" from the Shinnecock Indians. You can't miss seeing **Hook Mill,** a windmill located between North Main Street and Pantigo Road. Built in 1806, it has now been restored to serve as a landmark of the past.

EAST HAMPTON

East Hampton
Historical Society
101 Main Street
East Hampton 11937
516–324–6850

The **East Hampton Historical Society** is housed in the **Osborn-Jackson House,** dating from 1735. The house contains eighteenth- and nineteenth-century furnishings. Some rooms are used as galleries for temporary exhibits, and quilting and weaving are featured during the summer.

Clinton Academy was the first chartered academy in New York State; it dates from 1784. Boys came from New York City to study for college there. In 1815, 156 students were enrolled in a curriculum that included mathematics, navigation, surveying, geometry, accounting, Greek, and Latin. The house now contains East Hampton exhibits from the past.

Across the Green stands **Mulford Farm,** dating from 1680. A costumed interpreter will take you around the house, telling stories about the people and the items displayed there. Look for the patch of eel grass protruding from a hole in the wall up near the ceiling; although it was handy for insulation, inhabitants found that little creatures from the woods would hunker down in it during the winter and then find it difficult to get out. Displays include one on the maritime triangular trade, a chart of cattle ear marks so villagers could find their own animals, and a collection of wine bottles, silver, a delft platter in blue and white, and a pewter platter. Look for the "ghosts" of missing parts of hinges where the outline still reveals its original shape. The parlor is the place where the men entertained themselves; women chatted upstairs. Squared-off bottles fit into slots within a carrying case for travel; there's a case in the room. Clay pipes lie on the table—fastidious smokers broke off the tip before using a pipe. China in the cupboard was saved for special occasions. Look on the mantel above the fireplace for "spiles," which are curly wood shavings used to light the fire. The bedroom downstairs was used by the oldest and the youngest members of the family. The rope bed has straw on top and then a feather mattress. There's a twister to crank up the ropes on the bed—hence the phrase "sleep tight." Look for the "fleam," which was used to bleed people who became sick. They had to hold onto a pole tightly so the veins stood out for bleeding. Blood ran down the fabric wrapped around the pole, and the end result looked like a "barber pole." People used to congregate in the kitchen with its roaring fire to sew, weave on the loom, make candles in the mold, and cook in three-legged pots. Look for the "temse," a container covered with goatskin and pierced with nails, used as a sifter for hand-ground grain. And look for the unique waffle iron and toaster.

Don't miss **"Home Sweet Home,"** the childhood home of John Howard Payne, who wrote the song of the same name. You can see an eighteenth-century windmill, herb garden, gallery, and collection of English lusterware and ceramics.

"Home Sweet Home"
14 James Lane
East Hampton 11937
516–324–0713

The **Guild Hall** has changing exhibits, some from local artists who summer in town. There are 200 works in the permanent collection. The **John Drew Theater** (516–324–4050) offers a number of concerts, plays, and films.

Guild Hall
158 Main Street
East Hampton 11937
516–324–0806

The **East Hampton Town Marine Museum** has displays of early whaling history, fishing exhibits, models of fishing boats, and information on shipwrecks. Photos of the bulwark of the *Alice Reed* are there. Spoils of the ships turned up in "shipwreck" dresses that soon appeared on a number of women in town. One shipment carried shoes with metal tips, and the women tapped their way around town as well.

East Hampton Town
 Marine Museum
Bluff Road
East Hampton 11937
516–267–6544

Upstairs you'll find two "discovery rooms" for children, split into two age-groups. Here the kids can play and learn with lots of pieces to handle. Look out the window to see the jungle-gym trawler, just made for children to climb on.

Displays include a wetlands focus on the interdependency of all parts in the wetlands; shellfish and how they are harvested; cod trawling; dragging with cone-shaped nets; haulseining, wherein nets are set in boats and then hauled into shore with winches; harpooning by boat at sea; aquaculture, or fish farming; pound trapping as fish migrate; and a collection of lobster traps. Look for the underwater archaeological exhibit.

SOUTHAMPTON

Southampton is the oldest English settlement in the state; people arrived there in 1640 from Lynn, Massachusetts. The name was chosen by the Earl of Southampton to commemorate the colonization of our country. In 1898 the Southampton Colonial Society formed; it maintains many of the historical sites in town. We suggest a walking tour as the best way to see the center of this interesting old town; you can get a map from the **Southampton Chamber of Commerce** (76 Main Street; 516–283–0402).

The Historical Museum
17 Meeting House Lane
Southampton 11968
516–283–2494

The Historical Museum is housed in the home built by whaling captain Albert Rogers in 1843. There are a bedroom and a living room, both decorated as they would have been in his day; a colonial bedroom; the Shinnecock Room of Indian artifacts; and a collection of quilts, toys, china, glass, and old documents. Nearby are a one-room schoolhouse with the desks still in place, a whaling collection, farm equipment, weaving and spinning exhibits in the Red Barn, a carriage shop, country store and post office, blacksmith shop, carpenter shop, and an early drugstore.

The Old Halsey
South Main Street
Southampton 11968
516–283–3527

The Old Halsey was built in 1648 by Thomas Halsey, one of the town founders. It is now the oldest English frame house in the state. Phebe, the wife of Thomas, was murdered there by Connecticut Indians. The furniture is from the seventeenth and eighteenth centuries. Local garden clubs maintain the herb and border gardens.

The **Elias Pelletreau Silversmith Shop** was operated by a captain who was both a famous silversmith and a staunch Revolutionary War patriot. His silver is now very valuable and an expensive collector's item.

**Elias Pelletreau
Silversmith Shop
Main Street
Southampton 11968**

The **Parrish Art Museum** is the permanent home of the William Chase collection. There are special exhibitions of local artists as well as of internationally famous ones. The museum runs a series of workshops for children and concerts in the gardens during the summer, and other special events all year. As you will see, **Jobs Lane** offers one boutique, restaurant, and shop after another, inviting you to while away some time.

**Parrish Art Museum
25 Jobs Lane
Southampton 11968
516–283–2118**

Conscience Point, where the group from Lynn, Massachusetts, landed in June 1640, is off North Sea Road. There is a plaque attesting to their landing and subsequent founding of Southampton.

Take a drive out to the "estate" area along the shore. Some of the homes are weathered cedar shake, while others are brand-new. Most are large houses, with landscaping protecting them from the road and more landscaping protecting the dunes from beach erosion. The cedar-shake house used in the filming of one of Woody Allen's movies is along the row.

As in most of the beach communities in the Northeast, access to many of the beaches is restricted to residents only. The area of any beach between high- and low-water marks cannot be so restricted as long as you can find a way to get to it and a place to leave your car. If you walk or cycle, however, you have easy access to most of the beaches in the area. Check with the chamber of commerce on the location of beaches and parking facilities available to visitors. We suggest this because the town fathers may decide to place restrictions on a beach that has previously been open.

Have you heard about the "Money Wreck" or "Coin Beach"? If you happen to be on a beach in the Hamptons, look for gold coins in the sand. In November 1816 a ship mysteriously went aground on the bar opposite Shinnecock Bay. The ship was broken up and auctioned by local people; during the auction some gold coins were found. Two local whalers, Henry Green and Franklin Jagger, secretly searched on board at night, gathering as many coins as they could. Eventually the sea completed the job the wreckers had not finished, when one storm littered the beach for miles around with pieces of the hull. A number of years later, gold coins, dated between 1740 and 1790, began to surface on the beaches. Some farmers used their teams to plow the beaches; one found $60 in a day. Some local historians believe that this ship was one that was boarded off the Easthampton bar by a crew who murdered the men on board, removed what valuables they saw, lashed the wheel, hoisted sails, and pushed off as the ship headed for the beach.

Restaurants recommended to us include **Barrister's** (36 Main Street, 516–283–6206), **D'Antonio's Trattoria** (1580 North Highway, 516–283–3111); **Driver Seat** (62 Jobs Lane; 516–283–6606), **John Duck Jr.** (15 Prospect Street; 516–283–0311), **The Bowden Square** (Bowden Square; 516–283–2800), and **The Lobster Inn** (North Highway; 516–283–9828).

From the Shinnecock Canal we suggest an excursion to a stretch of the barrier beach via Lynn Avenue and the Ponquogue Bridge onto the spit at Shinnecock Inlet, where there is a county park. The beach community on the spit is housed between sand dunes and low pines. Drive along Tiana Beach on Beach Road and Westhampton Beach on Dune Road and turn back inland at the Swordfish Beach Club. Wend your way back through residential areas to Route 27A by any way that pleases you, or by Route 31 if you want to be direct. Then take Route 27 west to Shirley, turn left onto Route 46, and head for Fire Island across the Smith Point bridge.

FIRE ISLAND

Fire Island National Seashore is a 32-mile-long barrier beach that is kept in its wild state. You can park your car just over the Smith Point bridge, camp in the campground there, and walk into the park with your gear for the day. You can also take ferries from Patchogue, Sayville, and Bay Shore to reach the more remote areas. The **Visitors' Center** provides information and the beginning of the nature trail. Fire Island offers fishing—including excellent surf fishing—clamming, swimming, and bird-watching, among other recreational activities.

Fire Island Visitors' Center
Box 248
Sayville 11782
516–289–4810

Sailors have always been aware of the hazards—especially in storms—of this barrier beach enclosing the sheltered waters of Great South Bay. Added to natural hazards was the human element: Some residents misled ships by placing lamps in their windows, then salvaged the wreck that followed. One legend attributes the name "Fire Island" to these lamps; others say that it was originally "Five Islands" and that the name evolved from poor penmanship.

JONES BEACH

If you are not through swimming or beachcombing, you may want to drive out to Jones Beach, which is actually a series of beaches extending for 6½ miles. To reach it from the east, take the Robert Moses State Parkway and Causeway from Route 27 to Captree State Park; then head west along Ocean Parkway until you reach Jones Beach State Park. If you prefer swimming in a pool to swimming in the ocean, there is one available. Don't miss the Water Tower, reminiscent of the Campanile at St.

Mark's Cathedral in Venice. The **Jones Beach Theater** is also located in the park.

From Jones Beach you can take Meadowbrook State Parkway back to Southern State Parkway or the Long Island Expressway to New York City.

The next section of this itinerary follows the Hudson River to the north.

❧ *Hudson River Valley* ❧

The Hudson River was first discovered when Giovanni da Verrazano sailed along the coast under the flag of France in 1524. Not much was made of this discovery. When, however, the Dutch East India Company hired Henry Hudson to find a northwest passage to reach the riches of Asia, the river found a place in history. This inventive and aggressive English navigator hoped that he would find the way to the Orient as he sailed up the river in 1609 on his ship, the *Half Moon.* He sailed as far as Albany and, while disappointed to be unsuccessful in his original search, returned with enthusiastic reports of the fertile valley. Dutch settlers and traders led the way for other immigrants to follow.

The beauty of the Hudson River, with its tremendous cliffs amid views around each bend, has a geologic history of at least seventy-five million years. During the Ice Age the glaciers ground out the riverbed. The Continental Shelf was exposed long ago. Today the Hudson River channel is below sea level from Albany to the ocean. Therefore the river is tidal and saline partway up the 150-mile stretch to the Albany area.

Before the Revolution, use of the river was blocked by the Iroquois Confederacy; even during the early 1800s, the Mohawk and Oneida Indians controlled the Mohawk pass. Surrounded by steep walls of the cliffs, travelers did not have a chance against Indians poised to attack. During the Revolution about one-third of the battles took place somewhere along the Hudson River, since it was the main channel of communication between Canada and the colonies. The important Battle of Saratoga, regarded by some historians as the turning point of the war, kept the British from grasping that essential water route.

The Hudson River School of painters, active in the early- to mid-nineteenth century, had vibrant and majestic subjects for their work. This group of painters was the first in the country to band together. Led by Thomas

President Theodore Roosevelt's home in Oyster Bay.

SAGAMORE HILL, LONG ISLAND

View of the Hudson River from the West Point Military Academy.

WEST POINT

The Governor Nelson A. Rockefeller Empire State Plaza, cultural and governmental center of New York's capital.

EMPIRE STATE PLAZA

Doughty, Thomas Cole, Asher B. Durand, and William Cullen Bryant, they were instrumental in breaking away from the traditional American Academy of Fine Arts, run by John Trumbull.

A more liberal National Academy of Design was encouraged by Bryant, with Samuel Morse as president. As editor of the *New York Evening Post,* Bryant had the power to provide publicity through his paper. He was determined to see America develop an art of its own.

The early years of the nineteenth century also brought remarkable commercial significance to the Hudson. In 1807 Robert Fulton sailed his first steamboat, the *Clermont,* from New York City to Albany with remarkable speed, creating a new mode of transportation that would make development of the river possible. When the Erie Canal opened in 1825, the river really came into its own, because the Great Lakes and the West were finally accessible by water. Not until the railroads supplanted water transportation did the river begin to lose its central importance, and even that development began with Commodore Vanderbilt's water route, which is still one of the best ways to appreciate the beauty of the river.

Over the years a number of mansions were built along the Hudson, perched on hills or cliffs like the castles along the Rhine, yet in their opulence resembling more the collection of chateaus in the Loire Valley. Some of them are now in ruins, but others have been restored to the splendor of the past. You can also visit vineyards along the Hudson and taste their wines, as you can on the Rhine and the Loire. The Huguenots planted grapes in the seventeenth century; there are now many wineries to visit, mostly concentrated on the west side of the river in the section around Newburgh. If you take a cruise, you will catch glimpses of all of it at once—mansions, vineyards, cliffs—and perhaps add to your collection of lighthouses at the same time.

The mountains along the river are part of the Appalachian chain, consisting of several small ranges, including the **Highland, Taconic, Catskill, Shawangunk,** and **Helderberg mountains.** The Highlands extend from Poughkeepsie on the north to Peekskill and West Point on the south. There is a gorge between Cornwall-on-Hudson and Stony Point that is unusually deep, with the peaks ranging up to 1,400 feet above the river. James Fenimore Cooper's Natty Bumpo (in *The Pioneers)* remarked, "You must have seen them [the mountains] on your left, as you followed the river up from York, looking as blue as a piece of clear sky, and holding the clouds on their tops." Look for names such as Storm King, Breakneck Ridge, and Anthony's Nose in this area.

The Taconics lie east of the Hudson River, reaching 1,200 feet in height. The Catskills lie in an area bounded by State Highway 17 on the south, State Highway 23 on the north, U.S. Highways 209 and 9W on the east, from Kingston to Catskill, and from State Highway 30 south from Grand Gorge to State Highway 17 at East Branch on the west. The Shawangunk Mountains lie south of the Catskills. The Helderbergs run along the southern section of the Mohawk Valley on the west side of the Hudson River.

The geology of the Catskill Mountains may have been easy for geologists to uncover, because many identifying features are exposed—cliff faces, flumes (streams flowing over bedrock), and bare bedrock—which eliminates the need to dig and remove vegetation. The rock is sedimentary and thus retains more glacial scratches and fossils than igneous and metamorphic rock. Many of the fossils are of marine organisms, because the sea once covered this area. For more than fifty million years, erosion carried debris from the Acadians to an area known as the Catskill Delta. The delta rose up gradually and began to suffer from erosion, mostly from streams leading into the Hudson River. Glaciers advanced, leaving scratches and gouges; streams flowed beneath the glaciers as they melted, producing landforms such as kames, drumlins, eskers, drift pedestals, and kettle holes. As the glaciers melted, the land, which had been crushed by their weight, began to rise again; streams reversed their courses and produced waterfalls, rapids, and gorges.

There are hundreds of waterfalls for you to explore and photograph along the tributaries leading into the Hudson. A short list includes **Kaaterskill Falls, Bastion Falls, Haines Falls, Palenville Falls, Shinglekill Falls, Woodstock Falls, Glen Falls,** and the **Falls at East Durham.** James Fenimore Cooper wrote in *Leatherstocking Tales:*"The first pitch is nigh 200 feet and the water looks like flakes of snow afore it touches the bottom; and there the stream gathers itself together again for a new start and maybe flutters over 50 feet of flat rock before it falls for another hundred, when it jumps about from shelf to shelf, first turning this-a-way and then turning that-a-way, striving to get out of the hollow til it finally comes to the plain."

In spite of their proximity to New York City, the Catskills are still considered a wilderness area with peaks up to 4,000 feet, deep gorges, rocky crags, and impenetrable ravines. The Indians thought that the Great Spirit lived there and did not choose to live in the mountains; Dutch settlers found the fertile valley more profitable. Thus the Catskills were never developed and are today still a haven of natural beauty, with many remote areas prized by hikers.

If you are coming from New York City, we suggest that you begin this section at Tarrytown.

TARRYTOWN

Sunnyside
Route 9
Tarrytown 10591
914–631–8200

Tarrytown, dubbed so by Washington Irving after farmers' wives who apparently lingered when they went in to market, or after husbands who "tarried" at the tavern, is steeped in the legends of Sleepy Hollow. The town is located just north of The Tappan Zee Bridge at the widest section of the Hudson River.

Sunnyside, the home of Washington Irving, was described by him as "a little old-fashioned stone mansion all made up of gable ends and as full of angles and corners as an old cocked hat." Born in 1783 in New York City, Irving was named after General George Washington, whom his Scottish immigrant parents greatly admired. He remembered being patted on the head by General Washington when he was a child. In 1809 he published *Knickerbocker's History of New York,* a mixture of humor and satire about the Dutch settlers. Although the main character, Diedrich Knickerbocker, was fictitious, New Yorkers were also called "Knickerbockers." *The Sketch Book,* finished in 1820, first presented some of the characters that Irving is remembered for: Ichabod Crane, the Headless Horseman, and Rip Van Winkle. Irving also lived in Spain inside the famous Alhambra, as a guest of the Moorish Monarch of Granada, and developed his storytelling powers with *Tales of the Alhambra,* published in 1832.

After extensive traveling Irving returned home and purchased Sunnyside in 1835 from a member of the Van Tassel family, also featured in his writing. As you approach the house, look at the southerly view of the Hudson; once there were a beach and a boat dock, but when the railroad came through in 1849 the pleasures of the river were a little diminished. Look at the wisteria vine beside the front door; it was planted by Irving. The iron benches on the porch were housewarming gifts. Irving loved planning innovations for his house and invented a number of refinements that other homes did not have for years to come. For example, he was successful in creating a water system for his house that was unknown to anyone else around.

The Life of George Washington was written in this house and completed the year Irving died. His desk and books are still in the study as he left them, as is a couch where he slept when there were too many living in the house. His brother Ebenezer and his five daughters came to live with him, and later two of the girls, Sarah and Catherine, ran the house for Irving. The house is completely furnished, with his favorite chair poised by a window for the view and the dining room table set for dinner.

Follow Route 9 north of Sunnyside for 4 miles to visit **Sleepy Hollow Cemetery,** where Washington Irving is buried, and to immerse yourself in visions of Ichabod Crane, his horse "Gunpowder," and the Headless Horseman. According to the story, Ichabod Crane rode off on Gunpowder to visit Katrina Van Tassel and ask her to marry him. He was turned down, and, as he made his way home, "It was the very witching time of night that Ichabod, heavy-hearted, and crestfallen, pursued his travel homewards, along the sides of the lofty hills which rise above Tarry Town. . . . In the dark shadow of the grove, on the margin of the brook, he beheld something huge, misshapen, and mounted on a black horse of powerful frame. . . . Ichabod was horror-struck, on perceiving that he was headless! . . . If I can but reach that bridge, thought Ichabod, I am safe." He was, however, thrown from his horse by the "head" tossed at him by the headless horseman. In the morning Ichabod Crane was gone, his horse Gunpowder was there, and a pumpkin was lying in the road. The bridge where this cli-

**Sleepy Hollow
  Cemetery
Route 9
Tarrytown**

A•63

max of the story is set crosses the Pocantico River by the Old Dutch Church and the cemetery.

Lyndhurst
Route 9
Tarrytown 10591
914-631-0046

Backtrack a few miles to **Lyndhurst,** which really looks the way a castle should! This Gothic Revival gray-white marble mansion was designed by Alexander Jackson Davis in 1838 for William Paulding. The second owner, George Merritt, enlarged the house in 1865. The last owner was Jay Gould, who almost cornered the gold market and caused the Black Friday panic in 1869. Some of the original furnishings that Davis designed for the house remain there.

Philipsburg Manor
Route 9
Tarrytown 10591
914-631-8200

Philipsburg Manor has been restored to re-create the period from 1720 to 1750. After you leave the visitors' center you will cross a bridge over the river into that earlier era. Ducks and geese float and dive in the pond and a mill wheel turns with a splashing sound. The Dutch-style manor house was built for Frederick Philipse in the 1700s. His home was in Yonkers, but this house was used as headquarters for his business. The interior is quite spartan, with bare floors and no curtains. In the parlor is a Dutch cupboard with painted scenes on it. The bed in Adolph Philipse's bedroom can be folded when not in use—an early Murphy perhaps? Visit the gristmill for a demonstration.

Historic Hudson
150 White Plains
Road
Tarrytown 10591
914-631-8200

Historic Hudson, which operates Sunnyside, Philipsburg Manor, and Van Cortlandt Manor, offers a variety of programs throughout the year: candlelight tours, winter cookery, a flower festival, country dancing, sheepshearing, concerts, storytelling, and crafts. Write for a brochure of events.

Union Church of
Pocantico Hills
Route 448
Tarrytown 10591
914-631-8200

The **Union Church of Pocantico Hills** features stained-glass windows by Henri Matisse and Marc Chagall. Matisse designed a neo-Gothic rose window—in memory of Abby Aldrich Rockefeller, wife of John D. Rockefeller, Jr.—that was installed in 1956. Chagall created the "Good Samaritan" window in 1965, as well as eight side windows, seven of which represent Old Testament prophets.

Head north on Route 9 to the sign for Croton Point Avenue, which will lead you to **Van Cortlandt Manor.** In 1697 Stephanus Van Cortlandt's land was chartered by Royal Patent as the Manor of Cortlandt. Philip Van Cortlandt, his son, received the manor house and one-tenth of the land. He added a gristmill, store, church, school, and the Ferry House, which was an inn at the ferry crossing. Travelers came on the Albany Post Road and crossed the river on a family-owned ferry; local inhabitants frequented the taproom in the inn to get news from peddlers and other travelers. Philip Van Cortlandt's son Pierre was the first lieutenant governor of the state.

CROTON-ON-HUDSON

**Van Cortlandt Manor
South Riverside
  Avenue
Croton-on-Hudson
10520
914–631–8200**

Continue north on Route 9 to Route 403 and head into Garrison. The **Bird and Bottle Inn** dates from 1761, when it was known as Warren's Tavern, now a favorite spot for a meal or overnight. (Also see Inn appendix.)

GARRISON

Boscobel was begun in 1804 by States Morris Dyckman. The name Boscobel was taken from a home of the same name in Shropshire, England. Charles II had hidden inside an oak tree in the forest of Boscobel in 1651 following his defeat by Cromwell. Dyckman had two pieces of wood from the "Royal Oak" made into two snuff boxes, which are on display in the house. He died in 1806 and his wife, Elizabeth, finished the house.

**Boscobel
Garrison-on-Hudson
10524
914–265–3638**

In the early 1950s the house had fallen into disrepair and was slated for the wrecking crew when it was finally purchased for $35. People in the area dismantled the house and stored the pieces in their barns until it could be rebuilt. Lila Acheson Wallace of the *Reader's*

Digest generously financed the reconstruction of the house. The house was completely restored and refurnished with as much accuracy as could be obtained from old records. The dining room contains silver belonging to the Dyckman family. Note the unusual wine glass coolers and the washstand that was available for travelers who wanted to wash up before dinner. The center hall of the house is so large that it was frequently used for dancing. The living room is set up for tea; afterward the tea table would be moved so the guests could play parlor games. The next room is a more casual living room; look for the barrel organ.

Downstairs in the museum area is a collection of decorative arts and memorabilia. Look for the snuff box in blue and gold. Lemonade or cider and cookies are offered at the end of the tour. Ask about Boscobel's special candlelit tours if you are going to be in the area during an evening.

COLD SPRING

Preservation, Revitalization of Cold Spring Area 73 Main Street Cold Spring 10516 914–265–2111

Follow Route 9D into Cold Spring, a historic nineteenth-century village. A number of houses and shops are within the National Historic District. The West Point Foundry provided employment for workers who lived in Cold Spring; the Parrott Cannon, which some say won the Civil War for the North, was manufactured there. The village lures strollers with its many shops and restaurants. Write or call for information on walking tours.

FISHKILL

Van Wyck Homestead Museum Route 9 Fishkill 10524 914–896–9560

From Cold Spring follow Route 9D north to Beacon and Route 52 northeast to Fishkill. The **Van Wyck Homestead Museum** is in a restored Dutch Colonial home. In 1732 Cornelius Van Wyck bought 959 acres of land and built his home, adding another wing in 1757. Between 1776 and 1783 it was used by Washington's officers as a headquarters. James

Fenimore Cooper's novel *The Spy* used this house as a setting; in reality there was a trial for Enoch Crosby, a spy who was imprisoned and then allowed to escape.

From Fishkill continue north on 9 through Wappingers Falls to Poughkeepsie. The Young-Morse Site, called **Locust Grove,** was the home of Samuel F. B. Morse. The house was named for the black locust trees lining the drive; Morse bought it in 1847 and remodeled it into a Tuscan villa. Memorabilia from his inventions, including the telegraph, are on display. The property was sold to the Young family in 1901, and the furnishings and collections of china, glassware, fans, dolls, costumes, and books are mostly those of Martha Innis Young.

The **Hudson Valley Philharmonic** (914–454–1222) offers a concert series during the year, both in Poughkeepsie and in Kingston. The Philharmonic also sponsors an innovative fund-raising project called "Designer's Showhouse." Every year a house in the area that could use renovation is revamped by local designers and architects; each provides the construction materials and furnishings for one room. Visitors buy a ticket from the Philharmonic to visit the house, and the owners of the house then have the choice of buying the results of the reconstruction or not. In any case, structural changes, wallpaper, and paint have refreshed the room and stay in place even if the furnishings are removed.

The **Bardavon 1869 Opera House** presents a full season of performances including chamber music, opera, jazz, choir, drama, special programs, and a Young People's Theater series.

Cruises on the Hudson River are available from **Riverboat Tours** (310 Mill Street, Poughkeepsie; 914–473–5211). The *River Queen*

POUGHKEEPSIE

Locust Grove
Route 9
Poughkeepsie 12602
914–454–4600

Bardavon 1869 Opera
 House
35 Market Street
Poughkeepsie 12602
914–471–5313

schedules sightseeing cruises, some of which include lunch or dinner.

HYDE PARK
Springwood
Route 9
Hyde Park 12538
914-229-9115

From Poughkeepsie follow Route 9 north to the south fringes of Hyde Park. **Springwood,** the home of Franklin Delano Roosevelt, dates back to 1810; it was purchased by his father in 1867. FDR and his mother remodeled the house in 1915. As you stand in the entrance hall, look for the Dutch clock, purchased by James and Sara Roosevelt in the Netherlands in 1881, and the bust of Franklin D. Roosevelt, sculpted by Paul Troubetskoy. His mother called the little room to the left "the snuggery"—a place where she could write or talk with a friend.

During World War I a new living room/library was added; there are many portraits, including one by Gilbert Stuart; statues; books; and comfortable furnishings. Eleanor Roosevelt once told the story of the night the king and queen of England arrived. Franklin planned to give them a cocktail after their long journey, but Sara, FDR's mother, felt that they would prefer a cup of tea. After they arrived and were given their choice, the king remarked that his mother would have made the same offer, but, in fact, he preferred to have a cocktail.

The Dresden Room—the music room—is furnished with floral slipcovers, Dresden china, and many family photographs. The dining room table is set with family china and silver as if the family were about ready to gather together, and Franklin's chair is placed at an angle so he could move into it easily from his wheelchair.

As you approach the staircase, you can't miss the old Chinese temple bell, which was rung half an hour before meals and then again when everyone should be seated. At the top of the stairs is the room Franklin used as a boy; each of his sons used that room as he became too old for the third-floor children's room. Once when Jimmy Roosevelt was sleeping in that room, there was anxiety about burglars; Franklin sat on lookout by the window with a gun, and Jimmy remembers being scared to death.

The king and queen of England stayed in the Pink Room, where they felt at home with the English prints on the walls. FDR was born in the room over the snuggery, in the southeast corner of the tower. The furniture in the room is original to that period of time. Franklin's dressing room contains his campaign hat, Navy cape, wheelchair, photographs, and other memorabilia.

The porch holds special memories of its own; FDR and his mother met guests there, and friends arrived at the porch to congratulate him each time he was victorious in an election. The rose garden, where his mother picked roses until her death, is the burial site of both Franklin and Eleanor.

The **Franklin D. Roosevelt Library and Museum** was built on land given by FDR for this purpose. He knew that his papers could not be housed in his home, and he wished to provide a place where historians and others could work with documents from this important era in American history.

This stone building with shutters holds personal papers, prints, a collection of Hudson Valley history, books, ship models, FDR's collection of naval prints, gifts given to the Roosevelts, and much more—even two Hudson River iceboats. You can spend hours looking at a collection that includes FDR's christening dress, a Scottish Murray clan kilt that he hated to wear as a child, a lock of his blond hair cut just before his fifth birthday, a hobby horse, Harvard cap and gown, photographs of his honeymoon in Europe—including one of FDR changing a tire in France with Eleanor and Aunt Doe looking on—photographs of the Roosevelt

Franklin D. Roosevelt Library and Museum Route 9 Hyde Park 12538 914-229-9115

children, and an entire room filled with political photos and documents. The last-named exhibit re-creates each phase of FDR's career and gives visitors a great deal of information on the extraordinary accomplishment of the hundred days of emergency legislation in 1933, as well as on each phase of World War II.

The **Eleanor Roosevelt Gallery** in the FDR Library and Museum is symbolized by the engraved crystal flame depicting the spirit with which she lived and acted. You can see Eleanor's christening dress, photos tracing her unhappy early childhood (when her parents were estranged and then died), her wedding veil with orange blossoms, jewelry made from things her father collected on lion hunts in Africa, gowns, an oriental evening coat, an honorary doctoral robe from Oxford, and many travel mementos.

Val-Kill, situated on a more remote part of the grounds on a separate site (take a shuttle bus or drive), was a retreat for Eleanor. She thought it a much cozier home than Springwood. She built a furniture factory there, which manufactured reproductions of early American furniture and provided jobs for local farmers during the winters. After FDR's death Eleanor lived at Val-Kill, considering Hyde Park her real home even though she had an apartment in New York. Many distinguished guests visited her there, including Khrushchev, Tito, Haile Selassie, and Nehru.

Culinary Institute of America
Route 9
Hyde Park 12538
914–454–1700

Make an advance reservation at the **Culinary Institute of America,** where 1,850 students are enrolled in a twenty-one-month culinary arts program. Students learn the fundamentals and refinements of cooking, baking, and charcuterie in American, oriental, and international cuisines. Ninety chefs and instructors from eighteen countries teach them within a restaurant setting. The Escoffier Restaurant, The

American Bounty Restaurant, The Caterina de Medici Restaurant, and St. Andrew's Cafe offer an extensive menu for lunch and dinner. Be sure to make a reservation because these extraordinary restaurants are sometimes booked ahead for several months, particularly on weekends. Tours of the seventy-five–acre campus are available two days a week.

Just north of Hyde Park is the **Vanderbilt Mansion.** This fifty-four–room, Italian Renaissance mansion was built by Frederick William Vanderbilt just before the turn of the century. Stanford White and his partners designed the mansion; they were also the architects for the Boston Public Library, the Pierpont Morgan Library, Columbia University, and the Villard Houses (now the New York Palace Hotel) in New York City. Edith Wharton and Ogden Codman, Jr., authors of *The Decoration of Houses,* published in 1897, were instrumental in developing the mansion's interior design. The oval center hall features Italian marble, a mantel that came from a palace, and a tapestry bearing the coat of arms of the Medici family. The living room is paneled in walnut from Russia; it was often used for dancing to music provided by a small orchestra. The mansion was furnished with elegant, ornate period pieces, mostly from France and Italy. The dining room table could seat thirty persons in a luxurious setting. The Vanderbilts lived in the mansion from Easter to early July, spent the summer in Newport or Europe, then returned in the fall until it was time to go to New York City for the winter social season.

You can walk through the gardens among the forty varieties of trees. The grounds were developed as early as 1795 by previous owners. On your way out you can follow a road that leads down to the river, where the Vanderbilt yachts once docked.

Vanderbilt Mansion
Route 9
Hyde Park 12538
914–229–9115

STAATSBURG

Mills Mansion
Old Albany Post
Road, off Route 9
Staatsburg 12580
914-889-4100

A few mile north of the Vanderbilt Mansion is the **Mills Mansion,** the setting of Edith Wharton's *The House of Mirth.* She described the grounds with all of their "opulent undulations," and about the library she said:

> The library was almost the only surviving portion of the old manor-house of Bellomont: a long spacious room, revealing the traditions of the mother-country in its classically-cased doors, the Dutch tiles of the chimney, and the elaborate hobgrate with its shining brass urns. A few family portraits of lantern-jawed gentlemen in tie-wigs, and ladies with large head-dresses and small bodies, hung between the shelves lined with pleasantly-shabby books: books mostly contemporaneous with the ancestors in question, and to which the subsequent Trenors had made no perceptible additions. The library at Bellomont was in fact never used for reading, though it had a certain popularity as a smoking-room or a quiet retreat for flirtation.

Morgan Lewis and his wife, the sister of Chancellor Robert Livingston, bought the land in 1792 and built their home. Here the Lewises entertained many famous people, including Joseph Bonaparte and the Marquis de Lafayette.

The house was destroyed by fire in 1832 and rebuilt in Greek Revival style by the Lewises. Ruth Livingston Mills inherited the house and enlarged it in 1896 by adding two wings, balustrades, pilasters, and floral swags on the facade. Inside, marble fireplaces, gilded ceilings, and oak paneling enhance the ornate, carved and gilded furnishings, tapestries, paintings, and many art objects. As with many of the other mansions along the Hudson, Mills Mansion was occupied only a few months of the year.

The estate is part of **Mills-Norrie State**

Park, which offers boating, fishing, camping, golf, nature and hiking trails, and picnicking facilities. Norrie Point Marina is a state-operated boat basin with launching and mooring facilities. In the park the **Dutchess Community College Environmental Museum** offers an educational program on the natural history of the mid-Hudson area for both students and the public.

From Staatsburg continue north on Route 9 to Rhinebeck. Five Dutch settlers bought 2,200 ares from the Sepasco and Esopus Indians for "6 buffaloes, 4 blankets, 5 kettles, 4 guns, 5 axes, 10 cans of powder, 8 shirts, 40 fathoms of wampum, 2 drawing knives, 2 adzes, half an anker of rum and one frying pan." Although Rhinebeck was founded by the Dutch in 1686, a group of German settlers named it Rhinebeck because its setting reminded them of cliffs along the Rhine. Today you can stroll through the National Historic District, maintained as a nineteenth-century village, with a walking-tour map from the **Rhinebeck Historical Society.** The Beekman Arms dates from 1766, the Delameter House from 1844, and the Dutch Reformed Church from 1809.

The oldest hotel in America, the **Beekman Arms,** is still operating in Rhinebeck on Route 9 (914–876–7077). Built by Arent Traphagen, the inn has sturdy stone walls 2 and 3 feet thick, mammoth oak beams, and floor boards 14 inches wide. As you walk in, you will see that the original structure still has the ambience that greeted guests during colonial days. Stop for lunch or dinner in the Tap Room; the Pewter Room, where an antique corner cupboard and collection of clocks reside; the Wine Cellar Room; or the new glassed-in Greenhouse Room. You can also spend the night in the hotel, or at the Delameter House or the Carriage House. (See Inns appendix).

RHINEBECK

Rhinebeck Historical Society
Box 291
Rhinebeck 12572
914–876–4778

**Old Rhinebeck
Aerodrome
Stone Church Road,
off Route 9
Rhinebeck 12572
914-758-8610**

Old Rhinebeck Aerodrome houses a collection of aircraft dating from 1908 to 1938. Instead of Muzak your ears will pick up the ballads of World War I. On weekends there are air shows above your head, and you can also take a ride in open-cockpit biplanes.

GERMANTOWN

**Clermont State Park
Route 9G
Germantown 12526
518-537-4240**

Continue north on Route 9G to Germantown. **Clermont State Park** was the ancestral home of Chancellor Robert R. Livingston. His great-great-grandfather was born in Scotland in 1654, spent years in Holland, and arrived in America in 1673. In 1686 Governor Dongan granted him a manor of 160,000 acres of land along the Hudson River. As lord of the manor, Livingston had full control of both the land and his tenants, and he also had a seat in the Colonial Legislature. The British burned the manor house in 1777, but it was rebuilt with the same Georgian architecture; in the 1870s a French-style roof was added. The house may be toured during the summer.

Livingston and Robert Fulton became friends and then partners as they planned and built a steamboat, named the *Clermont* after the estate. Robert Fulton married Livingston's cousin, and the partnership was firmly established. The state park offers nature trails, hiking, cross-country skiing, picnic facilities, and fine river views. From the park continue north on Route 9G to Hudson.

HUDSON

Shades of Nantucket! In 1783 Seth and Tom Jenkins, worrying that the British would vanquish Nantucket in another attempt to regain control of the colonies, moved west to find another home. They chose Hudson as a site and moved there lock, stock, and barrel in their whaling ships, with a number of other families. Some lived on board ship while their houses were being constructed. The new residents built up a number of the businesses they knew, including, of course, shipbuilding, a distillery, a sperm oilworks, and a sail loft. The War of 1812 demolished much of their industry, but by 1830 whaling was again in full swing. Many of the old buildings have been restored: the **Robert Jenkins House** (113 Warren Street), the **Cyrus Curtiss House** (32 Warren Street), and the **Bank of Hudson** (116 Warren Street).

The **American Museum of Fire Fighting** houses one of the oldest and largest collections of equipment in the country. You can't miss the statue of a fire chief with his handsome blue and red coat, carved in the 1850s. Currier and Ives prints are also on display. Stroll among the decorated nineteenth-century fire engines until you come to the Weiner Hose Company's carriage, which was used only for dress occasions such as parades and thus maintained its glistening appearance.

**American Museum of Fire Fighting
Harry Howard Avenue
Hudson 12534
518–828–7695**

Olana, 5 miles south of Hudson, was the home of painter Frederic E. Church. Set on a bluff 500 feet above the Hudson River, this home looks out of place with its Persian-style exterior. Church, a member of the Hudson River School, studied with Thomas Cole and painted amazing landscapes with a fine depiction of light. The views he had from his home must have been inspiring indeed. He wrote: "About one hour this side of Albany is the center of the world. I own it."

**Olana
Route 9G
Hudson 12534
518–828–0135**

North on Route 9 is Kinderhook. Henry Hudson sailed his ship here in 1609, noticed the group of Mohican Indian children who had come to stare at his ship, and named the village Kinderhook ("Children's Corner").

KINDERHOOK

Lindenwald was purchased by President Martin Van Buren in 1839, while he was in office. His youngest son had the house remodeled as an Italian villa with a four-story brick

**Lindenwald
Route 9H
Kinderhook 12106
518–758–9689**

Van Alen House
Route 9H
Kinderhook 12106
518-758-9265

tower. Earlier, around 1800, Washington Irving had tutored the children who lived in the house. He was interested in local legends and eventually used some of them in his own writing. The **Van Alen House,** nearby, may have been inhabited by the model for one of Irving's characters, Katrina Van Tassel. The house, built of red brick, reflects typical Dutch architecture, with gables, separate outside doors for each room, and a steep roof. A collection of delft and Hudson Valley paintings is on display.

OLD CHATHAM

The Shaker Museum
Shaker Museum Road
Old Chatham 12136
518-794-9100

Nearby in Old Chatham **The Shaker Museum** preserves the history of a community founded by Mother Ann Lee in 1774. Born in 1736 in Manchester, England, she joined a sect of Quakers who were distinguished from others by the peculiarity that they would be aroused with "a mighty shaking" during their meetings. Ann's group also believed that men and women should be equal and celibate. She had a vision instructing her to travel to America, so with eight others she arrived in Watervliet on August 6, 1774, and set up their society. "Do all your work as though you had a thousand years to live and as you would if you knew you must die tomorrow" sums up their attitude toward work. Although they lived by the Millennial Laws that prescribed celibacy, separate schools for boys and girls, and the clothing that must be worn—and prohibited ownership of property—the Shakers were respected by the surrounding communities for the high quality of the goods they produced and for their hard work. This museum has exhibits of Shaker furniture, a blacksmith shop, a schoolroom, a collection of tools, nine rooms containing furnishings of that time, and a craft gallery.

At this point, if you are traveling a circular route up and down the Hudson River, head back to Route 9, follow it south through

Hudson, and cross over the river to Catskill. If you are heading for Albany and upstate New York, head west to pick up Route 9H north to its junction with I–90; follow I–90 into Albany.

The cities of Albany, Schenectady, and Troy are linked together at the junction of the Hudson and Mohawk rivers, forming the Capital District. Albany is the site of the capitol, a building in French Renaissance style. It is now overshadowed by the Governor Nelson A. Rockefeller Empire State Plaza, which contains the Institute of Performing Arts, the State Museum, State Library, and the Corning Tower Building. The plaza is a showplace complete with sculpture, pools, and the ripple of fountains.

The **New York State Capitol** looks like a French château. It took more than thirty years to build, from 1867 to 1899. Look at the elaborate carving found on the building, especially the head of "Liberty," which is surrounded by garlands, and "Plenty," a female with intertwining grapes. Don't miss the "million dollar staircase," where the stone carvers sculpted faces of relatives and friends. Search for faces!

Capitol Park, right next to the capitol building, is a great place to buy an ethnic lunch from one of many vendors. The park has formal gardens, fountains, and a statue of General Philip Sheridan.

Governor Nelson A. Rockefeller Empire State Plaza is a ninety-six-acre government office complex surrounded by shops, restaurants, and entertainment centers. Referred to as "the Mall," this marble complex was a gleam in Governor Rockefeller's eye in 1962—with an estimated cost of $350 million. Labor problems caused delays, however, and it was finally finished for more than $2 billion in 1978. The Mall contains sculptures created by contem-

ALBANY

Albany Convention and Visitors' Bureau
52 N. Pearl
Albany 12207
800–732–8259;
518–434–1217

New York State Capitol
Albany 12242
518–474–2418

Governor Nelson A. Rockefeller Empire State Plaza
Madison to State Streets
Albany

porary artists, including David Smith, Alexander Calder, Françoise Stahly, Dimitri Hadji, Donald Judd, Alexander Liberman, Clement Meadmore, James Rosati, and George Rickey. Below the plaza is a long hallway called "The Concourse." A contemporary art collection lines the walls of the hallway, leading to shops, restaurants, banks, and ticket offices.

The most striking building on the plaza is the **New York State Institute.** Locally known as "The Egg" because of its shape, the center features drama, dance, and musical performances. The Empire State Youth Theater, Empire State Youth Orchestra, and Noon Concert Series call the building home. There are two theaters: one seats 950, and the other seats 450.

The **New York State Museum** contains exhibits on three themes: Man and Nature in New York State, the City of New York, and the Adirondack Wilderness. See the film, *The Chronicles of Change,* which will give you an introduction to the exhibits. The museum added a life-size Mohawk Iroquois longhouse in October of 1992. This museum uses a variety of techniques to bring history alive for the viewer, including life-size dioramas of lumberjacks maneuvering logs down wild rivers, fishermen in action, and the sounds of birds coming from realistic woodland settings. The Adirondack Wilderness section begins with "Prehistoric Wilderness" and includes lifelike groups of animals and hunters. The geologic history of the Adirondacks illustrates the evolution of the mountains, beginning with the collision of two continents over a billion years ago. The museum also has a section on gems found in New York and an antique fire engine exhibit.

Robinson Square, on nearby Hamilton Street, was once slated for destruction until it was saved by the efforts of local residents. These brownstone row houses from the 1850s

New York State Theater Institute
Albany 12242
518–443–5222;
518–442–5373 (box office)

New York State Museum
Empire State Plaza
Albany 12223
518–474–5842

now contain shops, apartments, and restaurants.

Albany Institute of History and Art dates back to 1791. Exhibits depict life in the upper Hudson River Valley through period furniture, silver, china, pewter, and paintings. The institute holds lectures, concerts, tours, workshops, and classes throughout the year.

Albany Institute of History and Art
125 Washington Avenue
Albany 12210
518–463–4478

Ten Broeck Mansion was built for Abraham Ten Broeck in 1798. General Ten Broeck was a member of the Colonial Assembly, a delegate to the Continental Congress, brigadier general in the Revolutionary army, and mayor of Albany. The general and his wife were both sixty-three years old when they built the house. The Great Albany Fire of 1797 had destroyed their previous home, so Ten Broeck leased the land from his father-in-law, Patroon Stephen Van Rensselaer. Thomas Worth Olcott moved into the house in 1850, and his family lived there for the next hundred years. It is now maintained by the Albany County Historical Association. This Federal mansion contains Sheraton, Phyfe, Hepplewhite, and Italianate furniture. Recently a valuable collection of wine was discovered in a cellar under the structure. Much of the wine had been bought many years before in Europe or New York City, and some of the original cases remained intact. Heublein auctioned the wine, and the money received was used for restoration of the mansion.

Ten Broeck Mansion
9 Ten Broeck Place
Albany 12210
518–436–9826

Historic Cherry Hill, a Georgian-style home lived in by five generations of the Van Rensselaer/Elmendorf/Rankin families until 1963, was built in 1787 for Philip Van Rensselaer. Fortunately, because the house had never been sold outside of the family, all of their personal belongings and clothing were saved. Visitors enter the house through an orientation room, where diagrams of the family tree outline the sequence of those who lived in

Historic Cherry Hill
523½ South Pearl Street
Albany 12202
518–434–4791

the house. Philip and Maria Van Rensselaer were the first to do so, beginning in 1787. Philip was the grandson of Hendrick Van Rensselaer, whose brother Kilian was patroon at that time. Philip Schuyler, who built Schuyler Mansion, was his cousin; a portrait of their grandmother, Elsie Wendell Schuyler, is in the dining room. Maria was the granddaughter of Peter Schuyler, the first mayor of Albany. Philip and Maria were merchant farmers who also owned a town house on North Pearl Street; they had thirteen children. The last member of the family to live in the house was Emily Watkinson Rankin, who died in 1963.

Cherry Hill is an unusual preservation site because it shows the life of a family from the 1780s to the 1960s, rather than in just one era. Visitors can trace the changes in life through nearly two hundred years of American history by examining the personal belongings left in the house. The collection includes china, furniture, silver, textiles, portraits, and documents. As you walk through the house you will see a mixture of furniture styles, because each generation added new pieces to supplement the original Chippendale. Catherine Van Rensselaer Bonney, daughter of Solomon and Harriet Van Rensselaer, was a missionary in the Orient. She sent home many oriental furnishings and decorations, including mirrors, prints, and ceramics in the camphorwood trunks used for shipping goods. At another time an Albany cabinetmaker by the name of Reed made some pieces for the house. Look for the collection of "branded" furniture in the dining room. To enable recipients to identify their possessions in the eighteenth century, brands were placed on furniture when it was shipped at the docks.

The house also contains an extensive collection of women's clothing, most of it made by dressmakers. Two of the bedrooms contain examples of clothing that had been found carefully preserved in trunks in the attic.

You can trace the development of heating in this house, beginning with the fireplace, then a coal grate in the fireplace, stoves of various kinds, and finally a hot-air furnace leading to grated floor vents. Lighting also underwent a series of changes, from candles through oil, kerosene, and gas lamps to electricity. The first and second generations living in the house did not have indoor plumbing but were dependent on the outdoor "necessity" and chamber pots. Before you leave, ask about Jesse Strang's murder confession; apparently he shot the husband of his lover through a window of the house.

The **Schuyler Mansion** is also called "The Pastures"; the two acres of lawns and gardens affirm the name. As you approach this home from below you will see the large brick structure high on a hill with what was originally a fine view of the river. Lawns went all the way down to the river, and guests arriving by water were sure to be impressed. This Georgian home was built in 1761 by Philip Schuyler. Schuyler came from a prominent local family and distinguished himself during the French and Indian War. He received a captain's commission in 1755 as recognition for gathering enough men to accompany William Johnson in the battle of Crown Point. He was involved in the preparations for the Battle of Lake George but was, in fact, attending his own wedding to Catharine Van Rensselaer on September 7, 1755, while the battle was in progress.

Schuyler Mansion State Historic Site
32 Catherine Street
Albany 12202
518–434–0834

George Washington did visit here, as did Benjamin Franklin, Benedict Arnold, Baron von Steuben, Comte de Rochambeau, and even General Burgoyne. This last guest may seem surprising because he had ordered Schuyler's country house in Saratoga to be burned during the crucial Battle of Saratoga; actually, the defeated British general was a prisoner/guest in the house.

Look for the gash on the stair rail, which may have been made by an Indian tomahawk. Tories tried to kidnap Schuyler during the Revolutionary War, but he heard of their plot in advance and was able to hire guards to thwart the attack. Although records do not indicate that Indians were involved in that incident, there is a legend that one of his daughters had run downstairs to rescue her baby sister, somehow forgotten in her cradle in the living room. She was on her way back up with the baby in her arms when, reportedly, an Indian tomahawk was thrown at her and gashed the stair rail. The house is furnished with period furniture, including some from the Schuyler family; Chinese export porcelain; delftware; and English glassware. Originally the house contained a wing on each side to house the kitchen smokehouse, gardener's shed, icehouse, carriage house, barn, coach house, office, and nursery with adjoining kitchen.

Some good restaurant choices in Albany include **Cranberry Bog** (56 Wolf Road; 518–459–5110), **La Serre** (14 Green Street; 518–463–6056), **Ogden's** (Howard at Lodge Street; 518–463–6605), and **Parc V Cafe** (Albany-Shaker Road at Route 155; 518–869–9976).

SCHENECTADY

Algonquin Indians first lived on the land that is now Schenectady; then the Iroquois battled their way to the site. In 1661 Arendt Van Curler bought 128 square miles from the Indians and banded together with fifteen other families to form a patroonship, where they built homes within a stockade for protection against the French. By 1690 there were sixty houses and four hundred persons living in the stockade. That year, during King William's War, 114 Frenchmen serving under Le Moyne de Sainte

Hélène and 96 Indians from Canada attacked the stockade. Sixty persons were killed, twenty-seven were taken captive, and many others died from the cold after their homes were burned. Friendly Indians in the area convinced the few settlers who survived to stay on their land and rebuild, which they did. When the Erie Canal was completed in 1825, business began to boom in Schenectady. Engines were built by the Schenectady Locomotive Works beginning in 1851, and in 1886 General Electric was founded there by Thomas Edison, leading to one rather expansive sobriquet—"The City That Hauls and Lights the World."

The **Stockade** (bounded by State Street, Washington Avenue, Front Street, and Ferry Street) is a residential area on the site of the original stockade settlement founded in the seventeenth century. Some of the existing homes were built before the Revolution, and others date from the early 1800s. The first Dutch settlers built their homes in the fashion of their homeland, with houses set right on the street and deep narrow gardens behind. The **Schenectady County Historical Society** maintains a museum of exhibits from the area, a library, a genealogical collection, and a collection of many documents. The society also conducts a "walkabout" of the Stockade every September.

Schenectady County
Historical Society
32 Washington
Avenue
Schenectady 12305
518–374–0263

Whenever you come to the Stockade, you can catch glimpses of the gardens and note the high Dutch gables and gambrel roofs. If you want to take your own walking tour, start at the Historical Society. Cross over Front Street to the **Jacob Vrooman House** (3–5 Washington Avenue), which was built next to the toll-keeper's house by the Washington Avenue bridge. Turn down Front Street to the **Governor Yates House** (17 Front Street), which dates from 1760. In 1825 Major General the Marquis de Lafayette stayed in the house as a guest of the governor.

The next house is the **Jeremiah deGraaf House** (25–27 Front Street), now divided into two homes. Note the doorway of Number 25 with its elegant pilasters and the oval sunburst medallion.

Across the street is the **Hendrick Brouwer House** (14 North Church Street), owned by a fur trader known for his honesty in dealing with the Indians. At one time they spared his home when others were destroyed, and it may be that some parts of this house retain the original structure. Return to Front Street and walk to its intersection with North Street to see the **Johannes Teller House** (121 Front Street), which dates from 1740. The gambrel roof continues as a shed roof on the other side.

At the juncture of Front, Green, and North Ferry streets stands the statue of an Indian that was placed there in 1887 as a symbol of friendship with the Mohawks. These were the Indians who encouraged the white men to stay and rebuild their town after the massacre of 1690. The **Old Public Market,** dating from 1795, is on one of the corners, and **St. George's Episcopal Church,** from 1759, stands on another. The **First Presbyterian Church,** elegant in Greek Revival style, is around the corner on Union Street. Turn right on Union Street to the **Abraham Yates House** (109 Union Street), dating from 1700. It is the only house in the Stockade built with a steep gable on the street side and brick wall as a parapet above the roof. Don't miss the "butterfly" brickwork on the gables. Across the street is the **Old County Court House** in Greek Revival style. Next to the Yates House is the **First Reformed Church,** dating from 1863, standing as the sixth building on the site of the original church built by Dutch settlers in 1682.

Union College
Union & Nott
 Streets
Schenectady 12308

Union College was founded in 1795. The first planned college campus in the United States, Union was also the first institute of higher learning in New York State chartered by the Board of Regents. On the Nott Street side of the campus, **Jackson's Garden,** with sixteen acres of formal and wild gardens, including an evergreen garden and an herb garden, surrounds a brook; students and alumni often hold weddings under a geiko tree there.

Nott Memorial, at the center of the campus, is also worth a visit. Originally a gallery for sculpture, then a library, and now a theater-in-the-round, this sixteen-sided structure built over nearly forty years in the middle of the nineteenth century marks the transition from stone-and-wood construction to framing with iron and steel; its thin dome is made possible by the use of steel. Around its base, in Hebrew, is a rabbinical teaching: "The day is short, the task is great, God is urgent."

The Schenectady Museum and Union College are joint hosts for an **International Festival of Chamber Music** in the **Union Memorial Chapel,** which has fine acoustics. Eleven concerts are presented by groups from England, Czechoslovakia, Germany, and the United States.

Near the college you can enjoy lunch at **Van Dyck** (237 Union Street; 518–374–2406).

The **Schenectady Museum and Planetarium** has long-range plans to offer exhibits capitalizing on the advanced technological industries that developed in Schenectady during the nineteenth century; exhibits will be partly displays and partly participatory. The museum now offers classes in art, crafts, and antiques; a planetarium; exhibits on history, science, and industry; and other concert series with Union College. The museum also sponsors a number of popular annual events, including plant shows, a crafts festival, and a festival of nations.

Schenectady Museum began as a children's museum in the Schenectady City School District

International Festival of Chamber Music Union Memorial Chapel Schenectady 518–382–7890

Schenectady Museum and Planetarium Nott Terrace Heights Schenectady 12308 518–382–7890

in 1934. It outgrew its classroom and moved into the former County Almshouse for a thirty-year stay until the city decided to tear down the almshouse and build an elementary school on the site; then the present museum was built. Don't miss the clever hands-on exhibits for children. In the "Discovery Center" children will find a number of "discovery boxes" that may be checked out and taken home. A box may include a small student-type microscope, a button collection, old locks with keys, small and sturdy musical instruments, and other items of interest to children. Also notice a display of stuffed animals that came largely from local residents who had their pets stuffed, and a costume collection that stretches from the early eighteenth century into the twentieth.

Canal Square
State & Jay Streets
Schenectady

Canal Square has been the focus of a revitalization project to restore historic buildings around the central canal system of the city. **Jay Street Market Place,** just across State Street, is a continuation of shops, restaurants, antiques shops, and bookstores.

Proctor's Theater
432 State Street
Schenectady 12305
518–346–6204

Proctor's Theater is now housed in a restored 1926 vaudeville movie house. This theater, one of a chain of theaters, was owned by F. F. Proctor and completed in 1926 for $1.5 million. During the 1970s local residents banded together to restore Proctor's, and in 1979 the theater opened again with a full program of music, dance, and opera. Half the fun of going is looking at the elegant gilt and crystal chandeliers, the gold leaf on ceilings and walls, and the Louis XV marble fireplace.

Schenectady is part of the 23-mile **Mohawk-Hudson Greenway** hiking and biking path, which runs through Niskayuna, Schenectady, Glenville, Scotia, and Rotterdam. Along it you can watch canal activity at Locks 7, 8, and 9. Contact the Schenectady Chamber of Commerce for a map.

Schenectady Chamber
of Commerce
234 Canal Street
12305
518–372–5656

From Schenectady take Route 890 to I–90 east, then I–87 south to Catskill to continue the Hudson River route back to New York City. If you are linking with Itinerary B (Upstate New York), take I–87 north to Saratoga Springs.

North of Catskill is the **Bronck House.** Pieter Bronck built this house in 1663; other buildings on the property date from the same year, 1685, and 1738. Inside the house are paintings by Thomas Cole, John Frederick Kensett, Ezra Ames, Richard Hubbard, Benjamin Stone, and Ammi Phillips. Period furniture, china, and glass are exhibited. A Dutch barn, a Victorian horse barn, and an unusual thirteen-sided barn with center pole construction are on the property.

COXSACKIE
Bronck House
Route 9W
Coxsackie 12051
518–731–8862

The **Thomas Cole House,** or **"Cedar Grove,"** was built in 1815; artist Thomas Cole lived there from 1836 to 1848. A 1985 exhibit featured his series of allegorical subjects, *The Voyage of Life.* The four paintings in the original set were painted in 1849–1850 and are in the Munson-Williams-Proctor Institute in Utica. In 1852 one of Cole's proteges, De Witt Clinton Boutelle, completed the series. Today the house is open by appointment.

CATSKILL
Thomas Cole House
218 Spring Street
Catskill 12414
518–943–6533

The **Catskill Game Farm** is a large park showing wild animals in their natural settings. The African section features cheetahs, antelope, and rhinos; a train runs around a bird garden, offering views of rare mountain goats and sheep on the other side. You can see bears, baboons, giraffes, a pygmy hippo, kangaroos, prairie dogs, and many more species, as well as baby animals in the nursery. Bring a picnic, or have lunch in the cafeteria.

Catskill Game Farm
Off Route 32
Catskill 12414
518–678–9595

In case you aren't going to the Orient, you can see Buddhist temples in a very unlikely setting—the Catskills. South Cairo (on Route 23 west of Catskill) boasts three temples, the earliest constructed in 1971 as the first Buddhist pagoda in the United States. One of them contains an eighteen-foot golden statue known as the Buddha of Mercy. A seven-story pagoda was built in 1984 as a symbol of good luck.

One of the things that visitors like to do in winter is ski at one of the Catskill areas. It's nice to escape the winter doldrums by heading for the crisp air and falling snowflakes for cross-country or alpine skiing, snowboarding, or just looking at the view. Some of the areas also offer year-round activities, so you can indulge in tennis, golf, hiking, or simply enjoying the view when the slopes are green. All of the areas offer a nice escape from the city.

Ski Windham
Windham
New York 12496
800–729–4SNO

Ski Windham has recently built a large lodge with wraparound, picture-window views. Intermediate skiers may want to start out easily on the Whiteway triple chair lift up to Wheelhouse Lodge (great for lunch) and ski down What's Next for a warmup. Then take the Wonderama triple chair lift and try Wonderama, a nice, well-groomed, wide slope under the chair. Next take the same chair up and ski Warm Up, a wide, intermediate trail. Take the same chair again and move over one trail to Lower Wheelchair, which is a bit narrower; when we were there a NASTAR race was held on the slope. The Whirlwind triple chair lift (or Whistler double chair lift) drops you off at the top for a run down Upper Wraparound, which is winding but sometimes crowded with skiers, leading into Lower Wraparound, which is easy. Take one of the same chairs up again and try Upper Wraparound, head left on Waltz, then take a right on Upper Warpath, which is a little steeper, and into Lower Warpath, an easy trail. Next time take Upper Wraparound to Upper Wise Acres and Lower Wise Acres—nice with trees and winding. When you're in really good shape, you might try Why Not, marked expert, from the

Why Not triple chair lift. It is wide with some steep pitches but not double black diamond.

Belleayre has a separate area for beginners that can also be reached from the main area. Ski down from any trail behind the Upper Lodge to the Lower Lodge, and take the lift back up. Intermediate skiers can take the double chair on the left, looking up from the lodge to the top, and then ski along the ridge to the only intermediate trail up there, Roaring Brook. This is a wide, gentle slope that is well groomed and easy intermediate, with less pitch than other intermediate trails. Then take the middle triple chair and get off at the midstation, as the trails at the top of the mountain are expert. Then you can walk on the flat toward the easier intermediate trails to the right or take the T-bar. Esopus, Peekamoose, Pepacton, and Seneca are all wide with winding curves. Back on the left side of the mountain, take the chair to the midstation and try Winnisook, Tongora, Belleayre Run, and Wanatuska. Since the upper third of the mountain is rated expert, any advanced intermediate who wants to try trails there is advised as follows: The least difficult are to the right looking up from the lodge, that is, Upper Peekamoose and Upper Seneca. The next hard lie on the left: Upper Tongora, Belleayre, and Wanatuska. And the most difficult are in the middle: Upper Onteora, Yahoo, and Utsayantha.

Palenville (southwest of Catskill on Route 23A) is the legendary home of Rip Van Winkle because Washington Irving wrote *Rip Van Winkle* while living there. James Fenimore Cooper later wrote that Palenville was "the greatest wonder of American landscape." The first and the oldest arts colony, known as **Interarts,** was begun in 1979 by Kevin Kennedy. A full schedule of music, dance, and theater is available.

South of Catskill **Opus 40** was developed

Belleayre
Belleayre Road
Box 313
Highmount, New York 12441
914-254-5600

Opus 40
7480 Fite Road
Saugerties 12477
914–246–3400

by one man, Harvey Fite, who originally bought the quarry as a source of stone for his sculpture. He built a house and studio there, began to clear the piles of rubble, and, using a quarryman's hand tools, hammers, chisels, drills, and a boom with a tray to move rocks, made terraces, walks, and stone walls. Fite displayed his sculptures amid pools and fountains, and in 1962 he used only fulcrum and lever principles to raise a nine-ton stone into position in the center of his garden. He named his quarry Opus 40 because he thought it would take him forty years to finish it. During the summer months classical, folk, and jazz concerts are held there. The **Quarryman's Museum** contains Fite's collection of quarryman's tools.

Those who think of the Catskills as nothing but an extension of the crowds and bustle of New York City are mistaken. The forest primeval lures hikers all through the Catskills. Almost everywhere you can hike to a quiet mountain lake or enjoy an unspoiled view from the top of a peak. For example, the **Escarpment Trail** is one that provides hikers with one scenic view after another above the cliffs of Kaaterskill Clove. The route begins at the junction of Route 23A and Kaaterskill Creek and winds for 24 miles to East Windham on Route 23. **North Lake** is pristine, and nearby, at the site of the **Catskill Mountain House** (long since burned), there are panoramic views of the Hudson Valley, the Taconics, and the Berkshires. And to top it all, you are in the vicinity of Kaaterskill Falls, which has a longer drop than that of Niagara. That is the particular appeal of the Catskills—many treats within a small compass. Hikers and backpackers can approach these pleasures through the Appalachian Trail, which winds over the Catskills on its way from Pennsylvania to Vermont. Read some of John Burroughs's works to catch the particular flavor of these mountains.

For a pamphlet entitled *Catskill Trails,* write to the **Department of Environmental Conservation,** Region 4 Subregion Office, 439 Main Street, Catskill, New York 12414. Or you may call 518–943–4030. Topographic maps may be obtained from the **U.S. Geological Survey,** 1200 South Eads Street, Arlington, Virginia 22202.

The Catskills claim to have been the site of the first fly fishing. Try for rainbow trout on the upper Kaaterskill, brown trout farther downstream, and finally bass and panfish below High Falls. The Catskill Creek, with its tributaries, Ten Mile Creek, Basic Creek, and Shingle Kill, contains brown trout; upstream from Oak Hill rainbow trout inhabit it.

KINGSTON

After your excursions into the Catskills, return to the scenic river road, Route 9W, and continue south to Kingston. The original settlement, called Esopus, was built within a stockade for protection from the Indians, but the thatched-roofed houses were easily burned by Indians in 1663. The next houses were built of natural local limestone between 1670 and 1750. The rural Flemish style, originally a single room with a grain storage loft above, is also found in New Paltz. Just before the Revolution the residents began to build square, two-story town houses. The area is still referred to as the Stockade District.

The **Senate House** was the site of the first New York state senate. The house had been built by Wessel Ten Broeck and overlooked the Esopus Creek. Abraham Van Gaasbeek owned the house in 1777 when Kingston served as the capital of New York. The first meeting in his house was on September 9, 1777. By October 7, however, with the British advancing up the Hudson, the senate was moved to Poughkeepsie. Visit the Senate House Museum; it contains the largest collection of paintings by John

Senate House
312 Fair Street
Kingston 12401
914–338–2786

A•91

Vanderlyn, who was a native of Kingston. Vanderlyn studied under Gilbert Stuart and made copies of Stuart's famous George and Martha Washington portraits. Aaron Burr offered to become his patron and sent him to study in France. In the museum look for a painting entitled *Ariadne Asleep and Abandoned by Theseus on the Island of Naxos.* Another favorite of many viewers is the portrait of Mrs. John R. Livingston, in which a mirror catches her profile.

There are many stone houses to see in the Stockade District. You can take a tour using a map from the **Friends of Historic Kingston** (914–338–5100).

Head across town and down the hill to the **Roundout** area, a nineteenth-century waterfront district. Originally called Kingston Landing, it came into its own in 1828 when the Delaware and Hudson Canal opened. The shipping of Pennsylvania coal, Ulster County bluestone, and Kingston cement and brick was big business. Shipbuilders set up shop there, first in sailing vessels and then in steamboats, but the area went into a decline when river traffic became less efficient than railroads and highways. The area is now being revitalized; a number of shops are open, and work is continuing on others.

Hudson River Maritime Center
Rondout Landing
Kingston 12401
914–338–0071

The **Hudson River Maritime Center** opened in 1980 to preserve the maritime heritage of the Hudson River, especially in the form of historic vessels afloat and ashore. You will see the *Matilda,* an 1899 steam tug, sitting in her cradle. She was retired in 1969 by McAllister Towing Company of Montreal, Canada, as the last operating commercial steam tugboat in North America. She was on display at the South Street Seaport in New York City until she sank at her dock in 1976. She was then raised, repaired, and given to the maritime center in 1983. The *Rip Van Winkle* offers all-day tours and music cruises on Friday and Saturday nights.

The museum has exhibits from the *Mary Powell,* a Hudson River steamboat built in 1861. She steamed to Manhattan on a daily basis, and people up and down the Hudson enjoyed watching her come into view. You can have a tour through the boat-building shop to watch the restoration progress on recent acquisitions. Pete Seeger is featured in a video presentation on the river, including a favorite, "Sailing down My Golden River. . . ." The **Hudson River Chapter of the Antique and Classic Boat Society** has its headquarters in the museum.

Head south on I–87 to signs for New Paltz.

NEW PALTZ

In 1677 the heads of twelve families signed a treaty with the Esopus Indians for 39,683 acres of land. Four months later Governor Andros issued a patent for the lands, which were named a township, and in 1678 the twelve families arrived to settle on their patent. These settlers had originally come from Lille and Calais, France. As refugees from Catholic persecution in France, they lived near Speyer and Mannheim, Germany, in the province of "Die Pfalz," and so named their new town New Paltz. They were of the French Huguenot faith; *Huguenot* means "French Protestant" and may have been derived either from the Swiss Protestant *Hugues* or from the Flemish *Huis genooten,* which means "house fellowship," since the people met in homes to study the Bible and pray.

Abraham Hasbrouck, as the leader, was able to obtain a large tract of land for his people. The group set up a unique form of government called the *Duzine,* or "Rule of the Elders." Later one representative from each of the twelve families was elected to the Duzine.

Indians advised the twelve families to build on high ground because the river sometimes flooded the valley; the settled on what is

**Huguenot Historical
Society**
Box 339
New Paltz 12561
914–255–1660;
914–255–1889

now Huguenot Street. The settlers lived in log cabins until 1692, when they had enough stone to build stone houses like their homes in France. Although the original homes had one room with a cellar kitchen and attic above, they added on other rooms to become the larger homes we see today. Descendants of each of the original twelve families still maintain an interest in the houses; they have contributed some of the original furniture passed down through their families to be put on display. The houses today are owned by the **Huguenot Historical Society.**

The **Jean Hasbrouck House** has his initials carved in stone to the left of the door. Inside is a long central hall with two rooms on each side. In the living room the table is covered with a rug or tapestry; a dulcimer is in the corner, and a snodnose lamp (very early brass oil lamp) is on the desk. The kitchen contains furnishings that were in the family before 1700. A large Dutch *kaas* (cupboard) has several delft spice jars on top, and the Hudson Valley rush-bottom chairs are typical of the area. A collection of pewterware and a variety of cooking utensils are displayed. Upstairs in the attic you will see a beehive chimney, a loom, and an exhibit on the production of linen from flax. Don't miss the store in the house, which has a variety of goods common to the period. Another room contains a bar with what looks like a picket fence on top. Could it be so that patrons could not lean their elbows too long as they imbibed? No, it was used to dry clean glasses.

A large stone monument in the street lists the names of the original twelve patentees; this boulder was brought down from the mountains on a sledge in 1899. The cemetery contains the graves of all of the patentees and their wives. Look for the stone with primitive angels done by a local stonecutter. One gives the first letter of each word in the epitaph. On another stone

the cutter did not think ahead—several letters in
the name are stuck in above the line.

Locust Lawn, southwest of New Paltz,
was built in 1814 by Colonel Josiah Hasbrouck.
This Federal mansion contains period furniture,
china, books, and paintings by Ammi Phillips,
Alden Weir, and John Vanderlyn. The mar-
bleized plaster walls in the central hall were a
specialty of the architect, Cromwell. Outside are
a slaughterhouse, a wood house, a carriage
house, and a smokehouse.

Locust Lawn
Route 32
Gardiner 12525
914–255–1660

Mohonk Mountain House (Lake
Mohonk, New Paltz; 914–255–1000), located in
the Shawangunk Mountains right on a clear
glacial lake, offers Old World charm in a beautiful setting. Guests come for several days to take
a course such as Fall Photography or Scottish
Weekend or to enjoy the famous Mystery
Weekends, which were actually begun at
Mohonk. Dating back to 1869, when twin brothers bought the existing building and land
around it, Mohonk has been run by the same
family through its expansion from ten rooms to
300. Antique furnishings enhance this castlelike
escape from the real world.

Walkers and hikers enjoy the many trails
through this 22,000-acre estate. We especially
recommend a hike up to the tower at Sky Top,
where you can savor the view. Along the way
you will find gazebos built out over sheer
drops, deep crevasses, and unusual rock formations. Advance reservations for lunch will allow
day visitors in the gate, or you can pay for a
day pass in order to hike on the grounds of the
estate. (See Inns appendix.)

Take I–87 south to Newburgh.

Washington's Headquarters were in the
Jonathan Hasbrouck house from April 1782 to
August 1783. The army remained encamped at
New Windsor while negotiations prior to the

NEWBURGH

**Washington's
Headquarters
84 Liberty Street
Newburgh 12550
914-562-1195**

Treaty of Paris were in progress. In 1782 Washington turned down a proposal by some of his men to turn America into a monarchy and name him king. Did you know that Washington originated the Order of the Purple Heart here? On May 3, 1783, he awarded the first "Badge of Military Merit" for acts of bravery. There is a museum housing memorabilia from the Revolutionary War.

**New Windsor
Cantonment
Temple Hill
Newburgh 12550
914-561-1765**

New Windsor Cantonment, just south of Newburgh, is the site of the last encampment of soldiers during the Revolution. Seven hundred log cabins once filled the area, but now only one of the original cabins remains. The site includes reconstructed buildings, and there are periodic reenactments portraying the life of the soldiers.

**CORNWALL-ON-
HUDSON**

**Museum of the
Hudson Highlands
174 Main Street
Cornwall-on-Hudson
12520
914-534-7781**

**Storm King Art
Center
Old Pleasant Hill
Road
Mountainville 10953
914-534-3115**

The **Museum of the Hudson Highlands** contains live animals as well as natural history exhibits. You can take a self-guided nature trail walk. The **Ogden Gallery** features changing art exhibits as well as films and lectures.

Nearby **Storm King Art Center,** southwest of Newburgh on Route 32, is a display of more than two hundred sculptures on two hundred acres of landscaped gardens. You will find sculptures by David Smith, Barbara Hepworth, Henry Moore, Isamu Noguchi, Alexander Calder, Alexander Liberman, Louise Nevelson, and more.

From the early days when the Huguenots planted grapes along the Hudson Highlands in the seventeenth century to the present day, vineyards have flourished in the area. You can plan your own wine-tasting tour as you visit some of the vineyards: **Adair, Baldwin, Benmarl, Brimstone Hill, Brotherhood, Cascade Mountain, Chateau Georges, Clinton, Cottage, High Tor, Maganini Farm, Milbrook, North Salem, Royal Kedem, Walker Valley, West Park, Windsor,** and **Woodstock.** For more detailed information on each vineyard, get a current brochure on winery tours from one of the tourist offices in the area (Kingston, New Paltz, Newburgh, or Poughkeepsie).

From Cornwall-on-Hudson take Route 218 to West Point. The **United States Military Academy**, commonly referred to as West Point, was founded in 1802, although it had been in the planning stages since the Revolution. West Point was occupied from 1778 on; during that year the "Great Chain" was draped across the river to stop British ships. Benedict Arnold almost lost West Point to the British by betraying his country to Captain John Andre, an aide to General Sir Henry Clinton. Arnold made plans to sell West Point to the British for £20,000, but the plan backfired when Americans captured Andre near Tarrytown. Incriminating papers, which he had hidden in his boot, were sent to General Washington. Arnold then fled to the British ship *Vulture* and later served in the British army. Andre was tried and hanged as a spy.

Stop in the Visitors' Information Center located just outside the south gate (Thayer Gate) in Building 2607 for information on touring the grounds. The West Point Museum is located in Thayer Hall. A collection of military weapons and relics was begun in 1777, starting with British weapons used during the Battle of Saratoga. There are two chapels to visit. The Old Cadet Chapel dates from 1836 and stands in the West Point Cemetery. This Greek Revival–style building houses marble shields as memorials for officers during the Revolutionary War. The Cadet Chapel is bright with stained-glass windows. One of the largest church organs in the world is in this chapel.

Route 9W will lead you to signs for Bear Mountain State Park.

WEST POINT

United States Military Academy Information Center West Point 10996 914–938–2638

BEAR MOUNTAIN STATE PARK

Bear Mountain State Park (Route 9W; 914–786–2701) contained both Fort Clinton and Fort Montgomery during the Revolutionary War. British General Sir Henry Clinton was able to capture both forts in October 1777. The **Bear Mountain Historical Museum** stands on the original site of Fort Clinton; it contains exhibits on the history of the forts as well as mementos from the soldiers who fought there. Perkins Mountain Drive will take you to the top of the mountain. The park offers boat rentals, a swimming pool, hiking trails, and a roller-skating rink.

Routes 9W and 202 lead to Stony Point.

STONY POINT

Stony Point Battlefield
Route 9W
Stony Point 10980

Stony Point Battlefield, north of Stony Point, was the scene of one of the most daring attacks of the Revolution. In July 1779 the British held the fortifications there. General Washington commanded General Anthony Wayne to capture Stony Point. Wayne had ordered his soldiers to attack with bayonets, so that an accidental shot would not alert the British; just after midnight the Americans completely surprised the British, easily taking the fortifications. Wayne, who suffered a head wound, continued to direct his soldiers; he earned a gold medal for this exploit and the name "Mad Anthony."

Continue on Route 9W south to the Tappan Zee Bridge back to New York City. Or take Route 202 to the Palisades Parkway to the city. This completes itinerary A, covering New York City, Long Island, and the Hudson River Valley.

ITINERARY B:

Upstate New York

AUSABLE CHASM

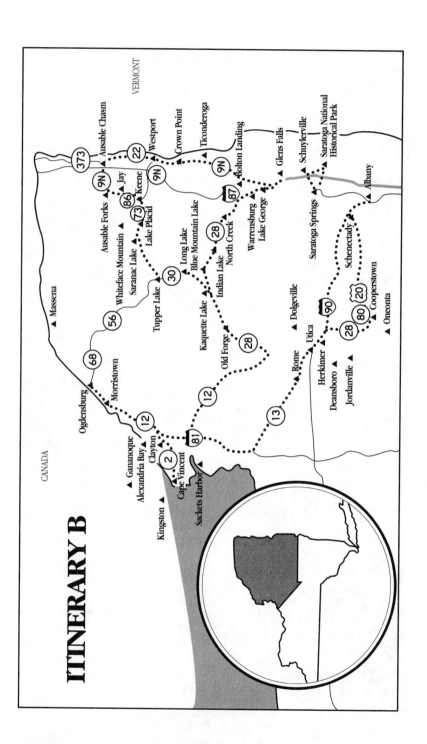

ITINERARY B

Upstate New York

John Godfrey Saxe

"Pray, what do they do at the Springs?"
  The question is easy to ask;
But to answer it fully, my dear,
  Were rather a serious task.
And yet, in a bantering way,
  As the magpie or mocking-bird sings,
I'll venture a bit of a song
  To tell what they do at the Springs!

Imprimis, my darling, they drink
  The waters so sparkling and clear;
Though the flavor is none of the best,
  And the odor exceedingly queer;
But the fluid is mingled, you know,
  With wholesome medicinal things,
So they drink, and they drink, and they drink,
  And that's what they do at the Springs!

Then with appetites keen as a knife,
  They hasten to breakfast or dine;
(The latter precisely at three;
  The former from seven till nine.)
Ye gods! what a rustle and rush
  When the eloquent dinner-bell rings!
Then they eat, and they eat, and they eat—
  And that's what they do at the Springs!

Now they stroll in the beautiful walks,
  Or loll in the shade of the trees;
Where many a whisper is heard
  That never is told by the breeze;
And hands are commingled with hands,
  Regardless of conjugal rings;
And they flirt, and they flirt, and they flirt—
  And that's what they do at the Springs!

The drawing-rooms now are ablaze,
  And music is shrieking away;
TERPSICHORE governs the hour,

And FASHION was never so gay!
An arm 'round a tapering waist—
How closely and fondly it clings;
So they waltz, and they waltz, and they waltz—
And that's what they do at the Springs!

In short—as it goes in the world—
They eat, and they drink, and they sleep;
They talk, and they walk, and they woo;
They sigh, and they laugh, and they weep;
They read, and they ride, and they dance;
(With other unspeakable things;)
They pray, and they play, and they *pay*—
And that's what they do at the Springs!

This itinerary begins in the pleasant town of Saratoga Springs, where visitors can discover intrigue among the Victorian personalities who once frequented the spa, bet on the horses at the track, bathe in the mineral waters, and attend concerts, ballet, and theater. To the north the Adirondacks beckon climbers, hikers, canoeists, sailors, and anyone else who enjoys the natural beauty of lakes and mountains. Lake Placid, the site of the 1932 and 1980 Winter Olympics, can be the jumping-off point for those who wish to explore the myriad lakes, rivers, and mountains in the wilderness area of the Adirondack Park. To the west is the St. Lawrence Seaway and the unique Thousand Islands area of New York State, where the confluence of five Great Lakes funnels into a single river that is used for both shipping and pleasure. At the conclusionn of this tour, you can either head back to Albany and south on the Hudson River section of Itinerary A or continue west to join Itinerary C in the Finger Lakes region.

☙ *Saratoga Springs Area* ☙

Saratoga Springs, the "Queen of the Spas," is located on top of a liquid gold mine. During the glacial era streams deep in the earth picked up minerals that formed natural gases, which escaped in the form of springs and geysers. Iroquois Indians joined the forest animals in drinking from these bubbling, saline waters because they believed the waters had powerful medicinal effects. In 1767 the Iroquois carried Sir William Johnson, the British superintendent of Indian affairs, on a litter to Saratoga to cure his gout with the miraculous waters. George Washington was another who visited Saratoga Springs to partake of the waters.

SARATOGA SPRINGS

New York State Spa
Saratoga Spa
State Park
Saratoga Springs
518–584–2000;
518–584–2010

Saratoga Springs
Convention and
Tourist Bureau
480 Broadway
Saratoga Springs
12866
518–584–1531

Today in Saratoga Springs you can drink the water from one of several fountains, buy bottled mineral water, or bathe in one of the bathhouses that are open to the public at **New York State Spa.** Take it from personal experience—the baths will relax you to the utmost. Each person has a private room for soaking in this soothing effervescence in a tub. You will find the tub quite long; for those of us under 6 feet, the tub has a little stool to hook your feet under so they won't float. The water is dark in color, hot, full of massaging bubbles, and conducive to a state of drowsiness until you are aroused by your personal attendant. You are wrapped in a hot sheet and allowed to continue your state of slumber. Eventually you will be awakened, and you must pull your renewed self together and return to the real world.

Architecture in Saratoga Springs ranges from the Greek Revival style of the early 1800s through the Gothic Revival style of between 1830 and 1855 to the Victorian style. Although many of the grand hotels of the Victorian age burned during the first half of the twentieth century, when they were undervalued and unappreciated, much of the business district still retains the feel of its original Victorian architecture, with some modern structures sandwiched in between. **Franklin Square** contains a number of Greek Revival buildings; take a look at the house at 59 Franklin Street with a facade resembling Greek temples. Gothic Revival cottages, with steep roofs and decorated gables, usually had a porch like the one at 198 Regent Street. Victorian structures in Saratoga include such variety as the Italian Villa, Lombardian, Italian Palazzo, Mansard or French Renaissance, and Queen Anne styles. If you drive the length of North Broadway, Circular

Street, Regent Street, and other streets on the east side of town, you will come across examples in all of these styles. Check at the **Saratoga Springs Urban Cultural Park Visitors' Center** in Drink Hall, across from Congress Park, for more detailed information about the historic homes in Saratoga Springs. The **Chamber of Commerce** also has information.

Drink Hall was originally a trolley station for the Hudson Valley Railroad. The arched windows and columns provide a neoclassical touch; if you are there in the spring the flowering trees in front provide color and fragrance. Inside there is a bas-relief of the Indians and Sir William Johnson arriving at High Rock Springs.

Stroll across the street into **Congress Park** a thirty-three-acre landscaped garden complete with fountains and sculpture. Notice the *Spirit of Life,* which was designed by Daniel Chester French as a memorial for Spencer Trask. In 1870 the elegant **Canfield Casino** was constructed in Congress Park by John Morrissey to provide a setting for balls and gaming; large stained-glass windows decorate this Italianate building. Diamond Jim Brady and Lillian Russell were among the prominent visitors to Canfield Casino. Brady had one evening ensemble glittering with 2,548 diamonds, which must have intensified the illusion of wealth in the many mirrors of the casino. After you have admired the public rooms on the lower floor of the casino, be sure to visit the mementos of the grand era of Saratoga in the **Historical Society of Saratoga Springs Museum** (518–584–6920), on the second and third floors, and the **Ann Grey Gallery** (518–584–6920), which displays contemporary art. During the last quarter of the nineteenth century, when Broadway was filled with massive and elegant hotels, Saratoga was ranked in the world of fashion and wealth with Tuxedo Park, Newport, and Bar Harbor.

**Saratoga Springs
Urban Cultural Park
Visitors' Center
465 Broadway
Saratoga Springs
12866
518–587–5030**

**Saratoga Springs
Chamber of
Commerce
494 Broadway
Saratoga Springs
12866
518–584–3255**

**Congress Park and
Canfield Casino
Broadway
Saratoga Springs
12866
518–584–6920**

Do you enjoy listening to a concert or watching a ballet on a balmy summer eveing? If so, you have come to the right place; the **Saratoga Performing Arts Center** provides pleasure for visitors and residents alike. In 1966 the shell amphitheater opened, seating 5,103. An additional 25,000 can relax on the lawn to enjoy the performances of the New York City Ballet in July and the Philadelphia Orchestra in August. You can buy tickets under the roof if you order in advance (and sometimes, with luck, on the day of a performance), or you can purchase lawn tickets for reasonable prices and bring your own blanket or lawn chair. Picnics on the grounds beforehand suit any style, from fast food to elegant gourmet treats. **Scallions** (404 Broadway; 518–584–0192) packs picnic baskets. In addition to the ballet and the orchestra, the **Spa Little Theatre** is also on the grounds, staging performances year-round. Besides this extraordinary selection of cultural fixtures, specials at SPAC include popular singers, jazz ensembles, and a variety of other nationally recognized entertainers.

Have you ever had breakfast at a Victorian racetrack? Try **Saratoga Race Course** (late July and August only), where you can combine the pleasures of the present and the past on a fresh, sunny morning when the dew is still clinging to the geraniums in the flower boxes. Make reservations and try to be at the track by 7:00 a.m. so you can get a ringside seat to watch the horses working out. An announcer calls out the name of each horse, stable, and trainer. Or come watch the thoroughbred racing in the afternoon. You'll have plenty of chances to admire the horses as they are being saddled in the tree-shaded paddock next to the track.

Open since 1863, Saratoga is the oldest track in the country, retaining its Victorian character not only in architecture but in ambience,

Saratoga Performing Arts Center
Saratoga Spa State Park
Saratoga Springs 12866
518–584–9330;
518–587–3330; during season

Saratoga Race Course
Union Avenue
Saratoga Springs 12866
212–641–4700;
518–584–6200; during season

by virtue of its exclusive right to run races in New York State during twenty-four days in August. For these four weeks the track and the town revert to the customs of a century ago— with "boxes" at the track and "cottage" lists locating visitors published in the newspaper, and grand parties in the old style, with elaborate printed programs and ample newspaper reporting. Perhaps nowhere else does so much of the spirit of the old ways of high society survive, untrammeled by tourism, as here during these four weeks each year.

If you are visiting during the second week of August, you can observe the annual **Fasig-Tipton Auction** of thoroughbred racehorses. Buyers sit inside the pavilion, signing their bids disguised by transparent signals like touching an ear or crooking a finger; the public is welcome to mill around outside the glass windows to watch the bidding and to stroll around the barns and paddocks, where some of the finest and most expensive derby winners of the future are waiting to be purchased. And as our young son once observed, there are few better places in the world to gaze at a collection of thoroughbred luxury cars; he found the Bentleys, Rolls-Royces, and Jaguars more fascinating than the horses.

Don't forget to visit the **National Museum of Racing and Thoroughbred Hall of Fame** opposite the race course. Visitors enter through starting gates and are immediately immersed in the world of horse racing. Full-size horses, jockeys, groomers, and patrons look almost real in their fiberglass bodies. Paintings, trophies, and racing silks compete with video presentations. A movie, *Race America,* begins with a truck tailgate opening at the track, the thundering as race horses jump right over the viewers, the roar of the crowds, and the excitement of the race.

And if you don't manage to get to Saratoga

National Museum of Racing and Thoroughbred Hall of Fame
Union Avenue
Saratoga Springs
12866
518-584-0400

**Saratoga Raceway
Route 9
Saratoga Springs
12866
518–584–2110**

**Skidmore College
North Broadway
Saratoga Springs
12866
518–584–5000**

**National Museum of
Dance
South Broadway
Saratoga Springs
12866
518–584–2225**

during the magic weeks of July and August, not all is lost. **Saratoga Raceway** stages races ten months a year in the evening. You can have dinner there while watching your favorite trotter; television monitors guarantee your vision all around the track. Though far younger than the flat track and less embellished with tradition, this track has established its own reputation for good racing and fine dining.

Skidmore College, once housed in some of the Victorian buildings along Union Avenue and adjoining streets, now has been in residence on the "New" Campus just off North Broadway for more than a decade. The red brick buildings, connected by covered walkways, are nestled in 800 acres of woods that are ablaze with color in the fall. This site, once filled with more than a dozen summer estates, was Lucy Skidmore Scribner's original choice for the campus, but it could not be acquired until 1965, when the college began developing a campus of forty-five new buildings that serve more than 2,000 students. If you want to take a look at this elegant new campus, drive up North Broadway to the entrance and follow the signs on the directory. If you want a guided tour, stop in at the Admissions Office, located in the carriage house adjacent to the Surrey, a country manor just across Broadway from the campus entrance.

If you're interested in dance, take a trip to the new **National Museum of Dance,** housed in a historic bath pavilion, the Washington Bathhouse, out on Route 9. The Mr. and Mrs. Cornelius Vanderbilt Whitney Hall of Fame resides in a lovely beaux arts foyer. Exhibits include costumes worn in Hollywood and Broadway productions, photos of dancers, and videos celebrating the lives of famous dancers.

The rose gardens at **Yaddo,** on the eastern side of Saratoga Springs where Union Avenue joins I–87, are a pleasant retreat on a hot day.

You can visit the gardens but not the buildings on the estate, for they are occupied by artists and writers in residence. Spencer and Katrina Trask bought the property in 1881, lived there with their children, and now are buried in the rose garden. Their little girl, Christina, called their residence, named "The Shadow," Yaddo, and the name stuck. The Trasks' wills left everything to a Yaddo foundation to provide a retreat and workplace for artists, writers, and musicians. Some of the literature and art that you enjoy may have been created in this peaceful setting. Each resident works all day in an individual house, studio, or room, having lunch there alone. In the evening the residents convene for dinner, relax, and perhaps attend a lecture or concert in town or at the college. Free of telephones and interruptions, these guests are able to compose, paint, or write more intensively than they could in less insulated surroundings—and this is the whole point of the Trasks' legacy.

Yaddo
Union Avenue
Saratoga Springs
12866
518–584–0746

Dining out in Saratoga can be a real treat, but it is a movable feast. We have tried almost all of the restaurants that seem to come and go each season and have returned to the old standbys time after time. A sampling includes **Ash Grove Inn** (Church Street; 518–587–1278), **The Caunterbury** (Union Avenue; 518–587–9653), **Chez Pierre** (Saratoga Road; 518–793–3350), **Gideon Putnam** (Saratoga State Park; 518–584–3000), **Hattie's Chicken Shack** (45 Phila; 518–584–4790), **Lillian's** (408 Broadway; 518–587–7766), **Mother Goldsmith's** (43 Phila; 518–584–9772), **Olde Bryan Inn** (123 Maple; 518–587–2990), **The Trattoria** (14 Phila Street; 518–587–0269), and **Wishing Well** (Route 9; 518–584–7640). The **Adelphi Hotel** (365 Broadway; 518–587–4688) serves meals during the summer season; stop after a SPAC performance for a special evening. For an evening of

SCHUYLERVILLE

**Saratoga National
Historical Park
Routes 4 and 32
Schuylerville 12871
518–664–9822**

folk music, try **Caffe Lena** (47 Phila Street; 518–584–9789).

You may want to take a side trip to **Saratoga National Historical Park,** located 12 miles southeast of Saratoga Springs and 8 miles south of Schuylerville. Drive south on Route 9 to Route 9P, where you turn east and drive around the south shore of Saratoga Lake. Turn right on Route 423, which is Battlefield Road, and meet Route 32, following signs to the battlefield. The visitors' center has an audiovisual presentation, a museum, and a special lecture series available on topics such as "Archaeology at the Saratoga Battlefield." From late spring to the fall, you can watch eighteenth-century crafts demonstrated by guides in period costumes.

The battles that are regarded as the "turning point of the Revolution" were fought here during the fall of 1777, when General Horatio Gates led the American troops on to victory over General John Burgoyne. The American commander, Heratio Gates, settled into position at Bemis Heights to wait for General John Burgoyne, the British commander. Benedict Arnold attacked the British at Freeman's Farm on September 19, 1777, and was relieved of his command by Gates for refusing to wait. He stayed near his troops, however, and reappeared in his general's uniform on Ocotber 7, riding his white horse at the head of his men. His courage enabled the Americans to take a redoubt located in an important position. Burgoyne's men were demoralized and hungry because the commissaries had not given them provisions. Having lost 1,200 men and surrendered 5,700 more, Burgoyne retreated to Schuylerville in a downpour, with his men slogging through the mud. When news of his defeat arrived in France, French military advisers decided to side with the Americans.

Take a self-guided tour of the battlefield on foot, by car, by bicycle, or on cross-country skis in winter. Along the route you will see markers for **Freeman Farm, American River Fortifications, Chatfield Farm, Barbers Wheatfield, Balcarres Redoubt, Breymann's Redoubt,** and **Burgoyne's Headquarters.**

Another Revolutionary War site lies nearby: **Schuyler House** is on the southern edge of Schuylerville. General Philip Schuyler lived in this pleasant estate setting; the original house was burned by the the British but rebuilt in 1777 after the vicotry. The **Saratoga Battle Monument** is on Burgoyne Road near Route 29.

Schuyler House
Route 4
Schuylerville 12871
518–695–3664

≋ *The Adirondacks* ≋

The Northway (I–87), one of the most scenic highways in America, will take you from Saratoga to the Adirondacks—8,900 square miles of lakes, forests, mountains, and wildlife. The **Adirondack Park** is the largest state park in the United States, larger than Glacier, Olympic, Yosemite, and Yellowstone parks put together. There are forty-six peaks that spire over 4,000 feet above sea level, and nine of these have rocky alpine summits. Mount Marcy reaches 5,344 feet and Mount McIntyre is 5,112 feet. Whiteface is 4,867 feet high. For orientation you may think of the Adirondacks in terms of four sections: the High Peaks in the northeastern region, the lake and river area in the center, Lake George and other lakes in the southeast region, and flat woodland leading to the St. Lawrence valley in the west.

The Adirondacks contain some of the oldest exposed rocks on earth; the mountains were probably formed by pressure inside the earth that pushed older rocks up to the surface. Geologists feel that these rocks are an extension of the same landscape covering the whole Labrador Peninsula and part of the Laurentians of Canada. Hard, crystalline rocks, shot through with colored mineral streaks, were not washed by the sea or buried in sediment but remained pure. They still contain valuable ores; iron deposits in the area can be strong enough to affect compasses. The last glacial ice scraped the rocks bare, inscribing its path as it moved.

Altogether, the northern section of New York State is remarkable for its natural beauty, much of it unknown to people from other regions who associate the whole state with New York City. The Adirondacks provide a wonderful getaway from the bustle of cities, a place where you can find peace and quiet while enjoying sports or simply looking at the view. You can count on finding wilderness in the Adirondacks because the state of New York has declared about a third of the area to be "forever wild," a conditon that has attracted visitors for many years. Teddy Roosevelt came for hunting, Robert Louis Stevenson spoke of the region as "Little Switzerland," and millionaires built elegant "camps," around the turn of the century.

The "Great Camps," as they were called, were not primitive in the least—nothing like tents beside a campfire. As word was passed about the scenery, fishing, hunting, and mountain hiking available in the Adirondacks, wealthy businessmen came for privacy while they relaxed and enjoyed their favorite sports. They built retreats surrounded by many acres of land so that each family could bring nannies, maids, guides, chefs, and other personnel to run their camps efficiently and yet not be bothered with neighbors. The architectural style that developed came to be known as the Great Camp style of the Adirondacks. Each "camp" contained a main lodge, guest lodges, dining room, social hall, kitchen, laundry, carpentry shop, blacksmith shop, boathouse, and other buildings as needed. The buildings were often linked by a covered walkway. Building materials consisted of logs, either peeled or unpeeled, and fieldstone common to the area. Other special features included bay windows, loggias, turrets, lintels, and porches. Most of the Great Camps are not open to the public; however, Sagamore Lodge and Conference Center, a former Vanderbilt camp, is open to the public in the summer (see page B•119).

History buffs will find in the Adirondacks relics and stories from the French and Indian War and the American Revolution, as well as from later eras of mining and lumbering.

If you have not visited the Adirondacks yet, you may have seen pictures or read literary accounts of the area. Winslow Homer spent time in Keene Valley and at the North Woods Club, near Minerva, where he painted extensively during the 1870s and sporadically until 1908. Other artists who have worked in the area include Asher Durand, Homer Martin, J. F. Kensett, Frederick Rondel, Arthur Fitzwilliam, James Smillie, and James E. Buttersworth.

A short list of writings about the Adirondacks would include James Fenimore Cooper's *The Last of the Mohicans*; Richard Henry Dana's "How We Met John Brown," in the *Atlantic Monthly*; Ralph Waldo Emerson's "The Adirondacks"; Kate Field's many magazine and newspaper articles during the nineteenth century; Hugh Fosburgh's *One Man's Pleasure*; Anne

LaBastille's *Woodswoman, Beyond Black Bear Lake,* and *Assignment: Wildlife;* William H. H. Murray's *Adventures in the Wilderness;* Francis Parkman's *France and England in North America;* Jean Rikhoff's *Buttes Landing, Where Were You in '76, Sweetwater,* and *One of the Raymonds;* Theodore Roosevelt's *Outdoor Pastimes of an American Hunter;* George Washington Sears's (Nessmuk) *Woodcraft;* Robert Louis Stevenson's *The Master of Ballantrae* and *The Letters of Robert Louis Stevenson to His Family;* Seneca Ray Stoddard's *The Adirondacks;* and Sloan Wilson's *All the Best People* and *Small Town, N.Y.*

Hikers can obtain trail guides and topographical maps from the **Adirondack Mountain Club** (R.R. 3 Box 3055, Lake George, New York 12845; 518–668–4447) or **Department of Environmental Conservation** (Hudson Avenue, Warrensburg, New York 12885; 518–623–3671).

GLENS FALLS

Exit 18 from the Northway will take you into Glens Falls, the site of battles during the Indian Tribal Wars as well as the Revolutionary War. Long ago Indians used the name "Chepontuc," which means "a hard place to get around," to describe this place on the Hudson where they had to carry canoes around the rushing waters. During high-water times the 60-foot fall provides a refreshing swish of water; it has powered the paper mills and other industries that are the economic basis of the city. **Cooper's Cave** (now closed) on Hudson River Island, located under the bridge to South Glens Falls, was an important setting in James Fenimore Cooper's *The Last of the Mohicans.*

The **Hyde Museum** is housed in the former home of Louis and Charlotte Hyde. Charlotte was the eldest daughter of Samuel Pruyn, a prosperous Glens Falls industrialist involved in mining, lumbering, canal transportation, and paper manufacturing. While attending a finishing school in Boston, Charlotte met Louis Fiske Hyde, a student at Harvard Law School. They married in 1901 and began collecting art. The Hydes returned to Glens Falls and built their Florentine Renaissance home in 1912 with plenty of room to display their art collection. Perhaps

Hyde Museum
161 Warren Street
Glens Falls 12801
518–792–1761

they were inspired by Isabella Stewart Gardner, who had her Venetian Renaissance home, Fenway Court, built to house her growing art collection. They traveled to Europe to collect furniture from sixteenth-century Italian and seventeenth- and eighteenth-century French styles. Tapestries, Aubusson rugs, and velvet draperies completed the warm and pleasant appearance of their home.

An interior courtyard is filled with plants, sculpture, and fountains. Windows on the second-story level open onto the courtyard. As you walk through the rooms, you'll notice many well-known works on display. The first major painting the Hydes bought was Turner's *Grand Canal.* In 1933 they purchased Rembrandt's *Portrait of Christ* from the Soviet Union. Other significant works in the collection include *Annunciation* by Botticelli, *Trees* by Cezanne, *Dancer with Red Stockings* by Degas, *Portrait of St. James the Less* by El Greco, *Portrait of the Artist's Son* by Hals, *A Good One, Adirondacks* by Homer, *Cartoon for the Mona Lisa* by da Vinci, *Two Draped Nudes* by Matisse, *Boy Holding a Blue Vase* by Picasso, *Portrait of a Young Man* by Raphael, *Portrait of the Artist's Mother* by Rembrandt, *Estelle in a Red Hat* by Renoir, *Head of a Negro* by Rubens, *Portrait of the Doge Alvise Mocenigo* by Tintoretto, *Portrait of Jan Woverius* by Van Dyke, *Corner of a Field* by Van Gogh, and *The Sea, Pourville* by Whistler, to name a few. In late 1985 the museum acquired *Show Horse* by Remington. A changing gallery displays local work and traveling exhibitions. A new addition opened in November 1989 providing space for galleries, concerts, and programs.

Chapman Historical Museum
348 Glen Street
Glens Falls 12801
518–793–2826

The **Chapman Historical Museum** illustrates the development of the area in an 1841 home. Zopher Isaac and Catherine Scott DeLong bought the house in 1860 and lived there with their eight children. In 1923 their granddaughter married Frederick Braydon Chapman. Juliet Goodman Chapman gave the home to the Historical Association in 1966. The museum has been developed to depict the home of a Victorian family. The fireplace in the Library–Music Room was made of black marble from a local quarry. The spiral staircase in the hall is unusual because the bannister is attached to the side of the staircase instead of standing on the treads. Walk through the parlor, with its white marble fireplace, to the "lady's morning room," which is part of the original 1841 house. The bay windows contain larger pieces of glass than were normally used during that period.

The Chapman is well known for its extensive collection of Seneca Ray Stoddard's photographs, paintings, and manuscripts. The toy and doll collection appeals to visiting children. A new wing has been added to house the gallery and gift shop. If you are there at Christmas, you will enjoy the special Victorian Christmas decorations in the museum.

If you're in the area during the latter part of September, you can attend the annual Adirondack Balloon Festival. Balloons have been coming here for the past fifteen years, and every year is better than the one before. Depending on wind and weather conditions, balloonists fly a couple of times a day over a four-day period.

Glens Falls restaurants include **Garden in the Park at the Queensbury Hotel** (88 Ridge; 518–792–1121), **Blacksmith Shop** (Aviation Road; 518–792–4550), **Hilander** (Haviland Road; 518–793–6363), **Log Jam** (Lake George Road; 518–798–1155), **Avanti** (Lake George Road; 518–668–4135), **Montcalm** (Lake George Road; 518–793–6601), and **The Coachman** (Lake George Road; 518–793–4455).

The Great Escape (518–792–6568) fun

**The Great Escape
Route 9
Queensbury 12804
518–792–6568**

**West Mountain Ski
Area
West Mountain Road
Glens Falls 12804
518–793–6606**

LAKE GEORGE

park becomes more elaborate every year. Started many years ago as "Storytown" by entrepreneur Charles Wood, its change of names reflects both growth and a wider range of interests. Poeple come for the day with their families, a picnic, and the stamina to keep moving around from one thrill to the next. (You also can come without a picnic as there are snack bars in the park.)

As you drive along the Northway, you'll see **West Mountain Ski Area** stretching its trails up into the woods. Intermediate skiers will probably want to warm up on the open slope, then take the Summit chair up to ski first Frolic and then Holy Mackeral (which is a little narrower and pleasant if it has snowed recently, as there is no snowmaking there at this time). Then take the triple chair up to try Mach II, which is wide with some dips and flats. Northwest Passage is also nice and leads into Mach II. Try Midway under the triple chair. On the outside AOA is nice but does not have snowmaking, so watch the cover.

From Glens Falls take either I–87 or Route 9 to Lake George.

"Lake George is, without comparison, the most beautiful water I ever saw; formed by a contour of mouuntains into a basin thirty-five miles long, and from two to four miles broad, finely interspersed with islands, its water limpid as crystal and the mountain sides covered with rich groves of thuja, silver fir, white pine, aspen and paper birch down to the water edge, here and there precipices of rock to checker the scene and save it from monotony. An abundance of speckled trout, salmon trout, bass, and other fish with which it is stored, have added to our other amusements the sport of taking them. . . ."— Thomas Jefferson (*A letter to his daughter, 1791*)

The best way to see Lake George is from

the water. Step on board one of the cruise ships in the village for a journey through pellucid blue water so clean you can drink it; past mountainsides coverd with hemlock and pine, clumps of rocky outcroppings at the shore, mansions and a grand hotel from the nineteenth century; and finally into the wilderness area of the lake toward Paradise Bay. You're in for a surprise there. Keep your eye out for some of the sleek classic antique boats such as *Hackers* or *Fay and Bowens;* their owners enjoy taking them across the lake for a spin, and you will be able to recognize them by their mahogany brightwork and sharp bows that cut easily through the chop. In the nineteenth century steamboats like the one you are on were the primary mode of transportation up and down the 32 miles of the lake surrounded by mountains, which had only a few primitive roads along parts of its shores and still has none in its middle section.

Keep a watchful eye as your ship steams along the west shore. The first mansion along **"Millionaires' Row"** is a half-timbered English Tudor building, enclosed within a wrought-iron fence, with broad green lawns and a view of the lake you won't believe. It was built by William J. Price and later owned by Charles J. Peabody. As you continue down the lake, look for a series of large docks and boathouses left over from the days when steamers plied the waters with passengers, supplies, and mail. Royal Peabody built a lovely mansion called Wikiosco, which has been renamed the **Blenheim;** a wide green lawn draws your eye up to the imposing stone-and-timbered building and to the green hemlock and pine trees beyond it. Your captain will tell you about some of the mansions still standing and in use as private homes (many others are now resorts), and you can read the stories about former inhabitants in several books that are available locally. Lake George was a popular summer resort for people from St. Louis, Philadelphia, and New York in the nineteenth century, and some of their descendants have chosen to live there permanently.

As you continue along the west shore, on one side of Green Harbor you will see a forty-two–room Italian Renaissance mansion; the estate is perched on a peninsula of craggy rocks and evergreens, with a terrace providing an endless view of lake and mountains. Harold Pitcairn gave the land to his wife and built the mansion as a birthday present many years ago; it is still used as a private home, but yachtsmen keep their boats there in slips or at anchor all around the harbor.

Offshore to the north **Canoe Island** is really two islands with a passage in between; the smaller is in private hands and the larger belongs to Canoe Island Lodge, which brings guests to it for barbecues and swimming on a natural sand beach. The American Canoe Association, founded in 1880 at Crosbyside and dedicated to setting standards and establishing competitions for a popular and growing sport, held its first sailing and paddling regatta at Canoe Island, thereby creating the name.

A mile farther north along the west shore, the **Lake George Club,** built in 1909, is housed in a wooden Victorian structure, with an octagonal peaked roof perched over the dance floor. The terrace is perfect for those who want to watch sailboat races or to savor the view of the mountains on the east side. (The club is private.) Below, a rocky path leads to the "Grotto," where there is a photograph of *El Lagarto.* Spencer Trask was the first president of the Lake George Club, and other founding members included William Bixby, Maurice Hoopes, Louis Hyde, George Knapp, Charles and George Foster Peabody, S. T. W. Sanford, Olin Stephens, and M. L. C. Wilmarth, among others.

Just beyond Basin Bay, north of the Lake George Club, Spencer and Katrina Trask, whose summer home Yaddo was at the edge of Saratoga Springs, built a retreat on a series of three islands. They called it **Triuna.** You will see a belfry and Gothic arch attached to one of the colonnaded bridges and walkways connecting the islands, with many guest rooms above the other bridge. Window boxes filled with flowers flourish all summer to complete this idyllic getaway spot.

Long before reaching Bolton Landing, you will see the gigantic white **Sagamore Hotel,** the scene of an international meeting with President Roosevelt during the thirties. The original developers bought Green Island for $30,000, built the hotel, and opened it in 1883. In 1893 the building went up in smoke, and its successor was completed the next year. Again in 1914 the Sagamore burned to the ground. The current structure was completed in 1930 and refurbished for the summer of 1985—once again providing a luxurious haven for visitors as well as a new convention center.

George Reis stayed with his parents at the Sagamore in the early 1900s. He was fascinated by the Gold Challenge Cup Race of 1914 when Count Mankowski raised hopes of a local winner but unfortunately struck a floating log. George bought a boat named *El Lagarto,* or the "Lizard," which you can see in the Adirondack Museum at Blue Mountain Lake; he won the Gold Challenge Cup Race in 1933 in Detroit and in 1934 and 1935 on Lake George in *El Lagarto.*

As you steam in between pine islands, you will notice that some of them consist only of rock and a few trees—great for a private picnic. Others are larger, with several picnic tables and facilities for camping. Your surprise is coming! Watch carefully as you steam into the very narrow channel behind **Sarah Island** and then into

Paradise Bay. Campers wave as you go by, and everyone waits for the proper maneuvering of your ship in the bay. Slowly she begins to back and fill, turning around, as if on a dime, within a few yards of shore. Boats at anchor toot their horns as she expertly completes her rotation without touching the shore or any boats, and everyone waves as she blithely departs through another narrow passage and heads off into the main lake again. Once while anchored in Paradise Bay, we were circled by an ancient but immaculate *Fay and Bowen* loaded to the gunwales with lovely young girls; suddenly they attacked us, laughing, with a barrage of water-filled balloons and then, like the steamer, sailed out through the channel and were seen no more. We might have been in the Greek isles or fairyland—of such stuff are the idylls of a timeless summer afternoon made.

As you enter the channel inside Fourteen Mile Island, on the east shore heading back south, you will see part of the **Knapp Estate.** In 1894 George Knapp bought the Hundred Island House, which had been a well-known hotel earlier in the century on a great deal of land. Later he built another home on the steep slope below the cliffs of Shelving Rock. This area contains some of the oldest exposed rock in the East—from the pre-Cambrian era. Just south of Red Rock Bay, you can still see marks made by the stone cutters as they quarried rock for the terraces and walls of the house. A cable-car railway was constructed to run from the shore into the cellar. In 1917 a fire started in the railway electrical system, spread into the house, and demolished it, but the chimneys and stone walls remain to this day. New York State bought much of the property and will preserve it as part of the wild forest that lines much of the eastern shore of the lake.

The return trip along the east side of the

lake will take you past a wilderness area where there are no roads. Wildlife abounds, and you may be lucky enough to see a doe and her fawn, even from the water. While you cruise along, you may decide you would like to return to the area to explore this marvelous yet accessible wilderness at a slower pace; there are two ways to do so. The first is by hiking or backpacking, depending on whether you prefer daytrips or longer excursions into the woods and mountains along the lake. There is an extensive, marked trail system on the east side of the lake beginning at an EnCon parking lot off Pilot Knob Road. (Call the Department of Environmental Conservation for trail information or write for maps.) The trails lead to **Pilot Knob, Buck Mountain, Sleeping Beauty, Black Mountain, Shelving Rock,** and several isolated mountain ponds. All of the mountains have extensive views of Lake George, beating anything that can be reached by road, which is as it should be for dedicated hikers. None of the climbs is too arduous for a day's hike, if that is your preference.

Department of Environmental Conservation
P.O. Box 220
Warrensburg 12855
518–623–3671

Black Mountain, the highest in the Lake George region, may also be reached in a more interesting way by taking a boat to Black Mountain Point and climbing a spectacularly beautiful trail to the summit, where there is an old fire tower (now abandoned, since helicopters cover fire watches in the forest preserve). From the top of Black on a clear day, you can see the high peaks of the Adirondacks to the northwest, Mount Mansfield in Vermont to the north-northeast, Mount Washington and the Presidential Range in New Hampshire to the northeast, Killington Mountain in Vermont to the east, and Mount Monadnock in New Hampshire to the southeast. Meanwhile the whole panorama of the northern two-thirds of Lake George is laid out below you. It's a view worth the climb.

The second way to explore the wilderness is by camping on one of the 179 state-owned islands in Lake George, all of which have beautifully maintained lakeside campsites with docks, tent sites, tables, barbecue pits, and outhouses. In some sites you have a small island all to yourself; in others your area, though generous, is contiguous to other campsites. Aficionados of the islands have their own favorites based on a special view or unusual privacy, but to newcomers, especially those who have camped elsewhere, all sites seem extraordinarily beautiful. The islands fall into three groups, with those in the **Southern Basin** administered by an EnCon Headquarters on Long Island (518–656–9426); those in the **Narrows,** the middle section loaded with islands, from Glen Island (518–644–9696); and those in the **Northern Basin** from Narrow Island off Hulett's Landing (518–499–1288). (For general information on all sections of the lake, call 518–644–9696 or 623–3671.) During busy times in the high season (July and August), it may be wise to make advance reservations for a site by calling 800–456–CAMP or by mailing forms available from **State Parks,** Albany, New York 12238 (518–474–0456). At less busy times simply go, take your boat to the island headquarters in the part of the lake you wish to stay in, and choose your island! In the spring and fall, local residents go where they please.

Out of the wilderness area, civilization returns with the sight of homes and sailboats patiently bobbing as they wait for someone to unfurl their sails. Around the next point you will see **Camp Chingachgook,** the Schenectady YMCA camp. Children from all over New York State have learned to swim, sail, and water-ski there. You will pass many private homes along **Pilot Knob, Cleverdale Point,** and **Assembly Point,** because this section of the lake is mostly residential. Land and homes command fantastic prices all along Lake George, and this shore is no exception. **Dunham's Bay,** another lovely, narrow bay, is filled with summer "camps."

As you return to the village, you will realize that of all the different views you have seen around the lake, none can be said to be choicer than the others. Residents feel that each view is unique, and as they visit one another they savor Lake George and the mountains from yet another perspective. The deep-blue water filled with islands, fringed by craggy gray-and-brown rocks and set against dark green mountains, has to be seen (or painted!) to be believed. Not all blue water is salt! For a cruise contact **Shoreline Cruises** (2 James Street; 518–668–4644) or **Lake George Steamboat Company** (Steel Pier; 518–668–5777).

After you've got your bearings on a cruise, you may want to stop in at the **Lake George Historical Association.** Dating back to 1895, when it was housed in a spare classroom in the Union School building, the association now resides in the **Old Court House and Jail.** The mid-nineteenth-century building is interesting, as it displays architecture from three periods— 1845, 1878, and 1900—and there are few jailhouse sites still standing.

Lake George Historical Association Canada Street at Amherst Lake George 12845 518–668–5044

The museum displays historical information concerning Lake George, including artifacts collected from the wars fought in this area. Look for the French and Indian War twelve-pound cannonball with a fleur-de-lis on it; the discovery of this cannonball indicates that Montcalm's artillery trench was on the present site of the Historical Association. An anchor from the steamship *Minnehaha* found on Meadow Point is also on display. Look for the large mural, *Lake George,* by David Cunningham Lithgow. The museum has an extensive collection of Stoddard prints from the nineteenth cen-

**Lake George
Battlefield Park
Lake George**

tury and Thatcher works from the late nineteenth century to the mid-twentieth century.

Lake George Battlefield Park, located between the lake and Route 9 near the **"Million Dollar Beach,"** contains ruins of **Fort George,** which replaced Fort William Henry two years after it had been burned by the French, in 1759. The park has a collection of valuable bronze monuments depicting the historical past of Lake George. There is a statue of Father Isaac Jogues, the first white man to see Lake George, when he was a prisoner of the Indians. He was the one who created its more poetic French name, *Lac du San Sacrement.* Another statue of an Indian with the mythical name *Horicon* is in the park. On September 8, 1903, Theodore Roosevelt was present for the dedication of a monument portraying William Johnson and Prince Hendrick, commemorating the importance of Fort William Henry during the French and Indian War.

The Battle of Lake George was actually a series of three conflicts that took place in September 1755. Both the British and the French wanted control of a water route to Canada. The French built Fort St. Frederic at Crown Point, which threatened the British stronghold at Ticonderoga. General William Johnson left Albany in August 1755 and slashed out a military road from Fort Lyman (later called Fort Edward) toward Lake George, on his way to Crown Point. French Commander in Chief Baron Dieskau heard about Johnson's plan to attack Crown Point and set out to meet the British, but General Johnson, General Lyman, and the Mohawk Indian chief, King Hendrik, were already encamped on Lake George. Colonel Ephraim Williams and King Hendrik led their men north to meet Dieskau; King Hendrik was killed by bayonet and Colonel Williams was shot. (You can see the marker where Williams was slain on Route 9. A gray rock inscribed E.E.

1755 marks his grave near Bloody Pond.)
Dieskau chased the Provincials to the area now
called Bloody Pond, and then to Fort William
Henry. A battle was fought at the fort and
Dieskau was taken prisoner. Johnson was inca-
pacitated with a leg wound, and his command
was taken by General Lyman.

Bloody Pond received its name after a
contingent traveled from Fort Lyman along the
military road and surprised 300 Frenchmen
there. Two hundred French soldiers were
thrown into it, coloring the water red for weeks
afterward.

A reconstruction of **Fort William Henry**
can be seen on Route 9, overlooking the southern end of Lake George. The original fort had
been built by William Johnson after the Battle of
Lake George and named after one of King
George's grandsons. The reconstruction has
stockades, dungeons, musket-firing demonstrations, exhibits, and an audiovisual program.
James Fenimore Cooper wrote about the retreat
of the survivors in *The Last of the Mohicans.*

**Fort William Henry
Route 9
Lake George 12845
518–668–5471**

To get a bird's-eye view of the lake and
the islands, you can drive up the **Veterans
Memorial Highway;** its entrance is located on
Route 9 across from the battleground campsite,
just north of Howard Johnson's. You also can
climb up a trail to the top of **Prospect
Mountain.** The mountain once had a cog railway to the summit to provide the same advantage for nineteenth-century tourists. Today's trail
uses the right-of-way for the old cog railway
and begins behind the high school and crosses
the Northway on a footbridge. The view from
the top is one you'll remember—panoramic to
say the least. During the winter the Memorial
Highway is open for snowmobiles and connects
with a number of other trails in the region.

**Veterans Memorial
Highway
Route 9
Lake George**

Other tourist attractions in the village of
Lake George include **Magic Forest,** horse-

drawn carriage rides, **Waterslide World,** golf, tennis, fishing, and boating. If you are here any weekend in February, you can attend the **Lake George Winter Carnival,** which has been held for a quarter of a century. Events include a polar bear swim, snowmobile races, motorcycle races, iceboat races, ice-fishing, parachute jumps, sleigh rides, snow sculpture, ice skating, snow-shoe races, and canoe jousting. When snow and ice conditions permit, a 64-mile cross-country ski race from Lake George Village to Ticonderoga and back is run.

There are so many good restaurants in the Lake George area that it is hard to choose among them; we will list some we have enjoyed. In Lake George: **East Cove** (Route 9L; 518–668–5265), **Boardwalk** (Amherst Street; 518–668–3242), **Capri Pizzeria** (221 Canada Street; 518–668–5027), **George's** (Route 9L; 518–668–5482; seasonal), **Mario's** (469 Canada Street; 518–668–2665); and **Shoreline** (4 James Street; 518–668–2875). In Bolton Landing: **The Algonquin** (Lake Shore Drive; 518–644–9442).

For a weekend getaway or special night out, try one of the following for superb cuisine:

At exit 23 turn toward Warrensburg and **The Merrill Magee House** (at the Bandstand, Warrensburg, New York, 12885; 518–623–2449), which is very popular for lunch, brunch, or din-ner among residents of the Glens Falls/Lake George area. The present tavern room was part of the original house dating from 1839; a Greek Revival section was built in front around 1850, and another section was added to the rear in the early 1900s. The house is filled with antiques, china, an 1864 rosewood piano, some original wallpaper, stenciled walls and . . . a surprise in the ladies' room. (For those of you who can't visit as soon as your curiosity would wish—there is a "lady in the tub" complete wilth blue-satin shower cap and jewelry visible above the permanent bubbles!) (See Inns appendix.) **The Grist Mill** (River Street; 518–623–3949) is housed in a renovated mill. Diners can sit beside the rushing river and imagine what it might be like in an open canoe. We tried that section once and found it "over our heads."

Bolton Landing is the site of the renovated resort hotel described on page B•119. **The Sagamore** (Lake Shore Drive; 518–644–9400) offers meals in several restaurants and a spectacular view of Lake George. You can have a continental breakfast, high tea, or late-evening libations complete with piano music in the Veranda; lunch at the poolside cafe or Mr. Brown's Cafe; nightclub entertainment at Van Winkle's; dinner in the Sagamore Room; or a very special dinner in the Trillium Room. (See Inns appendix.)

Near Chestertown, on Friend's Lake, are two inns featuring gourmet restaurant dining. **The Balsam House** (Friend's Lake, Chestertown, New York 12817; 518–494–2828) was built in 1845 as a farmhouse, with a bell tower and another floor added in 1891. Renovated several yars ago, the inn offered hospitality to Mary Frann, before her premiere in Bob Newhart's television inn. The dining room features a black marble fireplace with a copper hood that gleams under the lights. (See Inns appendix.)

The Friend's Lake Inn (Friend's Lake Road, Chestertown, New York 12817; 518–494–4251) began life in the 1860s and has been completely renovated following a number of years when the only inhabitants were a contingent of raccoons. The owners, ski instructors at Gore Mountain, did much of the renovation work themselves, then turned their attention to providing fine dining. (See Inns appendix.)

Take Route 9N out of Lake George Village

BOLTON LANDING

**Marcella Sembrich
Memorial Studio
Lake Shore Drive
Bolton Landing 12814
518-644-9839**

**Historical Museum of
Bolton Landing
Main Street
Bolton Landing 12814
518-644-9960**

and drive up the west shore to Bolton Landing to the **Marcella Sembrich Memorial Studio.** Marcella Sembrich, the famous opera singer, spent summers there, teaching and encouraging students in their study of opera. She performed in the great opera houses of Europe and was a member of the Metropolitan Opera Company. Visitors can see her musical scores and opera costumes and her personal collection of paintings and art objects. The setting of this stucco house on Lake George is very pleasant.

Also in Bolton Landing is the home of sculptor David Smith on Edgecomb Pond. His statuary is positioned on the grounds. Stop in the **Historical Museum of Bolton Landing** to see clippings and information on David Smith.

From Bolton Landing continue north on Route 9N over **Tongue Mountain,** where you can stop for a hike up to many outlooks for sweeping views of the Narrows of Lake George. The whole Tongue Mountain range, east of Route 9N, is forever wild; it includes 16 miles of trails over five peaks to Montcalm Point and back along the shore of Northwest Bay. Don't underestimate the rigor of the full circuit, as we once did; that 16 miles is mostly up and down the five peaks, 500 or 600 feet up and down each way much of it slow climbing or descending. Wear boots and watch where you put your hands, because timber rattlesnakes may be snoozing in the rocks. There are dens of them on Tongue Mountain; they are an endangered species, so just try to let them sleep. They are not at all eager to see you either, but if startled they could react. Professor William Brown of Skidmore College, an expert on the species and the area, suggests two simple rules: Don't disturb them (walk around), and don't put your hands or feet anywhere you can't see. Don't, though, let fear of the snakes keep you from the hike, which is magnificent on a clear day; we have done it in the fall during leaf season and on snowshoes in the winter, and the view of the Narrows 2,000 feet below changes its aspect every minute of the trail. If you start at the summit of Tongue Mountain (marked parking lot on Route 9N), you will come to a spur trail to Deer Leap after 0.6 mile; this leads to a cliff overlooking the Narrows where Indian lovers were supposed to have jumped off the edge to avoid separation. Then follows the series of five peaks, each with its own distinctive view, down the chain to the southernmost point 10 miles south, where the trail finally becomes easy and flat along the bay. If you want a shorter version of the hike, start at Clay Meadows (marked parking lot), which has a spur trail leading up to the main ridge trail.

From the ridge of Tongue Mountain, continue north on Route 9N through a long, lovely descent to **Sabbath Day Point,** the spot where General Amherst arrived in 1759 with 12,000 soldiers on the Sabbath and ordered religious services to be held. He was on his way to capture Fort Ticonderoga and Crown Point. Farther along this scenic drive, 4 miles north of Hague, you will come to **Roger's Slide,** which is famous for the legend of the snowshoes. During the French and Indian War, Captain Robert Rogers and his Rangers outfoxed the Indians who were chasing them by walking to the cliff's edge, tossing their packs down the cliff onto the frozen lake, then walking backward in their footprints in the snow to leave the impression that they had been forced to jump off the cliff. Fooled by this ruse, the Indians did not pursue them.

Continue north on Route 9N to Ticonderoga.

Fort Ticonderoga was built in 1755 by the French during the French and Indian War.

TICONDEROGA

Fort Ticonderoga
Ticonderoga 12883
518–585–2821

Originally named Fort Carillon, its position on Lake Champlain at the outlet from Lake George gave it control of the water route between New York and Canada. General Montcalm successfully defended the fort against the attacking force led by General Abercrombie in 1758, but the British captured it a year later. It remained in their hands until May 1775, when Ethan Allen, Benedict Arnold, and eighty-three Green Mountain Boys appeared without warning and easily captured it. In 1777 General John Burgoyne took the fort on his way to the crucial battle at Saratoga, after the Americans had evacuated, but it was eventually abandoned by the British, who burned all of the buildings. The restored fort contains a museum, barracks, a dungeon, and fortifications and has fife and drum music and cannon and mortar demonstrations. You can also visit **Mount Defiance** and **Mount Hope Battery** nearby, both of which were important in battles for the fort.

The Green Mountain Boys
William Cullen Bryant

Here halt we our march, and pitch our tent
  On the rugged forest-ground,
And light our fire with the branches rent
  By winds from the beeches round.
Wild storms have torn this ancient wood,
  But a wilder is at hand,
With hail of iron and rain of blood,
  To sweep and waste the land.

How the dark wood rings with voices shrill,
  That startle the sleeping bird!
Tomorrow eve must the voice be still,
  And the step must fall unheard.
The Briton lies by the blue Champlain,
  In Ticonderoga's towers,

And ere the sun rise twice again,
Must they and the lake be ours.
Fill up the bowl from the brook that glides
Where the fire-flies light the brake:
A ruddier juice the Briton hides
In his fortress by the lake.
Build high the fire, till the panther leap
From his lofty perch in flight,
And we'll strengthen our weary arms with sleep
For the deeds of tomorrow night.

Continue north on Route 9N and Route 22 to Crown Point. The visitors' center has displays on the French **Fort St. Frederic,** built in 1731, and the British **Fort Crown Point,** dating from 1759. The Green Mountain Boys, led by Colonel Seth Warner, captured Fort Crown Point in 1776, lost control, gained the fort back, and finally left for the last time in 1777 as General Burgoyne entered New York. There are self-guided tours and an orientation film. Special programs are planned during the year, including reenactments of battles, an encampment of soldiers demonstrating life at the fort during the period of the French and Indian War, and an archaeological program that winds up the season with an especially popular "Archaeology Day."

Although there are two ways to leave Crown Point to go to the next stop on the itinerary, our favorite is to backtrack from Crown Point to Ticonderoga and head west past Paradox Lake until you meet I–87 to go north. This part of the interstate is rated one of the most scenic stretches of interstate highway in the United States.

Along I–87 you will catch occasional glimpses of the "High Peaks" on your left, with the tallest, **Mount Marcy,** named for William Learned Marcy, one-time governor of New York.

CROWN POINT

Crown Point Visitors' Center
Route 9
Crown Point 12928
518–597–3666

HIGH PEAKS REGION

If you climb to the top of Mount Marcy you will see **Tear-of-the-Clouds** below, the mountain pond that is the source of the Hudson River; it was named by Verplanck Colvin in 1872. Almost thirty years later, Theodore Roosevelt stood on that very summit when President William McKinley was close to death from the shots of an assassin. By the time he arrived back in North Creek, the nearest railroad terminal, he was President of the United States.

Do you have aspirations to become one of the Forty-Sixers? The original three persons to lay claim to this physical feat climbed all forty-six high peaks in the Adirondacks (those at or above 4,000 feet) by August 1921. Their six-year quest to bag them all set the permanent standard for climbing in the Adirondacks. Sometimes they would knock off more than a few peaks in a single day, even though at that time only fourteen of the mountains had trails to follow. This tradition has continued over the years, giving pleasure to many hikers. Age is not a factor; in 1983 five-year-old twins became the youngest to achieve Forty-Sixer status. It is very difficult to recommend where to start—some peaks are easy, some are difficult, and some have more views than others on the way up.

If you're ready to begin climbing, continue on I-87 north to Route 73, then go west to Keene, the center of the region. Before you go, get a copy of *Guide to Adirondack Trails: High Peaks Region,* published by the **Adirondack Mountain Club** (R.R. 3, Box 3055, Lake George, New York 12845). You can stay overnight at one of the two lodges owned by the club: **Adirondack Loj,** located 9 miles by car from Lake Placid, and **Johns Brook Lodge,** accessible by foot on the trail system surrounding Mount Marcy; both make excellent bases for climbing Marcy and surrounding peaks.

A number of hikers feel that the High

Peaks are becoming much too crowded and that the trails and foliage are suffering from the tread of too many feet. They recommend that hikers try some of the less well-known mountain peaks. Others suggest climbing mountains that have more open terrain for terrific views much of the way up. The **Department of Environmental Conservation** has trail guides and maps available for a variety of destinations. You will also need a topographical map for accurate trail-finding. Within the High Peaks region, some rewarding alternatives to the overcrowded Marcy climb are **Cascade, Porter, Basin** (difficult), **Haystack, Giant, Owls Head,** and the **Crows.**

AUSABLE CHASM

If you are interested in walking through a spectacular river gorge and then visiting Whiteface Mountain and High Falls Gorge, continue north on I–87 to Ausable Chasm (518–834–7454), formed over 500 million years ago by the layering of "Potsdam Sandstone." These cliffs rise to several hundred feet on both sides of the river, which continually carves a deeper and deeper chasm as it drops from the eastern fringe of the Adirondacks into Lake Champlain. Bring your comfortable shoes to take a hike along walkways past Pulpit Rock, Elephant's Head, Jacob's Ladder, Mystic Gorge, and the Cathedral. You can also take a boat ride from Table Rock in a bateau with experienced boatmen. You'll go through a flume, whirlpool basin, and down rapids.

WILMINGTON

**Whiteface Mountain
Wilmington 12997**

From Ausable Chasm look for signs to Route 9N heading southwest toward Au Sable Forks and Jay, then turn onto Route 86 to **Whiteface Mountain,** in the town of Wilmington. The Whiteface Mountain Veterans Memorial Highway takes you near the top of the only one of the forty-six Adirondack High

**Whiteface Mountain
Ski Area
Wilmington
518–946–2223**

Peaks that is accessible by car. (If you see some hikers working on the forty-six, be prepared for some condescension!) President Roosevelt dedicated this highway to the men from New York who died in the two world wars. You will arrive within 500 feet of the top and can then walk or take an elevator to the **Summit House.** You can also take the chair lift at the **Whiteface Mountain Ski Area.** The cylindrical building at the summit is used for research by the **Atmospheric Science Research Center.** The view from the top includes nearby Adirondack peaks, Lake Champlain, the Green Mountains in Vermont, and the Montreal area. A nature trail tells the tale of weather erosion, alpine flora and fauna, and the changes that take place in such an exposed setting.

Whiteface Mountain ski area was the site of all the alpine events during the 1980 Olympics. The aftereffects of that world competition show in the many carefully groomed trails. During the Olympics busloads of spectators climbed up the sides of the trails to watch the best skiers in the world compete. We particularly remember Stenmark, whose impeccable runs in the giant slalom won him the Olympic gold medal. The area, which is usually uncrowded, is a delight for recreational skiers; its network of trails offers every degree of challenge to skiers of various abilities.

Whiteface offers plenty of beginner and novice slopes at the bottom of the mountain—a nice place to warm up. Intermediate skiers may want to take the Valley triple chair to the top the first time and ski down Boreen, which is wide and winding and has nice views. Take the same lift up again and ski Upper Valley or Broadway to the Little Whiteface lift. Go up and ski Excelsior to Upper Valley or On Ramp. Advanced intermediates can push themselves to take the Little Whiteface lift halfway up or take the Mountain Run lift to the same point. Ski Parkway; even though the upper is labeled expert, the slope is wide. Intermediates may continue to ride the Freeway lift halfway and ski Parkway. Ski all the way to the left, facing down, to try MacKenzie. If you'd like to go to the very top for a fine view of Lake Champlain and the high peaks—Mount Mansfield and Sugarbush—take the Valley triple lift up to the Summit triple lift and try Paron's Run, which at the top looks hard but really isn't. This joins Excelsior. If the snow is very good, highly advanced intermediates could try Lower Skyward, but only from the midstation of the´ Summit triple lift, not from the top.

Whiteface is superb for the expert skier. Once you get to know the mountain, you can see why the Olympics were held there. The top of Upper Cloudspin and Upper Skyward are true double diamond. No advanced intermediate should try the upper portions. In comparison with places that overrate difficulty, rating standards there seem closer to European standards. Believe the signs!

Southwest of Whiteface on Route 86 is **High Falls Gorge,** which may be seen from a series of paths and bridges. The Ausable River has been cutting its way down through the gorge for over a billion years, aided by wind and ice erosion. You can take a self-guided tour with stops at listening posts.

Continue on Route 86 and Route 73 into Lake Placid. (Or follow Route 73 from Keene into the town.) This is a pleasant resort town located in a broad valley surrounded by mountains. As the last glacier melted 14,000 years ago, gravel formed dams to create glacial lakes such as Lake Placid. Whiteface Mountain, with an elevation of 4,867 feet, provides a perfect contrast for the 300-foot depth of Lake Placid.

**High Falls Gorge
Route 86
Wilmington 12997
518–946–2278;
518–946–2211,
    off-season**

LAKE PLACID

As you enter town, you will see Mirror Lake first, as it lies along Main Street. During the summer you can bring a blanket and sit in the park overlooking the lake while listening to a concert. Motorboats are prohibited on Mirror Lake, so you can be assured of peace and quiet as you canoe, row, sailboard, swim, or just relax on its shores. Continue on to Lake Placid for a variety of recreational activities, including boat cruises.

Lake Placid is a center for a number of tourist attractions, including the extensive facilities built for both the 1932 and 1980 Winter Olympics. Stop in the **Olympic Center** for information and a map on Olympic sites. The **Olympic Arena Complex** is the center for ice sports, where four ice surfaces under one roof are maintained. The rinks are used for ice shows, hockey competition, professional hockey training, figure skating, and a summertime skating school. The **Olympic Speed Skating Oval,** where Eric Heiden earned five gold medals in 1980, is adjacent to the Olympic Arena. It is used by athletes in training and by the public during the winter.

**Olympic Center
Lake Placid 12946
518–523–1655**

Take a drive to the **Ski Jump Complex,** where you will see two towers next to each other. The 90-meter (225-foot) tower houses a glass-enclosed elevator, which you can take to the top for a view of the Adirondacks. During the summer plastic matting permits ski jumping, and a snow-making system is used to ensure plenty of snow all winter. The stadium there holds 25,000 spectators, with an electronic scoreboard to register distance, style, and total points.

**Mount Van
 Hoevenberg
 Recreation Area
Route 73
Lake Placid 12946
518–523–2811**

Mount Van Hoevenberg Recreation Area includes the Olympic bobsled and luge runs, an extensive network of Olympic cross-country ski trails, and a biathlon course. We have found cross-country skiing there to be pure delight on a clear, sunny morning after a fresh snowfall. The trails are wide and provide all varieties of terrain, from easy flats to difficult descents. If snow has not fallen recently, the trails are still kept in good shape and hold their snow much better than windswept mountaintops in the area. If you come on a weekend or in a holiday period, don't be put off by a crowded parking lot; the system of trails is big enough to swallow a lot of skiers and give them the sense of space they came for.

The **Lake Placid Center for the Arts** offers a full program of performances, such as dance companies, the Syracuse Stage Theatre, the Lake Placid Sinfonietta, the Sennel Theatre Group, the Community Theatre Players, and a classic film series. The gallery of fine arts features the work of current artists. The **Adirondack North Country Crafts Center** (518–523–2062), located in the library, sells Adirondack crafts.

**Lake Placid Center for the Arts
Saranac Avenue
Lake Placid 12946
518–523–2512**

The **John Brown Farm and Grave,** a historic site of New York, is located on Route 73, 2 miles south of Lake Placid. In 1848 John Brown arrived in Lake Placid, where he continued to strive for the freedom of the Negro. The house has been restored, and his mementos are on display.

**John Brown Farm and Grave
Route 73
Lake Placid 12946**

If you're looking for a place to lunch, there are many to choose from. Local friends recommend **Jimmy's 21** (21 Main Street; 518–523–2353), **The Cottage** (35 Mirror Lake Drive; 518–523–9845), **The Country Kitchen** (137 Main Street; 518–523–1799), and **Villa Vespa** (85 Saranac Avenue; 518–523–9959). For a special dinner (reservations suggested), try the **Lake Placid Manor** (Whiteface Inn Road, Lake Placid, New York 12946; 518–523–2573). The inn was built as an Adirondack camp in 1895 on the shore of Lake Placid with a view of Whiteface Mountain. The rustic simplicity of the lodge itself will not prepare you for its superb cuisine. (See Inns appendix.)

SARANAC LAKE

**Robert Louis
Stevenson Memorial
Cottage
11 Stevenson Lane
Saranac Lake 12983**

Continue on Route 86 to Saranac Lake to visit the **Robert Louis Stevenson Memorial Cottage,** where he lived from 1887 to 1888 when he came for a rest cure in a clinic directed by Dr. Edward Livingston Trudeau. Stevenson enjoyed the natural beauty of Saranac Lake and found the isolation and purity of the forest and lake conducive to his writing. He wrote much of *The Master of Ballantrae* as well as many articles in that house, and his bedroom is now a museum filled with memorabilia. Other rooms contain the furniture he used, including a desk; you can still see burns on the mantel from cigarettes he left burning there. Trudeau had told him to stop smoking and to stay in Saranac, and the cure worked. There are photos of a cast of Stevenson's hands from 1893, his velvet coat and cap, and a pair of ice skates that he used with pleasure on the lake.

In 1855 Queen Victoria's maid of honor, Amelia M. Murray, went on a camping trip in the Saranac Lake area with Horatio Seymour, governor of New York State, his niece, another man, and three guides. Murray wrote about seeing a loon for the first time and listening to its mournful calls, having freshly caught trout for dinner and partridge for breakfast, making a difficult portage around Raquette Falls, and other details of her trip.

In 1858, Ralph Waldo Emerson, James Russell Lowell, and eight other writers lived in "Philosopher's Camp" near Saranac Lake. Emerson wrote a poem describing the beauty of the place. Mark Twain had a summer camp on Lower Saranac Lake. Artists arrived to capture the landscape on canvas, and the Currier and Ives lithographs of the Adirondacks became popular.

Lake George, one of New York's most popular summer resort areas.

LAKE GEORGE

The indoor-outdoor Adirondack Museum on Blue Mountain Lake.

ADIRONDACK MUSEUM

Whiteface Mountain, site of all alpine ski events during the 1980 Olympics.

WHITEFACE MOUNTAIN

Before leaving the Saranac Lake area, you should decide whether to complete a short circuit back to Saratoga and Albany or contiune westward from the Adirondacks to the Thousand Islands region of the St. Lawrence.

BLUE MOUNTAIN LAKE

Adirondack Museum Route 28 Blue Mountain Lake 12812 518-352-7311

If you choose the short circuit, continue southwest on Route 3 to Tupper Lake and Route 30 to Long Lake and Blue Mountain Lake for a visit to the **Adirondack Museum.** This museum is both indoors and outdoors. Its exhibits are arranged both professionally (with just the right amount of information provided) and attractively (with plenty of space around them). We suggest heading first for the Conference Building to see an orientation film, *The Adirondacks.* This film focuses on people as well as issues in the Adirondacks. Exhibits are housed in cottages and buildings that are scattered around the grounds. Don't miss the logging exhibit. "Mining in the Adirondacks" is another new exhibit. The Rising Schoolhouse, dating from 1907, can be seen on the outside, but the inside is in the process of renovation. Outside, the steamboat *Osprey* and the excursion launch *Mountaineer* are moored in the boat pond. In the boat shed is *El Lagarto,* George Reis's elegant Gold Cup winner; there are also Adirondack guide boats, canoes, and a naphtha-fueled launch. A fully rigged racing sailboat from St. Regis Lake floats in a circular, glass-enclosed building. The exhibit on lumbering in the Adirondacks is a capsule history of the area's major industry. The diorama of Noah John Rondeau, who was something of a hermit, chopping wood will give you a sense of nineteenth-century life in the woods. If you press a button on the relief map, you will illuminate the lakes, rivers, and scenery of the Adirondacks. The "Oriental" is a private railroad car owned by August Belmont, representative of the way the wealthy reached their camps. It is elegant and paneled in mahogany. Don't miss the view of the surrounding area from the windows; we saw it in full fall, with oranges, yellows, and reds set against the blue of the lake.

Continuing the short circuit, follow Route 30 to Indian Lake and Route 28 through North River to Gore Mountain (518–251–2411) for a gondola ride up to the top. Looking down from a gondola is one of the best ways to enjoy fall colors. If you come in the winter, you will find a very fine major ski resort favored by local residents. It is run by the Olympic Authority, which also operates Whiteface Mountain.

GORE MOUNTAIN

Intermediate skiers visiting the **Gore Mountain Ski Center** may want to try the Sunway chair lift first to the midstation and then ski down to Jamboree. Take the same chair up all of the way and ski Sunway. Then take the East triple chair lift to Saddle Lodge and ski Sunway from the top—it is a nice wide "ego trail" to make skiers feel terrific. Take the same lift again and try Sleighride to Showcase to 2B. The same lift also offers the chance to ski Quick Silver, which has dips and some steep drops, and Twister, which is a curvy, fun trail. If you want to try the North Face, ski down Sleeping Bear and come up on the North chair to try Powder Pass, North Star, and Pete Gay. You can take the Summit chair up to the very top to try Cloud to Wood Lot. Stay up in the area to try Upper and Lower Steilhang. On the other side of the mountain again, the gondola takes you up to try a whole series of nice intermediate trails.

Follow Route 28 to North Creek.

**Gore Mountain
Ski Center
North Creek 12853
518–251–2411**

If you think of the Hudson as a stately, broad river flowing between palisades, which it is downstream, you'll get another vision of it during the springtime white-water season here.

NORTH CREEK

**Hudson River
 White-Water Derby
North Creek 12853**

Come during the first weekend in May, as thousands do, and watch the **Hudson River White-Water Derby,** which holds a slalom competition on a wild section in North River and a 7-mile downriver race from North Creek to Riparius. Spectators bring picnics and sit along the shores to watch participants paddle madly as they try to choose the best route through haystacks (the standing waves at the bottom of rapids that can swamp an open canoe) and avoid wrapping their canoes around rocks. The "Dean of American Canoeing," Homer Dodge (president emeritus of Norwich University), was still running the derby in his eighties. Downstream the section to the Glen also has a set of rapids, and ardent canoeists can continue on to Warrensburg through some Class-4 drops. (From damp personal experience, we recommend using a closed canoe, kayak, or raft for anything above Class 3.) The tributaries of the Hudson also provide a variety of white-water conditions. One of our favorite rivers is the Schroon, which ranges from flat water through the roughest water that an open canoe can handle. It has the advantage of also being available in the summer, because flow is controlled by a dam. Those who want wilder water can go to the Indian River or the Blue Ledges section of the upper Hudson, both of which require experts as guides. You can investigate taking a Hudson River rafting trip from **Cunningham's Ski Barn** in North Creek (518–251–3215), or **Adirondack River Outfitters** in Old Forge (315–369–3536).

For more precise information on specific canoe routes—anyone with white-water experience knows that you need it—write to the **Adirondack Mountain Club** for *Adirondack Canoe Waters.* Another helpful guide is *No Two Rivers Alike—Canoeable Rivers in New York and Pennsylvania,* by Alec Proskine (write to the Crossing Press, Trumansburg, New York 14866).

**Adirondack Mountain
 Club
Route 9N
Lake George, NY
12845
518–668–4447**

If you are interested in a flat-water canoe trip, contact the New York State **Department of Environmental Conservation** (50 Wolf Road, Albany, New York 12233, or 2 World Tade Center, Room 6126, New York, New York 10047; 212–488–2755) for information on canoe routes in the state. Ask for *Adirondack Canoe Routes: Lake Chains.* There are many choice circuits, including **Paul Smith's, Saranac Lake, Tupper Lake, Raquette Lake, Raquette River, Long Lake,** and the **Fulton Lakes Chain.** You can also go ski touring on the canoe portaging trails in this area. Although hiking trails are often steep, canoe trails tend to be flat and wide enough for maneuvering a canoe and thus make ideal cross-country trails.

To complete the short circuit, continue on Route 28 through Warrensburg, where you can pick up I–87 south to Sararoga Springs and Albany.

To continue the itinerary to the Thousand Islands area, either take Route 3 west from Tupper Lake to Route 21 west; Route 28 southwest from Blue Mountain Lake past Old Forge to Alder Creek, where you can pick up Route 12 northwest; or Route 30 north from Lake Clear Junction to Malone and pick up Route 37 west to Route 12. There are no direct, fast routes from east to west across this part of the state— the wildest and least developed in the Adirondack Park. Why should there be? There is, however, some virtue in the enforced slower pace through this section of the mountains, forests, and lake; appreciate them and remember that you are still in New York, not Montana.

RAQUETTE LAKE

If you choose the southernmost of the three routes to the Thousand Islands, you will pass Raquette Lake, much favored by canoeists. You can visit **Camp Sagamore,** built by

Sagamore Lodge and Conference Center
Raquette Lake 13436
315–354–5311

William Durant in 1897 and owned by the Vanderbilts beginning in 1903. This Tyrolean estate is a splendid example of the "Great Camps" of the area. During the summer a guided tour and slide presentation are offered. (The Sagamore also offers a variety of programs all year.) When we were there, we were entranced by the animal heads on walking sticks carved by the carpenter-in-residence in the carpenter's shop. When you visit the blacksmith shop, look for the champagne case drawer that says W. W. Durant on the bottom. The Wigwam guest cottage is the place to be if you like hearing the rushing water of a stream outside your door. In the Main Lodge look for the doorjamb where the Vanderbilt children marked their heights. Don't miss the covered bowling alleys that are still in use today.

From Raquette Lake take the scenic road through Inlet, and continue on to Thendara for a gourmet meal at **Van Auken's** (315–369–3033). This restaurant and inn is cheerful with hanging plants across the porch.

FULTON LAKES

Along the same route the Fulton Lakes Chain is very popular for canoe trips. Canoe liveries operating from Old Forge will help you plan your trip. They will pick you up at the conclusion of your route, perhaps the most important service one-way canoeists need. If you are there in the winter months, you will find alpine and cross-country skiing as well as snowmobiling trails. If you have children, you may want to

Enchanted Forest of the Adirondacks
Fulton Lakes
315–369–6145

head for **Enchanted Forest of the Adirondacks,** a theme park featuring make-believe, shows, and rides. It is open from June to September.

❧ *Thousand Islands Region* ❧

Although you may not wish to leave the wilderness of the Adirondacks, other pleasures await you in the Thousand Islands of the St. Lawrence. There may be almost 2,000 islands, depending on what you count, but a French explorer gave the area its name. These "jewels" in the river provide a perfect environment for water sports, natural beauty of a very high order, and a variety of historical and culinary attractions. Although some isalnds are quite small, including those of one-rock size, others house a one-family home with space to spare, and some have the dimensions for a whole village. On them you will see large stone mansions, luxury hotels, colonial houses of historical significance, and even a castle. You can take any one of a number of boat trips or rent a houseboat for your holiday, but be sure you do get on the water; there is no other way to appreciate the extraordinary beauty of the region.

Route 12 leads you to Clayton, where you can visit the **Shipyard Museum.** This museum has collected a unique group of antique boats, including dugout and birchbark canoes, St. Lawrence skiffs, turn-of-the-century launches, and speedboats from the Gold Cup era. *Dixie II,* the 1908–1910 Gold Cup champion, resides here. *PDQ,* short for "Pretty Damn Quick," George Boldt's 39-foot boat, was built in Ogdensburg. *Ariel,* a naphtha launch owned by President Garfield, was built between 1880 and 1884, and *Anita,* another naphtha launch, looks like a surrey with a fringe on top. She has a brass steering wheel, mahogany seats, and an engine in the stern. Skiffs, bateaux, Adirondack guide boats, and canoes are displayed in a shed behind the main building. A 10-foot-long dugout canoe on display was found exposed in a creek bank after a heavy rain.

Special exhibits in the museum include a life-size figure of Homer L. Dodge reclining in his sailing canoe. Mr. Dodge was born in 1887 in Ogdensburg and grew up canoeing and rowing his skiff on the St. Lawrence River. He

CLAYTON

Shipyard Museum
750 Mary Street
Clayton 13624
315–686–4104

became enthusiastic about white-water canoeing and particularly about conquering the treacherous rapids in the St. Lawrence in an open canoe (before many of the rapids were eliminated or modified by the Seaway construction). After years of preparation he did conquer the Lachine Rapids alone in an open canoe. In later years he won many trophies in white-water competition. We were fortunate enough to watch him skillfully maneuvering his canoe down the course in the Hudson White-Water Derby before he stopped canoeing at the age of eighty-seven.

The museum offers cruises on the *Narrah Mattah,* a 1902 cruiser in mint condition. Other boat trips are available from Riverside Drive in Clayton (315–686–3511).

CAPE VINCENT

From Clayton continue west on Route 12 toward Cape Vincent, a harbor settled years ago by the French. Look for **"Stone House"** on Main Street, one of many historic homes. If you are fascinated by ocean-going vessels, this is the place to stretch out on the grass and watch. You can see Carleton Island five miles offshore and the ruins of Fort Haldemand. Tibbett's Point Lighthouse is located at the junction of the St. Lawrence and Lake Ontario. Fishermen regard Cape Vincent as the black bass center of the area, and you can visit the **Cape Vincent Fisheries Station** to see its displays on the conservation of fish. If you are there in the middle of July, you can be involved in the **French Festival,** which brings the history of the area to life.

KINGSTON, CANADA

Since you are this close, you may want to make a side trip into Canada. You will need to go through Customs both ways, which does not take long. Check current regulations before you go. For example, we once came through with our dog and did not have her vaccination certificate with us, which caused some delay.

You can travel by ferry from Cape Vincent to Wolfe Island and by another ferry to Kingston, Ontario. Kingston, an early fur-trading center, was in a strategic location for military operations. **Fort Henry** was built in the years following the War of 1812; it has been restored and provides presentations during the summer season. The **Hockey Hall of Fame** is located in town. You can also take cruises to the Thousand Islands from Kingston.

The **Marine Museum of the Great Lakes** at Kingston has a variety of exhibits, including a blacksmith shop where the supplies necessary for shipbuilding were made, a steamboat display, a shipwreck chart, a display of half-models, a mast-step from a frigate used during the War of 1812, and a display on deep-sea diving. Signs invite visitors to hear a ship's whistle, rotate the dial on a radio direction-finder until the signals disappear, or pick up the telephone to hear the voice of the Coast Guard reciting weather conditions to mariners.

Stop in at the old **Prince George Hotel** (200 Ontario Street; 613–549–5440) for a Guinness or something else. It's right across the street from the **Visitor and Convention Bureau,** within sight of the waterfront.

If you drive northeast from Kingston on Route 2, you will come to the **St. Lawrence Island National Park,** where there is a visitors' center; check on the many activities available, such as hikes and interpretive programs.

From Kingston Route 2 will take you to the village of Gananoque, where you can shop endlessly for British china, woolens, and silver. This resort center has many water sports and various other activities for the visitor. During the summer season you can attend church services held from a rocky pulpit on the edge of a natural amphitheater at Halfmoon Bay. The congrega-

Fort Henry
Kingston
613–542–7388

Hockey Hall of Fame
 Alfred & Pine Streets
Kingston
613–544–2355

Marine Museum of
 the Great Lakes at
 Kingston
55 Ontario Street
Kingston
613–542–2261

Visitor and
 Convention Bureau
209 Ontario Street
Kingston

GANANOQUE

tion arrives by boat and views the service from the boats; canoe-paddling ushers distribute hymnals and collect offerings. Many Thousand Island boat trips begin at Gananoque.

The Thousand Islands Bridge is located east of Gananoque. This 7-mile crossing, dedicated in 1938 as a symbol of peace between Canada and the United States, provides magnificent views of the beautiful area. Park your car in the parking lot. A sky deck between spans of the bridge has an elevator to whisk you to a view ranging up to 40 miles. Ships flying different foreign flags thread through Seaway channels below as you look down from the top of the tower, and the vista of islands is spread before you. Don't miss it on a clear day.

ALEXANDRIA BAY

Boldt Castle
Heart Island
Alexandria Bay 13607
315–482–2501

Heading northeast on Route 12 from the I–81 junction will take you to Alexandria Bay. Look out in the river to see **Boldt Castle** on Heart Island. George Boldt, the owner of the Waldorf–Astoria in New York City, blasted the island into the shape of a heart and built this dream castle for his wife, but she died in 1902, four years after construction had begun. As a result, the castle was never occupied. This 300-room building was designed to look like a castle on the Rhine. There is a legend that Thousand Island dressing was first served aboard George Boldt's yacht during a cruise in the Thousand Islands. Boldt's steward served him a new dressing that he like so much that he decided to serve it in his hotel, naming it after his favorite vacation area. The steward was promoted and rose to fame as Oscar of the Waldorf.

A boat trip is the only was to explore the intricacies of the islands. **Uncle Sam Boat Tours** (315–482–2611) runs a variety of tours, including those on a new boat, the *Alexandria Bell*. **Empire Boat Tours** (315–482–9511) offers tripledeck boats. You will pass through "Millionaires

Colony," past the Devil's Oven, stop at Boldt Castle, then continue into Canada to cruise under the International Bridge, through Whirlpool Channel and Lost Channel, and past Fiddler's Elbow. Don't miss seeing the shortest international bridge in the world between two adjoining islands—one in Canada and one in the United States. Smugglers Cove was notorious as a meeting place for rum-runners; its seven entrances gave them a chance to get out without having to sink their bottles if the Coast Guard appeared.

Restaurants abound in Alexandria Bay: **Pine Tree Point** (Outer Anthony Street; 315–482–9911), **Riveredge Pancake House** (17 Holland Street; 315–482–9917), **Edgewood Resort** (Edgewood Road; 315–482–9922), and **Bonnie Castle** (Holland Street; 315–482–4511). Bonnie Castle is one of the old mansions on the river, dating from 1877.

MORRISTOWN

As you continue northeast (downriver) from Alexandria Bay on Route 12, you will find a number of state parks for leisurely stops. Route 12 merges with Route 37 near Morristown.

The **Red Barn Museum** has displays of some of the village's early residents, a blacksmith shop, and an icehouse. The **Stone Schoolhouse** in the museum dates from 1824. Typical desks, benches, and the schoolmaster's desk hold a collection of maps and books. As you might imagine, an old wood stove is in a prominent spot. The **Stone Windmill** was built in 1825 as a gristmill. Once it was used as a jail, and it saw action during World War II as an air warning observation post.

**Red Barn Museum
River Road
Morristown 13664
315–375–6390**

**Stone Windmill
Chapman Village Park
Morristown 13664
315–375–6390**

OGDENSBURG

Farther downstream, Ogdensburg has had a couple of forts in its history, including Fort Oswegatchie, which was built by the British in the late 1700s. The **Ogdensburg-Prescott**

**Remington Art
Museum
303 Washington Street
Ogdensburg 13669
315–393–2425**

International Bridge, the eighteenth-largest suspension bridge in the world, arches 125 feet above the river at the center.

The **Remington Art Museum** contains more of Frederic Remington's work than any other museum. The priceless collection includes 14 bronzes, 140 watercolors, 70 oil paintings, and many sketches. The gallery displays a selection of his work and features new acquisitions as they are received. Mementos from his travels also grace this museum. Educational programs for students are held throughout the year. Frederic Remington lived on Hamilton Street in Ogdensburg for eight years. He grew up during the time when horses were used all over town— horses and buggies, horses and carriages, work horses and wagons, racing horses, saddle horses, and fire horses. No wonder he chose to draw and sculpt horses.

**MASSENA
Robert Moses
 State Park
Barnhart Island
Massena 13662
315–769–8663**

Continue on Route 37 to Massena to **Robert Moses State Park,** where you can get information on the St. Lawrence Seaway as well as view some of the locks. Look for the original wooden map showing the adventures of Jacques Cartier as he discovered the St. Lawrence River. There is a 90-foot drop in the river here, which provides power for the Moses-Saunders Power Dam. The **FDR Project** on Barnhart Island has exhibits on river power developments.

After your tour of the Thousand Islands area, head south again on I–81 through Watertown.

SACKETS HARBOR

You may want to take a side trip from Watertown on Route 3 West to Sackets Harbor, a scene of fighting during the War of 1812. Some accounts claim that one American ship defeated five British ships, even returning the one ball that landed on shore to splinter the mast of the British flagship. General Zebulon

Pike, who discovered Pike's Peak as well as distinguished himself in the War of 1812, is buried in a military cemetery there.

Sackets Harbor Battlefield State Historic Site contains a visitors' center in the Union Hotel. There are lots of exhibits, dioramas, lectures, and special programs available. The site is right on the water, attractively landscaped with lawns and large maples. **Pickering Beach Historical Museum** is a historic home dating back to 1817. It contains items from the War of 1812, an antique doll collection, period furniture, silver, china, and other memorabilia. **Madison Barracks** on Pike Street was the site of training for a number of our most prestigious military leaders.

The remainder of this itinerary heads east to the Mohawk Valley and back to Albany. Take I–81 south from Watertown to Pulaski, then Route 13 and Route 69 to Rome. Alternatively, you can head south to join the Finger Lakes Itinerary.

**Sackets Harbor
  Battlefield State
  Historic Site**
Sackets Harbor 13685
315–646–3634

**Pickering Beach
  Historical Museum
503 West Main Street**
Sackets Harbor 13685

✑ *Leatherstocking Region* ✑

Sometimes regarded as the heartland of New York State, the Mohawk Valley has been called the "Leatherstocking" region because James Fenimore Cooper's book *Leatherstocking Tales* was set in this area. The name comes from the dress of woodsmen, who wore leather leggings to protect their legs from branches and thorns when blazing trails through the forest.

The Mohawk Valley was formed by the melting of glacial ice, which produced a wide river valley. The landscape is varied with rock groupings and precipices, forests, cataracts, and waterfalls dropping into jagged gorges. The Mohawk River begins just north of Rome and cuts a path through the Alleghany Plateau. This "river flowing through the mountains" is located between the Adirondacks and the Catskills, connecting the Great Lakes with the Hudson River. It flows for 150 miles until it dashes over the falls at Cohoes and into the Hudson.

Mohawk Indians lived there as "Keepers of the Eastern Door." These aggressive members of the Iroquois Confederacy protected the central part of New York State. Many of them prospered by farming their fertile land. As fur trade grew, the valley absorbed increasing numbers of men transporting pelts by canoes, bateaux, and barges. German settlers arrived in the 1720s, building sturdy stone houses as a deterrent against fire during Indian raids. In 1755 the British built a series of forts to interrupt trade along this crucial route.

ROME

Rome was originally called "the carrying place" by the Indians; there is a portage right in the center of town. Stop in the information center located in City Hall (315–336–6000) if you have some time to spend in this interesting small city.

Fort Stanwix
Rome 13440
315–336–2090

Fort Stanwix in the center of town was built in 1758 during the French and Indian War, then abandoned until 1776 when American soldiers rebuilt it. As you look at this star-shaped structure, you can imagine those inside using a pattern of crossfire to mow down attackers. A sentry from the Third New York Regiment, which was a colonial unit, is stationed at the drawbridge where visitors enter. At the visitors' center you can watch a film recounting the twenty-one-day siege by the British, then stroll around to see the men's quarters and other exhibits; you will hear the cannons boom on weekends.

Erie Canal Village
Route 49W
Rome 13440
315–336–6000

Erie Canal Village is an 1840s canal village complete with a train station, school, church, tavern, houses, shops, an icehouse, a steam-engine train, and a packet boat. The structures were taken apart and rebuilt in this location. You can walk along nature trails in the area, take a steam train for 4 miles, or take a boat, the *Independence,* pulled by Belgian horses. As you visit the buildings, you can watch blacksmiths, gardeners, weavers, and musicians at work, to name just a few of the trades and crafts practiced.

For a scenic drive in the area, take Route

46 north to North Western and continue along the gorge to Boonville. The **Black River Canal** is visible along part of this drive.

Or you can head southeast on Route 69 to **Oriskany Battlefield,** where a monument honors a group of colonial militiamen who were able to withstand an attack by Indians and Loyalists in 1777. There the "bloodiest battle of the Revolution" was fought during a period of six hours. General Nicholas Herkimer, commander of the militia, unknowingly led his men into an ambush in a ravine just south of the Mohawk. Herkimer was shot in the leg but refused to leave the battle. He sat on a log, with his sword drawn and his leg bleeding, and continued to direct his soldiers. When it was over, he was carried down the valley to his home, where his leg was amputated in an effort to save his life, but he died eleven days later.

Oriskany Battlefield
Route 69
Rome 13440
315–768–7224

Utica saw its real growth after the Erie Canal was completed in 1825. The **Munson-Williams-Proctor Museum** exhibits American and European art from colonial times to the present. The building was designed by Philip Johnson. Don't miss Thomas Cole's *The Voyage of Life,* which moves from childhood through youth and adulthood to old age. Next door is **Fountain Elms,** a decorative arts collection.

UTICA
Munson-Williams-
  Proctor Museum
310 Genesee Street
Utica 13503
315–797–0000

The **Children's Museum of History, Natural History, and Science** features a hands-on series of exhibits and has a variety of programs scheduled throughout the year. The **Utica Zoo** houses more than 300 animals, including reptiles, birds, mammals, and cats. Don't miss the special Children's Zoo, where your youngsters may pet the animals.

Children's Museum of
  History, Natural
  History, and Science
311 Main Street
Utica 13503
315–724–6128

Utica Zoo
Steele Hill Road
Utica 13503
315–798–3279

F. X. Matt Brewery (Court and Varick streets; 315–732–0022) offers tours, including a trolley ride to an 1888 tavern for tasting.

The **Stanley Performing Arts Center**

(259 Genesee Street; 315–724–1113) is a restored movie palace, now on the National Register of Historic Places. The building is shared by the Utica Symphony, the Central New York Community Arts Council Theater, and the Munson-Williams-Proctor Institute's great artists series.

**Musical Museum
Deansboro 13328
315–841–8774**

South of Utica on Route 12B, you will find Deansboro, the home of the **Musical Museum.** This family-owned collection has been called a "marvelous musical menagerie," and the best part is that visitors are encouraged to play the instruments. The collection includes a 1922 violina, which is to violins what player pianos are to pianos; a 1910 German player piano, which features pianists such as Paderewski, Saint-Saëns, and Grieg; and a Wurlitzer nickelodeon, an 1852 Cherry Valley emlodeon, music boxes, mechanical dulcimers, old phonographs, a Mississippi steamboat organ, and a hurdy-gurdy with mechanical monkey. Look for the French "Pochette," which was carried in a dancing teacher's coat pocket in the 1650s, a flute in a walking stick, and a blue-velvet music roll for carrying sheet music that was presented by Queen Victoria to an American singer in 1870.

**Remington Firearms
  Museum
Route 5S
Ilion 13357
315–894–9961**

From Utica take Route 5S to the **Remington Firearms Museum** to see antique and modern firearms. The first flintlock was designed by Eliphalet Remington in 1816. He soon switched to using a percussion cap that fired faster than the flintlock. In 1857 he produced his first revolver pistol, a .31 caliber "pocket" gun. Annie Oakley used Remington rifles.

Stop for lunch at the **Mohawk Station Restaurant** (96 East Main, Mohawk; 315–866–7460).

HERKIMER

From Ilion take Routes 28 and 5 to Herkimer. If you have always wanted to dig for gems, try **Herkimer Diamond Mines.** Silica deposits dating from Cambrian times grew into quartz crystals. You can use a two- or three-pound crack hammer and a bullpoint chisel to find your gems.

If you've read Theodore Dreiser's *An American Tragedy,* you'll find that the murder trial took place in Herkimer between 1906 and 1908. It seems that Chester Gillette may have murdered Grace Brown, pregnant with his child, on a trip to Big Moose Lake in 1906. He said that she committed suicide; others say that he drowned her in Punkey Bay.

If General Herkimer interests you, **Herkimer Home,** located beyond Herkimer and Utica, just east of Little Falls, is open to the public. It contains period furnishings and personal items belonging to General Herkimer. Maple sugaring and sheepshearing are demonstrated during the appropriate seasons. Don't miss the colonial garden.

Then head north on Route 167 to Dolgeville and the **Florence Jones Reineman Wildlife Sanctuary** for programs from the end of May through mid-August. Dorothy and Al Richard were given a pair of beavers by the State Department of Environmental Protection many years ago. The beavers, Samson and Delilah, made a dam at Middlesprite, where the Richards lived. They produced many litters of kits and grew tame enough to accept apples from a hand. At one point another beaver, Lilah, was caught in a trap and nursed back to health in the spare room at the Richards'

African violet lovers will want to head for **Lyndon Lyon Greenhouses** (14 Mutchler Street, Dolgeville), where table after table of pink, purple, white, and variegated violets bloom. We couldn't resist bringing home a large boxful.

Herkimer Diamond Mines
Route 28
Herkimer 13350
315-891-7355

Herkimer Home
Route 169
Little Falls 13365
315-823-0398

DOLGEVILLE

Florence Jones Reineman Wildlife Sanctuary
Off Route 29
Dolgeville 13329
518-568-7101

If you're heading into the Capital District, stop for a meal at **The Poplars Inn** (Riverside Drive, opposite exit 28; 518–853–4511) for dining on the Mohawk and a ride on the *Poplar Mist*.

JORDANVILLE

If you're on the way to Cooperstown, head south on Route 167 to Jordanville to see the **Holy Trinity Russian Orthodox Monastery.** Begun by two young Russian immigrants in 1930, the cathedral, with its gold onion tops, was completed in 1950; the main monastery building, which houses the printing press, refectory, and cells of the monks, was constructed later. The inside of the cathedral is beautiful, with icons and frescoes on the walls and ceilings. Women must cover their heads and wear a skirt, as slacks or shorts are not allowed.

COOPERSTOWN

National Baseball Hall of Fame Main Street Cooperstown 13326 607–547–9988

If you're starting from Utica, take I–90 east and Route 28 south to Cooperstown, a lovely town at the foot of Otsego Lake, with many attractions for visitors. It is the home of the **National Baseball Hall of Fame.** Fans can peruse the photographs, displays, artifacts, and memorabilia associated with baseball's greatest players. A life-size wooden sculpture of Babe Ruth greets visitors at the entrance. Look for the bat used by Mickey Mantle to hit a 565-foot homer; the scorecard from the first World Series in 1903; a cornerstone from Ebbets Field; Jackie Robinson's uniform; the first catcher's mask, dated 1876; and Joe DiMaggio's bronze plaque. On display is Babe Ruth's locker, with his uniform and personal items, such as his shaving brush. As you enter the third floor, you'll hear baseball music playing from an old Philco radio. One side of the hall is lined with baseball sheet music; the other, with baseball cards.

The **Farmers' Museum and Village Crossroads** is a re-creation of a typical village during the period 1790–1860. The village consists of twelve buildings. You'll begin your tour in the main barn, where there are displays depicting the hardships of families as they struggled to plant and reap crops. In contrast, they also had fun on skates, sleds, and even carousel horses. The Cardiff Giant, a 10-foot-long gypsum statue found in 1869, was originally thought to be a petrified prehistoric man. The hoax was created by George Hull. Upstairs in the textile loft, you can watch spinning and weaving. As you walk around the village, you'll notice wonderful aromas, which probably come from the kitchen at Lippitt Homestead, where guides are preparing food.

Cooperstown was named for Judge William Cooper, who founded the town in 1786. His son, James Fenimore Cooper, became a major American novelist and drew heavily on central New York for such work as *The Last of the Mohicans* and *Leatherstocking Tales.* **Fenimore House** contains James Fenimore Cooper memorabilia, a fine collection of American folk art, and life masks of prominent Americans molded by John Browere from 1817 to 1833. You'll see folk portraits, including "Who is it?" and "Who did it?" quizzes with three different doors to open to find the answer. Don't miss the portrait of the little girl with the defiant look on her face, entitled *One Shoe Off,* and *The Mariner* with spyglass in his hand. Nineteenth-century landscape paintings include *Escape of General Israel Putnam* from the Indians by Asher Durand and *Sugaring Off* by Grandma Moses, featuring vividly dressed people out in the white snow.

James Fenimore Cooper memorabilia include a pocket book with adjustable calendar, inkstand, incense burner, and razor. There are photos of Otsega Hall, where Cooper grew up, and Fenimore College, which once stood on the site of the present ballroom.

Farmers' Museum and Village Crossroads
Route 80
Cooperstown 13326
607-547-2533

Fenimore House
Route 80
Cooperstown 13326
607-547-2533

For a special dinner head north on Route 80 to **Hickory Grove Inn** (607–547–8100). The owner/chef specializes in veal, and every meal is cooked to order using fresh vegetables. (See Inns appendix.) In Cooperstown try **The Otesaga Hotel** (607–547–9931) for a meal in a grand old hotel.

Glimmerglass Opera House (Route 80; 607–547–2255) offers opera from June through September. The woodland setting on Lake Otsega is lovely. Performances are in English.

If you're ready for a hike, go to **Glimmerglass State Park,** which is 4 miles south of Route 20 (607–547–8662). There is a beaver pond to explore and plenty of hiking trails to follow.

ONEONTA

National Soccer Hall of Fame
11 Ford Avenue
Oneonta 13820
607–432–3351

For a side trip to Oneonta, take Route 28S and Route 88W to Oneonta to visit the **National Soccer Hall of Fame.** TV monitors show national and international matches. Pro games and local soccer games are also held there.

Oneonta is also the home of **Hartwick College** (800–828–2288, in state; 800–828–2200, out of state). The **Yager Museum** offers a collection of American Indian artifacts dating from 1000 B.C.

When you're ready for a meal, head for **Cathedral Farms** (Routes 23 and 205W) on the summer estate of millionaire Henry Buckley, who raised a prize herd of "Bigger and Better Guernsey Cows." Don't miss "Memory Forest," where 200 trees from friends were planted for his seventy-fifth birthday. If you're heading west, try two other restaurants run by the same group: **Christopher's** (exits 14 and 15, Routes 23 and 28; 607–432–2444) and **The Farmhouse** (Exit 16, Route 7; 607–432–7374).

I–88 East will take you to exit 22, the turnoff for **Howe Caverns.** Lester Howe discovered the caverns in 1842 and dared to squeeze himself inside to explore. With only the light from his oil lamp, Howe forced himself to crawl and slide farther in on each visit until he finally reached a large underground lake. Undaunted, he carried in materials to build a raft. On the other side of the lake, he found stalactites, stalagmites, and a variety of grotesque stone shapes. Today visitors take an elevator down and then walk on brick paths to view the sights of the cavern. You'll also take a boat trip to see even more wonders.

From Oneonta take I–88 East back to Albany (in Itinerary A) or Route 28 back into the Catskills.

Howe Caverns
Route 7
Howes Cave 12092
518–296–8990

ITINERARY C:

Western and Central New York

LANDMARK THEATRE, SYRACUSE

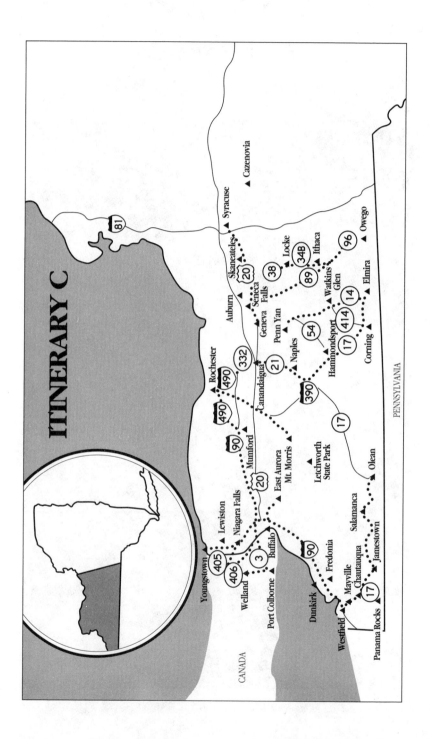

ITINERARY C

Western and Central New York

This itinerary can be the continuation of Itinerary B from the Thousand Islands section. It also links with Itinerary E: Western Pennsylvania.

⮿ *Finger Lakes Region* ⮿

The Finger Lakes region is one of wine and water—vineyards and even long, slender, and deep lakes left by departing glaciers. Waterfalls and gorges complete a water ambience of scenic splendor. The Iroquois believed that the Great Spirit placed his hand on this region and left behind his fingerprints. Other legends claim that the Creator reached to bless the land and left his fingerprints in the form of water-filled imprints. In fact, geologists report that the unique topographical contours of this area are the result of at least two Ice Age glaciers burrowing and grinding out long narrow lakes, gorges, and valleys. The earliest inhabitants were probably the Mound Builders. When Jesuit missionaries arrived from Europe, they found Cayuga, Seneca, and Onondaga Indians in residence. Many of the lakes bear Indian names, including Canandaigua, Keuka, Seneca, Cayuga, Owasco, and Skaneateles.

You can choose to tour some of the lakes on their northern side on Routes 5 and 20 with forays south at whim; along their southern side on Routes 13, 17, and 390 with jaunts north; or via several slalomlike sweeps around the lakes. For the purpose of this itinerary, we will move from one lake to the next in a westerly direction along a suggested route with side trips and options, leaving the final choice of route to be determined by your time and interests. You can also choose to cycle around the area if you are up to tackling the hills.

SYRACUSE

Syracuse Convention and Visitors' Bureau
Syracuse
315–470–1343

Syracuse, a gateway to the Finger Lakes, on the shore of Onondaga Lake, was first inhabited by Indians as early as 1570. Hiawatha selected this location as the capital of the Iroquois Confederacy. The Indians discovered salt on this site; in the seventeenth century Father LeMoyne discovered a salt spring south of Fort Sainte Marie de Gannentaha, which eventually led to the development of the salt industry in Syracuse. The fort was founded in 1656 but later succumbed to Indian attacks.

Visit the **Salt Museum** in Onondaga Lake

Park. A salt boiling block is on display there. Also in the park you can visit the reproduction of **Fort Ste. Marie de Gannentaha** (315–457–5715) to see guides engaged in cooking, carpentry, farming, log hewing, and blacksmithing. This seventeenth-century Jesuit mission presents a living history program.

**Salt Museum
Onondaga Lake Park
Syracuse
315–457–2990**

The Erie Canal also contributed to the growth of Syracuse. The **Erie Canal Museum** is housed in the only remaining weighlock of the original seven on the canal. This Greek Revival building contains a reconstruction of the west gates of the weighlock. In order to determine the toll owed by a canal boat, it was necessary to weigh the barge. After the water was drained from the lock, the barge remained on a giant scale that measured its weight. Tolls were abolished in 1883, and the building was used for administration; it was placed on the National Register of Historic Places in 1972. A replica of a typical canal boat lies inside the lock chamber. This museum is the only one in the United States concerned entirely with canal history and memorabilia. Special exhibits are featured at the museum, including a recent display on the canals of England.

**Erie Canal Museum
Erie Boulevard East at
  Montgomery Street
Syracuse 13201
315–471–7220**

The Erie Canal, dubbed "Clinton's Ditch" by those who doubted the value of Governor DeWitt Clinton's project, was dug by farmers and immigrant workers, who made 50 cents a day for very hard work. The canal was built 40 feet wide at ground level, 28 feet wide at the bottom, and 4 feet deep. A 10-foot-wide towpath ran along the bank; today the path is used for hiking and cycling. In 1836 the Erie Canal was deepened to 7 feet for boats carrying 240 tons, and in 1917 it was modernized. Eventually the paths along the canals will connect all the way from Buffalo to Albany. If you are interested in more extensive information on the canal system and its recreational opportunities, write for the brochure *Experience the Legend of New York's Canals* (**New York State Department of Transportation,** 5 Governor Harriman State Campus, Albany, New York 12232; 518–457–6376). Maps of trail segments along the canal may be obtained free of charge from Communications, **New York State Parks,** Empire State Plaza, Albany, New York 12238.

Discovery Center of Science and Technology
321 South Clinton Street
Syracuse 13201
315–425–9068

The **Discovery Center of Science and Technology** encourages participation by visitors in many of its exhibits. You can get your hands into exhibits on electricity, computers, energy, light, color, perception, sound, and the life sciences. Press a button and a special light will seemingly take the color out of you and your clothing. If you would like to see your hair stand on end, look for the static electricity globe. The planetarium is open daily for star shows.

Everson Museum of Art
401 Harrison Street
Syracuse 13201
315–474–6064

The **Everson Museum of Art** is considered to be one of the ten most architecturally interesting museums in the United States. It looks like a pinwheel with its cantilevered blocks around a central court. The collection includes both traditional and contemporary art from the nineteenth and twentieth centuries.

Landmark Theatre
362 South Salina Street
Syracuse 13201
315–475–7979

The **Landmark Theatre** was originally a Loew's theater and has been restored to all its glittering glory. Built in 1927, the interior features Persian and Moorish design. Programs include classic films, concerts, drama, and touring companies from Broadway.

Syracuse University offers a season of drama in the **Regent Theatre Complex** (820 East Genesee Street; 315–423–2708 for information, 423–3275 for the box office). **Salt City Center for the Performing Arts** (601 South Crouse Avenue; 315–474–1122) is open year-round for a series of musicals, comedies, and other dramatic performances. The **Syracuse State Theater** (820 East Genesee Street; 315–423–3275) is a professional theater featuring performers from

Broadway. The **Civic Center of Onondaga County** (411 Montgomery Street; 315–424–8200) is the home of the Syracuse Symphony Orchestra, the Syracuse Symphony of Famous Artists, and the Syracuse Opera Company.

The **New York State Fair** opened in Syracuse in 1841. It holds the record for being the longest-running state fair in the United States; it is open eleven days preceding Labor Day every year. Did you know that the first ferris wheel was built in Syracuse? In 1848 two canalmen with time to spare during the winter freeze constructed a four-car wheel that would hold twenty persons.

The newly opened **Burnet Park Zoo** offers nine exhibit areas in this "new breed of zoo." You can walk into a semidark replica of a prehistoric cave to view fish, amphibians, and reptiles whose ancestors have been here for millions of years. You can compare those that have changed a great deal from their earliest ancestors to those that have not changed at all. A multilevel walkway provides views of the collection of birds. Another area illustrates how animals adapt in order to survive in various environments. Exhibits on extinct and endangered animals are displayed.

Burnet Park Zoo
Wilbur and Coleridge
Avenues
Syracuse 13201
315–425–3774

A side trip from Syracuse can take you to the pretty town of Cazenovia. Located right on Cazenovia Lake, the town is full of elegant old homes. After the Civil War the town was discovered by wealthy families who wanted a cool, attractive summer residence. Stop for lunch at **Brae Loch Inn** (Route 20; 315–655–3431). When you open the door, you are greeted by bagpipe music; it's a wonderful way to set the mood. The inn is family-run, and everyone wears kilts. (See Inns appendix.)

CAZENOVIA

Greek Peak Ski Resort is located within

CORTLAND

C•167

Greek Peak Ski Resort
2000 New York Street
Route 392
Cortland 13045
607–835–6111

easy access of Syracuse, Binghamton, Ithaca, and the Finger Lakes. Snowmaking covers eighty-five percent of the area, so don't worry about thin snowcover on the way in—the slopes will be covered with a good base. Ask about the resort's "Guarantee Learn to Ski," wherein skiers can go to the red flag at the bottom of Chair II or III to meet an instructor who will offer instruction and encouragement until they can ski from the top to the bottom of the Alpha Slope.

SKANEATELES

William Seward, secretary of state during Lincoln's administration, called Skaneateles Lake "the most beautiful body of water in the world." The 18-mile-long lake is the highest of the region, at 863 feet above sea level. Hills green with forests converge into mountains at the head of the lake. The village of Skaneateles contains handsome homes, including **Roosevelt Hall,** which belonged to a cousin of President Theodore Roosevelt; this Greek Revival home overlooks the lake.

The *Mail Boat* brings mail, news, and guests to people living along the shore. You can ride on a "mail cruise" or take a luncheon or dinner cruise with **Mid-Lakes Navigation Company** (P.O. Box 61, 11 Jordan Street, Skaneateles, New York 13152; 315–685–5722). In fact, anyone fascinated by canal trips should look into this company's cruises that head west to Buffalo, east to Albany, and continue north to Whitehall, lasting several days. Traveling on the canals has been popular in Europe for years; now you can cruise leisurely closer to home.

Lunch or dinner at the handsomely restored **Sherwood Inn** (Route 20; 315–685–3405) takes you back in time. (See Inns appendix.)

Local inhabitants recommend **Doug's Fish Fry** (8 Jordan Street) for fish—it has no atmosphere but terrific food; in fact, its logo is

"Tourists Beware . . ." It is open seven days a week. **The Krebs** (53 West Genesee; 315–685–5714) has been in operation since 1899.

Follow Route 20 to Aubut, on Lake Owasco. This town contains a number of stately homes, including that of William Seward. **Seward House** displays many family furnishings, letters from Lincoln to Seward, gifts given to him from friends around the world, antique toys, and paintings. In fact, this museum has an unusually complete collection of original family belongings, because they stored a great deal in the attic and never threw anything away. Gowns, including wedding dresses, were wrapped carefully in tissue paper, often identified, and stored. Careful records of purchases and placement of furniture provided authenticity when the museum was being developed.

Built in 1816 by Judge Elijah Miller, the house was home to William Henry Seward after he married Judge Miller's daughter, Frances. The Sewards lived in Washington, D.C., Albany, and Auburn for nearly fifty years during his career as governor of New York, United States senator, and secretary of state. Seward signed the treaty for the purchase of Alaska at 4:00 a.m. on March 30, 1867. Emanuel Leutze captured this signing in his oil painting *Signing the Alaska Treaty,* which hangs in the Diplomatic Gallery on the second floor of the house.

Every room in the house is furnished with elegant original furniture and is decorated with personal family mementos as well as gifts given by heads of state. The dining room is set with the family china, as if for a holiday dinner. The family owned several complete sets of china, including Meissen, Canton, and Sèvres. A large silver well-and-tree platter has a section underneath for hot water; it weighs over thirty pounds when empty. Thomas Cole's painting of

OWASCO LAKE, AUBURN

Seward House
33 South Street
Auburn 13021
315–252–1283

Portage Falls, the largest canvas in the house, hangs in the drawing room. Also in the drawing room is a chair with a "musical message." Ask your guide to press the seat down, and you will hear a melody from the music box hidden underneath—that must have been a shock to guests!

Ten days before President Lincoln's assassination, Seward had a carriage accident that resulted in severe injuries to his jawbone, collarbone, shoulders, and arms. He was in bed at home the night John Wilkes Booth shot Lincoln. One of Booth's followers arrived at the Seward home and told the servant that he had medicine for Seward from his doctor. He went upstairs where he met Frederick, Seward's son, who told him he could not see his father. The intruder aimed a revolver at Frederick that misfired, then clubbed him and ran into the room to attack the nurse and finally Seward. He slashed Seward's face and throat, but the leather neck brace used to hold his jawbones in place saved Seward's life. Mrs. Seward died two months later from the shock of this attempted assassination of her husband.

Harriet Tubman Home
180 South Street
Auburn 13021
315–253–2621

Harriet Tubman Home was the site of the beginning of freedom for more than 300 slaves. The Underground Railroad was Harriet Tubman's prime concern during the Civil War. She also served as a spy and a scout for the Union army.

Schweinfurth Memorial Art Center
205 Genesee Street
Auburn 13021
315–255–1553

The **Schweinfurth Memorial Art Center** was opened in 1981. The center features exhibits of regional fine arts, photography, architecture, and children's art. There is a year-round series of workshops, concerts, and lectures.

A model of an Indian village depicting culture dating from A.D. 1100 is in **Emerson Park** on Owasco Lake. You can swim, fish, and go boating there as well. Follow Route 38 along the lake to **Moravia** and then to **Fillmore Glen**

State Park. Five waterfalls enhance this limestone and shale glen; a swimming pool is available. Millard Fillmore, our thirteenth president, was born near Moravia.

Follow Route 38 to Locke, then Route 90 to Route 34B, and head south toward King Ferry and Ithaca.

**Fillmore Glen
  State Park
Route 38
Moravia 13118**

Cayuga Lake, 43 miles long, boasts several colleges, including **Wells College** in Aurora, founded by Henry Wells, who also developed Wells Fargo and American Express. Ithaca has two colleges: **Ithaca College,** originally a conservatory of music, and **Cornell University,** founded by Ezra Cornell in 1865. You can visit **Cornell Plantations** to walk through the gardens, woodlands, swamps, and arboretum, all on 2,800 acres. The **Robinson York State Herb Garden** contains plants that have made a contribution to medicine or the culinary arts. For those who are interested in cultivating herbs to enhance cooking, this is the place to come. Don't miss the heritage garden that features plants popular in the 1700s–1800s. All of the plants are labeled so you can identify them.

**CAYUGA LAKE,
AURORA/
ITHACA**

**Cornell Plantations
One Plantations Road
Ithaca 14850
607–255–3020**

Sapsucker Woods is located 3 miles northeast of Cornell just off Route 13. In 1957 Cornell founded the **Laboratory of Ornithology** there as a research laboratory for the study of birds. The picture windows in the **Lyman K. Stuart Observatory** give the visitor a view of the pond, which is complete with microphones that transmit the sounds of birds as they feed. You can expect to see purple finches, downy woodpeckers, chickadees, and many waterfowl. Walking trails are open all year.

**Sapsucker Woods
159 South West Road
Ithaca 14850
607–256–5056**

If you're in the mood for food, you will find many fine restaurants in the sophisticated college town of Ithaca. **Turbacks** (607–272–6484) reportedly has the most extensive wine list in the area. It also notes where some of the special ingredients on the menu come from—all from local people in New York State. **Abbey's Restaurant** (309 Third Street; 607–273–1999), **The Greystone Inn** (1457 East Shore Drive; 607–273–4096), and **L'Auberge Du Cochon Rouge Restaurant Français** (Route 96B; 607–273–3464) have been recommended by local residents.

Buttermilk Falls State Park (607–273–5761) was the site of the filming of *Perils of Pauline.* The falls here are spectacular because of the height of the cascades that can be seen from the bottom. Hikers, however, will find many more cascades as they climb up to the bridge and climb down the other side. We chose to head up on the right side and back down on the Rim Trail, which took less than an hour.

OSWEGO

Tioga Central Rail Excursions
Route 38
Oswego 13126
607–687–0990

Railroad buffs may want to head south on Route 96B and Route 96 to Oswego for a trip aboard the Tioga Central train at **Tioga Central Rail Excursions.** You can stop during the 11-mile trip to visit the sites along the way. The railroad museum includes a collection of carriages, bicycles, tricycles, and antique automobiles. A Crowley's milk truck, a C-spring buggy made for a physician to use on his rural calls, and racing vehicles are on display.

ENFIELD

Robert H. Treman Park
Route 13
Ithaca 14850

Robert H. Treman Park is located on Route 13, 5 miles southwest of Ithaca near Enfield. A stone stairway will lead you down into the gorge for a series of vistas; cascades of water rather than a high waterfall provide the special beauty of this place. The park offers picnic tables, camping, swimming, hiking trails, and fishing.

Eight miles north of Ithaca, on Route 89 North along the west shore, is **Taughannock Falls State Park,** where there is a 215-foot drop into a mile-long glen. A great place for hiking, the park also offers camping, cabins, picnic shelters, a beach, biking trails, fishing, boat launching, and winter sports facilities.

The **Cayuga Wine Trail** consists of "estate" wineries where the owners grow their own special grapes for their wines. Vinifera grapes produce Chardonnay, Riesling, and Cabernet; French-American grapes produce Seyval, Cayuga White, Ravat, and Vidal; and native American grapes produce Concord and Niagara. As you taste wines along the wine trail, you will find that each has its own character. Traveling from south to north along Route 89, you will come to **Americana Vineyards, Lucas Vineyards, Plane's Cayuga Vineyard, Knapp Vineyards Winery, Lakeshore Winery,** and **Swedish Hill Vineyard.**

Taughannock Falls State Park
Route 89
Ithaca 14850
607–387–6739

Continue north along the lake on scenic Route 89 to Seneca Falls, famous as the birthplace of the women's rights movement. Both activist Amelia Bloomer and suffrage leader Elizabeth Cady Stanton lived there. The first Women's Rights Convention was held in Seneca Falls in 1848. A visitors' center is in the **Women's Rights National Historical Park.** The **Women's Hall of Fame** was established to pay homage to women who have devoted their lives to making life better in the United States. Women in art, athletics, business, education, government, humanities, philanthropy, and science have been honored. Exhibits include a photograph and biography of women such as Jane Addams, Marian Anderson, Susan B. Anthony, Clara Barton, Mary McLeod Bethune, Elizabeth Blackwell, Pearl S. Buck, Rachel Carson, Mary Cassatt, Emily Dickinson, Amelia Earhart, Alice Hamilton, Helen Hayes, Helen Keller, Eleanor Roosevelt, Florence Sabin, Margaret Chase Smith, Elizabeth Cady Stanton,

SENECA FALLS

Women's Rights National Historical Park
116 Fall Street
Seneca Falls 13148
315–568–2991

Women's Hall of Fame
76 Fall Street
Seneca Falls 13148
315–568–2936

Helen Brooke Taussig, and Harriet Tubman. Amelia Earhart's scarf was borrowed from the museum by Sally Ride and accompanied her aboard the space shuttle *Challenger*. It is displayed in a case along with other Amelia Earhart mementos.

Montezuma Wildlife
Refuge
Routes 20 & 5
Seneca Falls 13148
315–568–5987

Five miles north of Seneca Falls, the **Montezuma Wildlife Refuge** contains 6,432 acres as a habitat for birds, deer, and small animals. The refuge is also on the track for migrating geese and ducks.

Route 20 leads to Geneva.

SENECA LAKE,
GENEVA
Rose Hill
Route 96A
Geneva 14456
315–789–3848

Geneva, at the northern end of Seneca Lake, contains a series of stately homes overlooking the lake. **Rose Hill** was built by William K. Strong in 1839. In 1850 Robert J. Swan received the house as a wedding gift from his father. In 1965 Swan's grandson, Waldo Hutchins, Jr., purchased Rose Hill, then in ruins, for $15,000 and gave it to the Geneva Historical Society. Restoration was begun, guided by the administrator and curator, H. Merrill Roenke. During the process each one of the columns in front of the house was taken own; one contained more than 200 pounds of honey and a swarm of angry bees!

This Greek Revival mansion contains furniture of the period around 1840. Some of the furniture belonged to the Swan family, including a pair of rosewood armchairs dating from 1845, a marquetry tilt-top table, and a mahogany sofa with the original cut-velvet upholstery. Some of the furnishings were donated by Geneva families, who are pleased to see their treasured heirlooms preserved in this elegant museum. Records and documents have made it possible to furnish the house authentically. Upstairs you will see a red bedroom with a colorful quilt, a green bedroom, and an elegant blue bedroom. The grounds include a carriage house and boxwood gardens.

An earlier house, built by Robert S. Rose, a Virginian, is now used as a reception center.

Hobart and William Smith Colleges, now linked together as a single, coeducational institution, are also located at the northern end of Seneca Lake on adjoining campuses. The college owns a number of historic buildings; ask for a brochure of walking tours.

The **Crow's Nest on Seneca Lake** (490 Marshall Road, Waterloo; 315–781–0600) serves both lunch and dinner on the shores of the lake. There are slips for your boat if you arrive by water, and a deck for relaxing and enjoying the view.

Seneca Lake wineries include **Prejean Winery, Four Chimneys Farm Winery, Hermann J. Wiemer Vineyard, Inc.,** **Squaw Point Winery, Glenora Wine Cellars, Castle Grisch Winery, Rolling Vineyards, Chateau Lafayette Reneau, Hazlitt 1852 Vineyards,** and **Poplar Ridge Vineyards.**

Hobart and William Smith Colleges Geneva 14456 315–789–5000

Head south on Route 14 and drive the length of the lake to **Watkins Glen State Park,** a site well known for its natural beauty. Nineteen waterfalls, cascades, and grottoes may be seen along the walkway through the gorge. Pick up a brochure at the park office for your self-guided tour. While standing on Sentry Bridge you can see a hole cut in the rock where water used to flow on its way to the waterwheel of a gristmill. You can walk behind Cavern Cascade, if you don't mind a little spray. A trail leads from Spiral Tunnel, up the Indian Trail, to the Suspension Bridge. As you enter the Cathedral area, you will see a large stone with rippled surface; millions of years ago these ripples were in sand. Walk up through the Cathedral area to the Central Cascade, where you will see pools called "plunge pools." They were formed by waterfalls bombarding the

WATKINS GLEN Watkins Glen State Park Route 14 Watkins Glen 14891 607–535–4511

same spot for centuries. Pools that are not caused by waterfalls are called "pot holes." Rainbow Falls is so named because there is sometimes a rainbow in the spray. Frowning Cliff and Pluto Falls are located in a narrow, dark gorge (Pluto was the Greek god of the underworld). At Mile Point Bridge you can walk up to Jacob's Ladder or return by one of the trails. You can also take a shuttle up and walk down.

Although the Grand Prix Racing Circuit pulled out in 1981, there is racing at Watkins Glen once more, under new management. (Phone 607–535–2481 for tickets.)

From Watkins Glen you can make a side trip to Elmira via Route 14, Corning via Route 414, or Keuka Lake via Route 23.

ELMIRA

Elmira is especially famous for its former summer resident Samuel Clemens (Mark Twain), who wrote many of his best-known books there—*Tom Sawyer, The Adventures of Huckleberry Finn, The Prince and the Pauper, Life on the Mississippi, A Connecticut Yankee in King Arthur's Court,* and *A Tramp Abroad.* His connection with Elmira stems from a trip he took on the Mediterranean. He met Charles Langdon while cruising, saw a miniature portrait of Olivia, Charles's sister, and fell for her. They were married in 1870 and continued to spend summer vacations in Elmira. Olivia's sister, Susan Crane, built an octagonal room that resembled a Mississippi steamboat pilot house for him to use as a study. Mark Twain was delighted with this surprise and wrote, "It is a cosy nest and when storms sweep down the valley and the lightning flashes behind the hills beyond, and the rain beats over my head, imagine the luxury of it." Each morning, after his favorite breakfast of steak and coffee, he went up to this study and worked all day, without lunch, until time for dinner. While living and writing in Elmira, Twain liked to try out his lectures in front of a live audience, and the Elmira Correction Facility provided a local captive audience. He felt that they laughed more readily than some of his other audiences.

> When I was a boy of fourteen, my father was so ignorant I could hardly stand to have the old man around. But when I got to be twenty-one I was astonished at how much the old man had learned in seven years. —Mark Twain

You can visit the **Mark Twain Study** at **Elmira College.** It was given to the college by his grandnephew, Jervis Langdon, Jr. The view from the study is pleasant, similar to the view at Quarry Farm, with a pond and weeping willow to look at. Next to the study you will see a stone watering trough with his daughter Clara's name on it. He had four watering troughs made for the refreshment of horses on their way up the hill to Quarry Farm, each one carved with one of his children's names.

**Mark Twain Study
Elmira College
Elmira 14902
607–734–3911, ext. 233**

Quarry Farm was also given to Elmira College by Mark Twain's grandnephew. **The Center for Mark Twain Studies** is located there. Twain spent one last summer at the farm, in 1903. In 1904 he returned for Olivia's funeral, and in 1907 for the dedication of the organ in Park Church. He died in 1910 and is buried in Elmira's Woodlawn Cemetery. A monument was placed there as a memorial to Mark Twain and Ossip Gabrilowitsch, the first husband of his daughter Clara. Gabrilowitsch, a famous Russian pianist and conductor, wanted to be buried at the feet of Mark Twain.

If you've always had a yen to go soaring, you can do it here. **Harris Hill Soaring Corporation** (Harris Hill, near Elmira; 607–734–0641) offers you the chance to take off behind a tow plane and head up into the world of air currents, where you will soar silently over lakes, forests, and farms. An experienced pilot is at the controls, and you are free to take photos and enjoy the view.

National Soaring Museum
Harris Hill
Elmira 14902
607-734-3128

The **National Soaring Museum** is at the end of the runway at Harris Hill. You'll see a 1911 Orville Wright glider, a 1933 Albatross, a 1936 model with gull-like wings, and lots of exhibits with explanations. You can also sit in the cockpit simulator and imagine yourself in flight.

CORNING
Corning Glass Center
Corning 14830
607-974-8271

Route 17 will take you from Elmira into Corning. The **Corning Glass Center** encompasses the Museum of Glass, Hall of Science and Industry, and the Steuben Glass Factory. Begin your visit with a time-tunnel trip through the ages. Did you know that during the early thirteenth century, glass craftsmen were subject to death if they tried to leave the island of Murano, near Venice, with intent to use their knowledge elsewhere? These Murano craftsmen prized their fine filigree, diamond-etched, exquisite glass beads and vases. Don't miss the goblet, made by Verzelini in 1577 for Queen Elizabeth I. The Hall of Science will provide you with hands-on experiences in the world of glass. You can light ninety-six different kinds of light bulbs, bend sheets of glass, use a glass insulator to break the flow of high-voltage electricity, and dip glass in acid. Whether or not you have children, don't miss the magic show.

Rockwell Museum
Old City Hall
Denison Parkway &
Cedar Street
Corning 14830
607-937-5386

The **Rockwell Museum** contains the three collections of Robert Rockwell: western American art, Carder Steuben glass, and antique toys. Frederick Carder created his glass between 1903 and 1933 in Corning; 2,000 pieces are displayed in the museum. Paintings and bronzes by Frederic Remington, Charles Russell, Albert Bierstadt, and W. R. Leigh are also on display.

The **Market Street District** downtown has lots of shops and places to eat. During the summer you can ride around in an English double-decker bus.

At the southern end of Keuka Lake, you will find Hammondsport and wineries galore. **Bully Hill Vineyards, Cana Vineyards, Hunt County Vineyard, Vinifera Wine Cellars, Heron Hill Vineyards, Taylor, Great Western and Gold Seal Winery, Rolling Vineyards,** and **McGregor Vineyards** offer wine tasting. The **Glenn H. Curtiss Museum of Local History** honors this native son of Hammondsport in his role as "Father of Naval Aviation" with a collection of rare pieces from the early days of aviation. You can trace the development of aviation with models and photographs.

Something new has been added to Keuka Lake. *The Keuka Maid* cruises around the lake for lunch, dinner, and Sunday brunch. Hills and vineyards make this lake especially attractive during the day, and the cottage lights are pretty at night. (Call 607–569–BOAT or 569–3631.)

Follow the signs to I–390 to Cohocton, then Route 371 to Route 21 to Naples. The **Cumming Nature Center** is a division of the Rochester Museum and Science Center. This 800-acre center has nature trails, films, and an environmental education center. **Widmer's Wine Cellars** are located in Naples.

Continue on Route 21 to Canandaigua. **Sonnenberg Gardens** is a fifty-acre Victorian garden estate located just north of town. In 1857 Frederick and Mary Thompson bought Sonnenberg for a summer home. In 1902 Mrs. Thompson began planning gardens as a memorial to her husband, who had died. She traveled

KEUKA LAKE

Finger Lakes Association
309 Lake Street
Penn Yan 14527

Glenn H. Curtiss Museum of Local History
Main & Lake Streets
Hammondsport 14840

NAPLES

Cumming Nature Center
Gulick Road
Naples 14512
716–374–6160

CANANDAIGUA

Sonnenberg Gardens
Gibson Street
Canandaigua 14424
716–394–4922

to all parts of the globe visiting a variety of gardens and spent the next fourteen years designing gardens. There are eleven gardens, including the Japanese, Italian, Rose, Sub Rosa, Blue and White, Pansy, Moonlight, Conservatory, Colonial, South Lawn, and Rock gardens. The Rose Garden is planted in a design of arcs and interlocking circles, backed by a flawless green lawn. The Sub Rosa Garden is small and private; there are two cross-legged marble figures of Diana and Apollo beside the fountain. The blue and white garden, which Mrs. Thompson called her "Intimate Garden," contains peonies, phlox, snapdragons, vinca, delphinium, anchusa, salvia, and iris. The Victorians felt that pansies symbolized thought, so this garden is meant for meditation. As you see the multitude of pansies, check to see if their faces are smiling at you. The Moonlight Garden is planted with white flowers that glow in the moonlight; this garden was lost for some time but has now been restored. The Colonial Garden contains all of the old favorites set into a symmetrical pattern. The Rock Garden encircles a tower from which you can survey the blossoms of the season. The mansion itself has eight restored rooms decorated with period furnishings. Special events such as a Victorian weekend, pageants, poetry readings, drama, concerts, and barbershop quartets are held during the year.

Granger Homestead
295 North Main Street
Canandaigua 14424
716–394–1472

The **Granger Homestead** was the home of Postmaster General Gideon Granger, who served under Presidents Jefferson and Madison, and of Francis Granger, who served under Presidents Harrison and Tyler. Gideon Granger specialized in espionage work for the Jefferson administration; he discovered Federalist plots before they had been put into action. He retired from service in Washington in 1814 and began to build his mansion in Canandaigua, spending $10,098.11 on his house and $3,240 on the land, a large sum in those days. When it was complete, he sent for his wife, Mindwell, and their two sons. Although he had retired once, he was persuaded to stand for reelection to the State Senate. Granger was also involved in the promotion of the Erie Canal. He died at age fifty-five, and his son, Francis, lived in the house for seventy-six years until his death in 1868. During this time he added the north wing to the house. Francis's son, Gideon, was chairman of the war committee for raising troops during the Civil War.

This Federal mansion is furnished with period furniture, silver, and china. Note the extraordinarily high mantel in the South Parlour, with a portrait of Gideon Granger II over it. The three-part settee was constructed from three chairs; twenty matching single chairs are still in the house. The chandelier in the North Parlour was a gas fixture in use during the 1850s; later it was converted to electricity. The table in the dining room was originally in the White House; Gideon Granger purchased it after the executive mansion was burned by the British during the War of 1812.

The **Carriage Museum** at Granger Homestead holds fifty horse-drawn vehicles. An ointment wagon that was used to deliver patent cures is on display, as is a hearse with unusual lamps that are silver on the outside and gold on the inside.

❧ *Northwestern New York* ❧

In Northwestern New York—at least in this itinerary—you will visit the cities of Rochester and Buffalo.

Take Route 332 to I-90 to I-490 to Rochester. Rochester, the third-largest city in New York, is also known as the "Flower City." If

ROCHESTER

**Rochester Convention
and Visitors' Bureau
Rochester 14603
716–546–3070**

**George Eastman
House
900 East Avenue
Rochester 14603
716–271–3361**

you are there in lilac time, a treat is in store for you. Earlier it was called the "Flour City" because of its flour mills; waterfalls provided the power.

Internationally known for its **Eastman School of Music** (George Eastman was the inventor of Kodak cameras and founder of Eastman Kodak), Rochester's calendar of events overflows with many excellent music series. In addition to those offered by Eastman, the **Rochester Philharmonic Orchestra** offers a full program. There is also a theatrical season at the **Eastman Theater,** as well as performances by touring Broadway groups.

The **George Eastman House** reopened in January 1990 after being renovated and brought back to life as it was when Eastman lived there. He built the house between 1902 and 1905 using the finest materials, including plaster relief ceilings, carved woodwork, hand-painted window glass, and marble floors. He decorated his house with oriental rugs and appropriate furnishings to make fifty rooms seem homelike. Eastman and his mother lived in the house with a staff who provided fresh flowers from the greenhouses. After Eastman's death in 1932, the house was bequeathed to the University of Rochester, whose presidents lived in it for the next ten years.

Visitors may enter by the front door, which leads into a large hall and oriental-carpeted stairway leading upstairs. To the right is the living room, handsome with its newly re-created plaster ceiling, done in an ornate pattern depicting the four seasons in medallions up in the corners. A grand piano is open and ready for a concert, with violins resting on music stands nearby. Period furniture, fresh flowers, and bookcases lining the walls give this room a comfortable touch.

Across the hall the library has its Eastman system for cataloging books, with letters at the top of each case corresponding to a letter and shelf number inside each book. The bookplates portray Eastman, shown from the back reading in his chair. A collection of ivory miniatures is displayed in a glass case on one wall.

The teak-paneled billiard room contains a green-felt-covered table, as well as a sofa on a raised platform that has room under its step for billiard and game equipment, in addition to providing a birds'-eye view for those watching the game. Black leather sofas are casual, with a raccoon rug thrown across one corner. A cylinder phonograph and a classic radio blend in with family photographs.

The conservatory is a bright room with a two-story-high ceiling, lots of plants, and an organ. Eastman had a favorite group of women for lunch here every week—called the "Lobster Quartet" because they had lobster for lunch. These four younger women enjoyed his company and he theirs. The head of a life-size trophy is mounted high on the wall.

Visitors can walk back through the house, past the Dryden Theatre, solarium, galleries, and views of the garden outside the windows. The new wing at the back houses the International Museum of Photography, offering changing exhibits and demonstrations. Don't miss the photographs by Matthew Brady, which chronicle the Civil War at Gettysburg, Vicksburg, and Atlanta. Two Scotsmen, David Octavius Hill and Robert Adamson, photographed their countrymen as well as scenes in Edinburgh. In 1837 Louis Daguerre developed a method of etching images onto plates; this collection represents the beginning of the new field of photography. The galleries continue through the years with the work of Edward Steichen, Dorothea Lange, Cecil Beaton, and Ansel Adams. Stop beside the large glass windows to look down two more floors into the offices and storage areas for the motion picture collection of over 7,000 titles, photography print collection, rare photographs, books and manuscripts, and camera collection. Each of the areas is climate-controlled for its contents; some rooms are without windows for perfect control. The two lower floors are subterranean, allowing for more constant conditions for these priceless collections.

Rochester Museum and Science Center and Strasenburgh Planetarium
657 East Avenue
Rochester 14603
716–271–4320

The **Rochester Museum and Science Center and Strasenburgh Planetarium** produces elaborate space shows geared for all ages. *The Space Shuttle: An American Adventure* is the first film designed to be projected on a planetarium's dome. You might see Bob McGrath of "Sesame Street" conducting preschool-age children through introductory astronomy on film.

One of the permanent exhibits features the Seneca Iroquois collection. Demonstrations are given on the process involved in making cornhusk Indian dolls. The computerized planetarium offers both futuristic space programs and a glimpse of the sky in prehistoric times.

Also under the aegis of the RMSC is the **Cumming Nature Center,** located 35 miles south of Rochester on 900 acres. The Beaver Trail leads to an observation tower that has a view of a 35-acre beaver pond. You'll have a bird's-eye view of the habitat of the beavers— maybe a slapping tail or two to warn the young. The Conservation Trail leads to a sawmill that is actually running.

An outdoor art gallery features paintings by Jerry Czech along the Helen Gordon Trail. Don't miss the Iroquois Trail, which portrays the history of the Indians through the eyes of painter Ernest Smith. Programs there include hikes on the 8 miles of trails, cross-country skiing in winter, maple sugaring, and a host of other seasonal programs.

Seneca Park Zoo
2222 St. Paul Street
Rochester 14603
716–266–6846

The **Seneca Park Zoo** may be another stop on your itinerary, especially if you have children with you. Aim for feeding time, which is usually around 3:00 p.m.

The **Susan B. Anthony Home** was the headquarters for the women's crusade leading to passage of the Nineteenth Amendment. Her home contains the furnishings that were there when she entertained Elizabeth Cady Stanton and Frederick Douglass. It was here that Anthony was arrested in 1872—for voting. Walk up to the third floor to see her study, and a collection of items that include a horsehair couch, a black hat on a wighead, an evening wrap, and a black dress. The Museum Room on the second floor details the development of the woman's suffrage movement. The desk Anthony used is there too.

Susan B. Anthony Home
17 Madison Street
Rochester 14603
716–235–6124

The **Margaret Woodbury Strong Museum** contains toys, silver, furnishings, and glassware of the period 1820–1930. An extensive doll collection, including miniatures and dollhouses, is sure to delight the "little girl" in most of us.

Margaret Woodbury Strong Museum
1 Manhattan Square
Rochester 14603
716–263–2700

This is one of our favorite museums, with its attractive displays that are not overdone but tastefully arranged to give pleasure to the viewer. There is a clue to the exhibits: As you walk from one area to another, notice the floor—it changes style and material to fit each era about every 20 feet.

The first floor begins with a portrait of Margaret Woodbury Strong, a Kodak heiress who bought up the contents of whole houses in order to get what she wanted for her collection. Her father had been in the buggy whip business, until Henry Ford came along and put an end to that. The Orient was then the obvious place to conduct his business, and some of the collection was purchased there.

Margaret's wedding shoes from 1920, with white silk stockings to match, stand next to a wood carving of Barbara, done in 1930.

Some of the exhibits on the first floor are changing, but all are interesting, with more than enough to keep the eye moving. We were taken with an old rocking chair proclaiming "Our Mother" on the back.

A children's playroom features toys from years ago, and all of the children there were happily engrossed. If you want to play with Lincoln Logs again, here's your chance.

Margaret Strong's first love was dolls, and her collection is said to be the largest in the world. Upstairs they are standing in one case after another, carefully grouped and cataloged. You can even look up the details on any doll in the collection in the card catalog found beside each case. From wood, cloth, gesso, and bisque to felt, wax, and papier-mâché—they are all there. Dolls of all sizes, with plain or elegant clothing, stand ready to be played with. Perhaps at night they have a ball!

The dollhouses are of all sizes and types, including the ones Margaret played with as a little girl. We were told that Margaret was supposed to give away her favorite toy once a year; she said the doll didn't like her dollhouse all that much. The Doll's Mansion was made in Germany and features a string-operated elevator. Alice Steele, of West Cummington, Massachusetts, made eighty different rooms that she remembered from her past, and some of them are on display.

Toys include a cast-iron "burning building," a horse-drawn trolley, mechanical banks, battleships, automobiles, and much more.

When it's time for a meal, head for **The Spring House Restaurant,** dating from 1829, whose ballroom bounces when dancers enjoy themselves (3001 Monroe Avenue; 716–586–2300); **Rochester Club Restaurant,** once a men's club and now open to the public (120 East Avenue; 716–423–1948); **Chapel's**

Cuisine de Marche, located in former jail cells (30 West Broad Street; 716–232–2300); **Marketplace Inn,** for Sunday-night Irish singers (800 Jefferson Road, Henrietta; 716–272–1550); **The Depot Restaurant,** where you can dine in a restored railway car or the Station House (41 North Main Street, Pittsford; 716–381–9900); **Rooney's** (90 Henrietta; 716–442–0444); **La Petite Maison** (54 Park; 716–256–0390); or **Cafe Creme de la Creme** (295 Alexander; 716–263–3580).

Rochester has a number of fine recreational areas, including **Cobb's Hill Park** between Highland Avenue and Culver Road; **Upper Falls Park** on the Genesee River off St. Paul Street; **Manhattan Square Park** at Chestnut and Broad streets; **Mendon Ponds Park** at Clover Street and Pond Road; and the **Barge Canal Trail,** which connects Perinto Park, Pittsford Park, Lock 32 Canal Park, and Genesee Valley Park. (For information on the Barge Canal Trail, call 716–442–8550.)

Route 383 will take you southwest to Mumford and the Genesee Country Museum.

The **Genesee Country Museum** is a nineteenth-century village containing more than fifty homes, shops, and other buildings. An Iroquois word meaning "Pleasant Valley" brought us "Genesee." After the Revolutionary War soldiers who had fought under George Washington against the Iroquois in the valley chose to settle there. The first farmers who arrived on the scene had to carve out enough land from the wilderness to live on. After the hardships of the first year, when they had to build log houses and a lean-to for their animals, sow seeds, and burn logs to make potash, the settlers developed a life-style above mere subsistence level. Wheat grew easily, and the area became the "Granary of the East." The museum has been

MUMFORD
Genesee Country Museum
Flint Hill Road
Mumford 14511
716–538–6822

developed to show the evolution of daily living as buildings changed from log cabins to comfortable homes.

The **Hamilton House** appeals to visitors with its Victorian Italianate architecture. Built in 1870 by J. D. Hamilton, the house has fifteen rooms and a tower in the center on the front side of the building.

The **Octagon House** has a surprise for the visitor; look up into the cupola, which was specially designed to accommodate the belief that the spirit ascended directly into heaven when one died.

The **Jones Farm House** has stenciled walls in remarkable condition. In the kitchen the farmer's wife would make cheese to store excess milk; shelves are designed to hold this cheese. The kitchen always smells warm and fragrant because the guide does a great deal of baking and cooking. Farm animals are in the yard. Daphne is a hen who struts into the kitchen, hops into a basket, and lays an egg. She does this every day without fail. Bridget is another hen who appears on the scene now and then.

Livingston Manor is an elegant "city" house in style. One winter when the house was closed, the lovely gilt harp was almost destroyed by a raccoon that knocked it over. Apparently the raccoon came in through the chimney, which is four stories up. A harpsichord is displayed in the same room with the harp. The house is furnished with typical furniture of the 1827–1840 period. A beehive oven in the kitchen is used for baking during the tourist season. The formal garden beside the house has been planted in nineteenth-century–style patterns.

Genesee Country Museum schedules many special events, such as Fiddler's Fair, Salute to Autumn, Battle of Gettysburg, Fire Muster,

Mark Twain spent many summers in Elmira and wrote many of his best-known works here.

ELMIRA

The Falls, one of North America's greatest natural tourist attractions.

NIAGARA FALLS

The Turtle, a Native American Center for the Living Arts.

THE TURTLE

Dressage and Carriage Drive Competition, Black Powder Shoot, and Independence Day.

LETCHWORTH STATE PARK

You may want to make a side trip to Letchworth State Park (Route 36, off Route 19A, Castile; 716–493–2611), located just 35 miles southwest of Rochester. Take Route 390 south until you see signs for Mount Morris and the park. This 14,350-acre park is noted for the rushing Genesee River that tumbles over three major waterfalls; the highest is 107 feet. Genesee Gorge is 600 feet in height; if you are an aficionado of gorge scenery, don't miss this one. A restored **Seneca Indian Council House** and the **William Pryor Letchworth Museum** are there to visit.

Darien Lake Theme Park
Exit 48A off Route 90
Darien Center 14040
716–599–4501

Another side trip might be to **Darien Lake Theme Park,** a theme park on 1,200 acres with thirty-five rides, including a 165-foot giant ferris wheel from the 1982 World's Fair. Darien has a concert series, a nature trail, petting zoo, and picnicking and camping facilities.

BUFFALO

From Rochester take I–490 to I–90 to Buffalo. This city was not really named after the animal of the same name; some think it came from a mispronunciation of the French *Beau Fleuve,* or "Beautiful River." The Niagara River connects Lakes Ontario and Erie. In 1825, when the Erie Canal opened, Governor DeWitt Clinton carried a barrel of fresh water from Lake Erie on the first trip along the canal until he reached the Atlantic, where he poured it into salt water. Erie Canal had finally joined the Great Lakes with the Atlantic Ocean.

Buffalo has a number of distinct areas to explore. The downtown area contains some architectural treasures as well as modern structures. **City Hall** was built in 1932; the frieze on the front of the building characterizes workers of the 1930s. This Art Deco building has colorful mosaics. Take the elevator to the twenty-eighth-floor Observation Deck for a view. The statues on either side of the entrance are of Millard Fillmore, thirteenth president of the United States, and Grover Cleveland, the twenty-second president. The monument across from City Hall honors William McKinley, who was assassinated in 1901 while attending the Pan-American Exposition in town. The **Old Post Office** building is Flemish Gothic with lots of gargoyles, bison heads, and eagles on the facade. A 244-foot tower and skylight are above the inner court area. Erie Community College uses the building. **St. Paul's Episcopal Church** was built between 1888 and 1890 following a fire. The style is Gothic Revival; look for the Tiffany windows over the altar. The **Prudential/Guaranty Building** was among the first skyscrapers when it was built in 1896. The architect was Louis Sullivan, Frank Lloyd Wright's teacher and mentor. The terra-cotta exterior is in contrast to the mosaics inside. You can't miss the **Goldome Bank,** built in Beaux Arts Classical style in 1889. Someone figured out how to keep birds from spoiling the gold; fake rubber snakes strewn around up there seem to keep them away.

The Theater District is highlighted by **Shea's Buffalo Theatre.** This ornate gilt interior is bright with mirrors, marble, and crystal chandeliers. Paintings and sculpture complete an elegant atmosphere. Performances include ballet, musicals, rock concerts, and special galas.

Shea's Buffalo Theatre
646 Main Street
Buffalo 14240
716–847–1410

Allentown is an area that has come down through the years from the 1850s almost intact. It is on the National Register of Historic Places; homes have been restored to their previous appearance. Look for the row of "painted ladies"—San Francisco has nothing on Buffalo!

Allentown
45 Elmwood
Buffalo 14240
716–881–1024

Delaware Avenue is the epitome of the proverbial "Millionaire's Row." You will see one huge mansion after another. Some of them are still privately owned; others have been taken over by corporations.

Theodore Roosevelt Inaugural National Historic Site
641 Delaware Avenue
Buffalo 14240
716–884–0095;
716–884–0330

The **Theodore Roosevelt Inaugural National Historic Site** was the home of Ansley Wilcox and his wife, Mary, beginning in 1883. On September 5, 1901, President William McKinley came to Buffalo for the Pan-American Exposition. During a reception Leon Czologoz shot him twice at close range. Vice-President Theodore Roosevelt arrived in Buffalo and stayed with his friend Ansley Wilcox. When it appeared likely that McKinley would recover, Roosevelt went on vacation in the Adirondacks. Fortunately, he left his itinerary and addresses with Wilcox. When Roosevelt arrived at the cottage near Mount Tahawus, he and his family canoed to the upper end of Colden Lake, where they set up camp for the night. In the morning Roosevelt climbed Mount Marcy, the highest peak in the Adirondacks. As he was returning, he saw a man hurrying up the trail with a telegram informing him of the worsening condition of President McKinley. Roosevelt found a wagon with driver and set off for the railway station in North Creek. The 50-mile ride was difficult in the middle of the night, but with changes of horses they made it to the station. As he boarded the waiting train, he received the news that McKinley was dead. When the train reached Buffalo, Wilcox met Roosevelt, loaned him some clothes, and took him to his own home for the inaugural ceremony.

One of the most famous landscape architects of the time, Frederick Law Olmsted, designed five of Buffalo's city parks and a number of parkways. He also designed Central Park in New York. Frank Lloyd Wright designed several houses in Buffalo. One was built in 1904 with long, low lines reflecting Wright's prairie style. The **Martin House** is currently being restored; a great deal of work is going into the research for this project to maintain accuracy.

A number of literary and musical figures have lived and worked in Buffalo. Mark Twain lived there in the 1870s when he edited the *Buffalo Express.* Taylor Caldwell is a present resident, and Edwin P. Christy began his Christy Minstrel show there.

Buffalo has a number of museums for you to visit. The **Buffalo Museum of Science** contains two dinosaurs, mummies, Chinese jade, anthropological artifacts, and a variety of natural history exhibits. Don't miss the special "Discovery Room" for children; they can touch everything there. The museum has an observatory, a research library, a lecture series, and a nature preserve 3 miles out of town.

The **Albright-Knox Art Gallery** contains a collection of contemporary art that includes works by Jackson Pollock, Clyfford Still, William de Kooning, Frank Stella, Henry Moore, Jean Dubuffet, Robert Rauschenberg, and Roy Lichtenstein. Some of our favorites include Henry Moore's *Reclining Figure,* Raoul Dufy's *Place du Pantheon,* Paul Cézanne's *Morning in Provence,* Paul Gaugin's *The Yellow Christ,* Vincent Van Gogh's *The Old Mill,* David Smith's *Tanktotem IV,* and Winslow Homer's *Croquet Players.* In addition, the museum displays art dating from 3000 B.C. to Impressionism and Postimpressionism, Cubism, Surrealism, and Constructivism. The gallery holds classes in art and art history, photography, and film, as well as offering lecture series and seminars.

The **Buffalo and Erie County Historical Society** reproduces an 1870 street on the lower level of the museum. This street has a "company store," a bank, a dime store, a sporting goods store, a drugstore, a theater, a cigar shop, and several more stores. Another display, entitled "People of the Longhouse," depicts Indian

Martin House
125 Jewett Parkway
Buffalo 14240

Buffalo Museum of Science
Humboldt Parkway
Buffalo 14240
716-896-5200

Albright-Knox Art Gallery
1285 Elmwood Avenue
Buffalo 14240
716-882-8700

Buffalo and Erie County Botanical Gardens
South Park Avenue & McKinley Parkway
Buffalo
716-828-1040

**Buffalo Zoological
  Gardens
Delaware Park
Buffalo 14240
716–837–3900**

**Buffalo and Erie
  County Historical
  Society
25 Nottingham Court
Buffalo 14240
716–873–9644**

**Our Lady of Victory
  Basilica and National
  Shrine
South Park Avenue &
  Ridge Road
Lackawanna
716–823–2490**

**Naval and
  Servicemen's Park
1 Naval Park Cove
Buffalo 14240
716–847–1773**

life inside the longhouse and in the village. It includes some of the sports enjoyed by the Iroquois, such as lacrosse, hoop and javelin, and snow snake. The Canal Exhibit has artifacts, a replica of a canal boat, and the history of the Erie Canal. The Pioneer Life Exhibit concentrates on life along the Niagara Frontier during the early 1800s.

The **Buffalo Zoological Gardens** house over 680 animals in their natural settings. An Asian forest, a rain forest, a gorilla section, and a children's zoo are among the areas to see.

The **Buffalo and Erie County Botanical Gardens** contains twelve greenhouses growing exotic plants, palms, fruit trees, and flowers. Frederick Law Olmsted designed the gardens. When we were there, four bridal parties were smiling for photos among the plants.

Our Lady of Victory Basilica and National Shrine is an ornate Italian Renaissance cathedral. Inside, the stations of the cross are sculpted life-size from white Italian marble.

The **Naval and Servicemen's Park** has a collection of World War II vessels, including the USS *The Sullivans* and the USS *Little Rock*. The museum contains seafaring memorabilia, including models of Benedict Arnold's fleet on Lake Champlain in 1776 and a display of painted flags, such as the 1620 *Mayflower,* 1775 Bunker Hill, and first Navy Jack flags. The section on John Paul Jones contains photos of the chapel in Annapolis where his tomb lies, models of ships he served on, and Jones memorabilia.

The "new kid on the dock" is the SS *Croaker.* If you've always wanted to visualize life at sea on a sub you can walk through this one from stem to stern. Living quarters were cramped to say the least, and some men shared sleeping space with torpedoes. When we were there, one of her men from World War II days in the Pacific was on hand to talk with us. You can also take a cruise for a couple of hours or an evening on *Miss Buffalo* docked at Naval and Servicemen's Park; 716–856–6696 from May to September, or 716–822–1598 from October to April).

Buffalo's many recommended restaurants include **Chef's** (291 Seneca at Chicago; 716–856–9187) for Italian specialties such as spaghetti parmesan or veal cacciatore, **Crawdaddy's** (2 Templeton Terrace; 716–856–9191), **Buffalo House** (172 Franklin; 716–856–0404), **Shayleen's** (69 Delaware; 716–856–1737), **Anchor Bar** (1047 Main; 716–886–8920), **Garvey's** (414 Pearl; 716–856–3222), **Towne Restaurant** (186 Allen at Elmwood; 716–884–5128), **Garcia's Irish Pub** (74–76 Pearl; 716–856–0111), **Macaroni Company** (320 Pearl; 716–856–1081), and **Lord Chumley's** (481 Delaware; 716–8414).

☙ *Niagara Falls Area* ☙

Over 450 million years ago, a shallow, saltwater sea covered the Niagara Frontier area. Primitive marine plants and animals lived in this tropical climate. Gradually sediments washed down from the mountains and the sea disappeared. These sediments buried plant and animal remains that became fossilized as the layers turned to rock. You can see four different types of sedimentary rock in the Niagara gorge. The top layer is Lockport Dolostone, which contains highly compacted materials as well as animal and plant remains. The second layer consists of Rochester shale, which is much less resistant to erosion. The third layer is limestone, and the fourth and lowest is sandstone. Glaciers carved through the land and made it sag with their tremendous weight. As the melted basins were filled, the Great Lakes were created, and water continued to seek an outlet to the sea. The Niagara River flowed north from Lake Erie to Lake Ontario, at Lewiston met the escarpment, a 300-foot cliff, and plunged over it. Thus Niagara Falls was born 12,000 years ago.

Because water freezes and expands, cracks and joints built up hydrostatic pressure, widening the gaps and causing the less sturdy Rochester shale in the second layer to weaken and wash away. The top layer, the Lockport Dolostone, was left hanging and finally broke off and fell, time after time. In 1931, 185,000 tons fell near the American Falls; later another fall took out the Schoellkopf Power Plant. Geologists dammed the river and stopped enough of the flow to study the rock. Cracks were analyzed, and several overhangs were removed. The Niagara Escarpment has receded 7½ miles since its birth at a rate of 1 to 4 feet per year.

The falls have provided energy since 1895, when the world's first hydroelectric plant was constructed. While building that plant experts realized that less water flowing over the falls would mean less erosion as well as more power for eastern states. For once, industry and ecology were in perfect agreement. Because of the rapid erosion of the falls, both Canada and the United States have been controlling the flow of water above the cascades by the use of gates. Water is diverted into generating plants instead of wearing away the rock. In 1950 Canada and the United States signed an international treaty that determined the amount of flow over the falls. They were able to leave enough for scenic beauty and yet divert 50 to 75 percent of the flow for use in the power plants downstream. During the tourist season there is still a minimum flow of 100,000 cubic feet per second, yet in 1961 the Niagara Power Plant opened with a staggering total output of 2.19 million kilowatts.

That figure is not surprising when one thinks of the sources of so much hydroelectric power. All of the Great Lakes flow into the Niagara River and drop 326 feet, which produces tremendous force. The Niagara River at the Great Gorge Rapids is understandably the most turbulent in the country. There is one offspring of this marriage of convenience between industry and ecology: The daily change of flow influences the whirlpool 3 miles below the falls. The whirlpool was formed 75,000 years ago when the river collided with another river and began scouring out rock down below the surface. The whirlpool normally swirls counterclockwise, but when the flow is decreased the lower level of water redirects the flow and slowly reverses its direction.

Awe and wonder have always attended human perception of the unimaginable power of the falls and the turbulence of the river below. In 1678 a Fransiscan missionary, Father Louis Hennepin, was the first white man to see Niagara Falls. The view of this gigantic, roaring waterfall brought him to his knees. Earlier the falls had figured in Indian legends. There are several versions of the "Maid of the Mist" story. One has been attributed to the Seneca Indians, who reportedly sent a maiden over the falls, as Maid of the Mist, for thanks after a good harvest. According to one version, the custom was terminated after a chief died trying to save his only daughter as she paddled to certain death. Another legend is about a young girl who, after several misfortunes in her young life, despaired and decided to paddle her canoe over the falls to end her life. As she fell, her canoe was guided gently down under the falls, where she met the "Thunder Beings." They helped her to recover her confidence and, in fact, cured her so that she could go back to her people. Apparently a small snake had hidden in her dress before her bad luck began and was released under the falls, crawling away and out of her life.

In more recent times the falls have been associated with those who would like to be legendary. You must have heard about the Niagara Falls daredevils who risked life and limb to perform various stunts over the falls. Sam Patch was the first to dive, not once but twice, from Goat Island. Jean Francois Gravelet waked a tightrope over the falls in 1859 and 1860. Can you imagine turning a somersault up there? Well, he did! Annie Taylor, the first woman among these daredevils, went over the falls in a barrel in 1901, but several men died trying to duplicate her successful trip; the last persons to survive the episode were Peter De Bernard and Jeffrey Petkovich in 1989. Such publicity stunts are now illegal.

NIAGARA FALLS

There are actually three falls: the **American Falls** at 184 feet, **Horseshoe** (Canadian) **Falls** at 176 feet, and **Bridal Veil,** the smallest of all. Part of the fun of a trip to Niagara Falls is to see how many different ways you can view these dashing wonders. For a variety of vantage points, try some of the state parks, such as **Devil's Hole, Whirlpool, Upper Rapids,** and **Goat Island.** For a new perspective be sure to see the falls at night when they are illuminated for several hours. You can also join escorted groups to view the falls by bus, boat, or helicopter. Planning your tour of Niagara Falls is not easy when you survey all that is available for your pleasure. We will be concerned only with activities related directly to the falls themselves; the myriad attendant attractions could just as well be available in any other place in the country.

The elevator at **Prospect Point Obser-**

**Prospect Point
  Observation Tower**
Niagara Falls 14302
716–278–1770

Maid of the Mist
Niagara Falls 14302
716–284–8897 (U.S.);
416–358–5781
  (Canada)

vation Tower, enclosed in a steel and glass structure, will take you to the base of the falls as well as 282 feet above them. The view from the top is actually 100 feet above the cliff, a bird's-eye treat. At the bottom you will have a closer look at the falls. If you're eager for a really close look, take a trip on the ***Maid of the Mist,*** which leaves from the base of the Observation Tower. You don foul-weather gear and your boat chugs over to each of the falls and into the Horseshoe Basin; the boat bounces increasingly as you draw nearer to the tumbling water. The roar of the water and the spray on your face (and the rest of you) enhances your perception of the power of this plunging natural wonder. (You can also take the ***Maid of the Mist*** from the Canadian side, boarding at the Incline Railway at the foot of Clifton Hill.)

Goat Island is located in the middle of the falls; you can reach it by a bridge either on foot or by car. Many people come to Goat Island to run, hike, and cycle, and you can see both the Canadian and American falls from the island. You may wonder how the island got its name. During the winter of 1770, John Stedman placed a number of his animals on the island to protect them from wolves and bears. Because the winter was very severe, all of the animals died but one—a goat. Soon after crossing the bridge onto Goat Island, you can follow a path up the hill to the right beside a branch of the American rapids that flow over Bridal Veil Falls. Walk down the steps onto Luna Island, where you can see the crest of the Bridal Veil Falls. As you might imagine, Luna Island was named for the moon; around the time of a full moon you can stand on Luna Island and see a rainbow, or "Lunar Bow." The spray from the falls reacts with the refraction of moonlight to produce this sight. Back on Goat Island again, you will come to the **Cave-of-the-Winds** building. You can take a walking tour, dressed in foul-weather gear, to within 25 feet of the base of the falls. On the far side of Goat Island you will see the Three Sister Islands. Cross the first bridge onto Asenath Island, the second onto Angelina Island and the third to Celinda-Eliza Island. **Niagara Viewmobiles** (716–282–0028), which are sightseeing trains, run around Goat Island and Prospect Point. Commentary is available; you can also get out for a better view and hop onto another train later.

Cave–of–the–Winds
Goat Island
Niagara Falls

Farther downstream **Whirlpool State Park,** located on Robert Moses Parkway, overlooks the whirlpool from a high bluff. Hiking and nature trails are well marked.

Whirlpool State Park
Robert Moses
 Parkway
Niagara Falls

If you want to find out more about how it all began, stop in the **Schoellkopf Geological Museum** for the history of the falls area for more than 500 million years. An audiovisual presentation tells the tale of the development of the falls, and a variety of other exhibits are there for you to see. The museum runs an extensive program of trips and hikes in the area. It also has a full schedule for schools and groups.

Schoellkopf
 Geological Museum
Main Street near
 Rainbow Bridge
Niagara Falls 14302
716–278–1780

The **Turtle** is a Native American center for the living arts in a museum designed in the shape of a turtle. One Indian legend recounts that the earth was created on the back of a giant turtle. This museum houses a variety of collections, including a scene of life-size models who have faces made from masks of real people. George Washington is honored in an exhibit depicting the wampum belt given to confirm the Great Treaty of 1784; Washington promised to live in peace and not to take any territory from the six nations. The museum holds many special programs during the year, including arts and crafts shows, craft demonstrations, pow-wows, and dramatic performances.

Turtle
25 Rainbow Mall
Niagara Falls 14302
716–284–2427

There are several new shopping areas in Niagara Falls. **WinterGarden** is a glass enclosure brimming with green plants and waterfalls. A walkway system connects it with hotels, the **Convention Center,** and **Rainbow Centre,** another shopping mall.

NIAGARA FALLS, ONTARIO

If you cross over into Canada, you will have more views of the falls. (Don't forget, you'll have to go through Customs.) A **Great Gorge** trip, beginning with an elevator descent to the level of the river, is available. You can see the rapids of the Lower Niagara River from the boardwalk below. **Table Rock Scenic Tunnels,** reached by elevator, give you a chance to see both the Canadian Horseshoe Falls and the Niagara River.

Table Rock Scenic Tunnels
Niagara Falls, Ontario
416–358–3268

The Canadian side offers many other attractions, as well as magnificent public gardens full of beautiful plantings. The **Horseshoe Falls Incline Railway,** located next to Table Rock House, gives you a ride between Table Rock and the Minolta Tower. **Skylon Tower** (5200 Robinson Street) rises 160 meters (525 feet) above the ground and a total of 263 meters (863 feet) above the falls. On a clear day the view from the top is well worth the admission fee. The **Daredevil Gallery** (416–356–0943) includes exhibits showing the exploits of those who sought to challenge the falls. And don't miss the **Rainbow Carillon Tower** (416–354–5641) at Rainbow Bridge. Concerts are played on its fifty-five–bell set during the season.

Horseshoe Falls Incline Railway
Niagara Falls, Ontario
416–356–0943

Niagara Power Project Visitors' Center
5777 Lewiston Road
Lewiston 14092
716–285–3211

The **Niagara Power Project,** one of the largest hydroelectric facilities in the world, has the capacity of 2.4 million kilowatts. Seven other plants contribute to the hydropower supply for New York State. The Visitors' Center has a view of the gorge with thirteen large turbines on the left. Inside, displays include a robotic arm, a 1920 telephone, and a huge model of the Niagara Falls area with the river winding over the falls and continuing around the city.

Downstairs take a historical tour from the white-water rapids and falls, ranging from 10,224 B.C., the time of the last glacier; to the falls in 2024 B.C., when the Egyptian pyramids were built; to the falls at the birth of Christ; to the separation of the falls in A.D. 900; to the falls seen by Father Louis Hennepin in 1678; to today. Questions are posed and answers discovered by way of hands-on computers. A movie, *Niagara Then and Now,* presents quotes from presidents and poets, including Abraham Lincoln, Mark Twain (who said that the fish don't bite near the falls), Oscar Wilde, and Walt Whitman.

From Niagara Falls, Ontario, you can take a side trip to Niagara-on-the-Lake, the home of the **Shaw Festival.** This theatrical company produces the works of George Bernard Shaw and his contemporaries, and its season runs from early May through mid-October.

Fort George National Historic Park dates from 1797. It changed hands several times until it was finally abandoned in the early 1820s. The reconstructed fort is open to the public.

For a side trip to the Welland Canal from Niagara Falls, Ontario, take Route 405 to signs for the Welland Canal. (From Buffalo take Queen Elizabeth Way to St. Catharines.) The canal was built to connect Lake Ontario with Lake Erie, avoiding the insurmountable barrier of the Niagara escarpment. It was designed for vessels needing deep water and safe passage into the interior of our continent. There are seven locks to negotiate, and it takes about twelve hours to complete the trip. Each lock is 859 feet in length and 80 feet in width; the entire canal is 27 feet deep. Locks are filled or emptied by gravity. A vessel going upstream enters the lock, valves are opened, and water

NIAGARA–ON–THE–LAKE, ONTARIO

Shaw Festival
Niagara–on–the–Lake
800–724–2934
  (from U.S.) and
800–267–4759
  (from Canada)

Fort George National
  Historic Park
Niagara–on–the–Lake
416–468–2187

WELLAND CANAL,
ONTARIO

**Welland Canal
Viewing Centre
Canal Road
St. Catharines**

flows in; the vessel rises, gates are opened, and the vessel moves out. Lock 1 is on Canal Road north of Lakeshore Road in St. Catharines. Lock 2, located just north of Carleton Street, has picnic areas along the banks. The **Welland Canal Viewing Centre,** a large elevated platform, provides views of the lock procedures at Lock 3. Tourist information, a picnic area, and a snack bar are also available there. Locks 4, 5, and 6 offer simultaneous locking of ships going upstream and downstream. Lock 7, in Thorold, is the last lift over the Niagara escarpment.

An abandoned channel in Welland is now used for recreational purposes, such as picnicking, boating, and water-skiing. **Merritt Island,** on a strip of land between the Welland River and Welland Recreational Waterway, offers hiking, biking, and cross-country skiing. A lighthouse, tourist information center, and a park are located at Lock 8 in Port Colborne, very close to Lake Erie. The elevated observation deck provides a view of lock operations.

YOUNGSTOWN

**Fort Niagara,
Youngstown 14174**

Back on the American side, take I–190 and the Robert Moses Parkway to Youngstown. In 1726 Fort Niagara (716–745–7611) was built by the French; you can visit the fort on the state park grounds. It has been restored, and special reenactments are held to take you back into history. This fort was very active during the French and Indian War, the American Revolution, and the War of 1812.

A self-guided tour takes you to the Provisions Storehouse, Powder Magazine, Dauphin Battery, Gate of the Five Nations (a good place from which to view the mist above Niagara Falls on a clear day), the South Redoubt, 18-Pounder Battery, Land Defenses, North Redoubt, and around to the "French Castle." The castle, restored to its mid-eighteenth–century style, shows how the officers and men lived in those days. Rooms include storerooms, a powder magazine, chapel, guardhouse, and bakery. Stop to see the well that was used from 1726 until 1812. It was sealed at that time and reopened in 1927. You can hear the story of the headless ghost of a murdered French officer ⋅ who still searches for his head. Some say that he sits on the edge of the well at midnight and rises when the moon is full to continue his search. Major Robert Rogers (of Rogers's Rangers fame) was imprisoned in the castle for several weeks in 1768.

For a number of summers, archaeologists have conducted scientific excavations on the site. Each six-week dig takes place during July and August, and visitors are welcome to watch.

LEWISTON

On the way back from Fort Niagara, you may want to stop in Lewiston to stroll among buildings dating back to the War of 1812. Thirty-five thousand years ago Niagara Falls was located there. Later, Indians landed there to begin their portage around the falls. Father Hennepin, the first white man to see the falls, landed there in 1678.

Lewiston was located in a strategic position on the Niagara River, with access to the Great Lakes, so Indians, French, and British fought for control there. The first railroad in America was constructed by the British there as a tramway to carry supplies up the steep cliffs. American control was in force during the Revolution, and the town became a successful center for transportation as well as for trade.

Did you know that the first cocktail was created in Lewiston? Catherine Hustler, who owned a tavern on Center Street, mixed gin and herbed wine in a tankard and stirred it with a pheasant feather.

Artpark is a theater and art complex in a 200-acre state park. Visitors can walk around

Artpark
Lewiston 14092
716–745–3377

the park to see the sculptures made of wood, steel, masonry, and other materials. There are workshops for children and adults. Artists-in-residence create their works in open-air studios so everyone can watch the process. Preforming artists include musicians, mimes, actors, clowns, dancers, and storytellers. You can buy tickets for performances ranging from jazz to classical music. If you want to buy lawn tickets at a very reasonable price, plan to arrive early to stake your claim to one of the few flat pieces of grass on the hillside outside the stage; otherwise you may find yourself sliding downhill during the performance.

Lewiston is a great place to stay if you want to be out of the mainstream of the Niagara area, but close enough for convenient touring. A popular bakery in town is **DeCamillo Baking Co.** (535 Center; 716–754–2218). For lunch or dinner head for **Carmelo's Coat of Arms** (425 Center; 716–754–2311), which has a variety of continental dishes to offer, or **The Riverside Inn** (115 South Water Street; 716–754–8206), located right on the water.

From Lewistown retrace I–190 to Buffalo and take I–90 along the south shore of Lake Erie.

∼ *Southwestern New York* ∼

This part of New York State includes Dunkirk and Fredonia down to Salamanca and Olean.

DUNKIRK

Dunkirk is the largest city in Chautauqua County on Lake Erie. A revitalization program to restore the charm of this lakeside setting is under way. The natural harbor has lots of yachting activity because it is an easy sail to Canada from Dunkirk. Beaches, launching sites, and fishing piers are available for anglers interested in coho salmon, black bass, walleye pike, and pan fish.

Dunkirk is in the heart of the grape-growing area along the Erie shore. Geographically there is a 3- to 5-mile-wide strip of lowland bordering on Lake Erie that is perfect for raising grapes. The low altitude and the warmth of the lake provide a long growing season with delayed frost. The first grapes were raised in the country in 1818, and by 1859 the Concord grape became an important product. A dentist, Dr. Thomas Welch, created unfermented grape juice. Wineries include **Chadwick Bay, Johnson Estate, Merritt Estate, Roberian, Schloss Deopken, Veter,** and **Woodbury.**

The **Seaway Trail** was formally designated by the New York State Legislature in 1980. It was designed to commemorate the linking of the Great Lakes coastlines with the St. Lawrence Seaway, from the Pennsylvania border to the gates of the Eisenhower Locks at the end of New York's northern border with the St. Lawrence. Dunkirk is one of the stops on the Seaway Trail.

The **Dunkirk Lighthouse** dates from 1827. Originally the light coordinated with a pier-head beacon to guide ships safely into Dunkirk Harbor; it was the first oil-burning lighthouse on Lake Erie. The original tower and a brick lighthouse-keeper's house were replaced in 1875. The last lighthouse keeper lived there until 1951, when the light became automatic. A **Veterans' Museum,** containing artifacts, uniforms, and memorabilia from each of the armed services, has been opened in the lighthouse. Photographs detail the International Iceberg Patrol formed after the sinking of the *Titanic.* Photos of the original lighthouse show the amazing height of ice formations during one year; when lake ice moves under the force of strong northwesterly winds, it crunches every-

**Dunkirk Lighthouse
Point Gratiot
Dunkirk 14048
716–366–5050;
716–366–5765**

thing in its path. As you go up the stairs, look at the lovely carved capstan on the staircase.

FREDONIA

Follow Route 60 to Fredonia. This is a pleasant village with a number of stately homes dating from the 1830s to 1850s on the main streets. The **State University of New York College at Fredonia** is there. The **Michael C. Rockefeller Arts Center** on campus offers a year-round program of drama, music, film, and dance. The art gallery mounts exhibits by students and faculty as well as changing traveling exhibits.

Fredonia and the area claim a number of firsts: the first naval skirmish of the War of 1812 at the mouth of the Canadaway Creek (located just off Point Gratiot), the first grange in the world, the first Women's Christian Temperance Union organized at the Fredonia Baptist Church in 1873, and the first natural gas well in the United States.

Darwin R. Barker Museum
20 East Main Street
Fredonia 14063
716–672–2114

The **Darwin R. Barker Museum** has exhibits depicting the evolution of the town from prehistory to the present. The house was originally built in 1821 by Leverett Barker, who was a tanner. It was the first brick house built in Chautauqua County. The museum holds period clothing, military uniforms, books, documents, period furnishings, and portraits. A genealogical society reference library enables you to trace your ancestry in the region.

Continue south on I–90, a scenic route to Westfield.

WESTFIELD

In 1860, Grace Bedell, an eleven-year-old Westfield girl, sent a letter to President Lincoln suggesting that he grow a beard to improve his appearance. He replied by letter, and when his inaugural train stopped in Westfield on the way to Washington in 1861, Lincoln asked for her as he told her story to the assembled crowd. He alighted from the train, showed her his new whiskers, kissed her, and said, "You see, I have followed your advice." His letter brought $20,000 in 1966 when sold at auction in New York City.

Chatauqua County Historical Society is housed in a mansion built in 1818 by James McClurg. The mansion is furnished with period pieces, including a bull's-eye gilt mirror dating from 1795, needlepoint chairs original to the house, a Hepplewhite secretary from 1820, and many portraits.

Chautauqua County Historical Society Village Park Westfield 14787 716–326–2977

Barcelona Lighthouse, a 35-foot-high lighthouse built of fieldstone, cost $3,400 to build in 1828. It was the first building in this country to use natural gas for illumination. The light guided boats loaded with furs, logs, salt, and fish until 1859, when it was no longer useful because the railroad had garnered most of the transportation business.

Barcelona Lighthouse East Lake Drive Westfield 14787

In Westfield pick up Route 394 to Chautauqua Lake. **Chautauqua Institution** was founded in 1874 on the western shore. Although its original purpose was to provide educational training for Sunday-school teachers, the institution developed a program of activities for all ages in the form of lectures and entertainment in the arts, religion, education, and recreation. You can take summer courses as well as attend an opera, symphony, ballet, or play in the evening.

CHAUTAUQUA Chautauqua Institution Box 1095 Chautauqua 14722 716–357–6200

In the early days Chautauqua was controlled by several hundred families who passed on their heritage through the generations. After 111 years of self-governance, the trustees developed a land-use code in 1985. The goal now is to keep the old Chautauqua and yet allow realistic development in keeping with the old ideals. The typical wooden Victorian cottages with gingerbread on the porch eaves remain, and colorful displays of flowers enhance the homes. You must have a gate ticket to get into the grounds during the nine-week season.

You have probably heard about the Chautauqua tent shows that went from town to town, giving inspirational lectures. William Jennings Bryan was among the early traveling tent orators. Imitations spread rapidly, but of them all, only Chautauqua remains.

Among the famous visitors of the past are George Gershwin, who composed "Concerto in F" there in 1925, and Thomas Edison, who placed his new electric streetlights there in 1880. Leo Tolstoy came as a speaker, as did Henry Ford and Amelia Earhart. In 1936 Franklin Roosevelt gave his "I Hate War" speech there, and Teddy Roosevelt spoke of the Chautauqua Institution as "typical of America at its best."

Chautauquan fishermen know that the native muskellunge, or "muskie," lies in wait for unwary anglers who think it will be easy to land one. Try your luck at fishing. From Mayville you can cruise on the *Chautauqua Belle;* this replica of a nineteenth-century steamboat offers brunch and sunset cruises.

Sea Lion
Chatauqua Lake
Historic Vessels
Company
15 Water Street
Mayville 14757
716–753–2403

You can also have a ride on the *Sea Lion,* a replica of a sixteenth-century English merchant sailing vessel. In 1971 Ernie Cowan began researching the construction of sixteenth-century sailing vessels; then he started building his own ship. He found a stand of 350- to 400-year-old virgin white oak; this wood contains a natural fiber that seals wood pores and prevents leaking. This fiber bends easily and has a natural resistance to rot—qualities that appeal to any shipbuilder. By 1978 the framing and exterior planking of the vessel were completed. The hull was launched in 1984; masts and rigging were fitted before her launching in 1985. She flies three flags: the American flag, the Tudor Rose (the flag of the House of Tudor and Queen Elizabeth I), and the Cross of St. George (a plain red cross on a field of white—the flag flown in the sixteenth century in England).

From Chautauqua Lake you might want to take a side trip to **Panama Rocks.** This site can be reached from Route 474, heading west from the lake. These rocks were formed over 300 million years ago as sediment on an ocean floor. One million years ago the glaciers created this labyrinth of caves and passageways, twisting the rock as it moved. When the ice melted, crevices, cliffs, and caves remained; water and winds have further shaped and etched designs in the rock. The forest grew, with wildflowers, ferns, and mosses adding contrast to the rocks.

The rocks and caves were used for shelter in ancient times; part of a fireplace can still be seen near the top of one ridge. The Eriez Indians, sometimes known as the "Cat People," lived there until the Senecas conquered them. They sold lead ore, taken from a hidden spot on the ridge, to the settlers. During the 1800s the rocks were used by robbers as a perfect place to stash their loot. It has been reported that there is still some gold hidden deep in a cave or hole.

Jamestown is located on the southern tip of Chautauqua Lake. James Prendergast founded the town, and in 1811 he bought 1,000 acres where he built a sawmill and dam. Jamestown is still known for its production of furniture and other wooden products.

The **Fenton Historical Center** is housed in a mansion built by Governor Reuben E. Fenton. The museum includes a library, genealogical center, Swedish and Italian heritage rooms, archives of early Jamestown, and articles from the Fenton family. It also offers a self-guided tour of the nineteenth-century historic area.

PANAMA ROCKS

**Panama Rocks
1 Rockhill Road
Panama 14767
716-782-2845**

JAMESTOWN

**Fenton Historical
Center
67 Washington Street
Jamestown 14701
716-483-7521**

Art Gallery
509 Cherry Street
Jamestown 14701
716–484–7135

The **Art Gallery,** in the James Prendergast Library, contains collections of French, German, and American paintings, as well as a special collection of Scandinavian memorabilia.

Burgeson Wildlife
Sanctuary
Riverside Road
Frewsburg 14738
716–569–2345

The Jamestown Audubon Society sponsors the **Burgeson Wildlife Sanctuary.** It offers special programs on natural topics and the environment, workshops, and tours.

Lucille Ball grew up in Jamestown. Roger Tory Peterson, the author of *A Field Guide to Birds,* and Horace Greeley were residents of the town.

CONEWANGO
VALLEY

Northeast of Jamestown, in the Conewango Valley, is an area fairly recently settled by Amish families. Route 62 west from Ellington to Cowens Corners Road, to Route 241 north to North East Road to Chautauqua Road, will take you by bakeries, shops selling handcrafted quilts, chairs, cheese, antiques, and fresh fruit. (See a more complete description of the Amish on page F•263.)

SALAMANCA

Seneca–Iroquois
National Museum
Broad Street
Extension
Salamanca 14779
716–945–1738

Salamanca Rail
Museum
170 Main Street
Salamanca 14779
716–945–3133

Retrace your steps and take scenic Route 17 to Salamanca. It is the only city in the world right on an Indian reservation. The **Seneca-Iroquois National Museum** contains more than 300,000 items depicting the culture of these Indians. You will see displays from prehistory up to contemporary culture.

The **Salamanca Rail Museum** is housed in a 1912 passenger rail depot. Exhibits present the history of the western New York railroads. You can also take a scenic ride on a train during the season.

ALLEGANY
STATE PARK

Allegany State Park, located off Route 17, has 65,000 acres tucked against the Pennsylvania border. Open year-round, this park offers hunting, fishing, boating, swimming, tennis, and 75 miles of hiking trails. A nature education center is on the grounds. (For information call 716–354–2182).

Take Route 417 to Olean.

Rock City Park is dramatic with the remains of a prehistoric ocean bed. The world's largest deposit of quartz boulders is also on view. A mineral museum and a nature trail provide explanations for visitors.

OLEAN
Rock City Park
Route 16
Olean 14760
716–372–7790

This is the end of Itinerary C. You can continue south into the Allegany National Forest for more of the same beautiful scenery and vacation attractions; head west on I–90 to Erie (linking with Itinerary D); or drive back to the Finger Lakes area on Route 17.

ITINERARY D:

Northern Pennsylvania

KINZUA DAM

ITINERARY D

NEW YORK

Presque Isle ▲

▲ Erie

90

79

76

80

6

▲ Kinzua Dam

▲ Coudersport

▲ Grand Canyon of Pennsylvania

15

Williamsport ▲

180

Lewisburg ▲

Northern Pennsylvania

La Fayette
Dolley Madison

Born, nurtured, weeded, prized, within the pale
Of peers and princes, high in camp—at court—
He hears, in joyous youth, a wild report,
Swelling the murmurs of the Western gale,
Of a young people struggling to be free!
Straight quitting all, across the wave he flies,
Aids with his sword, wealth, blood, the high emprize!
And shares the glories of its victory.
Then comes for fifty years a high romance
Of toils, reverses, sufferings, in the cause
Of man and justice, liberty and France,
Crowned, at the last, with hope and wide applause.
Champion of Freedom! Well thy race was run!
All time shall hail thee, Europe's noblest Son!

This itinerary can be a continuation of Itinerary C, from Western New York, or it can be done in reverse from the South-Central area of Pennsylvania (Itinerary F). The routes include Erie, Presque Isle, and North-Central Pennsylvania.

❧ *Erie and Presque Isle* ❧

Did you know that at one time Erie was the scene of clandestine rum-running? Many of the local residents were in cahoots with each other, traveling in groups of two or three boats in case of trouble. Their boats were specially made for speed and built with heavier planking so that they could take the pounding the Coast Guard would inflict during the chase. They had aircraft engines, called Liberty engines, which were noted for their 500 horsepower. The boats were also built with a number of hatches to receive cases of liquor in a hurry. When the weather was favorable, they would cross the lake, sometimes managing to make it to land where cars were waiting to receive the liquor. At other times the Coast Guard received a tip and were on hand to meet them, lobbing a one-pound shell across the bow or opening machine-gun fire to stop the smugglers. Close calls were a way of life for those who engaged in rum-running.

The romance of days gone by is present not only in stories about rum-running but also in legends based on historical fact from the early days of Erie. The Underground Railroad is depicted in one of the houses open to the public. And, of course, Commander Perry brought fame to Erie through his seafaring ventures during the War of 1812. On one occasion the Marquis de Lafayette was the guest of honor at a dinner held on a bridge under an awning of sails from captured British ships.

ERIE

Erie was originally named for the Eriez Indians, a group of 12,000 strong at the beginning of the seventeenth century. The Indian Wars in 1653 and a pestilence destroyed this tribe. In 1753 the French built Fort Presque Isle, but they abandoned it in 1759. The British were on the scene until an Indian uprising—Pontiac's Conspiracy—demolished their outpost. In 1794 General Anthony Wayne succeeded in vanquishing the Indians during the Battle of Fallen Timbers. An American settlement was begun the next year.

At this writing Erie is undergoing extensive revitalization in the downtown historic area. As in other cities, some historic buildings were torn down in the past, but the existing structures are now being renovated and preserved. You will be amazed to see the finished sections of the district in this historic waterfront city.

Commander Oliver Hazard Perry supervised the building of ships in Erie during the War of 1812. The keels of the *Niagara* and the *Lawrence* were laid in March 1813, and the vessels were launched in June. On August 1 Perry undertook the task of floating the boats across the sandbar at the entrance to the bay with the aid of "camels," or empty tanks. On September 10 Perry and his men, on board the *Lawrence,* challenged the British and engaged them in battle. When the *Lawrence* was reduced to a hulk by British long guns, Perry and his remaining men dashed by boat to the *Niagara;* from this ship Perry reattacked the battered British fleet and decisively won the Battle of Lake Erie. He wrote: "We have met the enemy and they are ours: Two ships, two Brigs, one Schooner and one Sloop." Both the *Lawrence* and the *Niagara* were allowed to sink in Misery Bay after the battle. The *Lawrence* was raised in 1876 and, although she was not intact, was taken to Philadelphia for the country's Centennial and finally burned in a fire that consumed the Centennial buildings. The *Niagara* was raised in 1913 for the centennial of the battle; she was towed by the *Wolverine* to various ports on Lake Erie during that summer. She was brought back to Erie and remained in the water until the 1930s, when she was put into her cradle.

Niagara
164 E. Front Street
Erie 16507
814–871–4596

Until September 1987 visitors could climb aboard the *Niagara* and look up to see the flag flying from the shrouds: "Don't give up the ship." The original flag that Perry carried over his shoulder as he boarded the *Niagara* is on display at the Naval Academy in Annapolis, Maryland. The *Niagara* was the only remaining brig-of-war from that period, but two other 1812 ships survive. The *Constellation* in Baltimore is now the centerpiece in the waterfront historical development area, and the *Constitution,* "Old Ironsides," is still afloat at Charlestown Navy Yard in Boston. The *Niagara* is a square-rigged vessel with two masts: the foremast is 92 feet in height, and the mainmast is 100 feet. She carries eighteen thirty-two-pounders, which were very effective at close range. Her two 12-pounders in the bow are known as chasers. She needed a crew of more than 140 men to set sails, steer, man the guns, and perform other necessary functions. Visitors could also go below to see the very sparsely furnished captain's quarters, officers' quarters, the sail bin, quarters for the men who slept on the gun deck in hammocks, and a life-size cockpit scene with Usher Parsons, a surgeon's mate who was the only doctor available to treat ninety-six men on the *Lawrence*. He received his medical degree from Harvard after the war.

In September 1987 the *Niagara* was completely dismantled, and salvageable pieces were stored. She has been rebuilt using some of the original 1813 timbers. She was launched on September 10, 1988, and now rocks at her mooring.

Nearby there's a reproduction of one of the yawl boats carried by Commodore Oliver Hazard Perry's flagship *Lawrence* and the *Niagara* during the 1813 Battle of Lake Erie. The yawl boat is built of Douglas fir and white oak in a lapstrake design (the planks overlap each other). She was used to ferry supplies between ships in the squadron and from the shore.

Walk up State Street to the **Old Custom House,** which was built in 1839 as a bank with Andrew Jackson as president and used as a custom house from 1849 to 1888. This Greek Doric structure, built of white Vermont marble, now houses the **Erie Art Museum.** The walls, doors, and windows of the original building are still intact, but the museum added an inner wall for the gallery. Look at the ceiling of plaster over lath that highlights elaborately decorated classic Greek motifs, such as acanthus leaves and Greek fret in a circular pattern.

Old Custom House
411 State Street
Erie 16502
814–459–5477

Right next door is the home of the **Erie County Historical Society** in the **Cashier's House.** Also of Greek Revival design, this building was constructed in 1839 as a home for the cashier of the bank next door. Inside you will find a surprise if you try to open the doors along the right side of the hall: There is nothing but plaster on the other side! Some of the furniture in the hall came from the SS *Wolverine*, including the sofa and the campaign-style desk. Ask the guide to tell you stories about Captain

Erie County Historical
Society
Cashier's House
417 State Street
Erie 16501
814–454–1813

Dobbin and some of the other people in portraits on the walls. There are collections of copper luster china used on the *Wolverine,* and a blue-and-white platter that was used at the banquet for Lafayette in 1825. Look for the furniture decorated with "feathering" (painted with a feather). The **Erie Society for Genealogical Research** is located in the museum, if you would like to look up your past in the region. You can do your own research or ask the staff to work for you.

Dickson Tavern/Perry Memorial House
201 French Street
Erie 16502
814–453–5811

Walk around the corner to **Dickson Tavern/Perry Memorial House.** John Dickson built this house in 1815; at that time it was on the waterfront. Look out of one of the front windows toward the hospital, and you will see the site of a historic banquet. In June 1825 Lafayette toured the country he helped save. Tables were set on the 170-foot-long bridge on Second Avenue, which is now behind the hospital. Sails from British vessels vanquished by Perry provided an awning for diners, and flowers and greens decorated the banquet area. This grand feast cost $2.00 per person, according to the bill received by Giles Sanford.

You may hear local legends about the secret passages in the basement of this house, which were used by runaway slaves in the Underground Railroad. The theory was that they crawled down under the fireplace into a tunnel below, yet there is no structural evidence of an opening under the fireplace. It is known, however, that the Underground Railroad did exist in the area—in one residence or another. You can see an exhibit of two slaves in hiding as you peek into a basement window. The tavern taproom in the basement features two male mannequins drinking from pewter tankards. They may have been drinking "flip," which was a combination of beer, rum, and water stirred with a hot poker to give it a pungent flavor. Or it may have been punch made with a rum or tea base and flavored with lime or lemon juice. The building also has a diorama showing some of the vessels built in Erie, including the *Scorpion, Tigress, Porcupine, Ariel, Niagara, Somers, Lawrence, Caledonia,* and *Ohio.*

Next head to Sixth Street, where you will find **Perry Square.** Look for the statue of Perry erected for the two hundredth anniversary of his birthday on August 23, 1985. He is shown as he went aboard the *Niagara,* with the flag draped over his shoulder.

Continue on Sixth Street to the **Erie Historical Museum.** H. F. Watson built this Romanesque-style house in 1895; Felix Curtze bought the house in 1924. Look for the many stained-glass windows and friezes; some in the dining room have cherubs on them. The den has an Eastern look with its carved wooden trim and vaulted ceiling. Mr. Watson kept his insect collection in the rows of shallow drawers there. A peacock frieze is in the gift shop, and dolphins are on the stained-glass windows. The striking fireplace in the hall displays gold, marble, and delicate carving, and there is a clock next to the staircase that belonged to the Watson family. Upstairs look for Winifred's bedroom—a perfect room for a little girl—with steps leading up to a balcony, shelves, and a three-dimensional window with pansies in soft shades of green, yellow, white, and blue. The museum contains exhibits on the Battle of Lake Erie, ship models, and the history of commercial fishing in Erie. Look in the carriage house for the planetarium, which offers classes in astronomy.

**Erie Historical Museum
356 West Sixth Street
Erie 16507
814–453–5811**

The **Firefighters' Historical Museum** is full of firefighting equipment, including fire extinguishers, fire alarm systems, uniforms, an 1830 hand-pumper, and an 1886 hand-pulled hose cart.

**Firefighters' Historical Museum
428 Chestnut
Erie 16502
814–456–5969**

Stop for lunch or dinner in the **Pufferbelly**

Restaurant (414 French Street; 814–454–1557), which is housed in the original Fire House Number 1. Various items from firefighting in the past decorate the restaurant. **Farrell's** (1535 West 26th Street; 814–453–4911) features thirteen mouth-watering variations of veal.

PRESQUE ISLE STATE PARK

Adjoining Erie on Route 832 is Presque Isle State Park (814–871–4251). This 3,202-acre sandy peninsula extends into Lake Erie for 7 miles. As you drive out you will see Presque Isle Bay on your right and Lake Erie on your left. The bay provides shallow "nursery" waters where fish spawn and propagate. Among the fish you might catch in the lake are walleyes, smallmouth bass, largemouth bass, muskies, northern pike, blue gills, perch, carp, and bullfin. Fishermen and visitors alike have been delighted to see the lake coming back after a murky period when it was polluted. A local fisherman remarked that previously he could see only about 10 feet down into the lake to spot his yellow downrigger balls, but now he can spot them at 40 feet. The quality of the water is improving every year.

Besides fishing, you can swim along the 7-mile stretch of sandy beach on Lake Erie or hike, jog, cycle, and picnic at the many tables. There are six launching ramps, a marina, and a boat livery where you can rent canoes, row-boats, and motorboats. During the winter cross-country skiing, ice skating, and ice-fishing are popular. A nature center provides exhibits and special programs. Because hundreds of species of birds, ducks, geese, and several kinds of cranes live in the park, ecologists come to study plant and animal life in the ponds, bay, and lakeshore areas. While you are in the park, look for the Perry monument; it is a memorial to those who died during the Battle of Lake Erie.

≋ *North-Central Pennsylvania* ≋

An alternative route if you want to head east instead of south to Pittsburgh is to take Route 19, than Route 97 to Route 6. This Grand Army of the Republic Highway was named to honor the veterans of 1861 and 1865. Earlier it was known as a forbidden Indian trail; the Seneca Indians denied the white man passage. It has been named as one of the top ten scenic routes in the United States.

KINZUA DAM

From Warren take Route 59 for 6 miles to **Kinzua Dam** and the **Allegheny Reservoir.** During the summer visitors can enjoy swimming, boating, fishing, and hiking in the area. Kinzua Dam and the Allegheny Reservoir were designed in 1936 as a flood control measure; the dam was completed in 1965. Hydroelectric power is another result of the project; the **Big Bend Visitor Center** demonstrates this process. The word *Kinzua* means "land of Many and Big Fishes." Look upstream of the dam to see a "trash boom," which is a line of floating timbers to catch debris before it enters the sluiceway. Rim Rock provides a scenic view of Wolf Run.

Back on Route 6 you'll pass Kane, then Mount Jewett, and finally the **Kinzua Bridge,** built in 1882. At that time it was the highest railroad bridge in the world, at 301 feet. The Pittsburgh, Bradford, and Buffalo Railroad ran from Knox, Pennsylvania, to Marienville, Pennsylvania, by 1881 and continued on to Kane in 1882. A legend dating back to 1893 has sent people to look for $50,000 buried somewhere within sight of the bridge. A gunman robbed the company store in Palmerville and made off with his loot. Later, searchers found a young man who was delirious with fever—he kept muttering something about "the money," "see the bridge," "glass bottles," and "three-cornered stone" before he died.

Continue on Route 6 past Coudersport for

10 miles to the **Pennsylvania Lumber Museum.** Much of the white pine and hemlock lumber came from the state of Pennsylvania, and two of the largest sawmills in the world were in the area. Here's the place to see how the "woodhicks," or lumbermen, lived in camps. Conditions were terrible, and the pay was as low as $1.50 a day. Visitors walk from building to building to see the engine house, loader shed, logging cars, stable, filer's shack (where the men sharpened their tools), blacksmith-carpenter shop, bunkhouse, mess hall, kitchen, and sawmill.

Pennsylvania's Grand Canyon is located west of Wellsboro. The canyon is 50 miles long and 1,000 feet deep. Overlooks provide spectacular views. Visitors can cruise the canyon by canoe and raft. Leonard Harrison and Colton Point State parks lie within the Grand Canyon.

WILLIAMSPORT

**Little League
 Baseball Museum
Route 15
Williamsport 17701
717–326–3607**

Turn south on Route 15 to reach Williamsport, the home of the **Little League Baseball Museum.** Here's a hands-on museum enough to delight any youngster. The kids can swing bats, throw balls, and push buttons. A video replay captures each participant's actions and plays back the results. Don't miss the World Series Room to see forty years of Little League World Series Championship on film. A special room of memorabilia contains the collection of George Bebble, one of the founders of the program.

**Lycoming County
 Historical Museum
858 West Fourth Street
Williamsport 17701
717–326–3326**

The **Lycoming County Historical Museum** offers Indian artifacts collected in the area. Exhibits trace the history of life for the first settlers until the present day. You'll see a one-room country school of 1900, the inside of a home from the frontier era, a blacksmith shop, carpenter shop, and a Victorian parlor. Don't miss the displays of children's toys, including a doll's house. The train collection is one to delight all ages.

Continue south on Route 15 to Lewisburg, which contains a lot of Victorian and Federal-style homes. The Packwood House began as a 1796 log cabin and ended up a three-story building used as a hotel and tavern. John and Edith Fetherston bought the house during the 1930s, named it Packwood House after the Fetherston mansion in Warwickshire, England, and furnished it with their personal collection of art objects. One of the original log walls remains in the "log wall room." Edith became a painter, and there is a gallery displaying her work. She also established a Chinese garden complete with bronze statues.

ITINERARY E:

Western Pennsylvania

INCLINE RAILWAY, PITTSBURGH

Western Pennsylvania

Pittsburgh Area

～ *Pittsburgh Area* ～

Where was your town on the list when Pittsburgh was rated Number 1 as a place to live by Rand-McNally? In spite of the grousing by those of us who live elsewhere, let's give Pittsburgh a chance! It was once a grimy, smoky city, but in the late 1940s a countywide smoke-control program began to clear the air. In the 1950s Gateway Center and Point State Park were developed over the rubble of downtown gloom. Since then a number of skyscrapers and new stores and restaurants have been added to the scene. Visually you will be amazed to discover the Gothic influence in the city—gargoyles, stained glass, arches, turrets, and pinnacles.

PITTSBURGH

George Washington was responsible for the choice of the "Golden Triangle"—where the Ohio, Allegheny, and Monongahela rivers meet—as the location for a fort. Fort Prince George was in the process of construction when a flotilla of bateaux and canoes arrived, carrying both French and Indians. Surrender was inevitable, with only forty men available to defend the new fort. The French disassembled the stockade and made use of the beams as they built Fort Duquesne. In 1758 General John Forbes took the fort from the French, but they blew it up as they retreated. He began construction again and changed the name to Fort Pitt, named for William Pitt, the prime minister of England, who was respected by the colonists. The blockhouse was built in 1764, with two rows of holes for firing on attackers. You can visit the

Fort Pitt Blockhouse
Point State Park
Pittsburgh 15222
412–471–1764

Fort Pitt Museum
Point State Park
Pittsburgh 15222
412–281–9284

Fort Pitt Blockhouse, the only remaining structure of Fort Pitt, located in **Point State Park.** Walk around in the park to see some of the bastions and earthworks of the old fort. The **Fort Pitt Museum,** located near the blockhouse, has exhibits, models, a reconstructed trader's cabin, displays of frontier life, and materials on early Pittsburgh. If you're there in June, the **Three Rivers Arts Festival** will be in full swing.

As Pittsburgh developed industrially, its

Gateway Center in downtown Pittsburgh.

PITTSBURGH

The Tropical Marsh Room of the Aviary-Conservatory.

PITTSBURGH

Carnegie Institute, the realization of Andrew Carnegie's dream of two museums and a music hall under one roof.

PITTSBURGH

E•231

position at the junction of three rivers was very advantageous. Coal dug locally, a glassworks, and a blast furnace were the forerunners of the tremendous steel and iron industry. During the late nineteenth century, Andrew Mellon, Henry Heinz, Andrew Carnegie, and Henry Clay Frick developed their empires. The name "Iron City" and then "Smoky City" were not without claims to truth. Theodore Dreiser lived in Pittsburgh in 1894 as a newspaper reporter. In *A Book About Myself,* he describes his arrival by the river Monongahela and seeing the rosy glow from the stacks pouring forth an orange-red flame. He goes on to mention the pounding and cracking noises that sounded as if they emerged from subterranean depths.

During both world wars Pittsburgh's industries were able to produce the materials needed for the war effort. After World War II Richard King Mellon was largely responsible for the anti-smoke campaign, the clearing of outmoded downtown areas, the construction of architecturally interesting buildings, and the creation of **Mellon Square Park** as a beauty spot. Although coal and steel still play a major role in the life of the city, their presence is unobtrusive and controlled. The renaissance of Pittsburgh is a transformation much admired by old and new visitors alike.

Our first impulse when traveling to a city new to us in Europe or the United States is to climb centuries-old worn steps up to the steeple of a cathedral, to shoot up to the top of a skyscraper in an outside elevator, or to take a funicular or cog railway to the peak of a mountain for the view. In Pittsburgh you can take one of the two remaining incline railways (simply called "inclines") to the top of Mount Washington for a view of the city across the river. The **Monongahela Incline** was originally built in 1870 so that people who lived on top of

Mount Washington could travel down to their jobs easily. It has been renovated several times and now has new cars that carry twenty-five persons up the 635 feet of vertical rise. You can catch the "Mon" at the Carson Street Station Square and ride up to Grandview Avenue. The **Duquesne Incline** travels from Fort Pitt Bridge up 400 feet to an area of several restaurants. These cars have handsome, carved cherry panels with bird's-eye maple trim and amber glass transoms. Take a look at the large collection of postcards of cable cars and cog railways from all over the world in the waiting room. For a spectacular evening, have dinner on the top of **Le Mont** (1114 Grandview Avenue; 412–431–3100), where you can watch the sunset reflecting in clouds, lights turning on, the 200-foot fountain spraying in Point Park, and lights glinting on the sparkling glass skyline of Pittsburgh.

There are several ways to see the city, including a customized tour by **Pittsburgh Panorama** (120 Beech Street; 412–731–6044). Knowledgeable guides will plan a tour with your interests in mind; you can relax and leave the driving to someone else.

Among the new downtown buildings you can't help but admire is the new **PPG Place,** which looks like a crystal castle complete with spires, towers, turrets, and a real fairyland ambience. The forty-story office tower shimmers and reflects everything around it. Particularly notice the inside Wintergarden with its great profusion of greenery.

The **National Steel Center** in downtown Pittsburgh is shaped in the form of a triangle. Its restaurant, located sixty-four stories up, has a view that is worth the trip. We were told that the columns in this building have water in them as protection against fire.

Gateway Clipper Fleet offers visitors

**Monongahela Incline
Carson Street
Pittsburgh 15219**

**Duquesne Incline
Fort Pitt Bridge
Pittsburgh 15211
412–381–1665**

**Gateway Clipper Fleet
Station Square Dock
Pittsburgh 15219
412–355–7980**

**Station Square
One Station Square
Pittsburgh 15219**

**Westin William Penn
  Hotel
William Penn Place
Pittsburgh 15219
412–281–7100;
800–228–3000**

**The Carnegie
4400 Forest Avenue
Pittsburgh 15213
412–622–3172,
 exhibitions;
412–622–3289, tours**

views from the river, complete with narration. You can choose a dinner cruise, a sightseeing cruise, or one on the *Good Ship Lollipop* with Lolli the clown, if you are traveling with children.

Station Square, located right on the Monongahela River across the Smithfield Bridge, is a restored historic site with boutiques and restaurants. The **Grand Concourse Restaurant** (412–261–1717) offers a fine view of the busy river, which has a constant stream of tugs and barges going up or down; a train whizzed by in front of us as we were having lunch. This restaurant is in the terminal building, which was built around the turn of the century. Look up at the domed roof with its yellow stained-glass windows, carved woodwork, and marble columns. Complete renovation has made these rooms a romantic reminder of the Golden Age of Rail.

Another historic building in Pittsburgh is the **Westin William Penn Hotel,** built in 1916 by Henry Clay Frick. Make a date to have afternoon tea, Sunday brunch, or pretheater dinner there. If you have a chance to see the Ballroom, on the seventeenth floor, don't miss it. This two-story room has a gilded balcony, crystal chandeliers, and elegant furnishings. (See Inns appendix.)

Pittsburgh has more colleges and museums than you may have time to explore, so we will describe a sampling of them. Andrew Carnegie is a name you can't miss as you visit Pittsburgh. He was intensely interested in many of the arts and built everything on a large scale. The **Carnegie** contains both the **Museum of Art** and the **Museum of Natural History.** Within the Museum of Art you can see the permanent American art collection in the Sarah Mellon Scaife Gallery. Silver, furniture, and porcelain from England, France, and Germany are in the Ailsa Mellon Bruce Collection. The Museum of

Natural History has more than 10,000 items on exhibit, including Dinosaur Hall, Polar World, Hillman Hall of Minerals and Gems, Indian relics, wildlife, anthropology, and the Walton Hall of Ancient Egypt. The Benedum Hall of Geology opened in 1988. The **Carnegie Library,** at the same address, is gigantic, with more than four million entries in the catalog.

Our favorite tower is located right on the campus of the University of Pittsburgh. **The Cathedral of Learning** is a forty-two–story Gothic structure containing twenty-three "nationality classrooms," rooms decorated and designed by artists from each of the ethnic groups that settled in Pittsburgh. The design of each room reflects cultural and aesthetic influence, and the emphasis is on the roots of the people prior to 1787, the date of the United States Constitution. Authenticity of each room has been ensured by the expertise of the designers, many of whom were born and educated in the respective country. Studying in these rooms creates an appreciation and understanding of America's heterogeneous cultural heritage; nationality committees promote that understanding by sponsoring scholarships, lectures, exhibits, and programs for visitors from abroad.

The center of the building is magnificent with its four-story Gothic columns and vaulted ceiling. The classrooms line up on all four sides of this central Commons Room. The Chinese Classroom exhibits an ornate painted ceiling with a golden dragon in the center. In the English Classroom you can see items saved from the House of Commons after bombings in 1941, including a fireplace with a monogram of Queen Victoria on it. Coats of arms from a number of English cities are set into stained-glass windows. The German Classroom will please children with its scenes from Grimms' fairytales

**Cathedral of Learning
University of
  Pittsburgh
Pittsburgh 15260
412–624–6000**

**Heinz Memorial
 Chapel
University of
 Pittsburgh
Pittsburgh 15260
412–624–4157**

**Frick Art Museum
7227 Reynolds Street
Pittsburgh 15208
412–371–7766**

on stained-glass windows. In the Norwegian Classroom look for the tapestry done in reds and blues; the theme is the biblical story of the five wise and the five foolish virgins. If you are there during December, you will find the rooms decorated to represent each nationality's celebration of the holiday.

Walk across the lawn to the **Heinz Memorial Chapel,** which was fashioned after Sainte Chapelle in France. This French Gothic interdenominational chapel has 73-foot-high stained-glass windows. You can spot hundreds of historical and religious figures in the windows. Special concerts and programs are held in the chapel.

The **Frick Art Museum** is located in an Italian Renaissance building. The collection includes Flemish, Italian, and French paintings and furnishings. Several paintings dating from the thirteenth century are on display. Look for the Savonnerie rug made for Marie Antoinette and furniture owned by Marie Antoinette and Madame Adelaide, Princess of Orléans. Italian Renaissance bronzes, Russian silver from the seventeenth century, and a Florentine fifteenth-century plaque from the atelier of Andrea della Robbia are in the collection.

Nearby **Frick Park** offers nature trails, a nature museum, tennis courts, picnic facilities, and a parcourse fitness circuit. Other parks in the city include **Schenley Park,** which has a lake, walking trails, golf, roller skating, ice skating, cross-country skiing, tennis, and baseball. Pittsburgh supports numerous free concerts, as well as drama and special programs in the parks. Ask for a copy of *The Citiparks Guide,* published by the Department of Parks and Recreation, which lists all the performances and special events. For example, the Three Rivers Regatta, Renaissance Fair, Grand Prix boat racing, sternwheeler competitions, skydiving show, hot-air balloon races, and more are held each August.

The **Phipps Conservatory,** is a two-and-one-half-acre conservatory under glass. A variety of different plant species may be seen in the thirteen sections of the conservatory.

Sports fans will enjoy the $22 million, circular **Civic Arena** located downtown across from the Hyatt at Chatham Square. The stainless-steel dome is partly retractable. The arena houses the Pittsburgh Penguins hockey team. **Three Rivers Stadium** is home to the Pittsburgh Pirates and the Pittsburgh Steelers.

If you have children with you, don't miss the **Children's Museum,** located in the Old Post Office Building. Six areas have been built to encourage hands-on learning for young children.

The newest building in town is quite dramatic with its very modern design right on the water. **The Carnegie Science Center** features four theaters, over 250 hands-on (or feet-on) exhibits swarming with children, a planetarium, and the Omnimax theater. Plan to spend many hours there; your children won't want to leave. There are learning centers for children ages three to six and seven to thirteen, with a limited number inside at one time. Children can pet live animals, work with computers, engage in water play, and avail themselves of a variety of educational toys.

Outside, the USS *Requin,* which was commissioned in 1945, rebuilt as the first U.S. Navy Radar Picket Submarine in 1946, and saw duty in the Arctic Circle, Atlantic, Caribbean, Mediterranean, and South America, arrived on the scene in September 1990. Visitors can go aboard for a tour to see how men lived and worked there.

You may not be able to keep your mind on the performance when you sit beneath the glittering chandelier set in the gilded, domed

Phipps Conservatory
Schenley Park
Pittsburgh 15213
412–255–2376

Civic Arena
Auditorium Place
Pittsburgh 15219
412–642–2062

Three Rivers Stadium
North Shore Drive
Pittsburgh 15212
412–323–5000

Children's Museum
1 Landmarks Square
Allegheny Center
Pittsburgh 15212
412–322–5058

Carnegie Science
 Center
One Allegheny
 Avenue (North Side)
Pittsburgh 15212
412–237–3400

ceiling of the newly renovated **Benedum Center** (719 Liberty Avenue; 412–456–2600). The old Stanley Theater, dating from 1928, has become the Benedum, home of the Pittsburgh Ballet Theater, the Pittsburgh Opera, the Civic Light Opera, and the Pittsburgh Dance Council.

Clayton
7227 Reynolds
Pittsburgh 15208
412–371–0606

Clayton is the Henry Clay Frick estate, which has been renovated over a six-year period to the tune of $6 million. It was opened to the public in September 1990. Visitors walk first into the Carriage Museum, which has a 1931 Lincoln, a 1902 Spider phaeton, a 1903 country omnibus with white wool seats to protect evening clothes, an 1888 Victoria (which is open and used only in summer), and an 1880 Brougham with mirrors, a shade, map pocket, and bell. Inside the house visitors will see original pieces kept in the family over the years.

Also on the grounds is the **Frick Art Museum,** containing the art collection of Miss Helen Clay Frick. The museum was undergoing renovation when we were there, but we understand that the collection is priceless.

There are a number of side trips to take from Pittsburgh. Some of them are on the way to Gettysburg, the first stop on Itinerary F.

OLD ECONOMY VILLAGE

Route 65 heading northwest from Pittsburgh will take you to Old Economy Village, on Fourteenth and Church streets, in Ambridge (412–266–4500). This village was once the home of a Christian communal society called the Harmonists. Eighteen buildings, dating from 1824, are open and furnished with pieces belonging to the Harmony Society. Guides are dressed in the period costume worn by the sect. The community was once very prosperous, producing wool, cotton, silk, textiles, and shoes. Its Great House, originally owned and occupied by George Rapp, who was the founder of the village, is a thirty-five–room mansion.

Fort Necessity (take Route 51 to Uniontown and Route 40 to the fort) was the scene of George Washington's first military action in 1754. Virginia's Governor Dinwiddie sent Washington on a difficult assignment, with poor supplies of food, equipment, and weapons. His men were inexperienced and discouraged. The battle at the fort marked the beginning of the French and Indian War. Visitors can tour a reconstructed stockade that encloses a storehouse. **Mount Washington Tavern** is a restored inn, which was frequented by stagecoaches during the nineteenth century. Look for the "coachman's horn," which the driver blew to announce his arrival. He could alert the innkeeper to prepare a hot meal and have drinks waiting on the bar.

FORT NECESSITY

**Fort Necessity
  National Battlefield**
Farmington 15437
412–329–5512

From Fort Necessity take Route 381 to Ohiopyle and the **Ohiopyle State Park.** The name comes from an Indian name meaning "White Frothy Water." The Youghiogheny River flows through the area, providing white-water canoeing, a scenic gorge, and Cucumber Falls. Outfitters offer group rafting trips, which include transportation to the river and a promise to hold your car keys safely in case you inadvertently take a swim. The park offers picnicking, a nature center, fishing, boat launching, hiking, and camping. Ohiopyle is also the jumping-off point for the **Laurel Highlands,** a region of Pennsylvania noted for its great natural beauty. Visitors are attracted to this area for hiking and for other recreational pleasures. Ohiopyle State Park is the southern end of the 70-mile **Laurel Highlands Hiking Trail,** which is accessible in a number of places.

OHIOPYLE

Continue on Route 381 to **Falling Water,** one of Frank Lloyd Wright's spectacular homes. Did you think that the name "Falling Water" refers only to the waterfall under the home

Falling Water
Route 381
Mill Run 15464
412–329–8501

Frank Lloyd Wright designed for Edgar J. Kaufmann? Recently an architectural historian, in writing about the way architects "sign" their work, proposed that Wright used words instead of the usual red tile bearing his initials. The word *Fallingwater* contains his initials—F, L, and W—as well as the vowel A, the double LL, and the final strong consonant T. Very clever indeed!

This sandstone house has balconies cantilevered from gigantic boulders and a waterfall below the main terrace. Inside the living room is a glass hatch that may be lifted to reveal a set of steps leading down to the rushing water, thereby cooling the room. As you move up through the house you will feel drawn out to each terrace, to savor the views and wonderful sounds as the water dances downward.

Seven Springs Mountain Resort
Champion 15622
800–452–2223

To the northeast of Falling Water is **Seven Springs.** This year-round resort offers a variety of activities, including golf, tennis, swimming, hiking, and skiing. Skiers of all ages will find hours of fun here. Intermediate skiers will find that the double chair lift, Lift 5, in the front of the lodge will take them to Upper Fawn Lane Trail, which is gradual, leading around a corner into Fawn Lane Trail, then Cortina Trail, which is a wide, easy slope all the way down. Take the same lift up and try Stowe Trail into Cortina Trail. The quadruple chair, Lift 4, will take you to the very top, and you can ski Upper Fawn into Santa's Beard and Cortina. Lift 6, a triple, takes you just a bit short of Lift 4, so ski Deer Pass to Blintzen or Alpine Meadows, both rated intermediate. Lift 3 services Stowe Slope and Tyrol Slope, both intermediate. If you want to try the North Face, take Lift 4 and ski across the top in front of Tahoe Lodge and try Turtleneck Trail and Slope. Lift 11 will take you up to the same place for a trip down Little North Face Trail and Slope. Take Lift 8 up to ski Sunset Slope under the lift.

Fort Ligonier can be reached by following Route 381 and turning west on Route 30. (From Pittsburgh take I–76 to Route 30.) General John Forbes built Fort Lingonier to stand as a base in the attack against the French. Today's full reconstruction of the 1758–1766 fort contains barracks and a museum. The parlor of General Arthur St. Clair, a local resident who was very helpful during the war, is in the museum. There are mannequins in the Officer's Mess Building, the Officer's Quarters, and the Supply Room. The town of Ligonier has been restored in eighteenth-century Georgian style. There are Sunday-evening concerts in the bandstand on the square during the summer.

When it's time for a meal, head 3 miles east of Ligonier on Route 30 to the **Ligonier Country Inn** (Laughlintown; 412–238–3561) or west on Route 30 to the **Mountain View Inn** (Greensburg; 412–836–1123 or 836–1138). (See Inns appendix.)

LIGONIER
Fort Ligonier
Route 30
Ligonier 15658
412–238–9701

If you enjoy seeing historic battlefields, take a side trip to **Bushy Run Battlefield.** Take Route 30 west to Jeanette, turn north at Lowry Avenue, then take Route 130 west to Route 993 east. The battlefield (412–527–5584) is 1 mile east of Harrison City. Bushy Run Battlefield was the location of a battle in August 1763 between the Indians and the British, led by Colonel Henry Bouquet. Through careful strategy, Bouquet diverted the Indians, who had stronger forces than he did. This victory prevented the Indians from driving out the British and from capturing Fort Pitt. It marked the turning point in Pontiac's war and decided the territorial fate of the frontier. It also reopened the line of communication and supplies. The museum contains exhibits relating the details of the battle. You may picnic on 183 acres.

BUSHY RUN
BATTLEFIELD

JOHNSTOWN

For another side trip from Ligonier, take Route 271 into Johnstown for a ride on the **Inclined Plane** (814–536–1816). Look up the unbelievably steep tracks to the top; then drive your car onto the platform and move on up! The structure was built in 1891, after the Great Flood of 1889, as a "lifesaver," to carry people to safety during future floods (which included the 1936 and 1977 devastations).

**Johnstown Flood
  Museum
Washington &
  Walnut streets
Johnstown 15907
814–539–1889**

The **Johnstown Flood Museum,** housed in the former Carnegie Library, tells the tale of the 1889 flood with exhibits, including a giant animated model that shows the path of the flood. You will feel as if you were there on that fateful day in 1889 as the dam broke. Don't miss the collection of articles recovered from the flood. You will see a pinwheel-design quilt that became a lifeline used to pull people from the water into a house. There is also a handkerchief that was found in the pocket of a man who did not survive.

Before you leave Johnstown, stop by the **Community Arts Center of Cambria County** (1217 Menoher Boulevard, Route 271; 814–255–6515), which is in an 1834 log house. You can stroll through arts and handicraft galleries and attend classes, concerts, and craft fairs there.

HUNTINGDON

What kind of ears does a train have? (Engineers.) You might hear more of these jokes if you catch an Amtrak train from Johnstown to Altoona. Our jovial conductor kept us entertained during the trip.

Or you can drive from Johnstown to Altoona on Route 219 north and Route 22 east. Then continue east to Huntingdon to see

**Lincoln Caverns
Route 22
Huntingdon 16652
814–643–0268**

Lincoln Caverns and the adjoining Whisper Rocks. The stalactites gleam with crystals, and the formations look like a fairy castle.

Can you believe a lake without cottages ringing the shoreline? Huntingdon's **Raystown Lake** was created during the 1970s for flood control and is now used for recreation. You can take a cruise from **Seven Points Marina** (Heston; 814–658–3074) or **Lake Raystown Resort** (Entriken; 814–658–3500).

From Huntingdon take Route 22 to Mount Union, Route 522 to Route 30, and head into Gettysburg. If you are coming from Pittsburgh, take I–70/76 to Route 30 to Gettysburg.

ITINERARY F:

South-Central Pennsylvania

GETTYSBURG

ITINERARY F

South-Central Pennsylvania

The Blue and The Gray
Francis Miles Finch

By the flow of the inland river,
  Whence the fleets of iron have fled,
Where the blades of the grave-grass quiver,
  Asleep are the ranks of the dead:—
Under the sod and the dew,
  Waiting the Judgment Day:—
Under the one, the Blue;
  Under the other, the Gray.

These in the robings of glory,
  Those in the gloom of defeat,
All with the battle-blood gory,
  In the dusk of eternity meet:—
Under the sod and the dew,
  Waiting the Judgment Day:—
Under the laurel, the Blue;
  Under the willow, the Gray.

From the silence of sorrowful hours,
  The desolate mourners go,
Lovingly laden with flowers,
  Alike for the friend and the foe:—
Under the sod and the dew,
  Waiting the Judgment Day:—
Under the roses, the Blue,
  Under the lilies, the Gray.

So, with an equal splendor
  The morning sun-rays fall,
With a touch impartially tender,
  On the blossoms blooming for all:—
Under the sod and the dew,
  Waiting the Judgment Day:—
Broidered with gold, the Blue;
  Mellowed with gold, the Gray.

So, when the summer calleth,
  On frost and field of grain,

With an equal murmur falleth
The cooling drip of the rain:—
Under the sod and the dew,
Waiting the Judgment Day:—
Wet with the rain, the Blue;
Wet with the rain, the Gray.

Sadly, but not with upbraiding,
The generous deed was done.
In the storms of the years that are fading
No braver battle was won:—
Under the sod and the dew,
Waiting the Judgment Day:—
Under the blossoms, the Blue;
Under the garlands, the Gray.

No more shall the war-cry sever,
Or the winding rivers be red:
They banish our anger forever
When they laurel the graves of our dead!
Under the sod and the dew,
Waiting the Judgment Day:—
Love and tears for the Blue;
Tears and love for the Gray.

This itinerary can be traveled from the end of Itinerary E eastward or done in reverse from the Philadelphia area westward. The route includes Gettysburg, York, Harrisburg, Hershey, Lancaster, Lititz, Ephrata, Reading, Hopewell Village, Valley Forge, Chadds Ford, and Kennett Square.

☙ *Gettysburg Area* ☙

The Civil War had been waged for two years when Confederate General Robert E. Lee marched into Pennsylvania on June 3, 1863, with 75,000 soldiers from the Army of Northern Virginia. General George G. Meade had 97,000 men ready under the Union flag of the Army of the Potomac. The greatest battle of the Civil War—at Gettysburg—came about by accident.

Before the battle Gettysburg was a peaceful little town, known to few except those who chose to live there. At that time Lee's troops straggled out in a lengthy line running from Chambersburg almost all the way to Gettysburg. He decided to move his soldiers together; Gettysburg seemed to be a convenient location to consolidate them. During this time his soldiers had been garnering supplies from around the area; on July 1, 1863, a group led by General Harry Heth started out toward Gettysburg to find shoes, which they badly needed. On the way they encountered John Buford's cavalry just by chance, and so the battle began.

Eyewitness Billy Bayly and two other young boys were picking raspberries when they were surprised to hear the sound of cannon. They ran to the blacksmith shop and straddled the fence there to watch the fight. As they watched, the Yankee cavalry dismounted and fought hand to hand with the Confederates; then reinforcements arrived, and, when the action got too close for comfort, the boys "skedaddled" out of there.

Much of the fighting on the first day took place around McPherson's barn on McPherson Ridge. John Burns, a Scotsman who lived in Gettysburg, had earlier tried to enlist but was turned away because of his age. At age seventy-two he was still determined to fight, so when the fighting broke out he took his musket and joined the soldiers heading for the McPherson Farm. When he arrived on the line, some of the soldiers in the 150th Pennsylvania Volunteers gave him one of their more modern muskets in place of his antique firearm. He was wounded several times but kept on fighting—an inspiration to the younger men around him. You can see a statue of John Burns, musket in hand, standing on a boulder on the site of that day's fighting.

Why did General Lee, who had sent out his cavalry leader, Jeb Stuart, to scout for him, not know that the Federal army was drawing near? During Stuart's ride he managed to circle around the enemy and trap himself so that he could not get back to his own men.

Both sides jockeyed for position and clashed during the rest of the day, received reinforcements, and geared themselves up for the battle the following day. By July 2 the armies were a mile apart on parallel ridges. Lee and his Confederate forces were on Seminary Ridge, while Meade and the Union army had dug into Cemetery Ridge. Amazing as it may seem, these two generals who were about to fight each other with such vigor remained on friendly terms after the war. At one point Lee asked Meade why his beard was so gray. Meade replied, "You have to answer for most of it."

Lee advanced first and pushed the Union forces back through Devil's Den, Little Round Top, the Wheatfield, the Peach Orchard, and finally back to Cemetery Ridge. On the second night of battle, the Union army had decided neither to advance nor retreat—but watched preparations for the final assault they knew would come. Confederate General George Edward Pickett led the flamboyant onslaught, which was clearly visible to the waiting men on the other ridge. Perhaps the style of the charge, which in some ways resembled the recent but ill-fated Charge of the Light Brigade in Crimea, suited the man. (It has been reported that Pickett was quite vain about his perfumed and immaculately trimmed hair. General Lee, when asked for a lock of his hair, told the lady that, although he did not have any extra, Pickett certainly did. Apparently Pickett failed to see the humor in this comment.) In "Pickett's Charge" the long gray line advanced in unison, with red flags flying, through streams, over hills, through orchards, meadows, and cornfields. In fact, they were a perfect target; artillery shells and rifle fire ravished the advancing line. Fewer than 5,000 Confederate soldiers reached Cemetery Ridge.

The Battle of Gettysburg took a tremendous toll on the young men of America—51,000 casualties were recorded. Although the Civil War continued for another two years, the Confederacy never fully reconstituted its army after the mangling at Gettysburg. "The world will little note, nor long remember, what we say here; but it can never forget what they did here." Abraham Lincoln solemnly spoke ten sentences that said it all. On November 19, 1863, the cemetery at Gettysburg was dedicated.

Lincoln's Gettysburg Address

Fourscore and seven years ago our fathers brought forth upon this continent a new nation, conceived in liberty, and dedicated to the proposition that all men are created equal. Now we are engaged in a great civil war, testing whether that nation, or any nation so conceived and so dedicated, can long endure. We are met on a great battlefield of that war. We have come to dedicate a portion of that field as a final resting-place for those who here gave their lives that that nation might live. It is altogether fitting and proper that we should do this. But in a larger sense we cannot dedicate, we cannot consecrate, we cannot hallow this ground. The brave men, living and dead, who struggled here, have consecrated it far above our poor power to add or detract. The world will little note, nor long remember, what we say here; but it can never forget what they did here. It is for us, the living, rather to be dedicated here to the unfinished work which they who fought here have thus far so nobly advanced. It is rather for us to be here dedicated to the great task remaining before us, that from these honored dead we take increased devotion to that cause for which they gave the last full measure of devotion; that we here highly resolve that these dead shall not have died in vain; that this nation, under God, shall have a new birth of freedom, and that government of the people, by the people, and for the people, shall not perish from the earth.

GETTYSBURG NATIONAL MILITARY PARK

Gettysburg National Military Park Visitors' Center Route 134 Gettysburg 17325

When you visit Gettysburg National Military Park, be sure to look for the visitors' center entrance. You can get information on both self-guided and guided tours there. Allow two to three hours for a trip around the park by automobile. There are also hiking trails of varying lengths. The well-organized center has many displays and presentations to enhance your visit. Don't miss the electric map, which pinpoints each section of the three-day battle with colored lights. A short walk from the visitors' center, the **Cyclorama Center** features a painting of Pickett's charge by Paul Philippoteaux that is accompanied by a sound and light program in the circular auditorium. You can also see a ten-minute film, *From These Honored Dead,* and view a number of exhibits.

Eisenhower National Historic Site Gettysburg 17325 717–334–1124

While you are in the visitors' center, you can buy bus tickets for the **Eisenhower National Historic Site.** (The tour starts and finishes at the visitors' center.) The tour itself is free; you pay only a nominal sum for the bus. This 230-acre farm was owned by Dwight and Mamie Eisenhower; it was given to the U.S. government in 1967, effective upon their deaths. As you walk through the house, you will see their paintings, gifts given to President Eisenhower, photographs, and their furniture. Look for the ornate marble fireplace in the living room, which was given to them by the White House staff. A collection of porcelain and figurines is in a glass cabinet. The Eisenhowers rarely used the living room; they spent their time on the porch, which has one wall of glass and is especially bright and cheerful. The white chairs are contrasted by touches of red; memorabilia from their travels fit into the decor. Ike's easel stands ready for a painting of the view, the card table for a relaxing game, and the television for Mamie's favorite "soaps." You may walk through all of the rooms on the first floor, then proceed to the second floor along the hall to look into the bedrooms and sitting room. Look for oil paintings created by Eisenhower; there are seven in the house.

Take a look at the "bank barn." The cattle and horses lived on the bottom floor; the top floor was a hayloft accessible from the outside by a sloping bank. Don't miss seeing the attractive barbecue area, where Ike loved to grill steaks for his guests. In the garden you will see the "Frisco Bell," which was given to him by the St. Louis–San Francisco Railway Company, and a putting green presented to him by the Professional Golfers Association. Peek into the garage to see the "Surrey with the Fringe on Top," their favorite means of getting around the farm with their guests.

If you want a bird's-eye view of the expanse of the national park, ride the elevator up **National Tower.** At the top follow signs first to a circular, carpeted, glassed-in, and air-conditioned deck, where you will be directed to stand in the white section to hear a recording of the events of the first day of battle while you look out at the actual site. The recording will ask you to move to the next sector (green) to see the site of the second day, then back to the black sector for more of the second day, and on to the blue sector for the third day. There are two observation decks up above; both have telescopes and maps mounted for your use.

The **Lincoln Room Museum** has a collection of Lincoln memorabilia. Lincoln stayed

National Tower
Route 134 or Route 97
Gettysburg 17325
717–334–6754

**Lincoln Room
Museum**
12 Lincoln Square
Gettysburg 17325
717–334–8188

Lee's Headquarters
401 Buford Avenue
Gettysburg 17325
717–334–3141

The Conflict
213 Steinwehr Avenue
Gettysburg 17325
717–334–8003

Jennie Wade House
Route 97
Gettysburg 17325
717–334–4100

**Gettysburg Travel
Council**
35 Carlisle Street
Gettysburg 17325
717–334–6274

there in 1863, working on his famous Gettysburg Address in the house. There is a presentation of the Gettysburg Address in stereophonic sound.

Lee's Headquarters is the site of Lee's development of strategy for the battle. Although he usually slept in his tent, just like his men, he slept in this house just before the battle. There are exhibits of both Confederate and Union clothing, and military equipment. The house dates from the 1700s.

The Conflict is a four-section documentary produced by six projectors and stereo sound-tracks to reproduce the sights and sounds of the Civil War. During the summer you can also see a fifth film, entitled *Three Days at Gettysburg*.

Gettysburg has a heroine named Jennie Wade. The **Jennie Wade House** was actually the home of her sister, Mrs. Georgia McClellan. Jennie had chosen to stay with her sister, who had had a baby a few days before the battle began. She was baking bread for the family as well as for Union soldiers when a Confederate cannonball zoomed through two doors in the house and hit Jennie in the back. At the time of her death, twenty-year-old Jennie had in her dress over her heart a picture of her childhood sweetheart, Jack Skelly, and a letter confirming his wish to marry her. She never knew that he too had been killed in battle. Jennie was the only Gettysburg civilian to die in the battle; her grave in **Evergreen Cemetery** is marked by a statue and a Union standard that flies around the clock by Congressional Proclamation.

If you are interested in a walking tour of downtown Gettysburg, stop in the **Gettysburg Travel Council** office. You will receive a map with historical data on the Civil War period, and you can pick up a calendar of annual events.

For a special dinner try the historic **Dobbin House** (89 Steinwehr Avenue; 717–334–2100).

Reverend Alexander Dobbin built this house in 1776 on 300 acres of land. He established a classical school in his home, where a number of prominent men were educated. Later, in the mid-1800s, runaway slaves hid in a secret crawlspace behind sliding shelves. After the Battle of Gettysburg, the house was used as a hospital for soldiers from both armies. This stone house has 2-foot-thick walls and seven fireplaces. It is furnished with antiques, including four-poster beds with canopies. Diners sit "in bed" for dinner. Waitresses in colonial dress will bring you a "compleat" dinner.

The **Farnsworth House** (401 Baltimore Street; 717–334–8838) dates back to 1810. Some people believe that Jennie Wade was shot from the garret on the top floor. You can dine in a restored dining room or in the garden beside a stream.

The area around Gettysburg is attractive, with farmland and gently rolling hills. You can continue to explore more of the many museums and attractions in Gettysburg or spend time in the country cycling, hiking, or driving on a scenic tour, perhaps to **Mount Newman.** The Gettysburg Travel Council will provide you with details.

Route 30 east will take you right into York. Or you can first take a side trip to Hanover on Route 116. A third alternative is to skip Hanover and York and go directly to Harrisburg, via Route 15.

Hanover Shoe Farms, 2 to 3 miles east of Hanover, claims to be the finest standardbred horse farm in the world because it produces record-breaking trotters and pacers. Several large stallion barns are open. If you can go in April, May, or June, you may be on hand when some of the foals are born.

There is a battle monument in Hanover

HANOVER

Hanover Shoe Farms
Route 116
Hanover 17331
717–637–8931

Square dating from the Battle of Hanover in 1863, just prior to the Battle of Gettysburg.

YORK

During the fall of 1777, British troops were on the march to Philadelphia, inspiring members of the Continental Congress to flee toward the west to a more secure place for conducting their affairs. They crossed the Susquehanna River and took lodgings in York. From September 30, 1777, to June 27, 1778, York was the national capital. There the Continental Congress adopted the Articles of Confederation that provided a legal national government.

Historical Society of York County
250 East Market Street
York 17405
717–848–1587

Visit the **Historical Society of York County** to see a museum featuring daily life in York County in a village square, exhibits from the War of 1812 and the Revolutionary War, and a library of books, manuscripts, and historic newspapers. The society sponsors several historic houses. **Bonham House** is decorated in several different periods, including federal and Victorian. The **Golden Plough Tavern** was built in the 1740s and retains a German style of architecture with William-and-Mary-period furniture. It has now been combined with the **General Gates House** so you can walk from one to the other. As you walk through the tavern, look for sections exposed to show the original construction. A settee from 1710 still has its original hide. The fireplace has a hole where hot coals could be pushed through to heat the next room. You will see the taproom where the men sat smoking their pipes and drinking ale.

Bonham House
152 East Market Street
York 17405

Golden Plough Tavern
157 West Market Street
York 17405
717–845–2951

In this house, where General and Mrs. Gates lived in 1778, Lafayette was instrumental in preventing the ousting of George Washington as chief of the army. The toast he gave to Washington was the signal for the end of the plots to remove him. The guide will tell you about the "soul hole," which in German belief was important to have in a house; should someone die, the soul could escape quickly and not be trapped in the house. Note the short bed that must have forced sleeping in a semisitting position; perhaps the prevalence of respiratory problems caused by dampness and cold made this position more comfortable.

Next door you will see the **Barnett Bobb House,** which contains furniture decorated with a quill dipped in paint. Look for the chest that seems as if it were painted with a corncob.

York is known for the markets where farm families sell their farm produce as well as Pennsylvania Dutch and German special foods. **Central Market House** (34 West Philadelphia Street), **Farmers Market** (380 West Market Street), and **New Eastern Market** (201 Memory Lane) are three to visit.

Cultural offerings include the **York Little Theater,** which presents six drama productions each year, five productions especially for children, and five "Studio Five" productions. The **Strand-Capitol Performing Arts Center** presents a variety of live entertainment, including comedy, big bands, drama, and children's theater. You can also see classic movies there. The **York Symphony Association** is a community orchestra that plays five to seven concerts every year.

Special events in York include a St. Patrick's Day parade, a street fair in May, a Bavarian festival in August, an art festival in August, an agricultural fair in September, an oyster festival in October, a Halloween parade, and a Yuletide festival.

From York I–83 will take you north to Harrisburg.

York Little Theater
27 East Belmont
York 17405
717-854-3894

Strand-Capitol Performing Arts Center
50 North George
York 17405
717-846-1111

York Symphony Association
13 East Market
York 17405
717-854-0906

❧ *Harrisburg and Hershey* ❧

Harrisburg and Hershey offer you glimpses of two eras in the historic development of South-Central Pennsylvania.

HARRISBURG

Etienne Brulé first spotted this location in 1615 as he was traveling on the Susquehanna River. In 1710 John Harris opened his trading post there; John Harris, Jr., provided ferry service across the river in 1753. He insisted that the name of the town be changed from Louisbourg to Harrisburg, contingent on selling land to the legislature. Harrisburg became the state capital in 1812, and the **Capitol Building** was begun in 1819. (The State Capitol complex is between North and Walnut streets, and Third and Sixth streets.) This Italian Renaissance structure is a work of art, with a dome very much like that of St. Peter's in Rome. The marble staircase imitates the staircase at the Paris Opera. Don't miss the bronze doors and stained-glass windows. George Grey Barnard sculpted the two groups at the central entrance area.

State Museum of Pennsylvania
Third & North Streets
Harrisburg 17105
717-787-4978

The **State Museum of Pennsylvania** is housed in a circular six-story building, adjacent to the Capitol building. There are exhibits on Indian life, natural history, archaeology, geology, and military history, antique cars and carriages, and period furnishings. Don't miss the painting by Rothermel entitled *The Battle of Gettysburg,* which is among the largest framed paintings in the world. A planetarium has scheduled shows.

Governor's Home
Front & Maclay Streets
Harrisburg 17105
717-787-1192

The **Governor's Home,** planned in Georgian style, was completed in 1968. In 1972 Hurricane Agnes flooded the basement and first floor; the house was then remodeled. It is furnished with period Pennsylvania antiques, including a mahogany cylinder Hepplewhite desk.

In addition to the State Museum, Harrisburg features a number of free attractions, including the Planetarium, the Harrisburg Area Community College Friday Night Film Series, band concerts at Italian Lake, lunchtime concerts at Market Square, and a downtown walking tour.

Special events include the Pennsylvania

Farm Show in January, Pennsylvania Relief Show and Sale (featuring crafts and foods) in April, Harrisburg Arts Festival in May, July Fourth Regatta on the Susquehanna, Antique Auto Club of America Fall Meet in October, and several flea markets throughout the year. The Kipona Celebration on Labor Day weekend (*Kipona* means "Summer's End") includes water sports and boating on the Susquehanna, with daily events such as water-skiing and boat and canoe races. There are craft demonstrations and art shows in Riverfront Park, magicians, concerts, a 10-kilometer run, a bicycle race, and more.

Go east to Hershey via Route 322/422.

Hershey was founded and developed by Milton S. Hershey as a planned community. He built his chocolate factory in 1903, and the town grew around it. If you loved *Charlie and the Chocolate Factory* or if you are a confirmed "chocoholic" you will feel at home with the ambience of Hershey. Even the streets have names like Chocolate Avenue and Cocoa Avenue, and the streetlights are shaped like candy kisses. On the other hand, if all of this turns you off with images of modern "fun" parks and artificial tourist traps, take a second look. We first entered Hershey with some skepticism and emerged with a great deal of respect for the vision of the founder and the institutions his ideas created. Here is a "new town" with its own stamp and integrity, dreamt and built long before the end of the Second World War spawned many other "fun" parks in America and Europe.

Stop in the information center at the entrance to Hersheypark, where you can pick up a map of the area to plan your day. Right next door is **Hershey's Chocolate World,** which is free of charge. In plush automatic vehicles you will ride by artistic exhibits of typical

HERSHEY

**Hersheypark
Information Center
Hersheypark Drive
Hershey 17033
717-534-3005**

**Hershey's Chocolate
World
Hersheypark
Hershey 17033
717-534-4900**

Pennsylvania Dutch farms and cacao tree plantations in Africa and watch the process of turning the raw material into chocolate bars. Don't panic as you begin the journey through a roasting oven—it gets warm but not roasting temperature. And just see if you can resist buying a gigantic chocolate chip cookie after you emerge!

Hersheypark
Hershey 17033
717-534-3916

Hersheypark offers areas depicting themes from Pennsylvania Dutch, German, and English origins. Anglophiles will enjoy Tudor Square, where buildings imitate that architectural style right down to the leaded glass windows. Carousel Circle features an antique carousel, built in 1919, where music is provided by the original Wurlitzer band organ. The Pennsylvania Dutch place contains crafts such as pottery, candle-making, and leatherwork, and silversmiths and a blacksmith. Typical Pennsylvania Dutch foods and gifts are sold by staff in costume.

How would your children like to engage in "ball crawling"? An area called Kid Stuff has 40,000 balls to crawl in, a tubular sliding board, teeter-totter horses, a fairly-tale teller, and a Hound Dog Jamboree. A dolphin and sea lion show is presented in a circular theater around a water tank. For the feeling of being in Germany, visit Rhine Lane, where painted walls, geraniums flowing from window boxes, and guides in German costume enhance the shops.

Hershey Museum
Hersheypark 17033
717-534-3439

The **Hershey Museum** near the visitors' center has remarkable collections. For a peek into a typical Pennsylvania German household, look at the reconstructed home of Adam Danner, who was both a weaver and a farmer. This house was built inside the museum from lists of his household belongings and includes a weaver's loom and various kinds of equipment used in the early 1800s. The Apostolic Clock is one of the most popular exhibits in the museum. This 1878 clock shows the procession of the apostles before Christ; he comes out of one door and they all file by, turning to him, except for Judas. Time, Manhood, Old Age, and Death are also represented here.

ZooAmerica houses more than 200 mammals, reptiles, fowl, and fish within five distinctive regions. The evergrèen forests planted in "North Woods" feature three peregrine falcons, great horned owl, black bear, and timber wolf. "Gentle Woodlands" duplicates the fields and wooded areas of Eastern North America with raccoon, otters, wild turkey, bobcats, and deer roaming among wildflowers, flowering dogwood, mountain laurel, hemlock, and red oak. The Southern Florida Everglades are represented in "Grassy Waters," where you can see alligators, long-legged birds, and fish. "Big Sky Country" has been landscaped to represent the Western Grasslands and Rocky Mountains. Don't miss the antics of the prairie dogs, who are on constant show; you also will see a bison, a puma, and a golden eagle. In the "Cactus Community" you will enter a semidark corridor to see nocturnal animals awake and active. These creatures include tarantulas, gila monsters, sidewinders, ringtails, and spotted skunk.

ZooAmerica
Hersheypark
Hershey 17033
717-534-3860

Hersheypark Arena is home to the Hershey Bears of the American Hockey League. Basketball games are played there; ice-skating shows and entertainers come on tour. The **Hersheypark Stadium** hosts college and high-school football, rodeos, concerts, and special sports events. Golf is very popular in Hershey; there are seventy-two holes on five courses, and three of them are championship-level courses.

The **Milton Hershey School,** founded in 1909, provides education for children who have lost one or both parents. Hershey believed that all students should learn a vocational skill before graduation, that they should have religious training, and that they should have experience working on a farm. He also insisted that

Milton Hershey
School
Route 322
Hershey 17033
717-534-3500

every graduate should be given $100 as he or she left school. This may be related to the story told about his own experience as a young man. He was trying to find a job in Denver when he saw a sign, BOY WANTED. After he had entered the room, he realized that the boys there were being "railroaded" to a mining camp as captives. He pulled out a gun, demanded to be released from the locked room, and was lucky enough to escape. Because he had $100 in his pocket, he was not destitute; he felt both relieved for himself and disturbed about the captives inside who were down on their luck without any means of remedy.

Hershey Gardens
Hersheypark Drive
Hershey 17033
717–534–3531

Don't miss the **Hershey Gardens,** which opened in 1937 with just roses and now display thousands of flowers on twenty-three rolling acres. Follow the path through twelve areas blooming at different times of the year. There are six theme gardens: English Formal Garden, Italian Garden, Fountain Garden (don't miss the statue of the little boy holding a boot with water spurting from a hole in it), Colonial Perennial Garden, Japanese Garden, and Rock Garden. The Colonial Garden is especially attractive; much of the information about plant species for this garden was discovered in the garden records kept by Thomas Jefferson. The garden maintains collections of many different trees and shrubs all year. If you come during spring, summer, or fall, you can expect to see tulips, dogwood, azaleas, magnolias, and flowering cherries in April and May; rhododendrons, viburnum, irises, and peonies in late May and June; roses from June to October; daylilies, herbs, and annuals in July and August; and chrysanthemums and late-season roses in September and October. Bird-watchers will see a variety of birds, including warblers and hummingbirds, among the more than forty species that have been spotted there.

Hotel Hershey (800–533–3131), an elegant, Mediterranean-style building, was built in 1932 from a picture on a postcard given to the architect by Mr. Hershey. Enjoy the reflecting pool and formal gardens, the fountain lobby, and the quiet elegance of this hotel on a hill. It has an ambience all its own, one that seems to hold its place without being pretentious in this town of unique institutions. You can enjoy lunch or dinner there, as well as spend the night. Both Hotel Hershey and **Hershey Lodge and Convention Center** (800–533–3131) offer special rates for getaway weekends.

From Hershey take Route 743 south and Route 283 to Lancaster, the first town to see in the Pennsylvania Dutch region.

∾ *Pennsylvania Dutch Region* ∾

Beginning in 1727 the Amish, also known as the "plain people," emigrated from Europe to find freedom from persecution. The Pennsylvania Dutch region is a fascinating place to visit because of what you can learn about the Amish people and their way of life.

Because the Amish were persecuted in Germany, they don't wear anything of a military nature. They do not wear buttons, because military uniforms have brass buttons. Pockets are removed from their shirts, and a jacket or vest must cover any shirt buttons. They wear suspenders (belts are considered too modern), black shoes, and broad-brimmed hats. Men may wear a beard after they are married. Small girls can have buttons and dresses in blue, green, purple (or pink, under age six). Women wear the same colored dresses with a black apron. Single girls wear a white apron on Sundays. Women's dresses are fastened with about thirty pins. When they marry, they take off the white apron and do not wear it again until they die; when someone in the family dies, they wear black dresses. Women part their hair in the middle and pull it back into a bun, covering the hair with a white organdy prayer veil or a black bonnet. Children may play with dolls as long as certain restrictions are observed. In earlier days dolls did not have faces; now commercially made dolls are acceptable if the original clothing is replaced by Amish clothing.

The Amish are well known for their superior farming results; they work very hard to plan and produce their crops as well as keep up with new techniques of soil conservation. The typical farmer tills about sixty acres of grain, alfalfa, corn, and tobacco. (The usual cash crop is tobacco.) He uses horse-drawn equipment that he laboriously repairs and rebuilds. He grows almost everything the family needs. Dairy herds are found on most farms. Any profits are put right back into the farm, because frugality is a virtue. As you drive past their farms, you will see that there are no electric lines leading into their homes; they do not use electricity; nor do they own telephones. Yet the first-time visitor is likely to be amazed by the apparent prosperity of these small, "uneconomical" farms in splendid repair, with huge barns clustered together on tiny parcels of land like the houses of a village. Sixty acres would not support a single family in Iowa or Nebraska, but here they sustain extended families.

Inside the house the kitchen is the room the family uses much of the time in cold weather because it contains the wood-burning stove. The Singer treadle sewing machine is a necessary item to make clothing for the family. If the machine breaks down and parts are unavailable, the family may buy an electric model and convert it into treadle. There are no pictures or photographs on the walls; the Amish firmly believe that their own likenesses go against the biblical commandment "Thou shalt not make to thyself a graven image, nor the likeness of anything that is in heaven or in the earth beneath."

Within each Amish house is a room reserved for church services. Thirty Amish families in the district take turns having services in their homes. The meal is provided by the host family and consists of sandwiches, salads, and hot coffee. Men and boys eat first; women and girls, afterward. Church services take place from 8:00 a.m. until noon, using the Martin Luther Bible as well as the King James Version. Interpretation of the Bible is literal; they accept the words of the Bible by faith. The Amish do not believe in infant baptism. They wait until the child is at least age fourteen to ensure that he understands the full meaning of commitment. Anyone may choose to leave the faith before that time, but if one chooses to leave after baptism he is shunned for life by the community. The Amish believe in a close brotherhood and will gather to help each other when needed. In fact, they do not carry insurance against natural disasters; after tornadoes or floods they will bring food to neighbors and get to work rebuilding their barns and houses.

Weddings are in November on Tuesdays or Thursdays; November is the least busy month for the men, and Tuesdays or Thursdays are the least busy days for the women. The guests bring dishes of food to the wedding,

The Golden Plough Tavern, oldest (1741) surviving structure in York.

YORK

The Hotel Hershey, built in 1933 and fashioned after many European resorts visited by Milton Hershey and his wife.

HERSHEY

An Amish horse and buggy in the heart of Pennsylvania Dutch country.

LANCASTER

but gifts are given later. The couple will spend the first night in the home of the bride's parents, then will honeymoon until March, spending one night with each of the wedding guests and receiving gifts at that time. They receive two gifts from each wedding guest: The man receives farming equipment or animals, and the woman gets something she can use in her home. In March they settle into their own house and farm, given to them by the groom's parents. The bride's parents give them furniture and perhaps a dairy herd.

No motorist can be unaware of the buggies in this part of Pennsylvania, because they have their own marked highway lane, but the uninitiated may miss the meaning of the type of black buggy they see. Unmarried Amish ride in an open "courting" buggy; no chaperone is needed, as anyone can see what is going on! Married couples have a closed buggy, designed in a rectangular shape with glass in front. Both types of buggies are graceful and well sprung, with contours fitted to the human body that no modern automobile can match.

LANCASTER

Visitors' Information Center
501 Greenfield Road
Lancaster 17604
717–299–8901

Stop in the **Visitors' Information Center** located just off the Route 30 bypass east of Lancaster. There you can see a film, *The Lancaster Experience,* that will give you information about the Amish people and their way of life.

Amish Homestead
2034 Lincoln Highway East
Lancaster 17604
717–291–0832

For a closer glimpse of Amish life, continue east on Route 30 to Route 462 and look for the **Amish Homestead.** This house was built in 1744 by Thomas and Richard Penn, sons of William Penn. An Amish farmer and his family now live in the house and farm the property. Here you can walk through the barns to see the animals; the buggies are on display in the next building. Be sure to take advantage of the buggy ride to get the feel of traveling in these marvelous machines. You also can go inside the house.

Lancaster Walking Tour
100 South Queen Street
Lancaster 17604
717–392–1776

Downtown Lancaster has enough historical buildings and cobblestone courtyards dating from the days of the Continental Congress to give the visitor a strong feeling of the past. The **Lancaster Walking Tour** includes an audiovisual presentation and a ninety-minute tour with costumed guide. The tour covers a 6-block area and fifty sites.

The **Heritage Center of Lancaster County** has a collection of household furnishings, clocks, pewter, silver, samplers, rifles, and various crafts typical of the area.

Wheatland was the residence of President James Buchanan. He bought the mansion in 1848 and used it during his presidential campaign. Guests were entertained there by his niece and "First Lady" Harriet Lane. The building is Federal in style with Empire pieces in the dining room and Victorian furniture in the parlor. Look for the large porcelain Japanese goldfish bowl and the zinc-lined tub.

Lancaster Central Market is the oldest operating market in the country. Andrew Hamilton arranged for the land for a market in 1730, and in 1742 King George II proclaimed the site as the Central Market. There are fruits, vegetables, cheese, poultry, meat, seafood, and flowers—all ready to be taken home.

Did you know that the **Conestoga wagon** was first used on the turnpike between Lancaster and Philadelphia? This type of large, four-wheeled wagon was usually drawn by either four or six Conestoga horses. The wagon was a boat-shaped bedframe made from white oak, with poplar boards for the floor. It was made with a sag in the middle, which distributed the weight from the end gates—a useful feature for rolling hills. Hoops were attached to the side boards and then covered with a white canvas or homespun top. The axles, hubs, and wheels needed to be sturdy for use over rough roads. One of the most important items taken on a trip was an iron jack capable of raising loads weighing many tons. The wagons carried a set of bells made of brass or iron. If you got stuck in the mud, you had to wait until some-

Heritage Center of Lancaster County
Penn Square
King & Queen Streets
Lancaster 17604
717-299-6440

Wheatland
1120 Marietta Avenue
Lancaster 17604
717-392-8721

Lancaster Central Market
Penn Square
Lancaster

one came along to help; then you had to give him a set of bells. When you arrived in town "with bells on," it meant that you had not had trouble on the road; but if you came without bells, you were in disgrace. The drivers led a rough life, sometimes carrying brass knuckles or a blackjack to deal with problems. They often smoked "stogies," cigars that were supposed to keep the dust out of their throats. Sometimes the drivers would pick up a little boy to help, and he would run and hop onto the "running board." On the wagons there was actually a shoe on the brake—hence the name "brake shoe." You can see Conestoga wagons in various museums around the county.

Special events in the Lancaster area include an antiques show in March; sheepshearing in April; an old-fashioned country hoedown in May; a woodcarving show in June; craft days and country fair in July; a carriage, sleigh, and antique auction in August; Harvest Days and Octoberfest in October; and various events during the Christmas season.

Landis Valley Museum
2451 Kissel Hill Road
Lancaster 17604
717-569-0401

Head north from Lancaster on Route 501 to Route 272 to the **Landis Valley Museum.** Henry and George Landis pulled together the implements, tools, and furnishings of various eras and established them in appropriate buildings to create this museum of rural life and culture. The museum is divided into three chronological areas, which cover the time span from the colonial period to the end of the nineteenth century. The first area centers on a settler's farmstead of 1750–1800. It is a treat to stroll into this peaceful setting on a sunny summer day and watch the animals walking around the yard. The farm has a typical Pennsylvania "bank barn"; you get to the top level by walking up a bank at the back; the livestock live in the lower level. Walk into the settler's cabin to see a costumed guide weaving a basket or at some other task.

The second area is built around a Federal farmstead depicting the 1815 period, with an adjoining "grandmother's" house. The third area has been designed as a typical village crossroads of the 1825–1900 period. It includes craft buildings, a tavern, and a hotel. Don't miss the museum and its variety of exhibits. A group of women were quilting when we were there. The museums hosts special programs, including the Harvest Festival in October; crafts, seminars, workshops, and an institute in June; a country picnic day in August; and a Christmas program with a candelit tour in December.

LITITZ

Return to Route 501 and head north to Lititz, settled in 1743 by Moravians who named the town for their hometown in Bohemia. Take a walk along Main Street to see eighteenth-century homes that are still lived in today. Although most of the buildings are not open to the public, the **Johannes Mueller House** is the home of the **Lititz Historical Foundation,** where you can get information on the town.

Johannes Mueller House
137–139 Main Street
Lititz 17543

Across the street is the **Moravian Church Square;** you can visit the **Brethren's House** to see the collection of church archives by appointment. **Linden Hall,** one of the two oldest girls' schools in the country, is located in this square.

From Linden Hall cross the street again for a stop in the **Sturgis Pretzel House,** where Julius Sturgis made the first pretzels. If you love soft pretzels, you won't want to miss this stop; you can even help twist some pretzels!

Sturgis Pretzel House
219 East Main Street
Lititz 17543
717–626–4354

From Lititz take Route 772 and look for signs to Ephrata, where you can visit the **Ephrata Cloister.** This eighteenth-century German Protestant monastic group cultivated choral music known as *Vorspiel*—musical drama (presented today by performers) that will give

EPHRATA

Ephrata Cloister
632 West Main Street
Ephrata 17522
717–733–6600

you an idea of the way of life in this communal settlement. The **Pennsylvania Historical and Museum Commission** now runs the Ephrata Cloister; you can tour the grounds as well as buy tickets for the Vorspiel. The settlement was founded by Conrad Beissel, a German Seventh-Day Baptist. He led a hermit's life and then gathered a group of celibate recluses, both male and female. Besides a male order and a female order, there was a third order, that of householders. These married men and women lived in the community, worshiped there, and supported the work of the Cloisters. They believed in a life of simplicity and self-denial. Because they baptized converts in the river, they were sometimes called the "Seventh Day Dunkers." These people were well known for their art, music, and their calligraphy called *Fraktur*. This term describes the eighteenth- and nineteenth-century colorfully painted or printed, watercolor documents common in their German community. The letters in these documents look "fractured." The collections include writing exercises, bookmarks, birth and baptismal certificates, marriage certificates, and valentines.

The Cloister Press published a great many books, including the *Martyrs Mirror* for the Mennonites in 1748. With 1,200 pages this book was the largest to be printed in America during the colonial period. As you tour the cloister, you will have to bend your head to enter each room and move single-file through the very narrow halls. Don't miss seeing the narrow wooden beds with wooden blocks for pillows! The society was closed in 1934, partly as a result of diminished membership.

As you travel around Pennsylvania Dutch country, you will have the opportunity to taste wine at a number of wineries, sample wares from farmer's markets, and have a meal in one of the fine restaurants that feature typical food of the area. Try **The Cameron Estate Inn and Restaurant** (Donegal Springs Road, Mount Joy; 717–653–1773) for some delectable food. For family-style dining head for **Groff's Farm** (Pinkerton Road, Mount Joy; 717–653–2048).

Tucked back on a wooded hillside between Lititz and Ephrata you will find the **Log Cabin** (11 Lehoy Forest Drive, Leola; 717–626–1181). During Prohibition, liquor was hidden under the wooden booths in the front room. You will need local directions to find it because it once was a hideaway. On the way you will pass through the Rose Hill covered bridge; did you know that a kiss exchanged on the bridge will bring good luck? These "kissing bridges" are also called "wishing bridges," so if you are alone when you cross, just make a wish.

In case you have been wondering about the **hex signs** you have seen on barns in the Pennsylvania Dutch region, there seems to be a difference of opinion as to their significance. Some people stoutly claim that they were used just for decoration; others maintain that they would keep lightning from striking; and still others report that the signs were used as a fire mark for insurance purposes. No matter which theory you espouse, it is fun to look for new shapes and patterns as you travel around the area.

From Ephrata head north toward Reading via Route 222. Along the way you will pass many large barns with hex signs on them.

READING

The area south of Reading is now "John Updike" country. There are no landmarks to guide you, but Updike set a number of his early novels in this area where he grew up. **Shillington** is 3 miles south of Reading, between it and Plowville; in Updike's books "Olinger" is between Alton (or Brewer in the Rabbit novels) and Firetown. If you enjoyed *The Centaur,* you will probably recognize the high school where John's father, Wesley Updike, taught mathematics. John was editor of the high school newspaper; old copes of his teenage work are kept in a vault in the new high school across the road.

If you head south on Route 222 from Reading (this route is called Lancaster Avenue here), you will come to a building called **Mifflin Plaza.** The words *Shillington School* are engraved in the stone at the top; John Updike attended this elementary school. The **Town Hall,** a red-brick building, is also still there. From the Town Hall turn onto Route 724; 2 blocks down you will see **177 Philadelphia Avenue,** where Updike lived until he was thirteen years old. The Updikes planted the dogwood tree there when John was born. Head south on Route 10 to Plowville, where the **Robeson Lutheran Church** stands; it was built by Updike's grandfather, among others. His father and all of his grandparents are buried there.

Reading is a major center for factory outlet stores. As you enter town, you will see numerous signs for the factory outlets. Pick up a map and brochure in the first store you enter.

HOPEWELL VILLAGE

Hopewell Village National Historic Site
Route 345
Birdsboro 19508
215–582–8773

Take Route 422 and Route 345 from Reading to **Hopewell Village National Historic Site.** The National Park Service has completely restored the original village surrounding **Hopewell Furnace.** This village is an authentic example of eighteenth- and nineteenth-century iron-making villages.

Mark Bird developed Hopewell Furnace in 1771 on French Creek. Four essential natural resources made the location a good one for an iron furnace: fast-flowing water to turn the waterwheel and provide mechanical power for the bellows; a supply of limestone; many hardwood trees to be cut and burned into charcoal to fuel the furnace; and easily mined iron ore near the surface of the earth. Mr. Bird paid his employees good wages, and by the time of the American Revolution the village was making skillets, pots, pans, stoves, and pig iron. During the Revolution Hopewell Furnace produced cannon, shot, and shells. Mark Bird commanded the second battalion of Berks County Militia and also bought uniforms, tents, and provisions for 300 men. In 1778 he sent a thousand barrels of flour down the Schuylkill River to Valley Forge to feed Washington's starving men. Unfortunately, Mark Bird fell deeper and deeper into debt during the war; in 1788 he lost Hopewell Furnace. A number of other owners tried to make the furnace prosper, but by 1808 the furnace was closed again. In 1816 it was fired once more because the iron industry was booming. By 1820 there were more than 150 employees, and the village was thriving. Five years later the Schuylkill Canal opened, so the wagons did not need to travel as far; the canal increased the range for Hopewell products to New York and Boston. In 1838 the Reading Railroad further increased the customers for Hopewell. Wagons brought in goods from Reading, Wilmington, and Philadelphia and took out iron products. But as the middle of the century approached, new technologies for iron-making began to make these older furnaces obsolete. In 1853 Hopewell built an anthracite furnace, but finally Hopewell closed in 1883.

The "Big House" was the center of activity for the village; sometime thirty people lived there along with the ironmaster and his family. Visiting businessmen came to sell or buy; because the village was so remote, they were always invited to stay overnight. The villagers gathered in the house for parties, marriages, deaths, and other occasions. The ironmaster himself was a key figure in the community; he had to be an expert in personnel, technology, production, and transportation control, as well as a salesman, expeditor, currency expert, marketing analyst, credit manager, bill collector, purchasing agent, investment counselor, and bookkeeper. This heavy load was shared with the company clerk, who also lived in the Big House. The clerk spent all of his time in the village store, where he was the storekeeper and the furnace paymaster. Most village workers were not paid in cash, but instead they charged their purchases against their earnings. Many of the men who worked in Hopewell were skilled workers, including the founder, who was responsible for producing quality iron; the molder, who poured the liquid iron into molds; and the blacksmith, who made mine and furnace tools and repaired the machinery. Unskilled labor included the wood cutters, colliers, and miners. Men worked in twelve-hour shifts to tend the furnace when it was in blast.

Stop in the visitors' center for an audiovisual program on iron making and the village during its heyday. As you walk around the village, you will see a demonstration of the charcoal-making process, which shows all of the layers added to the conical pile. It took almost four days to complete the process; a good collier would get thirty-five to forty bushels of charcoal per cord of wood. Walk into the furnace building, look at the giant waterwheel, and listen to its slap-slap-slap as it turns. You can visit tenant houses, barns, the blacksmith shop, office store, and the Big House.

There are several state parks in the area where you can stop for recreation or for a picnic lunch. **French Creek** (adjacent to Hopewell Village) offers picnic facilities; swimming in a pool; a nature center and interpretive trails; fishing; boat mooring, launching, and rental; hiking trails; horseback riding trails; and camping. During the winter you can skate, ice-fish, cross-country ski, and use the snowmobile trails. **Marsh Creek** (south of French Creek near I–76) provides picnic facilities; swimming in a pool; fishing; boat mooring, launching, and rental; hiking trails; horseback riding trails; ice skating; and ice-fishing. **Ridley Creek** (east of West Chester) offers picnicking, a nature center and interpretive trails, hiking trails, horseback riding trails, cycling, and cross-country skiing.

From Hopewell Village take Route 345 south to Route 23 east to Route 113 south to Clover Mill Road for a visit to a winery, **Fox Meadow Farm** (call for opening times). The winery is located on a farm originally owned by Zachariah Reis, who arrived in 1751. This farm and others nearby housed and fed Anthony Wayne's two divisions after the Battle of the Clouds during the Revolutionary War. French-American hybrid vines were planted there in 1980, and the resulting high-quality wines have won many awards.

Fox Meadow Farm
1439 Clover Mill Road
Chester Springs 19425
215–827–9731

If you're ready for a meal, try **The Country House** (215–933–8148) off Route 113 in Kimberton. It's just 6 miles west of Valley Forge Park.

Retrace back to Route 23 and head for Phoenixville. From Phoenixville follow Nuff Road, turn at the light at Fountain Inn on Bridge Road, which becomes Charlestown Road, until you reach **Swiss Pines,** to see the **Gardens of Japan.** The teahouse was designed by Katsuo Saito. Stone lanterns decorate the grounds, which include a stone garden, waterfalls, a variety of trees, and flowering shrubs.

Gardens of Japan
Malvern 19355
215–933–6916

You may want to drive along Yellow Springs Road to **The Yellow Springs Inn** (215–827–7477). We have friends who go there every Sunday night for dinner. The seafood entrees are a specialty. Once a colonial-period health resort, this building served as a hospital during the Revolutionary War, a Civil War hospital, an orphanage, and a summer campus for the Pennsylvania Academy of the Fine Arts.

Continue on Route 422 or Route 23 to signs for Valley Forge.

VALLEY FORGE

**Valley Forge Visitors'
Center
Route 23 & Outer
Line Drive
Valley Forge 19481**

Begin your tour at the visitors' center, where you can view an audiovisual presentation on the events of 1777–1778. And yes, George Washington really did sleep here! You will see his canvas tent, 53 feet in circumference, which was used as his office and his bedroom. Information on the park is available in the center; you can take a self-guided tour or a bus tour with a taped narration, which you can leave and rejoin as you wish.

Had Washington had his way, the troops would have spent that winter of 1777–1778 in Wilmington, Delaware, where equipment and supplies could be brought by water and the men could be housed comfortably. The Pennsylvania legislature, however, demanded that the troops remain out in the country to prevent British foraging parties from ransacking homes and villages. Washington responded to the legislature that it was easy from their vantage point in their warm and comfortable homes to send his men out into the cold, seemingly with little pity; Washington knew what their misery would be and felt sorry for them.

Accounts written by men on the march describe the snow and cold, the lack of food, and their fatigue and utter despair. As Washington rode beside a group of men without shoes, he asked the colonel why he had not provided them; he was told that the supplies had run out. The outlook was bleak when the troops arrived at Valley Forge, with its few stone houses and the ruins of an old sawmill. They went to sleep by their campfires, too tired to put up tents. Ironically, the next day was proclaimed Thanksgiving; they received half a gill of rice with a little vinegar to ward off scurvy.

The priorities of the winter encampment were to rest the troops, encourage them to stay the winter, and then train them. They built log houses 14 to 16 feet in length and half as wide, with a fireplace and bunks. As the winter progressed, many men died and many more deserted and returned home. The men learned, and what's more, gained confidence from their new skills, which raised their morale.

As you progress along your tour, you will first see **Muhlenberg Brigade,** where the militia defended the outer line of the area. The **Memorial Arch,** dedicated in 1917, will almost make you think you are in Paris viewing the Arc de Triomphe. General Anthony Wayne's statue is made of bronze; he is seated on a horse facing the direction of his own home. A local resident told us a story about Wayne, who was sometimes known as "Mad Anthony Wayne." On his way home from fighting Indians in the Northwest Territory, Wayne died in Erie (this is a very eerie story!); his son, Isaac, came about thirteen years later to recover his father's bones from Presque Isle. When they unearthed the body, it was completely intact. Isaac had the surgeon boil the body and bury the remains on the grounds; the bones were taken home. But because the roads were very bumpy, the bones kept falling out of the box. So every January 1 General Wayne gets on his horse Nancy and goes out looking for his bones.

Can you manage another Wayne story? Hannah Wayne, who lived in the Wayne mansion in the 1860s, went up to the attic to get something, carrying a candle with her to light the way. She got caught on the opening of the attic door; the flame ignited her clothing and set her on fire. She tried to kick out a window to get the attention of people outside the house. The women who were out in the garden heard her screams, but by the time they reached her it was too late. But the men in the fields never heard her at all. Later, during a dinner in the 1960s when the house was being restored, both men and women were sitting around the dining table when the women heard screaming from the attic and the crashing of glass; the men did not hear a thing.

The **Isaac Potts House** was Washington's headquarters. The **Dewees House** and adjacent huts for his lifeguards are also in this particular group of buildings. Nearby Redoubt 3 and 4 are the sites of the earthenworks where cannons were placed in the indentation in the center with men behind to load and fire them. **Artillery Park** contains a concentration of cannon; artillery was stored there ready for deployment where needed. **General James Varnum's Quarters** were in an early eighteenth-century farmhouse that looks down on the **Grand Parade. Washington Memorial Chapel** contains stained-glass windows tracing the founding of our country. Look up to see forty-eight ceiling sections inscribed with the states' arms. The bell tower contains a fifty-eight-bell carillon. The **Museum of the Valley Forge Historical Society,** located adjacent to the chapel, contains a collection of articles saved from the terrible winter of 1777. William Trego's famous painting *The March to Valley Forge* is in the museum.

Museum of the Valley
Forge Historical
Society
Valley Forge 19481
215–783–0535

During the year Valley Forge holds four special events: one on Washington's Birthday weekend (he celebrated his forty-sixth birthday there), December 19 to honor the Continental army, May 6 when the French joined the American side, and June 19 to celebrate the climactic moment when the army broke camp and charged after the British.

If you're ready for lunch, try the **Kennedy-Supplee Mansion** (Route 23; 215–337–3777), a restored 1852 mansion run by Valley Forge. It is elegant, with chandeliers, silver, and bone china.

From Valley Forge head south on Route 252 to Paoli. **The Wharton Esherick Studio** is located in Esherick's home in a lovely woodland setting up on a hill. Esherick was an artist, sculptor, and furniture craftsman who did his most notable work in the early 1900s. You can't help but notice the unusual lines of his garage (none are straight), the hexagonal building in three parts features dovetailed corners with a curved base, and the studio has to be seen to be believed. Inside the studio the visitor is confronted with a variety of Esherick's work—each piece distinctive and unusual. Favorites include a blue horse, sandstone pelican, Winnie-the-Pooh, a dancer in two pieces, and a spiral pole. Although Esherick began as a painter, he quickly moved into making his own furniture as well. Two desks have slots for papers; a toggle "boomerang" mechanism to open the doors, drawers, and top that pull out on runners; and a light that turns on when the desk is opened. His three-legged stool was very popular among his clients. The studio contains his own design for hinges, andirons, carved doors, copper sinks, steps, and a special row of coat pegs caricaturing each of the workmen. The stair rail going upstairs is really a mastodon tusk.

PAOLI

The Wharton Esherick Studio
Box 595
Paoli 19301
215–644–5822 (call for reservation)

⁓ *Brandywine Valley* ⁓

The Brandywine Valley begins along the banks of the meandering Brandywine River in southeastern Pennsylvania and ends in confluence with the Delaware River at Wilmington. Rich in pleasant, rolling landscape, the valley attracted settlers in colonial times. Industrialists who wanted to use its water power, people who came later to build country estates, and painters who captured the charm of the valley on canvas have left their mark on this lovely valley.

CHADDS FORD

From Valley Forge follow signs to Route 202 south and proceed to Route 1 to Chadds Ford. Shoppers will enjoy the village shops, which sell stained glass, antiques, china, bakery goods, Wyeth reproductions, carvings of bears, general store goods, silver, dried flower arrangements, fudge, and pottery. **Chadds Ford Inn** (215–388–7361) is a pleasant place for a meal. Built for Francis Chadsey in the early 1700s as a home, it later was used by his son, John, as a tavern. John's nephew, Joseph Davis, entertained American officers there just before the Battle of Chadds Ford on September 11, 1777. Another place for a meal is **The Country Kitchen** (on Route 1, 4 miles south of Route 202; 215–388–7700).

Chaddsford Winery
Route 1
Chadds Ford 19317
215–388–6741

You can visit **Chaddsford Winery**, located across the river from the Brandywine River Museum. Watch the process of wine making from the grape crushing through fermentation and bottling. The owner did careful research to find the right grapes to produce full-bodied and earthy serious reds and light and fresh spring wine, like a Vouvray.

If you come during September, you can participate in Chadds Ford Days. This special weekend features colonial craftsmen, art, country rides and games, antiques, and lots of food. It is held in a meadow at the edge of town.

Brandywine
Battlefield
Chadds Ford 19317
215–459–3342

Brandywine Battlefield is the site of the battle between George Washington's soldiers and the British in September 1777. Stop in the visitors' center to see a slide narration and exhibits. You can visit the farmhouse, owned by Gideon Gilpin, that was used by General Marquis de Lafayette. It is half-timbered with rubble construction. This is a typical Penn-plan house: two rooms on the first floor and two on the second. A carriage used by Lafayette is on display. Next door is the reconstructed house used by General Washington; it was owned by

Benjamin Ring. Washington stayed there for two nights before the battle.

Before the battle Washington's men were stationed along the east side of Brandywine Creek from Pyle's Ford, south of Chadds Ford, to Buffington's Ford toward the north. Under cover of fog the British began marching toward the American troops, pausing for a wine party at Jeffery's Ford on the way. Unfortunately, Washington did not receive enough accurate information about troop movements, so the British had the advantage. The American militia fought valiantly and were able to slow the British advance—they pushed them back many times—but eventually had to admit defeat. Although victorious, British General William Howe was not able to crush the Americans completely. Washington told Congress, "Notwithstanding the misfortune of the day, I am happy to find the troops in good spirits; and I hope another time we shall compensate for the losses now sustained."

If you're ready for a day of canoeing on the lovely winding Brandywine, call **Northbrook Canoe Company** (215–793–2279 or 793–1553) and find out about the various places upstream where you can begin your paddle, ending up at Northbrook. It is also possible to paddle south from Northbrook and be picked up at the designated spot. You can canoe for an hour or all day if you wish.

The **Brandywine River Museum** is housed in Hoffman's Mill, a gristmill constructed in 1864. When it faced extinction at auction in 1967, local residents formed the Brandywine Conservancy, which bought the mill. The group then spearheaded a funding program in 1968 to restore the building and turn the interior into a sparkling new art gallery. This was a $3.6-million project. A new wing is striking with its twin turrets and glass tower. Large windows enable

Brandywine River Museum
Route 1, west of Route 100
Chadds Ford 19317
215–459–1900

you to see prospects of the river from several different angles. A restaurant takes up a floor of the glass-walled tower. Take a look at the remarkable lighting that allows the natural light to focus on the paintings and statues in the gallery. If you are there during the Christmas season, you will see the model railroad in one gallery: Five miniature trains zoom along the track past villages and bridges and through farmlands. Christmas trees fill another gallery, complete with life-size animals.

The museum has a research library, which includes books, periodicals, letters, scrapbooks, and diaries. More important, the museum contains paintings by three famous American artists from a single family: N. C., Andrew, and Jamie Wyeth. The museum also includes works by John McCoy, Maxfield Parrish, Horace Pippin, Harvey Dunn, George Cope, and Howard Pyle. Although the museum contains much variety in its permanent collections and special exhibits, many visitors regard it as a place to study the development of artistic talent in a remarkable family.

N. C. Wyeth was noted as an illustrator. He painted the title page for the boy's *King Arthur* in 1917, the cover for *The Mysterious Island* by Jules Verne, and the cover for the 1919 edition of *The Last of the Mohicans* by James Fenimore Cooper. Look at his painting *Blind Pew*, which focuses on a man wearing a huge soaring cloak, feeling with his staff for his lost three-cornered hat. The moonlight lands on his tooth and his buckle with brilliance. Also poignant is *Treacherous Trail*, with snow blowing on a cliff and men struggling along through the drifts. A recent N. C. Wyeth acquisition, *In a Dream*, depicts the artist standing on a scaffolding talking to George Washington, who is asking directions. Rolling hills in the background reveal soldiers on a march, and Andrew Wyeth is pictured on the left, as a boy with his sketchpad. There are two worlds of N. C.'s son, Andrew Wyeth: Chadds Ford and Maine. One of his favorite paintings, called *Trodden Weed*, focuses on a pair of boots given to him by his wife, Betsy, as a Christmas present. He was supposed to use them in his paintings but instead put them on and found they fit beautifully. As he was recuperating from a serious illness and needed to get exercise, he put them on and went out walking. The painting may be considered a portrait of his recuperation. Look for his portrait of Betsy, which shows a strong, attractive face within an embroidered frame.

The Andrew Wyeth Gallery contains many new paintings, including the 1991 *Ring Farm*, with its beige hills and white fence. *Night Sleeper* features a dog with its eyes almost closed, and perhaps Andrew himself on a night train to Needham, Massachusetts, to visit his grandparents. *Sunday Times* is an attempt to express anger at pollution, as someone has left a paper in the park lying on the white snow. *Snow Hill* features a maypole with streamers, people, a man with a hook hand, Helga with braids, and a white streamer left for Andrew. A 1991 tempera focuses on a naked woman in water up to her shoulders. *Widow's Walk* offers the contrast of his Chadds Ford house on Route 1 with Maine in the background. Portraits include *Maga's Daughter, Betsy,* and *Helga. Fast Lane* almost got Andrew in trouble as he stopped to sketch a dead squirrel on Route 1 near his home: A policeman was ready to write up a ticket, asking, "Who do you think you are, Andrew Wyeth?" until he found out the truth.

Jamie Wyeth, following in his father's footsteps, is also revered as a fine artist. Look at his painting *Roots* for the feeling of intense detail. He was also very fond of pigs, and his portrait of Den-Den is on display. *Pig* brings forth the rough texture of the fur, the smooth pink nose, and the curly tail. This nursing mother almost seems to smile.

Trompe l'oeil, or "fool the eye," paintings include one by DeScott Evans entitled *Free Sample—Try One,* which is painted on canvas that looks like wood with broken glass over it.

Don't miss the wildflower gardens around the museum. For another Wyeth experience stop

Christian C. Sanderson Museum Route 100, north of Route 1 Chadds Ford 19317 215–388–6545

at the **Christian C. Sanderson Museum,** located across the river from the Brandywine River Museum. Chris Sanderson, always called "Sandy" by the Wyeths, was a close friend of the family. He was a teacher, musician, poet, actor, lecturer, humorist, writer, traveler, sportsman, radio commentator, historian, and—above all—collector. Chris began collecting at the age of ten while living in Washington's headquarters near Chadds Ford. He moved into the house that is now his museum in 1937; he saved the front half for a museum and the other half to live in. After his death his friends, headed by Andrew Wyeth, formed a corporation to continue his collection, which now fills the whole house.

What is in the museum? Everything and anything. Besides his personal collection, there are items saved by his mother, artwork from the Wyeth family, and mementos sent to him by friends. A favorite painting is one painted by Andrew Wyeth in 1937—a portrait of Sandy. Most of the Wyeths signed his guest book many times, sometimes with a little sketch—don't miss the one of Den-Den by Jamie Wyeth. You can see a piece of bandage used on President Lincoln during his final moments; it was obtained from a physician who attended Lincoln. Two little bottles of water that were once ice from the South Pole sit on a shelf. Look for the finial from the fence at London's National Gallery; a British soldier gave it to Eleuthère Du Pont during the VE Day celebration in London.

The soldier wanted him to have it as a memento "from his country to an American soldier in thanks for helping to win the war." Easter eggs from 1886 are in the collection. Look for "Jennie Wade's Pocketbook," which was given to Chris by Jennie's sister. This pocketbook was in her apron when she was killed in her sister's home during the Battle of Gettysburg. There is a sign made by N. C. Wyeth to hang outside the Sanderson home when Chris lived in Washington's headquarters. At one time Chris played Rip Van Winkle; he wanted an autograph of Joe Jefferson, who was the first to play Rip Van Winkle. Knowing that Joe was a close friend of President Grover Cleveland, Chris wrote the president to ask if he could get an autograph—which he received. Look for the upside-down sketch, which you can see in a mirror on the ceiling. Andrew Wyeth sketched on both sides of the paper, and Chris wanted to save both.

A few miles to the east on Route 1 brings you to the **Franklin Mint Museum.** If you're a collector of sculpture, dolls, jewelry, antique car models, plates, or coins, you'll enjoy this museum. The Faberge collection includes a mystery clock, crown, eggs, flowers, butterflies, and an Egyptian necklace (the original is in the Louvre). Porcelain "songbirds of the world" feature a blue-winged warbler, among others. We were especially entranced with a 1909 Rolls-Royce, the "Silver Ghost." Commemorative medals include one of Columbus.

Franklin Mint Museum
Franklin Center 19091
215–459–6168

Continue west on Route 1 to **Longwood Gardens.** William Penn originally sold this land to George Peirce in 1700. As this horticultural family passed the land down through the decades, the garden grew and an arboretum was developed. In 1870 Pierre S. Du Pont bought the estate and 203 acres of the famous

KENNETT SQUARE

Longwood Gardens
Route 1
Kennett Square 19348
215–388–6741

gardens. As the Du Ponts traveled abroad, they developed ideas to use at home, including the special features of English, French, and Italian gardens. The outdoor gardens are set beside two lakes, with fountains bursting forth in formal gardens and forests with tall trees for accent. You can stroll through 350 acres and see an astounding 14,000 varieties of species. Pierre Du Pont took great pleasure in designing the system for the fountains and waterfalls, which are illuminated with colored lights and sometimes enhanced by fireworks as well. He was an MIT graduate with a penchant for putting his engineering expertise to work. The collection is continually being increased by horticulturists who travel around the world and bring back exotic plants for the gardens.

As you walk through the arboretum building, watch for automatic sprinklers that might give you a shower. A favorite area for many young visitors is the topiary display, in which animals are designed on metal frames, using Styrofoam® and sphagnum moss. Plants used in this type of garden include fig, ivy, baby's tears, ferns, spider plants, and succulents. One room contains a large pool that is sometimes drained for a concert. The orchid room is a real treat, with many different colors in the various species; there may be as many as 25,000 species gathered from throughout the world. In tropical areas you will see the tropical pitcher plant, Spanish moss, pineapple, and the Panama hat plant. Medicinal plants used to make lotions, tonics, and healing ointments grow there; a strychnine plant is set back away from visitors' hands. The rain forest room has a walkway all around so you can view the palms from all angles.

Don't miss the giant waterlilies outside that can hold a hundred pounds of weight. The shiny huge leaves with a turned-up edging repel water; they are sometimes more than a few feet in diameter. The best time to see them is from July to September. Look for the cute scarecrow in the outdoor vegetable garden. Head for the bell tower and walk up the steps past green shrubs and trees to the "eye of water," which was built in 1968. It was inspired by a similar structure in Costa Rica. The eye sits above the reservoir for the main flower garden. Surplus water flows through the eye to the nearby waterfall. An initial morning surge of 8,000 gallons per minute begins the ripple and flows over the eye. The rate soon drops to a steady 5,000 gallons per minute for the rest of the day. The pattern of the flow changes as you watch the eye.

You can become a student at Longwood; courses in horticulture are offered as well as a variety of lectures and programs. Stop in at the tourist information center at the entrance to Longwood Gardens (215–388–2900) for information.

The **Terrace Restaurant** at Longwood Gardens serves lunch, or you can head into Kennett Square for lunch in **The Market Place** (215–388–7810). Look around at the gourmet foods offered for sale, including wild rice, spices, tofutti ice cream, cranberry relish, juices, Perrier, Cold Duck, sparkling cider, and freshly baked bread. After lunch stop in **Phillips Mushroom Place** (215–388–6082), which has a museum and gift shop. Mushrooms in the cooler there are the most pristine we have ever seen—nary a bit of earth on them. Also in Kennett Square you will find the **Longwood Inn** (Route 1; 215–444–3515), which features mushroom specialties and seafood.

Itinerary F ends here. You can head into Philadelphia and go north to the Poconos and Delaware Water Gap (Itinerary G) or go south into Delaware (Itinerary H).

ITINERARY G:

Eastern Pennsylvania

PHILADELPHIA

Eastern Pennsylvania

This itinerary begins in Philadelphia and then heads north through Bucks County, the Delaware Water Gap, and the Poconos. It can also connect with Itinerary H to Delaware, the Delaware shore, the Jersey shore, and Princeton. Or it can link with Itinerary F at the Brandywine Valley for exploration of Valley Forge, Lancaster, Hershey, Harrisburg, York, and Gettysburg.

⇜ *Philadelphia* ⇝

The "City of Brotherly Love" was so proclaimed by William Penn, who believed that settlers should be free to live by their own laws and that no one should be "molested or prejudiced for his or her own conscientious persuasion or practice." As a wealthy Quaker, Penn was determined to develop a colony in the New World that would provide anyone with freedom to practice his own faith. He convinced King Charles II to provide him with a tract of land in payment for a debt owed by the Crown to his father, Admiral Sir William Penn. The charter he received for "Sylvania" gave him full authority to impose taxes "by act of Parliament." He arrived in 1682 and named the colony Pennsylvania, "Penn's Woods," in honor of his father. Then he named Philadelphia after a Christian city in Asia Minor.

Inaugurating one of the first attempts at city planning, Penn was determined to lay out the streets on a grid pattern. When Charles Dickens visited in 1842, he commented that Philadelphia was a "handsome city, but distractingly regular." Penn's surveyor, Captain Thomas Holmes, also planned five squares to provide the residents with greenery, fresh air, and sunshine. By 1776 Philadelphia had become the second-largest English-speaking city in the world.

In 1774 the First Continental Congress met at Carpenters' Hall in Philadelphia. The Second Continental Congress met at Independence Hall, then called the Pennsylvania State House. Thomas Jefferson worked arduously drafting the Declaration then gave it to his colleagues to approve, and it was signed. (You can see the inkwell used to sign the Declaration of Independence as you walk through Independence Hall.) The Declaration of Independence was read in the State House yard on July 8, 1776. In 1787 the Articles of Confederation were revised by the Constitutional Convention here. Philadelphia remained the capital of our nation until 1800.

PHILADELPHIA　　　　　　　We suggest beginning your adventure back into time with a walking tour of the "most historic square in America," **Independence National Historic Park.** Several walking tours are available. Visit the **National Historical Park Visitor Center,** where you can watch the film *Independence,* consult with park rangers on your choice of tour, and buy one of several books on walking tours of the park. If you would like to hear historical explanations as you walk (from a cassette player carried on your shoulder), go to the **Norman Rockwell Museum** and ask for **AudioWalk Tour** (6th Street and Walnut; 215–925–1234). You will receive a map to follow, with the tour well marked. Pleasant harpsichord music on the tape sets the stage for eighteenth-century colonial life. You will learn little known facts not found anywhere else as you travel along the route.

The **Liberty Bell Pavilion** in the Independence National Park is an appropriate place to begin your tour. The bell is now housed in a glass-enclosed structure so visitors can see it twenty-four hours a day. Records in January 1750 detail the need for a steeple super-structure as a "suitable place thereon for hang-ing a bell." The arrival of the bell was to coin-cide with the Fiftieth Anniversary of William Penn's Charter of Privileges, which ensured freedom of faith for the citizens of Pennsylvania Colony. The bell was ordered through the colo-nial agent of the province in London in November 1751. The specifications included "Get us a good bell, of about two thousand pounds weight, the cost of which we presume may amount to one hundred pounds sterling, or perhaps with the charges something more. . . Let the bell be cast by the best workmen, and examined carefully before it is shipped. . . ." The bell arrived aboard the vessel *Myrtilla,* sailed by Captain Richard Budden. But as luck would have it, the bell cracked the first time it was rung.

National Historical Park Visitor Center
3rd & Chestnut Streets
Philadelphia
215-597-8974

Liberty Bell Pavilion
Independence National Historical Park
Market Street, between 5th & 6th Streets
Philadelphia

Two Philadelphia foundrymen, John Pass and John Stow, recast the bell in 1752; because the tone was not ideal, they recast it again, using an additional one and one-half ounces of copper per pound to change the quality. The new bell was installed in June 1753 in the steeple of the State House, but it was fated to be peripatetic. During the Revolution the bell resided in Allentown from September 1777 to June 1778. After its return it was placed in the tower until 1846; in the Assembly Room until 1872; then in the hallway of Independence Hall. In 1875 it was moved into the Supreme Court Chamber; in 1877 it was suspended on a chain from the ceiling in the hall; it was moved back to the Assembly Room in 1878; it was placed in a glass case and moved back to the tower in 1896. Finally, in 1915, the glass case was removed so visitors could touch the bell. During the Bicentennial year, 1976, the bell was moved to its final resting place in the new glass pavilion. With a history as unsettled as the country it represents, this movable bell deserves a rest! No one knows for sure how the bell got its name, but in 1839 a pamphlet dealing with antislavery referred to it as the "Liberty Bell." William Ross Wallace wrote, "That old bell is still seen by the patriot's eye, And he blesses it ever, when journeying by. . . ."

The bell was apparently rung too loudly and too often according to some of the neighbors; in 1772 there was a petition asking for moderation in the ringing of the bell. Apparently it was rung to call members into session both morning and afternoon, as well as for various public functions. Some of the more memorable ringings include 1753, rung for the first time to call the Pennsylvania Assembly together; 1757, Franklin left for England to solicit redress for grievances; 1761, King George III acceded to the throne; 1763, end of the French and Indian War;

1765 (with the bell muffled), when ships carrying stamps for Pennsylvania, New Jersey, and Maryland sailed up the Delaware River; 1771, calling the Assembly to petition the king for repeal of the tax on tea; 1774, news received on the closing of the port of Boston; 1775, news of the battle of Lexington; 1775, George Washington's acceptance of the appointment of commander in chief of the Continental army; 1776, proclamation of the Declaration of Independence; 1787, adoption of the Constitution of the United States; 1799, the death of George Washington; 1801, inauguration of Thomas Jefferson as third president of the United States; and 1824, welcome to General Lafayette to Philadelphia. In 1835 the bell cracked while it was being rung on Washington's birthday; later that year it cracked during the funeral for Chief Justice of the United States John Marshall. Since that time the bell has been tapped only for very special occasions.

Independence Bell

There was tumult in the city,
  In the quaint old Quaker town,
And the streets were thronged with people
  Passing restless up and down—
People gathering at the corners,
  Where they whispered lip to ear,
While the sweat stood on their temples,
  With the stress of hope and fear.

As the bleak Atlantic currents
  Lash the wild Newfoundland shore,
So they beat about the State House,
  So they surged against the door;
And the mingling of their voices
  Swelled in harmony profound,
Till the quiet street of Chestnut
  Was all turbulent with sound.

"Will they do it?" "Dare they do it?"
"Who is speaking?" "What's the news?"
"What of Adams?" "What of Sherman?"
"Oh, God grant they won't refuse!"
"Make some way, there!" "Let me nearer!"
"I am stifling!" "Stifle them!"
When a nation's life's at hazard
We've no time to think of men!"

So they surged against the State House,
While all solemnly inside
Sat the Continental Congress,
Truth and reason for their guide;
O'er a simple scroll debating;
Which, though simple it might be,
Yet should shake the cliffs of England
With the thunders of the free.

Far aloft in the high steeple
Sat the bellman, old and gray;
He was weary of the tyrant
And his iron-sceptered sway.
So he sat with one hand ready
On the clapper of the bell,
Till his eye should catch the signal,
The expected news to tell.

See! See! the dense crowd quivers
As beside the door a boy
Looks forth with hands uplifted,
His eyes alight with joy,
Hushed the people's swelling murmur
As they listen breathlessly—
"Ring!" he shouts; "ring, grandpapa!
Ring! oh, ring for liberty!"

Quickly at the welcome signal
The old bellman lifts his hand;
Forth he sends the good news, making
Iron music through the land.
How they shouted! What rejoicing!
How the old bell shook the air,
Till the clang of freedom echoed
From the belfries everywhere.

The old State House bell is silent,
Hushed is now its clamorous tongue,
But the spirit is awakened
Still is living, ever young.
And we'll ne'er forget the bellman
Who, that great day in July,
Hailed the birth of Independence,
Which, please God, shall never die.

Walk down the mall to **Independence Hall,** built in 1732 and the scene of a major portion of the history of our fight for freedom. In this building the Second Continental Congress met; George Washington was appointed commander in chief of the Continental army; the Declaration of Independence and the Articles of Confederation were adopted; the American flag was received as official; and Cornwallis's defeat in Yorktown and the end of the Revolutionary War were announced. Unfortunately, most of the original furniture was burned as firewood by the British in 1777. Look for the "Rising Sun" chair in the Assembly Room, which was used by George Washington during the Constitutional Convention in 1779. The silver inkstand on his desk was used by the signers of the Declaration of Independence and the Constitution. The Supreme Court Chamber did not have fireplaces, so little boxes of hot coals were provided to warm feet. Look for a 7-foot painting in the bell tower showing a view of early Philadelphia. The Long Gallery has served as a banquet room, meeting room, prison for American officers during the British occupation, and a museum. Look up to see the handsome brass chandeliers; the one in the center dates from 1740.

The man most frequently associated with Philadelphia during the Revolutionary era, Benjamin Franklin, was born in Boston in January 1706. Although his father, Josiah, wanted

**Independence Hall
Independence
National Historical
Park
Chestnut Street
Philadelphia 19106**

him to train as a minister of the Gospel, Franklin chose to train as a printer's apprentice and to teach himself a wide range of subjects. He went to New York in 1723 to find work but was not successful, so he went on to Philadelphia. There he landed, a seventeen-year-old youth who walked through the streets hungry, looking for work. In front of Franklin Field, the athletic stadium of the University of Pennsylvania, you can see a statue of him with his sack and a walking stick. Within five years Franklin had bought a printing business, then a newspaper, *The Pennsylvania Gazette,* and, at the age of twenty-seven, he began to publish *Poor Richard's Almanac.* His desire was to become wealthy so that he could have free time to pursue his interests to further society; he was not interested in joining the aristocracy. Within twenty years he was able to retire and begin his career as statesman, politician, and diplomat. He was involved in the first firefighting company in America, a fire insurance company, an academy that grew to be the University of Pennsylvania, the local hospital, and a local militia. A creative genius, he developed experiments and inventions with electricity, lightning rods, and the "Franklin stove." He was made clerk of the Pennsylvania Assembly in 1736, a member in 1750, and deputy postmaster-general of America in 1753.

Franklin's house on Market Street between Third and Fourth streets was in the process of construction in 1764 when he was called back to London. His wife, Deborah, stayed behind to oversee the house construction, which progressed with many difficulties. Franklin did not return for ten years, and Deborah died just before he arrived. The next year he was sent by Congress to France, along with Silas Deane and Arthur Lee, to try to persuade the French to sign treaties with America. He settled into a house in Paris and was sought after by the court of Louis

XVI and Marie Antoinette. In Philadelphia his house was confiscated for a while by British General Sir Charles Grey and his officers. In 1778 treaties between France and America were signed, and in 1785 Franklin returned home. Franklin was honored with the title of President of the Pennsylvania State Council, even though he was in poor health and in his early eighties. Some politicians accused him of senility because he had chosen to take on such a demanding job; Franklin wrote: "I had not firmness enough to resist the unanimous desire of my country-folks; and I find myself harnessed again in their service. They engrossed the prime of my life. They have eaten my flesh, and seem resolved now to pick my bones." In 1787, when the Constitutional Convention convened in Philadelphia, Franklin contributed his intellect and persuasive powers during the revision of the Articles of Confederation. He also entertained many members of the convention in his home, including George Washington. He died at age eighty-four. The house was razed in 1812; the National Park Service began archaeological excavations in 1953 to uncover the foundation as well as artifacts.

As you visit **Franklin Court,** the site of his home, you will find the restored office of the *Aurora and General Advertiser,* a newspaper published by Benjamin Franklin Bache, his grandson. Next door you can see demonstrations of eighteenth-century printing and bookbinding, reminiscent of his early trade. An exhibit of architectural interest promotes proper construction to prevent fire. A colonial post office where you can buy commemorative stamps is also on the site; letters are hand-canceled with a special Franklin postmark. The **U.S. Postal Service Museum** is next with a variety of exhibits. From the courtyard take a ramp into an underground museum. Look for the tele-

**Franklin Court
Market Street,
  between 3rd & 4th
  Streets
Philadelphia**

Penn's Landing
Delaware Avenue
Philadelphia

Port of History
 Museum
Delaware Avenue &
Walnut Street
Philadelphia 19106

Philadelphia Maritime
 Museum
321 Chestnut Street
Philadelphia 19106

phone "hotline," where you can dial Franklin's friends both in America and Europe to hear them tell stories about him.

After you have visited some of the many other sites of interest in the park, you may want to have lunch in **City Tavern** (Second and Walnut streets; 215–923–6059). This reconstructed eighteenth-century tavern serves typical colonial food, and the waiters and waitresses are dressed in period costume. Originally built over 200 years ago, this site has seen the likes of John Adams, Paul Revere, Thomas Jefferson, and George Washington, to name but a few.

Walk down to Philadelphia's waterfront area, **Penn's Landing,** where you can stroll along the park through a sculpture garden and into a new amphitheater area. There fountains play, and performances are given on a barge anchored in the river. While at the landing stop in the **Port of History Museum** for a look at the show "Philadelphia: Visions and Realities"; exhibits on regional, national, and international arts and crafts; and an extensive maritime collection. A few blocks away another museum, the **Philadelphia Maritime Museum,** contains ship models, figureheads, scrimshaw, paintings, and other marine exhibits. This museum also has **Workshop on the Water** at Penn's Landing in a converted 1935 barge, where you can see small-craft exhibits and attend classes to learn how to build boats.

You can visit a number of other interesting vessels moored at Penn's Landing. *Gazela of Philadelphia* (215–923–9030) is an 1883 Portuguese square-rigger used in conjunction with a fleet of small dory cod-fishing boats. Each year she sailed from Lisbon with a crew of fifty men to the fishing banks off Newfoundland. After the crew filled her hold with salted cod (sometimes taking as long as six months), she would return to port. Her spars, hull, and boom

were cut from Portuguese pine originally planted by Henry the Navigator in 1460. The **USS
Becuna** (215–922–1898), a guppy-class submarine, was commissioned in 1944 to serve in the
South Pacific. If you've always wanted to go
below on a submarine, here's your chance! The
USS Olympia was once Admiral Dewey's flagship in the Spanish-American War. Models portray life on board. Look for the antique copper
tub in the Commodore's Quarters.

Society Hill is a historic district, near the
river, that has been restored by the residents.
Walk on the cobblestone streets past Georgian
and Federal houses lighted by Franklin lamps.
Head House Square was originally a marketplace dating back to 1745. Renovated in the
1970s, it is now a red-brick collection of shops
and restaurants. Try **Dickens Inn** on Second
Street between Pine and Lombard. The original
Harper House dates from 1788
(215–928–9307). Nearby **South Street** is a sight
to behold if you are there during the evening—
people stroll around to be seen in outlandish
dress and hair arrangements. There are many
shops and ethnic restaurants in this area.
Downeys (Front and South streets;
215–629–0525) is a good choice for Irish specialties. Look for the unique collection of
antique radios perched on high shelves in each
room.

If you're hungry and want an unusual
experience, head for the **Reading Terminal
Market** for some taste treats. Merchants are
there six days a week; on Thursday, Friday, and
Saturday Amish farmers bring in their produce
and homemade products. In this large enclosed
market, you can also have lunch while you listen to musicians.

Philadelphia has more extraordinary museums than you can visit in a day or two. Drive
out Benjamin Franklin Parkway to the **Franklin**

**Reading Terminal
Market
12th & Arch Streets
Philadelphia
215–922–2317**

**Franklin Institute
20th Street &
 Benjamin Franklin
 Parkway 19103
Philadelphia
215–564–3375;
215–448–1200, taped
 message**

**Please Touch Museum
 for Children
210 North 21st Street
Philadelphia 19103
215–963–0666**

**Academy of Natural
Sciences Museum
19th Street &
 Benjamin Franklin
 Parkway
Philadelphia 19103
215–299–1020**

Institute. Four floors await you and your comfortably shod feet. Don't miss the walk-through heart, which is an interesting sensation. Anything you can think of in the realm of science and technology is on display. Much of the museum is available for hands-on exploration. The **Fels Planetarium** features seasonal constellation shows among other programs.

One of the most charming museums we have seen is the **Please Touch Museum for Children.** Exhibits have been planned for children seven years of age and younger. If older children come along, they may spend time in an adjacent area working on computers. We were enchanted with the large elephant that greeted us at the top of the ramp. He is built with wire framework from a wooden base and is adorned with much-loved toys donated by hundreds of children. Every time they visit the museum, children can find and touch their favorite toys on the elephant. You and your child can interact with each other and the touchable exhibits as you progress from the rural area to the urban, the contemporary to the future. There are clothes to dress up in, dolls to play with, hopscotch and other street games to try, video presentations to look at, and live animals to watch. Children learn from their play, and there is more than enough here to keep them inspired and happy.

The **Academy of Natural Sciences Museum** welcomes you with a roaring dinosaur at the entrance. Don't miss "Outside-In," an outdoor exhibit indoors telescoped down to child's size. You can see a working beehive in a tree, safely enclosed in glass. You can crawl through a fossil cave to see the skull of a saber-toothed tiger. The saltwater aquarium has fish, and the salt marsh has miniature sand dunes. Have a look through a microscope at one of the creatures who live there.

Continue on out the Benjamin Franklin

PHILADELPHIA

The Mummers Parade on Market Street.

MORRISVILLE

Pennsbury Manor, the country home of William Penn.

NEW HOPE

A mule-pulled barge on the Delaware Canal.

Parkway to the **Fairmount Park** area. This is the largest landscaped park in the world. You can walk, jog, cycle, ride horseback, canoe, sail, play tennis, golf, swim, or see one of a number of performances. You also can take the Fairmount Park Trolley Bus (215–879–4044) to view a number of sights, if only fleetingly; **Horticulture Center and Arboretum, Japanese House and Garden, Fairmount Waterworks,** several eighteenth-century homes, and **Memorial Hall.**

**Philadelphia Zoo
34th Street & Girard
Avenue
Philadelphia 19104
215–243–1100**

Don't miss the **Philadelphia Zoo,** where more than 1,600 mammals, birds, and reptiles live. The highlight here is the Treehouse, where visitors can have the sensation of what it is like to be the animal. Look out through the eyes of a frog, hatch out of an egg in the Everglades Swamp, climb through a 35-foot-tall honeycomb to see what a bee's-eye view is like, and swing inside a cocoon. Don't forget to nudge Daisy, the 2,000-pound fiberglass dinosaur—she will roar for you. Ask for your magic ring so you can press yellow lights to make the action happen. You can also tour the park on the Safari Monorail.

Try to be in town on New Year's Day for the **Philadelphia Mummers Parade,** which is like nothing you've ever seen before. The parade brings out 20,000 costumed participants who march for twelve hours. The lead mummers begin their march at 7:45 a.m., so don't oversleep. The first parade was sponsored by the city in 1901; however, local ethnic groups had been celebrating at that time of year a long time before. Origins of these customs include the shooting of guns by Swedes and Finns; Mumming plays by the English and Welsh; the celebration of Belsnickle (similar to Santa Claus) by the Germans; the carnival of horns and other noisemakers; and the theme song, "Oh, Dem Golden Slippers," by Southern blacks. Marchers include clowns, string bands, and brass bands.

Many clubs make identical costumes for their members, some of them costing as much as several thousand dollars each. If you go, you may be drawn into the festivities along the route—or you can always watch it on television.

This is the end of the Philadelphia section. Now for a tour in the country.

≈ *Bucks County* ≈

A getaway to Bucks County will take you out of the city and into lush green rolling hills, past large farms with sleek horses and woods and meadows interlaced with many gushing creeks and meandering rivers. Peace and beauty abound in these 620 square miles.

For over 300 years Bucks County has been significant in American history. You can stand on the spot where William Penn built his summer mansion or where our colonial forebears settled as they arrived from England, Sweden, Ireland, Wales, Holland, Germany, and many other countries. This area was known to be a haven to those who had been persecuted for their religious beliefs. Several men who signed the Declaration of Independence lived in the county. During the Revolutionary War George Washington crossed the Delaware to surprise the British on the other side. The Delaware Canal played a major role in developing the commerce of the nineteenth century, by providing a more direct route for the transportation of goods. Later residents of the county have included Henry Chapman Mercer, Pearl Buck, James A. Michener, and Margaret Mead.

From Philadelphia take Route 13 to signs for Pennsbury Manor, magnificently situated on a bend of the Delaware River. (The manor's mailing address is Morrisville, but it is a distance from the town.) William Penn chose this location for his country home from the twenty-three–million acres granted to him for the state of Pennsylvania. Although the land had been given by King Charles II of England, Penn instructed William Markham, his secretary, to buy it from King Sepassing of the Delaware

PENNSBURY MANOR

**Pennsbury Manor
Visitors' Center
400 Pennsbury
Memorial Lane
Morrisville 19067
216–946–0400**

Indians. William Penn met with three tribes—the Lenni-Lenape, the Mingoes, and the Shawnees—to consummate this "Great Treaty of Friendship" in 1682.

James Harrison directed the construction of this English manor house for Penn, beginning in 1683. The next year, when the house had not yet been completed, Penn was forced to return to England to oppose challenges to his proprietorship of Pennsylvania. He carried on a detailed correspondence with Harrison as the latter finished the house, constructed outbuildings, and developed the gardens. Penn returned from England in 1699. The family, which included his second wife, Hannah; newborn son, John; and twenty-one-year-old daughter, Letitia, moved into Pennsbury Manor in the spring of 1700.

The house required a large staff to provide a smoothly run household, to tend the gardens, and to operate the entire plantation. Crops included corn, wheat, barley, vegetables, and fruits, and the plantation made its own cider and beer. Like the streets of Philadelphia and English formal gardens, Penn's gardens were laid out in a geometric pattern. He encouraged his gardeners to transplant native plants from the woods into the gardens; seeds, roots, and trees were also imported from England.

Although the original house was destroyed, all of the buildings are reconstructions based on records. Inside the house rooms are furnished with period furnishings, but only one armchair belonged to William Penn. The outbuildings include a bake-and-brew house, smokehouse, plantation office, icehouse, stable, and barge house. The Penns traveled between Pennsbury Manor and Philadelphia on their own 27-foot river barge—a five-hour trip with six oarsmen, a coxswain, and a boatswain. A replica of the English river barge is on display. A number of domestic animals live on the plantation, just as they would have in Penn's day, and horticulturists maintain seventeenth-century gardens and orchards. Picnic facilities are available near the visitors' center.

Head back to Route 13 and turn right; you will see signs for Fallsington, a village that has preserved 300 years of history—from log cabins to Victorian mansions. Some of them are inhabited by descendants of the first settlers. The **Burgess-Lippincott House** dates from 1780; its doorway is considered to be one of the most handsome in the county. Inside look for the matching parlor mantel and the second bannister on the stairway. The **Stage Coach Tavern** operated from the 1790s until the 1920s, when Prohibition forced it to close. The **Moon-Williamson House,** dating from 1685, is one of the oldest houses in Pennsylvania still on its original site. Two fieldstones on the **Schoolmaster's House** bear the date 1758. William Penn traveled from Pennsbury Manor to attend the **Friends Meeting House.** Stop in the visitors' center (215–295–6567) for a walking-tour map and the audiovisual presentation.

From Fallsington continue on Route 13 to Morrisville, where you will meet Route 32 as it begins to wind along the Delaware Canal.

FALLSINGTON

Historic Fallsington, Inc.
4 Yardley Avenue
Fallsington 19054
215–295–6567

Morrisville was the home of two signers of the Declaration of Independence, Robert Morris and George Clymer. The house they each owned, at different times is called **Summerseat.** It was built in the early 1770s by Thomas Barclay; George Washington slept here on December 8, 1776. Robert Morris bought it in 1791; George Clymer, in 1798. Each room in the mansion has a fireplace.

MORRISVILLE

Summerseat
Hillcrest & Legion Avenues
Morrisville 19067
215–295–7209

Continue on Route 32 to **Washington Crossing Historic Park,** which is in two sec-

WASHINGTON CROSSING

**Washington Crossing
  Historic Park
Route 32
Washington Crossing
18977
215–493–4076**

**McConkey's Ferry
Washington Crossing
  Historic Park
Washington Crossing
18977**

**Thompson's Mill
Washington Crossing
  Historic Park
Washington Crossing
18977**

tions. The first is **McConkey's Ferry;** the second is **Thompson's Mill.** During the winter of 1776, the campaigns of George Washington had not been successful; his men were near starvation, and many had deserted. He knew that a victory was needed more than ever before. Fortunately, Washington was experienced in handling riverboats; only the weather could defeat his daring plan to surprise the British at Trenton. If the river froze, all would be lost, for the ice would not be thick enough to support troops, horses, and heavy equipment. Meetings to prepare for the crossing were held in the **Keith House,** the **Merrick House,** and the **Thompson-Neeley House,** at the foot of Bowman's Hill.

On Christmas Day 1776 the password among the troops was "Victory or Death" as they prepared to advance into a dark, gray, ice-strewn river. As they walked toward the boats 200 yards north of McConkey's Ferry, men without adequate shoes left blood on the snow. They embarked at 6:00 p.m. to ensure that the six-hour crossing would be completed in the dark. The weather turned from snow to sleet, slowing their progress through the ice floes, but they made it! You can see the famous painting *Washington Crossing the Delaware,* by Emanuel Leutze, in the **Washington Crossing Memorial Building.** A nearby building, the **Durham Boat House,** has reproductions of eighteenth-century cargo boats and exhibits about transportation on the Delaware.

Across the Delaware
Will Carleton

The winter night is cold and drear,
  Along the river's sullen flow;
The cruel frost is camping here—

The air has living blades of snow.
Look! pushing from the icy strand,
With ensigns freezing in the air,
There sails a small but mighty band,
Across the dang'rous Delaware.

Oh, wherefore, soldiers, would you fight
The bayonets of a winter storm?
In truth it were a better night
For blazing fire and blankets warm!
We seek to trap a foreign foe,
Who fill themselves with stolen fare;
We carry freedom as we go
Across the storm-swept Delaware!

The night is full of lusty cheer
Within the Hessians' merry camp;
And faint and fainter on the ear
Doth fall the heedless sentry's tramp.
O hirelings, this new nation's rage
Is something 'tis not well to dare;
You are not fitten to engage
These men from o'er the Delaware!

A rush—a shout—a clarion call,
Salute the early morning's gray;
Now, roused invaders, yield or fall:
The refuge-land has won the day!
Soon shall the glorious news be hurled
Wherever men have wrongs to bear;
For freedom's torch illumes the world,
And God has crossed the Delaware!

Three and one-half miles up the road, you
will come to the Thompson's Mill section of the
park, which includes **Thompson Mill Barn,** a
restored eighteenth-century barn. **Thompson
Grist Mill** is now an operating mill, rebuilt in the
style of 1870. The Thompson-Neeley House dates
from 1702; a number of crucial meetings took
place there during the Revolution. **Bowman's
Tower** was constructed in 1930 on the site of the
Continental army's observation point.

David Library
Route 32
Washington Crossing
18977

Bucks County Tourist
  Commission
P.O. Box 912
Doylestown 18901
215–345–4552

NEW HOPE

New Hope Mule
  Barge
New Hope 18938
215–862–2842

You can have a picnic in one of the several picnic pavilions in the park or head back to the junction of Route 32 and Route 532 near the McConkey's Ferry section to have lunch in **The Blue Ram** (215–493–1262). If you are interested in seeing a collection of original Revolutionary War manuscripts, stop in the **David Library,** located 1 mile north of Washington Crossing.

As you head north again on Route 32, you will pass a covered bridge, one of thirteen remaining of the original thirty-six in the county. The **Van Sant Bridge** is 86 feet long and was built in 1875. It is sometimes called Beaver Dam Bridge. For a brochure on the other twelve bridges in Bucks County, contact the Bucks County Tourist Commission.

As you enter New Hope, you will see the barge landing on the towpath. Don't miss the one-hour trip on the canal that will take you past one garden after another, the homes and studios of local residents, and railroad tracks with a number of restored coaches from the days of railroad prosperity. The canal was built between 1827 and 1832 to support the coal industry; barges also carried limestone, grain, lumber, and a multitude of other goods. The bargemen told us that the canal was dug by hand. Apparently there was considerable feeling between the "canalers" and the towpath strollers elegantly dressed in hoop skirts and top hats, since some canalers took delight in throwing coal to knock off those tall top hats. Young boys at the tender age of eight or nine began training to act as guides for the mules that pulled the barges. Now the barges are pulled by two horses led by their guide. We were treated to musical selections on a dulcimer, "bones," and a mouth organ. "Haul those barges up and down, Haul them up and down" was the refrain from the Delaware Canal Song. "Whiskey for Breakfast" came from an

Irish folk song. As we leisurely drifted along, the fragrance of honeysuckle wafted over us; the sight of hemlock, sumac, and maples added spring-green color; and only ducks punctuated the stillness with their quacks to each other.

As you stroll around New Hope—a retreat for artists, writers, and visitors alike—you will have a choice of many shops and boutiques. The historic **Van Sant House,** dating from 1743, was damaged by British shelling in 1776. Grapeshot can still be seen in the attic walls. The **Parry Mansion** is a restored stone house that was built in 1784 by Benjamin Parry, a wealthy lumbermill owner. The New Hope Historical Society has furnished the rooms in different styles, including the 1775–1800 period; 1800–1825, or the American Empire period; Victorian; and turn-of-the-century period. Look for the progression from candles to oil lamps as you view the room.

If you are in New Hope in the evening, you may want to attend the **Bucks County Playhouse** (215–862–2041) or the **S. J. Gerenser Theater** (215–862–2432), which overlooks the river and serves continental cuisine in elegant style.

The New Hope area makes a convenient and pleasant base for side trips in Bucks County. Besides the accommodations in town, you will find quite a few on Route 32 north. You can be refreshed and pampered in the elegance of years gone by. (Some of these inns are listed in the Inns appendix.)

Go north from New Hope on Route 32 to **Ringing Rocks,** found near Narrowsville, which really do ring when hit with a rock or hammer. Visitors enjoy hiking and picnicking in a number of parks all along the Delaware. You can also take canoe, raft, or tube trips on this section of the river. If you are there during the

**Van Sant House
Mechanic Street
New Hope 18938**

**Parry Mansion
Main & Ferry Streets
New Hope 18938
215–862–5652**

**EXCURSION NORTH
OF NEW HOPE**

**Ringing Rocks
Route 32
Narrowsville**

spring, the white-water season will be in full swing. Five covered bridges are along this stretch or just inland.

**Ralph Stover
State Park
State Park Road &
Stump Road
Point Pleasant
215–982–5560**

The **Ralph Stover State Park** is located 2 miles north of Point Pleasant. If you are there during a period of high water, you can try canoeing, rubber-rafting, or tubing on Tohickon Creek in the park. The course is challenging, so closed-deck canoes are recommended. For a view of the horseshoe bend in the creek, head for the High Rocks section of the park. Hiking, fishing, and picnicking are available to visitors. You can also rent one of six cabins by the week; contact the park office because they are booked by a lottery system prior to the opening of the season.

**EXCURSION WEST OF
NEW HOPE**

From New Hope head west on Route 202 to visit the numerous antiques shops concentrated along this road. Lahaska is the site of several complexes of shops, boutiques, and restaurants. Don't miss **Peddler's Village** with its ducks quacking and splashing in a pond set into landscaped gardens. The **Cock 'n' Bull Restaurant** (215–794–7438) is a convenient place for lunch.

Continue on Route 202 to **Doylestown** to visit the "Mercer Mile," where you will find an

**Fonthill
Court Street
Doylestown 18901
215–348–9461**

unusual medieval castle named **Fonthill** built by Henry Chapman Mercer. Fonthill contains Mercer's collection of tiles, prints, and engravings. Next door is the **Moravian Pottery and Tile Works,** where you can watch tiles being made, see a slide presentation on all three Mercer sites, and browse in the gift shop, which has sconces, paperweights, hot plates, and tiles. In the summer Shakespearean plays are produced outdoors on the grounds. The **Mercer**

**Mercer Museum
Pine Street
Doylestown 18901
215–345–0210**

Museum features an extensive collection of early American tools and folk art. If you are there at the right time in the spring, you will be surrounded by blooming forsythia. The **"Folk**

Fest" held on the second weekend in May includes sheepshearing, folk dancing, wagon rides, woodcarving, folk art, tinsmithing, black-smithing, and other eighteenth-century crafts. Across the street is the recently opened **James A. Michener Arts Center,** which is located in the beautiful stone building that was the Bucks County Jail in the 1800s (215–340–9800).

Take Route 313 from Doylestown to **Dublin** and the home of Pearl S. Buck at **Green Hills Farm.** Her gravesite is on the left as you drive in. She lived in China from the age of three months, taught at Mankin University, married John Buck there, and had a child, Carol, before returning to the United States in 1935. This house was her home for many years with her growing number of children; she adopted Eurasian children, and her foundation still supports many children of mixed races. Pearl Buck received the Pulitzer Prize in 1932, the Nobel Prize in 1938, and the William Dean Howells Prize. The house is alive with memories of this intelligent, energetic, and caring woman. Look for her medals, the desk where she wrote some of her books, her exquisite ceremonial Chinese robes, interesting Chinese chests, and other furnishings, including Peking carpets. Among her books on display are *The Good Earth* and *This Proud Heart.* Outside the grounds and flagstone patios were colorful with hanging pink plants when we were there.

**Green Hills Farm
Dublin 18917
215–249–0100;
1–800–523–5328**

From this point you need to decide if you will return to Philadelphia via Newtown and Langhorne; drive north to Bethlehem via Routes 313, 212, and 412; or go north to the Delaware Water Gap and the Poconos. If you are going north, take Route 113 to Route 611 and I–80 north to Stroudsburg for more views along the Delaware River. For a faster trip to Stroudsburg, take Route 113 to Route 611 to Route 22 west to Route 33 north, to Route 209 east.

NEWTOWN AND LANGHORNE

**Sesame Place
Route 1
Langhorne 19047
215–767–1100**

For those heading back to Philadelphia, return to Doylestown and head south on Route 611. Or, you can take Route 423 south through Newtown, which contains a number of eighteenth- and nineteenth-century buildings, and then go on to Langhorne, the home of **Sesame Place.** This educational play-park, adjacent to Oxford Valley Mall, helps children explore the worlds of science and technology; there are a computer gallery and a variety of exhibits. Physical skills are developed by climbing, jumping, bouncing, and sliding activities. Bring a change of clothing for the water activities.

BETHLEHEM

Bethlehem was founded on December 24, 1741, when Count Nicholas Ludwig von Zinzendorf celebrated a communion service with a group of newly arrived Moravian settlers in their first house. Their Protestant religion began with Jan Hus during the fifteenth century in Czechoslovakia, and they came to America to spread the Gospel to the Indians. The Moravians brought their traditions with them; advent stars with twenty-six points beam from almost every front porch. Their music is a highlight, as it combines voice, organs, woodwinds, strings, and brasses; we attended a concert we will long remember.

Moravian community *putzes,* or miniature nativity scenes, are assembled by volunteers, who arrange the tiny wooden and ceramic figures, gather pine boughs, and crawl under the stage to install the lighting prior to the Christmas season. The *putzes* include both sound and light. Visitors enter a darkened and quiet room, waiting for the first spotlight to appear on a scene. Voices describe the nativity story, and one scene after another is illuminated. It is a moving experience.

Traditionally, on December 1 the city is suddenly illuminated on the north side with thousands of white lights on trees and on the south side with colored lights. An 81-foot-high star gleams from the top of South Mountain. Guides in Moravian dress lead tours through the historic district.

The Gemein Haus, which is the oldest building in town, was built in 1742 and held all 56 settlers. The original concept of the church was its communal plan—all worked for the church and lived in separate "choirs" according to sex and age. By 1700 this plan was not needed, as families chose to build their own homes. The Gemein Haus is now the **Moravian Museum.** Saal Hall, which was the original place of worship, is within the house; services were conducted two or three times every day. A 1530 Nuremberg Bible is on display there. The room that the count stayed in is there, complete with a brown leather chair and ornate black wrought-iron hinges on the door. Quilts, such as one made by "Christine," were made from scratch—the Moravians sheared the sheep, dyed the wool, carded it, and wove the cloth. The music room contains an old flute, trombones with their cases, and a serpentine-shaped wooden horn covered with leather with fish skin in between.

The **Old Chapel,** the second place of worship in Bethlehem, dates from 1751. Movable wooden benches provided flexibility for the congregation. An open Bible stands on a table. Indians were baptized there. Our guide explained the significance of ribbons on caps: Red was for little girls, burgundy for teens, pink for those confirmed, blue for married women, and white for widowed women. Women wore a gray jacket, gray skirt, gray woolen cloak, and white apron.

The **Central Church** was completed in 1806, and the Bell House clock was placed in the belfry in 1824. Private residences include the Sisters' House, dating from 1744, which is

**Moravian Museum
66 West Church Street
Bethlehem 18016
215–867–0173**

where single women lived and worked, and the Widows' House. The Brethren's House, dating from 1748, was where single men lived. Now it is part of Moravian College's music department.

JIM THORPE

**Carbon County
Tourist Promotion
Agency
Railroad Station
Jim Thorpe 18229
717–325–3673**

Jim Thorpe was named for an athlete who never lived there—the American hero of the 1912 Olympics in Stockholm. If you'd like to visit the town, take Route 78 to Route 9 to Route 209. In the early 1950s two towns, Mauch Chunk and East Mauch Chunk, decided to merge. Mrs. Patricia Thorpe heard about the merger and was impressed with the community spirit, as citizens donated 5 cents a week to the economic development fund. Because the state of Oklahoma, where Jim Thorpe was born, would not provide a memorial for him, she offered his name and his body to the merging towns. A granite mausoleum was built to honor Jim Thorpe. In fact, the name change has meant an economic upswing for this community and its citizens.

**Asa Packer Mansion
Jim Thorpe Lion's
Club
Jim Thorpe 18229
717–326–3229**

The **Asa Packer Mansion,** dating from 1861, contains the original furnishings as the Packer family left them. This Victorian Italianate home gives visitors a glimpse into life in the late 1800s. The library contains Mr. Packer's safe and a blue glass chandelier from the 1876 Centennial Exposition in Philadelphia. The parlor contains rose velvet draperies that were made for the Packers' fiftieth wedding anniversary. Don't miss the carved cameo glass turquoise vase that is worth $40,000. Two paintings by George Henry Boughton hang there; he also painted *First Thanksgiving.* A replica of the gasolier chandelier was used in the movie *Gone with the Wind.* Upstairs in the hallway stands a Welty Orchestrian—a Swiss roller organ, bought in 1903 for $500.

≈ *Delaware Water Gap* ≈ *and the Poconos*

The Middle Delaware River region, which stretches for 40 miles between Stroudsburg and Milford, Pennsylvania, is a recreational area for those who enjoy hiking, canoeing, swimming, photographing a series of views around each bend of the river, and exploring the many waterfalls on tributary streams along the way. Since the 1960s the government has been developing this area for recreation. The river runs through a narrow valley, with the Kittatinny Mountains on one side and the Poconos on the other, producing the gorge and natural beauty of rushing waters at Delaware Water Gap. The name Pocono may have been derived from the Indian *Pocohanne,* which means "A River between Mountains."

The region is close to both New York City and Philadelphia, so it's easily accessible for daytrips and getaway weekends. There's an abundance of resorts to suit any taste or style.

Begin your exploration of the area with a stop in the **Kittatinny Point Information Station,** located just off I–80 west of the southern end of the Gap. For an overview of the river both north and south, climb to the top of **Mount Minsi.** The trail begins from the parking lot of the information station.

DELAWARE WATER GAP

Bushkill Falls is located a few miles north of Stroudsburg. Be prepared to do some walking, unless you choose to stop at the lookout situated a short distance from the parking lot. The main Bushkill Falls cascades down 100 feet over a series of rocks. You can also hike for 1 mile up the **Bridal Veil Falls Trail,** which has several waterfalls to photograph. There are a number of bridges over Little Bushkill Creek and Pond Run Creek and at the juncture of the two creeks.

**Bushkill Falls
Route 209
Bushkill 18324
717–588–6682**

A Bushkill legend involves a Lenni-Lanape Indian maiden named Winona and a young Dutchman named Hendrick van Allen. The couple fell in love and spent their time canoeing on the Delaware and climbing the mountains for the views. Whether he told her the news that he had to return to Holland or one of their families would not approve of their marriage is open to conjecture; in any event, they were found at the bottom of a cliff beside the waterfall. **Winona Falls,** several miles away, now bears her name; it is no longer open to the public.

**Pocono
Environmental
Education Center
Route 209
Dingmans Ferry 18328
717–828–2319**

Continue north on Route 209 to signs for the **Pocono Environmental Education Center,** a regional study center. From the center Keystone Junior College and the National Park Service explore the 200,000 acres of public land stretching through forests, across fields, beside ponds and waterfalls, and along a fossil slope—both to study and preserve it. This residential center attracts groups of students, teachers, scouts, and members of other organizations for its workshops and family vacation camps.

Dingmans Falls is a preserve along a streambed run by the National Park Service. A twenty-minute walk will take you through a forest of hemlocks and rhododendrons to Silver Thread and Dingmans Waterfalls. This is an extremely pleasant area without any of the trappings of commercialization. The **Dingmans Falls Visitors' Center** focuses on the river, mountains, and area wildlife, such as black bears and bald eagles. Picnic facilities are available, and the park service offers a variety of trips all along the Delaware Water Gap.

**Dingmans Falls
Visitors' Center
Route 739
Dingmans Ferry 18328
717–828–7802**

If you're planning a vacation that includes canoeing on the Delaware, you may want to contact one of the following outfitters: **Adventure Tours** (Box 175, Marshalls Creek, Pennsylvania 18335; 717–223–0505); **Shawnee Canoe Trips** (Box 189, Shawnee-on-Delaware, Pennsylvania 18356; 800–SHAWNEE), or **Kittatinny Canoes** (Dingmans Ferry, Pennsylvania 18328; 717–828–2700).

Milford can be reached by heading north once more on Route 209. Mary Pickford and

Lillian Gish came to Milford to film *The Informer* in 1912. **Grey Towers** was originally built as a summer home for James W. Pinchot. This forty-room mansion in medieval style was designed by Richard Morris Hunt in 1886. Pinchot's son Gifford became governor of Pennsylvania and first chief of the U.S. Forest Service. The mansion is the home of the **Pinchot Institute for Conservation Studies.** Visitors may enjoy terraces, lawns, and hiking trails to nearby **Sawkill Falls.**

Grey Towers
Route 6
Milford 18337
717–296–6401

A number of state parks lie to the west of the Delaware Water Gap. From Stroudsburg scenic I–80 will take you to **Big Pocono State Park,** one of the highest points in the Poconos. From the elevation of 2,131 feet you can see the Catskills of New York on a clear day. Park facilities include picnicking, cross-country skiing, hiking, equestrian trails, and hunting.

POCONO MOUNTAINS

Big Pocono State Park
Box 173
Henryville 18332

Hickory Run State Park offers picnicking, swimming, a nature center, fishing, hiking, and camping. The area just north of Hickory Run contains a number of ski resorts, as does the area to the northeast surrounding Skytop. **Camelback Ski Area** (717–629–1661) is located in Tannersville. Take exit 45 from I–80. Camelback has a vertical drop of 800 feet. (Free ski reports for Camelback are available from Pennsylvania phones: 800–532–8201; from other states: 800–233–8100.)

Hickory Run
State Park
RD1, Box 81
White Haven 18661
717–443–9991

Intermediate skiers at Camelback can feel confident taking the Marc Antony chair (Lift 3) up the first time and skiing down Julius Caesar and Rappahannock Ramble. Take the same chair up again to try Marc Antony and Cleopatra. For variety try the Bailey Chair (Lift 6) and ski King Tut and the Meadows. Be leery of the Birches Trail, as people tend to bunch up at the crook of the arm and delay everyone. In the center of the mountain, Big Pocono is nice but ski it in the morning before it becomes crowded; it also tends to "bump up," as more skiers turn in the same places. Camelback is basically a great mountain for intermediates—even the black diamond trails are not horrendous.

Big Boulder Ski Area (717–722–0101) is located off exit 43 from I–80 in Lake Harmony. The vertical drop there is 475 feet. Big Boulder is a pleasant area consisting of a wealth of easy slopes leading up to a few black diamond runs on the left side looking up. Try the Edelweiss triple lift first and ski down Edelweiss; then take the Little Boulder lift to ski Little Boulder and the Tannenbaum lift to ski Tannebaum. Move to one of the three lifts bunched together: Merry Widow I, Merry Widow II, and Black Forest. From the top ski Merry Widow or take the outside road marked Bunny Schuss.

Jack Frost (717–443–8425) is located on Route 940, 4 miles east of the Pocono interchange of the N.E. Extension of the Pennsylvania Turnpike, near White Haven. Its vertical drop is 500 feet. Jack Frost divides itself into an experts' system on the right, looking down; intermediate slopes in the center; and beginner slopes on the left, going down halfway. For a warmup try Snow Flake, Powder Puff, or Frosty down to lifts marked Easy Way and Snow Ridge. The next run down try the same at the beginning and ski onto Easy River or Ridge Run. Take the lift marked Diversion up to the top. In the center of the mountain, DeMatte's Demise, Exhibition, Tobyhanna, and Lehigh all lead down to two lifts: Blaze and Counterpoint.

Shawnee Mountain (717–421–7231), near Shawnee-on-Delaware, is accessible from exit 52 from I–80. The vertical drop of Shawnee is 700 feet. **Tanglwood Ski Area** (717–226–9500) is 3 miles north of I–84. Take Route 390, then Route 507 and Route 6 to Paper Birch Mountain (Lake

Wallenpaupack, Box 56, Tafton, Pennsylvania 18464). Tanglwood's vertical drop is 415 feet.

I–80 and I–380 lead to **Tobyhanna State Park,** which offers picnicking, swimming, a historical center, fishing boat rental, boat launching and mooring, hiking, bicycling, and camping.

Near Tobyhanna State Park **The Sterling Inn** (South Sterling, Pennsylvania 18460; 717–676–3311 or toll-free from Connecticut, New York, New Jersey, Maryland, Delaware, and Washington, D.C., 800–523–8200) offers lunch and dinner in the cozy dining room. You may feel so much at home that you will want to stay overnight. (See Inns appendix.)

Perhaps you would like to head north from Stroudsburg. Take Route 447 along the Brodhead Creek past Canadensis and Route 390 past Skytop to **Promised Land State Park,** which offers picnicking, swimming, a nature center, fishing, boat rentals, boat launching and mooring, hiking, horseback riding, and camping.

Lake Wallenpaupack lies a few miles north of Promised Land; this man-made lake, 15 miles long, is a popular recreation area. During the summer visitors water-ski, sail, swim, scuba-dive, fish, play tennis or golf, and hike along marked trails at the Ledgedale and Shuman Point areas. Alpine and Nordic skiing are available during the winter.

Route 84 leads westward to Scranton, a city we had not visited until a couple of years ago; since then we have been back three times, with pleasure. In the 1840s four anthracite blast furnaces were built. Molten iron flowed from the furnaces into forms where they were cast into rectangular shapes called "pigs" and then formed into rails. The glowing furnaces lit the sky until 1902, when the company moved to Lake Erie. The **Scranton Iron Furnaces** can be visited in downtown Scranton.

Tobyhanna State Park
Box 387
Tobyhanna 18466
717–894–8336

Promised Land
State Park
RD1, Box 96
Greentown 18426
717–676–3428

SCRANTON

Scranton Iron
Furnaces
Between Lackawanna
Avenue & Moosic
Street
Scranton 18501
717–463–3208

**Steamtown National
Historic Site
150 South Washington
Avenue
Scranton 18503
717–961–2033**

Steamtown National Historic Site can be found a block west of the furnaces in the former Delaware, Lackawanna, and Western Railroad yards. Here's the place to see a great collection of locomotives and rolling stock. A park ranger will take you on a tour to see the Little Red Caboose, built in 1920; a 1926 baggage car that was once part of the Phoebe Snow train; a wrecking crane called Big Hook; and lots of locomotives.

Phoebe Snow was created by the DL&W Railroad as an advertising gimmick. Earlier, travel by train was dirty, as smokestacks spewed out soot. With the advent of anthracite, or hard coal, passengers were relieved to enjoy trips in comfort and cleanliness. Phoebe Snow wore a white gown, and ads portrayed her speaking in rhyme, such as "Says Phoebe Snow about to go, upon a trip to Buffalo, 'My gown stays white from morn to night upon the Road of Anthracite.'"

Visitors can take a short train ride within the yard or a three-hour trip from Scranton to Kingsley and back. Be sure to ask for the "hobo" handout before your trip so you can interpret the stick-figure signs used by real hobos.

**Pennsylvania
Anthracite Heritage
Museum
RD1,
Bald Mountain Road
(McDade Park)
Scranton 18501
717–963–4804;
717–963–4845**

The **Pennsylvania Anthracite Heritage Museum** offers displays on the lives of people living in this hard coal area. Visitors will see a collection of the tools used by the miners, displays of Indian lore and railroad transportation, and the textile mills where both women and children worked.

**Lackawanna Coal
Mine
Scranton 18501
717–963–MINE**

The **Lackawanna Coal Mine** is adjacent to the Heritage Museum. Visitors almost step inside a miner's boots as they get into a car for a ride down into the mine. The depth at the bottom where we got out was 250 feet; the temperature is about 50 degrees year-round, so wear a jacket. In the early days mules were taken down there, never to emerge into daylight, as their stables were at the bottom. Miners passed through levels after working as laborers for three years, taking a test, and finally receiving mining papers. The men spent every day drilling 8-foot-long holes, inserting dynamite, yelling "Fire" several times, setting off the blast, and removing the coal. Some of them had to work on their stomachs in areas a few feet high. As you walk through the mine, you'll see models of miners at work, wearing caps and looking grimy. One little boy with his donkey looked sad and vulnerable. Child labor laws were in fact initiated by experience in the mines. As we passed an open office door, the "fire boss" was relaxing with his feet on his desk. Startlingly, two hands waved at us from the ground. At the end of the tour, we each received a "miner's certificate."

The **Everhart Museum** contains collections of nineteenth- and twentieth-century American art, folk art, Dorflinger glass, European art, Native American art, and science displays. A new "dinosaur hall" houses a 20-foot skeleton of a stegosaurus; a tyrannosaurus head is also there. The Environmental Gallery contains exhibits on acid rain, animal species that are now extinct, and a chronology of disasters such as the *Exxon Valdez* oil spill. The Spitz Planetarium is the oldest in the United States, and programs are given. Don't miss the beehive in the basement—you can watch the queen bee and all of her workers at work.

Everhart Museum
Nay Aug Park
Scranton 18501
717–346–8370

Montage Ski and Summer Recreation Area (800–847–7669 or, in Pennsylvania, 800–468–7669) is located just outside of Scranton on Montage Mountain Road. The area offers skiing in the winter and both waterslides and an alpine slide in the summer. The adjacent stadium is very popular for sports events much of the year.

Continuing our research for the intermediate skier, we recommend beginning on the

triple chair E, marked "Shuttle." Ski both
Mainline and Highball, which are both well
groomed and easy. Triple chair C, "Iron Horse,"
leads to six trails (Upper Fast Track, Upper
Runaway, Whistler, Switch, Spur, and Spike),
with crossovers in between most of them.

Elk Mountain (800–233–4131) is located
on Route 374 off of I–81. Intermediates will
enjoy taking Middle chair D for a warmup on
East and West slopes. Then try East chair B to
the top and take Tioga around the west side; it
leads back into East and West slopes. Take chair
B again and ski Tioga to Lenape, which is intermediate. On another run try Tioga to Lower
Tunkhannock, which is under the lift. Moosic
and Schuylkill are other options from Tioga.

This is the end of Itinerary G. You can
head northeast toward the Hudson Valley on
I–84, drive east toward New York City on I–80,
or return to Philadelphia on the N.E. Extension
of the Pennsylvania Turnpike.

ITINERARY H:

Delaware

Zwaanendael Museum, Lewes

ITINERARY H

Wilmington ▲

New Castle ▲

Odessa ▲

13

NEW JERSEY

Dover ▲

113

13

113

1

▲ Lewes
▲ Cape Henlopen State Park
▲ Rehoboth Beach

Delaware

This itinerary features Delaware. It links with Itinerary F (South-Central Pennsylvania) in the upper Brandywine Valley, with Itinerary G (Eastern Pennsylvania) in Bucks County, and with Itinerary I (New Jersey) along the Atlantic Ocean coastline.

≈ *Delaware* ≈

We begin our tour of Delaware in Wilmington, in the Brandywine Valley, then head south to Dover, Lewes, and Rehoboth Beach.

WILMINGTON

The New Sweden Company founded Wilmington as Fort Christina in 1638; the name was changed by Quakers who developed the town a hundred years later. The **Fort Christina Monument** stands where Peter Minuit landed after his voyage from Sweden; the sculptor was none other than Carl Milles from Stockholm. **Holy Trinity Church,** sometimes called Old Swedes Church, is the oldest active Protestant church in North America. The building dates from 1698 and is still in use. Adjacent to the church is **Hendrickson House,** dating from 1690, which contains a museum containing seventeenth- and eighteenth-century exhibits.

Holy Trinity Church
606 Church Street
Wilmington 19899
302–652–5629

Brandywine Park follows the river between the Augustine and Market Street bridges. Frederick Law Olmsted designed the park; one of its highlights is the garden with 188 Japanese cherry trees. The zoo in the park has Siberian tigers, monkeys, lions, bears, and a number of other animals.

Delaware Art Museum
2301 Kentmere
 Parkway
Wilmington 19899
302–571–9590

The **Delaware Art Museum** accents American art from the past 150 years. The Bancroft collection displays English Pre-Raphaelite paintings created by artists in the late nineteenth century. There are paintings by Howard Pyle, known as the father of the Brandywine School of painting, who immortalized legendary heroes like King Arthur, Sinbad, and Robin Hood. The museum also highlights the Phelps collection of Andrew Wyeth's paintings.

The Historical Society of Delaware operates the **Old Town Hall.** You can't miss the 9-foot statue of George Washington on the first floor. Exhibits include Delaware silver, period furnishings, a special children's room with a dollhouse and toys, a restored jail, and Revolutionary and Civil War artifacts.

For a special night out after touring downtown Wilmington, try **Sal's Place** (Lincoln Street at 6th Street; 302–652–1200), a culinary treasure hidden behind an unpretentious facade.

Nearby the **Delaware Museum of Natural History** has one of the most extensive shell collections in the country, thanks to the late John E. Du Pont. Du Pont, a naturalist, had collected shells for many years. The museum also leads you across Australia's Great Barrier Reef, a reconstruction placed under glass that you walk over. The Hall of Birds represents some extinct species, other exotic birds, and their eggs, including the large bird egg—that of the Elephant Bird, which weighs in at twenty-seven pounds.

The **Rockwood Museum** (610 Shipley Road, Wilmington; 302–761–4340) is housed on a nineteenth-century estate. Exhibits feature American, English, and continental decorative arts from the 1600s to the 1800s.

Winterthur Museum and Gardens, one of the most remarkable museum complexes we have ever visited, emphasizes the decorative arts made or used in America between 1650 and 1850. This massive and comprehensive collection of furniture, silver, paintings, textiles, and art objects is displayed in a series of period rooms. The gardens and arboretum extend their textured beauty over 200 acres; a tram ride with narration is a good way to get an overview of

The Historical Society of Delaware
515 Market Street Mall
Wilmington 19899
302–655–7161

Delaware Museum of Natural History
Route 52
Greenville 19807
302–658–9111

Winterthur Museum and Gardens
Route 52
Wilmington 19899
302–888–4600;
800–448–3883,
out-of-state

them. Visitors need to make reservations for some of the longer tours within the house, but others are available without reservations.

Winterthur took its name from the Swiss city of Winterthur, home of James Antoine Bidermann. In 1816 Evelina Gabrielle Du Pont married Bidermann, and in 1837 they bought 450 acres north of Wilmington and built their home. Their son, James Irénée Bidermann, inherited the estate but lived in France; his uncle, Henry Du Pont, bought the property in 1867.

The Bidermanns' great-nephew, Henry Francis Du Pont, was the moving force behind the further development of the mansion to house his growing collection. He started with the purchase of a Pennsylvania-made chest dated 1737, studied and learned about American crafts at a time when little research had been done, and continued collecting. He also became interested in the decorative art objects found in early American homes. His collection expanded to include textiles, needlework, ceramics, glassware, metalwork, paintings, prints, books, and newspapers. Further, he collected interior woodwork, paneling, fireplace walls, and doors from houses built between 1640 and 1840. Interiors from houses all along the Eastern seaboard were dismantled and reassembled in his mansion. A newspaper reporter once asked Du Pont who his collection agent was and received the reply "You're looking at him." Du Pont gave his estate to the Winterthur Corporation in 1951, and the museum opened later that year.

The Montmorenci Stair Hall is one of the most striking exhibits in the museum. This free-hanging staircase flows upward in a graceful curve; it was removed from a North Carolina house and dates from 1822. The Commons Room from the Red Lion Inn is decorated with clay-pipe holders and political posters of the nineteenth century and has the decor of a taproom for men only. The Du Pont Dining Room displays Federal furniture grouped around a mahogany dining table with an inlaid eagle in its center. The table is set with porcelain dessert dishes, including *glacières* to keep ice cream cold. On the sideboard are silver tankards designed by Paul Revere. Visitors can see almost 200 different room settings within the museum, all furnished with period pieces.

Henry Francis Du Pont was known as the "Head Gardener" because of his zealous interest in developing the gardens. He created pleasing combinations of color and texture, often moving large trees several times until they were just right. Du Pont's goal was to provide a different view for every turn of one's head, and he achieved it. Displays for all seasons alternate throughout the gardens. Spring is especially colorful, with daffodils and spring bulbs blooming all along March Walk and five acres of azaleas, rhododendrons, and woodland flowers. Most of the azaleas came from cuttings of the original plants Du Pont bought in 1917. These plants had formed an exhibit, with many others, of Kurume Azaleas at San Francisco's Panama-Pacific Exposition in 1915; a nursery on Long Island purchased the entire exhibit and sold Du Pont seventeen plants that it could not use. Visitors can take a tram around the gardens or walk to have more time to enjoy the fragrance and take photographs. Look for the large sycamore tree that had an unusual type of surgery. A tree surgeon split it down the back, took out diseased tissue, filled it with bricks and rubble, and replaced the flap. If you walk around to the back, you can see the bricks.

The Winterthur shops and galleries sell an impressive line of Winterthur reproductions, including furniture, textiles, wall-coverings, silver, pewter, porcelain, glass, clocks, brass, and carpets.

Many special events are scheduled at Winterthur throughout the year. The Point-to-Point horse race takes place in May, when jockeys ride four 3-mile steeplechase races over post-and-rail fences. In December Yuletide decorations culminate in an 18-foot-tall Christmas tree. You can enroll in graduate programs in Early American Culture, Conservation of Artistic and Historic Objects, or the History of American Civilization through the University of Delaware.

Hagley Museum
Route 141
Wilmington 19899
302–658–2400

The **Hagley Museum** is a 230-acre complex on the Brandywine River. Originally the site of the E. I. Du Pont black powder works, the museum was developed in 1952 to portray American industrial growth during the eighteenth and nineteenth centuries. To get an overview of the site, stop in the museum first for background on the development of the valley; dioramas, films, and exhibits provide clear explanations of both the technological and economic aspects of the industries clustered along the river. Power from the Brandywine River enabled men to build a variety of mills. One exhibit shows a gristmill and the step-by-step process of grinding grain and producing flour. A Delaware engineer and millwright, Oliver Evans, used waterpower to mechanize the milling process. The hydraulic turbine replaced the waterwheel by the middle of the nineteenth century. Industry grew in the area as cotton mills and tanneries were built. At this stage of industrial development, you could tell what a man did by looking at his hands: The man who worked on stone wheels in the mill had little chips of stone embedded in his hands; the man who tanned leather had brown hands from the tannin in the leather; the man who worked in an office had smooth hands; and the farmer had hands full of calluses.

In 1802 Eleuthère Irénée Du Pont bought land in the area. He constructed a powder yard at Hagley because two necessary ingredients were there: water and willow trees to make charcoal. He built his home, named Eleutherian Mills, on the hill above the powder mill at Hagley; with a speaking trumpet he could direct the operation of the mill from his balcony. On the second floor of the museum is a statue of Don Pedro, the prize ram purchased by Irénée Du Pont in 1805. Wool was an important commodity for mill owners, and Don Pedro sired enough lambs to become well known. Thomas Jefferson sent a letter of condolence when Don Pedro died in 1811. His image is also on the weathervane on the roof of the museum.

As the country expanded the need for powder grew, and the Du Pont Company became the largest in America. Immigrants who had been starving in Ireland came to work in the mill. They worked six hours a day, seven days a week, with two holidays a year: Christmas and the Fourth of July. When there was an explosion at the mill, anyone in the area lost his life. Sometimes the bodies were blown across the river; the expression "across the creek" came to mean that someone had died. Du Pont and his family took a risk in building their home so close to the mill. There were explosions that damaged the house, and his son Alexis was killed in one of the explosions. But Du Pont's motto was "safety first," and he felt that there were fewer explosions because he lived on the site.

You can take a bus along the river or walk with a map in hand. Although the area looks like a park today, it was once a busy, dirty industrial site. The workers lived up the hill; archaeological digs in process at this writing are recovering artifacts that will reveal the everyday lives of these families. You can visit the **Gibbons-Stewart House,** which has been restored to represent the home of a foreman and his family; stop for lemonade and Mrs. Gibbons's cookies. **The Brandywine Manufacturers' Sunday School, Stable,** and **Springhouse** are all open to the public. The **Hagley Yard** itself is a series of reconstructed shops and mills strung along the river, each one demonstrating part of the carefully controlled manufacturing process needed to make a substance as volatile as gunpowder. The yard consists of the Millwright Shop, New Century Power House, Steam Plant, Eagle Roll Mill, Graining Mill, Birkenhead Mills, and Engine House.

The family house, Eleutherian Mills, contains furnishings that belonged to the family. Du Pont's great-granddaughter, Louise Du Pont Crowninshield, was the last person to live in the house. The first floor remains much as she left it when she died in 1958. The artist who created the murals on the dining room walls had not been to America; he knew that Indians wore feathers on their heads, so he gave them peacock feathers. Follow the elliptical staircase up to the second floor, where there is an original Rembrandt in the Blue Room. The family used armoires because closets were taxed as rooms when the house was built at the beginning of the nineteenth century. Look for the collection of children's toys in the nursery; on Sunday children were allowed to play with the Noah's Ark but no other toys. The library contains a collection of furnishings from China and India. Because Irénée was in charge of the Crystal Palace Exhibit for the World's Fair, he went to the Orient at that time and brought back a Cantonese table with marble inlay and a hand-carved Indian chair so intricate it might have taken a man his entire life to carve.

On the grounds outside the main house, the **Old Stone Office** served as a company office. Inside look at the old typewriter, with gold-leaf decoration; it even has characters on a cylinder like modern typewriter print wheels. The garden has espaliered apple trees in a diamond shape and pear trees shaped into cones like those on a pine tree. Eight parterres on the inside contain flowers and vegetables; companion planting was used to ward off bugs. A compost pile grew huge pumpkins, some weighing over one hundred pounds. Deer, woodchuck, and rabbits still frequent the garden. A Conestoga wagon is on display.

Nearby **Nemours Mansion and Gardens** is a 102-room Louis XVI chateau on the estate of Alfred I. Du Pont. The name was taken from the Du Pont ancestral home of the same name in France. The mansion was designed by Carrere and Hastings of New York. It contains furnishings, tapestries, and paintings dating back to the fifteenth century. The gardens, developed from Du Pont's travels in Europe, were based on French models. You must call ahead to make a reservation to see Nemours.

Route 141 or Route 9 will take you to New Castle.

Nemours Mansion and Gardens
Route 141
Wilmington 19899
302-651-6912

Fort Casimir was the first name for this attractive town, then New Amstel, and finally New Castle. The **Green,** laid out by Peter Stuyvesant in 1655 during the years when it was called Fort Casimir, is still there; weekly markets and "great fairs" were held on it. Restored buildings lining the sides of the Green include the **Old Court House,** the **Town Hall,** and the **Old Dutch House.** You will find signs all over town telling you what happened where. In **Packet Alley,** for example, you can read the following: "Packet boats from Philadelphia met stagecoaches here for Maryland, the chief line of communication from the north to Baltimore and the south. Andrew Jackson, Daniel Webster, Henry Clay, David Crockett, Lord Ashburton, Louis Napoleon, Stonewall Jackson, Sam

NEW CASTLE

Old Court House
Delaware Avenue
New Castle 19720
302-323-4453

Old Dutch House
Third Street
New Castle 19720
302-322-9168

Houston, and Indians led by Osceola and Blackhawk en route to visit the Great Father in Washington all passed this way."

As you stroll around these streets, you will see window boxes filled with impatiens, heavy door knockers, painted shutters and doors, and a variety of iron fences. Another sign tells you that the site is the "Landing Place of William Penn. Near here Oct. 27, 1682 William Penn first stepped on American soil. He proceeded to the fort, performed livery of seisen [the act of taking legal possession of property], he took the key thereof. We did deliver unto him one turf with a twig upon it, a porringer with river water and soil in part of all."

George Read II House
42 The Strand
New Castle 19720
302–322–8411

The **George Read II House** is a Georgian house overlooking the Delaware River. The house was built between 1797 and 1804 by the son of a signer of the Declaration of Independence. Read wrote to his brother in 1802: "I have very nearly finished my new building which considering the magnitude of the undertaking is a very gratifying circumstance." The house has elaborately carved woodwork, gilded fanlights, and silver door hardware. Three rooms are preserved in the Colonial Revival style of the 1930s. The garden surrounding the house was developed in 1847 from the design of Andrew Jackson Downing.

Route 9 and Route 13 will take you to Odessa.

ODESSA

Odessa has a historic district of restored and preserved eighteenth- and nineteenth-century homes. During the early nineteenth century, grain was shipped from this port. The name of the town came from the Ukrainian seaport Odessa, which also exported wheat. Up until 1855 the town had been called Cantwell's Bridge.

Winterthur Museum owns and operates two historical houses and the Brick Hotel Gallery.

The **Corbit-Sharp House** was built by William Corbit, a Quaker tanner, in 1774. Some of the furnishings still in the house belonged to the Corbit family; others were made by local Delaware craftsmen. The **Wilson-Warner House** was owned by David Wilson, who was a local merchant and the brother-in-law of William Corbit. The house is furnished as it was when Wilson's son sold it in the early nineteenth century. The **Brick Hotel Gallery** contains the Belter collection of American-Victorian furniture.

From Odessa take Route 299 and Route 9 to Bombay Hook.

Bombay Hook began its recorded history in 1679 with the sale of marshland to Peter Bayard by Mechacksett, chief of the Kahansink Indians. The refuge totals 15,122 acres of predominantly brackish tidal marsh. The rest of the area comprises freshwater pools, agricultural land, and swamp. Migrating and wintering ducks, geese, and the bald eagle live there; the tidal marsh provides them with a natural habitat and plenty of available food. Ornithological groups take field trips into the refuge, where more than 300 species have been sighted. You may also see whitetail deer, red and gray fox, river otter, muskrat, Virginia opossum, eastern gray squirrel, woodchuck, and beaver. The refuge has observation towers, nature trails, and an information center.

Route 9 and Route 13 will take you to the **Delaware Agricultural Museum,** near the junction of Route 13 and alternate Route 13. This museum displays agricultural artifacts from the early settlements in Delaware to the mid-1940s. The collection of horse-drawn equipment is housed in a large hall. Buildings include a gristmill and sawmill, blacksmith, and wheelwright shop.

Continue on Route 13 into Dover.

Historic Houses of Odessa
Main Street
Odessa 19730
302-378-2681

Brick Hotel Gallery
Main Street
Odessa 19730
302-378-4027

BOMBAY HOOK NATIONAL WILDLIFE REFUGE

Bombay Hook National Wildlife Refuge Information Center
Route 9
Smyrna 19977
302-653-6872

Delaware Agricultural Museum
866 North Du Pont Highway
Dover 19901
302-734-1618

DOVER

Dover Visitors' Center
Federal and Court
  Streets
Dover 19901
302–739–4266

Hall of Records
Legislative Avenue
Dover 19901
302–736–5314

State Museum
316 South Governor's
  Avenue
Dover 19901
302–735–4266

Dover was originally proclaimed the seat of Kent County in 1683 by William Penn. It became the state capital after the British captured New Castle in 1777. Take Route 13 and Route 113, turn west at the Court Street traffic light, and bear right at Legislative Hall onto Duke of York Street. At the end of Duke of York Street, turn left on Federal Street and follow signs to the parking lot at the **Dover Visitors' Center.** You will see the **Green,** laid out by William Penn, where a portrait of King George III was burned after the ratification of the Declaration of Independence. (Delaware has the honor of having been the first state to ratify the U.S. Constitution in Dover, on December 7, 1787.) Also on the Green stood "Red Hannah," the last whipping post to be used in the United States, which was used until 1952. Look at the eighteenth- and nineteenth-century homes around the Green and north and south of State Street.

Delaware's **State House,** located on the Green next to the visitors' center, is the second-oldest seat of government in continuous use in the United States. The building was restored in 1976 for Delaware's Bicentennial celebration; it contains a courtroom, a ceremonial Governor's Office, legislative chambers, and county offices. Look in the Senate Chamber for the large portrait of George Washington, commissioned in 1802. The State House remains the symbolic capitol of Delaware, although the General Assembly meets in Legislative Hall. The **Hall of Records** (adjacent to Legislative Hall) houses important documents, including the original Royal Grant from King Charles II.

Delaware's **State Museum,** 1 block west of the Green, is composed of two buildings, including the Meeting House Gallery in a 1790 Presbyterian Church. An 1880 gallery next door houses shops and crafts exhibits depicting

Delaware around 1900. Annie Jump Cannon, who became a famous astronomer, is the subject of one of the changing displays in the museum. She began her career looking at the stars from the roof of her home, and later she created a special prismatic type of telescopic photography. During the first part of the twentieth century, she worked at the Harvard Observatory, classifying more than 400,000 stars. She was also the first woman to receive an honorary degree from Oxford.

Drive south on Route 113 to Kitts-Hummock Road and turn east to reach the **John Dickinson Mansion.** John Dickinson, sometimes called the "Penman of the Revolution," was a prolific writer for the colonists. It has been reported that he drafted the Articles of Confederation in 1778. This restored colonial home from Dickinson's boyhood contains furnishings of the period and a formal English garden.

John Dickinson Mansion
Kitts-Hummock Road
Dover 19901
302-736-4266

Continue south on Route 113 to Route 120; then drive northeast 6 miles to South Bowers Beach. This area is interesting because of uncovered artifacts revealing the settlements of prehistoric Indians who lived there during the eighth century. In 1928 workmen building a road unearthed human bones, presumably Indian, and reburied them in nail kegs. The **Island Field Archaeological Museum and Research Center** has displays portraying the culture of these early inhabitants.

Route 113 and Route 1 will take you to Lewes.

SOUTH BOWERS BEACH

Island Field Archaeological Museum and Research Center
South Bowers Beach
302-335-5395

Lewes dates back to Henry Hudson's discovery of Delaware Bay in 1609 and the subsequent settlement of a whaling colony on Lewes Creek in 1631. The unlucky colonists were murdered by the Indians, but more settlers arrived

LEWES

in 1659. Lewes led a maritime existence through its involvement with shipwrecks, pirates, and privateers during the Revolution and the War of 1812. Lewes was raided several times by pirates. In 1698 fifty men led by a French pirate plundered every house in Lewes and escaped with their booty. In 1708 pirates burned. and sank three vessels off Cape Henlopen within four days, causing William Penn's secretary to write, "The coast begins to be intolerably infested." In 1709 another French pirate made off with loot from the town. Later the government built the Delaware Breakwater and the Harbor of Refuge for ships to anchor in. Lewes prospered as a port with fish coming in and farm produce going out until the advent of the dual highway rolling down the center of Delaware. Today Lewes is the site of the **College of Marine Studies of the University of Delaware.**

The **Lewes Historical Complex** (212 West 4th Street; 302–645–8073) contains a group of restored buildings that have been moved into the area. The **Cannonball House Marine Museum** dates back to 1797. It was struck by a cannonball when the British bombarded Lewes in April of 1813. The **Early Plant House,** furnished as a settler's cabin, is probably the oldest building in the complex. The **Burton-Ingram House,** dating from 1789, is furnished with Chippendale and Empire antiques. Don't miss the **Thompson Country Store,** which was managed by the Thompson family from 1888 to 1962.

Zwaanendael Museum
Kings Highway &
 Savannah Road
Lewes 19958
302–645–9418

Zwaanendael Museum looks as if it had been transplanted from Holland. In fact, the building is a replica of the town hall in Hoorn, Holland. It was constructed in 1931 to commemorate the 300th anniversary of the first settlement in Delaware. Exhibits include a 1625 logbook, written by Robert Jewett, describing the bay as seen from the deck of Henry Hudson's *Half*

Moon. An exhibit entitled "Great Guns at Night" refers to April 6, 1813, when the British began a long-range bombardment of Lewes because the people refused to supply the fleet with food and water. Hannah Wolfe Burton wrote that she began to hear many great guns at night until bedtime and on Wednesday "30 before breakfast, 15 while we were eating."

Other displays deal with more peaceful aspects of the town's history. The lighthouse built in the 1760s was made of granite and stood almost 70 feet tall; on April 23, 1926, it toppled into the sea. Look for the "merman" in a glass case, with the head and arms of a monkey and the tail of a fish. Such stuffed animals were known as devil fish; in the nineteenth century making monsters was a common prank. Upstairs there are collections of coverlets, samplers, china, silver, models, dolls, doll cradles, accordions, puzzles, and a Dutch costume from Marken, Holland.

The **Lewes Chamber of Commerce** has written a walking-tour guide complete with a map. This is a pleasant town to stroll through. Stop for lunch or dinner at **Fisherman's Wharf Lighthouse Restaurant** (by the drawbridge; 302–645–6271).

Lewes Chamber of Commerce
Fisher Martin House
Kings Highway &
Savannah Road
Lewes 19958
302–645–8073

The **Lightship** *Overfalls* is on display at a wharf on Pilottown Road. The U.S. Coast Guard gave her to the Lewes Historical Society in 1973; she was one of the last lightships functioning on the East Coast. Drive on another mile on Pilottown Road to see the **deVries Monument and Fort Site,** which was the 1631 settlement of the whaling colony of Zwaanendael. The monument is placed on the site of the north bastion of the fort.

One mile east of Lewes is Cape Henlopen. It has always been a crucial landmark for sailors and other seamen. Once you've made it around

CAPE
HENLOPEN

this low sand spit into Delaware Bay, you're home free. Although the stretch of beach from Cape Henlopen to the Maryland border is only 25 miles long, it was littered with more than 200 shipwrecks during the early years of our country. Pirate activity was also rampant, and stamped silver bars from their hauls are still found by those who seek the best "coin beaches" in the country.

Legends abound about the *deBraak,* which foundered in 1798. In 1797 this ship was sent as an escort from Plymouth, England, to America and thence from the Delaware River to the Chesapeake. During a period of stormy weather, she and her crew became separated from the rest of the convoy, spotted a sloop that they could easily seize, and brought its cargo of cacao and copper ingots on board. The vessel finally arrived off Cape Henlopen; a sudden squall capsized her and she sank about 1 mile off Cape Henlopen light. The British Admiralty authorities in Philadelphia tried to salvage her, unsuccessfully. Yet her masts still showed above water, and everyone knew of the treasure she carried. She was retrieved in 1986.

In 1785 the *Faithful Steward* left Londonderry, Ireland, for Philadelphia. She carried 249 passengers, goods in her hold, and a large consignment of copper coins. When she went aground, her mainmast was cut away to lighten her. She got free but was unable to beat against a rising wind and gain sea room. She went aground again 10 miles south of Cape Henlopen, totally helpless in the huge seas of what may have been a hurricane. Residents of Lewes were not able to reach her and watched lifeboats coming ashore empty because there was no way to get passengers into them. Eventually the ship broke up, and four out of every five persons on board drowned. Coins from her cargo began washing up one hundred years later, no doubt adding to coins from other shipwrecks in the past. The **Delaware Coin Beach** is located just north of the Indian River Inlet. More coins have been found there over the years than anywhere else in the country. The U.S. Coast Guard searched the beach in this area after every storm in the 1930s and retrieved buckets of coins. Even a treasure chest reportedly 3 feet square and weighing 400 pounds surfaced, but it never reappeared.

Cape Henlopen State Park is a sandy peninsula with a 4-mile beach and crashing Atlantic waves. An 80-foot sand dune, the highest between Cape Hatteras and Cape Cod, rises above the beach. The park offers nature trails, crabbing, fishing, swimming, picnicking, tennis, basketball, softball, and camping.

Delaware Coin Beach
Delaware Seashore
 State Park
Cape Henlopen

Cape Henlopen
 State Park
Cape Henlopen
302–645–8983

Have you ever had the chance to look over your toes at the beach while floating peacefully a few yards offshore? Try Rehoboth Beach early in the morning when the boardwalk shops and arcades are closed. Unless you get up very early indeed, you won't be alone. Seagulls lay first claim to the beach as they stalk around looking for tidbits left over from the day before. While we surveyed the beach from our endlessly rocking cradle, larger birds located a couple of crabs washed in on a wave. Several men were walking back and forth with metal detectors—finding money, watches, and rings. The beach had already been cleaned by trucks dragging a rotating sweeper making neat rows of furrows that could soon disappear. Two fishermen with long poles stuck in the sand were hoping for a strike by a passing snapping blue or sand shark. Joggers, cyclists, and walkers made their way down the boardwalk, and seashell collectors walked barefoot in the white sand by the water's edge. A catamaran was tilted on one hull waiting for its owner. We were

REHOBOTH BEACH

Rehoboth
 Beach–Dewey Beach
 Chamber of
 Commerce
Rehoboth Beach
19971
800–441–1329

the only swimmers, floating peacefully watching the town awaken. Vacationers would soon fill the beach with their umbrellas, lunch coolers, beach towels, and thongs. After our swim we climbed the steps to the boardwalk, found a faucet to wash the sand from our feet, put on our thongs, and headed up to breakfast with the feeling that we had begun this day right.

If you are a beach person, Rehoboth is a fine place to come—the white sand is free of stones and stretches for miles. There is one shop after another to explore, and arcades offer more diversion. The ambience of the boardwalk is low-keyed and pleasant for a family-oriented beach holiday.

But if you can't stand any sight of beach "civilization," head south for the more isolated beach of **Delaware Seashore State Park.** This narrow strip between ocean and bay provides miles of pristine beach, and you can camp there as well. The park offers a marina with docks and hookups. Another park awaits you close to the southern border of Delaware—**Fenwick Island State Park**—just before the high-rises of Ocean City, Maryland, bring the city back to the sea with a vengeance.

From this point you can proceed to Ocean City, Maryland, to link up with Itinerary I, or you can continue on to New Jersey. If you are going on to New Jersey, return to Lewes to take the Cape May/Lewes Ferry (follow the signs to the ferry) for a seventy-minute crossing of Delaware Bay. (For ferry information, call 302–645–6313 from Delaware; 609–886–2718 for New Jersey.)

ITINERARY I:

New Jersey

Cape May

ITINERARY I

Princeton ▲

95

571

195

9

Toms River ▲

37

9

Pine Barrens ▲
Island Beach State Park ▲

Barnegat Light ▲

72

Wharton State Forest ▲

Batso ▲

New Gretna ▲

542

Long
Beach
Island

Smithville ▲

Holgate

9

Edwin B. Forsythe
Nat. Wildlife Refuge

295

ATLANTIC CITY EXPRESSWAY

Atlantic City

Margate City

Ocean City

GARDEN STATE PARKWAY

Stone Harbor ▲

Cold Spring ▲

Wildwoods ▲

Cape May ▲

DELAWARE

New Jersey

This itinerary through New Jersey links with itinerary H (Delaware) and itineraries J (Maryland) and K (Washington, D.C. and Virginia) along the Atlantic Coast.

≈ *New Jersey* ≈

Although some people think of New Jersey in terms of the megalopolis viewed from the New Jersey Turnpike, there is another, quiet side consisting of beaches, lakes, streams, pinelands, and marshes. The Appalachian Trail goes through the state. New Jersey is surrounded by water except for the border it shares with New York. Vacationers enjoy the Delaware River, Hudson River, and the barrier beaches along the Atlantic Coast.

Historically New Jersey is packed with reminders of her past dating from Henry Hudson's appearance in 1609. The Continental army crossed the state four times during the Revolutionary War.

For the purposes of this itinerary, we will begin in Cape May, head up the eastern coast, then turn west to Princeton and the Delaware River.

CAPE MAY

Victoriana is in full swing in Cape May. Houses with lacy gingerbread woodwork racing up and down each peak look as if they'd just been painted. The entire town has been included on the National Historic Landmark list. You wouldn't think that a disastrous fire, the Great Fire of 1878, would have had such a silver lining. But when the ashes of the past had barely cooled, people started building their Victorian dream homes. Queen Victoria was responsible for the popularity of this architectural style both in England and the United States. Visitors from this country and abroad felt right at home as they vacationed in Cape May.

This ocean resort is the oldest in the United States. Cornelius Jacobsen Mey named the peninsula while on a trip of exploration from Holland in 1620; for the next hundred years, the village led a quiet agrarian life. Then came the explosion as vacationers discovered

Cape May; in 1761 it became the first seashore resort in America. Famous visitors included Abraham Lincoln, Robert E. Lee, William Sherman, James Buchanan, Franklin Pierce, Ulysses S. Grant, William Harrison, P. T. Barnum, and John Philip Sousa.

Today a walking tour is the best way to see Cape May. Look for captain's walks, fretwork, cupolas, stained-glass windows, crowned dormers, rocking-chair porches, fancy fences, gazebos, and Victorian flower gardens. With several hundred houses to choose from, you and your camera can have a field day. Start your tour at **Cape May's Welcome Center,** where you can pick up a map and other information. This building was once a church; the "onion" dome on the tower is reminiscent of both the Orient and Bavaria. Visit the cluster of houses on Congress Street, including **Congress Hall** (Beach and Congress); **Annie Knight's and Joseph Evans's houses** (203 and 207 Congress Place), with captain's walks on their roofs; **Dr. Henry Hunt House** (209 Congress Place); and a "wedding cake" house, **Pink House** (33 Perry). Stroll down the mall where shops line both sides of the street, and head onto Washington Street. **Alexander's Inn and Restaurant** (653 Washington) is said to be the oldest house in town. On the corner of Washington and Franklin is the **Fireman's Hall History Museum,** which houses a 1928 American La France fire engine. Across the street is the **Church of the Advent,** which has wonderful stained-glass windows. Dip down Washington to the **George Allen House** (720 Washington), designed by Samuel Sloan as an Italianate villa, and walk around the block to see it from all angles. Take Corgi to Franklin and jog to Hughes to a row of Victorian homes beginning with Number 664 on the corner. This house is painted rose, gray, and white and is a

**Convention and
Visitor's Bureau
800–5–BUREAU**

**Cape May's Welcome
Center
405 Lafayette Street
Cape May 08204
609–884–9562**

I•349

photographer's dream, without phone wires across its facade. Turn left on Stockton to the **Mainstay Inn** (635 Columbia), originally a gambling house and club known as Jackson's Clubhouse. From the corner of Columbia and Howard, you can see the **Chalfont Inn** (301 Howard), the only hotel that did not burn during the Great Fire (and therefore the oldest hotel in town). (See Inns appendix.) Cut across 2 blocks to Gurney Street and **The Abbey** (Columbia and Gurney); then stroll past a row of identical houses to the **Inn of Cape May** (Beach and Ocean), where Wallis Warfield, the Duchess of Windsor, had her coming-out party.

Emlen Physick House and Estate
1048 Washington Street
Cape May 08204
609–884–5404

The **Emlen Physick House and Estate** was designed by the famous Philadelphia architect Frank Furness. The city of Cape May has leased this estate to the **Mid-Atlantic Center for the Arts;** if you're there in the summer, you can attend its theater (609–884–ARTS). Visitors during mid-October throng to the Victorian Week festival presented by the Mid-Atlantic Center. There are house tours, boat trips, an antiques show, vaudeville, a marionette opera, a Victorian fashion show and lawn party, a grand ball, and more. The center also offers trolley tours, either by an enclosed bus or in an open-air trolley, and an evening tour called "Mansions by Gaslight."

The **Cape May County Art League** maintains headquarters in the old carriage house on the estate amid ornate iron grillwork on the horse stalls and natural wood paneling. Physick's grandfather, Philip Syng, was the silversmith who designed and made the inkwell used by the signers of the Declaration of Independence that is now on display in Independence Hall.

The carriage house was built in 1876, and the main house was begun in 1878. The stick-style construction, added to many gables, ridges, dormers, and chimneys, gives a cubical, top-heavy look to the house. Inside look for the different kinds of lincrusta wall-covering, an oil-based papier-mâché type of product (which, when made with molasses, attracted vermin and needed to be replaced!). The house has two different types of light fixtures: Electricity was used only until 10:00 p.m., when gas or candles were used. Look for the elegant soup tureen with three-dimensional carving; it was a housewarming present. The brass chandelier in the formal parlor has porcelain inserts. The house contains a collection of Victorian furnishings, clothing, toys, tools, and memorabilia. During the restoration process a clock was stolen and later found by a dog underneath a local porch; it seems fitting that a man who kept fourteen dogs during his lifetime should have his clock found by a dog.

The Mad Batter (at the Carroll Villa Hotel, 19 Jackson Street; 609–884–5970), offers breakfast/lunch, and dinner. Highly acclaimed for its changing, innovative menu, this is a place where guests will never go away hungry. Everything is fresh, attractively served, and delicious. **The Lobster House** (Fisherman's Wharf; 609–884–3064) offers dining rooms, take-out foods, a fish market, and a light menu in the Raw Bar. It's located right on a working fishing dock, and the fish couldn't be fresher.

CAPE MAY POINT

Cape May Point is the place to pick up "Cape May Diamonds," which are actually pieces of quartz that have been smoothed by the action of the waves; some people make them into jewelry. You might also be on hand when silver begins to surface from the *Juno,* a thirty-four-gun Spanish frigate that foundered off Cape May in 1802. In 1801 Spain was facing bankruptcy, so silver was shipped from Mexico to Spain on armed naval frigates instead of on the slower galleons. The *Juno* had over ten tons of Mexican silver on board as she headed for Spain; she encountered rough weather and put into San Juan, Puerto Rico, for repairs. She departed in October 1801 with 1,000 passengers, seamen, and soldiers on board. Gale winds swept away the mainsail, damaged a mast, and opened up seams in the hull. In an effort to lighten the sinking vessel, her anchors and many guns were tossed overboard. Emergency caulking and pumping below decks, and trying to lash sails to the hull on the outside to slow the leaks, took the spirit right out of the entire crew. An American schooner, the *Favorite,* came upon the rapidly sinking ship, stood by to help as they saw her riding low, but then lost track of her during a storm. Although no one saw her position as she sank, some believe that she lies in 90 feet of water about 25 miles east of the mouth of Delaware off the tip of Cape May. The value of her silver has been estimated to be $4 million. The vessel's 7,100-pound anchor was snagged by a fisherman in June of 1968, 12½ miles off Cape May. It stands on the sea side of the Congress Hotel.

Cape May Point Lighthouse is one of the oldest functioning lighthouses in the country. As aficionados of historic lighthouses, we hope that money will be raised so that renovation can continue. You can climb the 199 steps to the top for a 360-degree view of Cape May. A number of lamps have been used in the tower, beginning with a classic lens installed in 1857 (now in the County Museum), a hydraulic float lamp from 1878, an incandescent oil-vapor lamp from 1910, and electrified lamps in 1938. Beginning that year lighthouse keepers were no longer required to live at the tower. The present light is visible 19 miles out at sea and flashes every ten seconds.

Cape May Point State Park offers a bird observatory, nature trails, a natural history museum, picnicking, and fishing. A museum on the grounds contains a tank with live lobsters, crabs, fish, and snails. Look for a smaller tank with a jaunty live seahorse strutting around. You'll also see fossil shells, a mastodon molar dredged off Cape May, a walrus tusk, ear bones of a right whale, honeycomb coral from the Devonian Age, and part of the rigging from an old sailing vessel. There is an exhibit of bird's nests, ranging from the smallest—a chipping sparrow who made a nest from wool left drying on a line by a weaver—to a large long-billed marsh wren nest. If you haven't seen Cape May diamonds before, you can see them here. You'll see clear, milky-clouded, orange-yellow, and smoky stones.

Take a walk on the boardwalk through the wildlife sanctuary, where you can enjoy sunshine without wind because of towering swamp grasses on both sides. You'll come out alongside several ponds, and there are benches for a rest while bird-watching.

After you emerge from your walk, join others on the Hawk Watch Platform. A posted list keeps you informed as to the number of species sighted to date. Cape May Point is said to be the best vantage point for bird-watching during migration, because of the location of this natural funnel. Active flights take place following a cold front—several thousand birds can be spotted in a single day. Roger Tory Peterson names Cape May as one of the dozen birding hotspots in North America.

Nearby, on the other side of the Cape May Canal, **Historic Cold Spring Village** is a re-created historical village. Fifteen restored buildings house crafts shops and a country store. Craftspeople are at work in their shops, and some of them give lessons at scheduled times. A working farm and petting zoo are also on the grounds. Stop in the **Old Grange Restaurant**

Cape May Point State Park
Cape May Point 08212
609-884-2159

Historic Cold Spring Village
735 Shore Road
Cold Spring 08201
609-898-2300

The Hedge Gardens
159 Fishing Creek
Road
Cold Spring 08201
609–886–5148

(609–884–3373) for a meal. In the vicinity **The Hedge Gardens** exhibit more than 175 green sculptures made from hedges.

From Cape May heading north toward Atlantic City, you have two choices. You may take Route 9, the shore road along the barrier beach, which is often slow and exasperating with many stoplights in built-up areas but provides some glimpses of the ocean. Your other alternative is the Garden State Parkway on the mainland proper, which provides faster, uninterrupted travel. The season, the weather, and your inclination should dictate the best choice on a given day.

THE WILDWOODS

Five miles of beaches and 3 miles of boardwalk at the Wildwoods add up to crowds during the season. The first beach area north of Cape May, it is one of the safest in New Jersey because the surf line stands 1,000 feet from shore. **Hereford Lighthouse** dates back to the 1800s and is listed on the National Register of Historic Places.

Follow Route 9 to Stone Harbor.

STONE HARBOR

Stone Harbor Bird
Sanctuary
111th to 117th streets
between 2nd & 3rd
Avenues
Stone Harbor 08247
609–368–5102;
609–368–1211

The **Stone Harbor Bird Sanctuary** provides a home for many species, including American egret, Louisiana heron, green heron, black crowned and yellow crowned night herons, cattle egret, and glossy ibis. Although visitors are not permitted inside the sanctuary, there is a visitors' center on Ocean Drive where you may spot birds flying.

Wetlands Institute and
Museum
Stone Harbor
Boulevard
Stone Harbor 08247
609–368–1211

The **Wetlands Institute and Museum** offers an observation tower, salt marsh trail, and Wetlandia Museum. This is the place to go to observe birds in a protected salt marsh and tidal creeks. There is no visitors' center, but you can put coins into mounted binoculars to view birds.

OCEAN CITY

Continue on Route 9 to Ocean City, which

ATLANTIC CITY

A typical nightime scene on Atlantic City's famed boardwalk.

WINTERTHUR

Eleutherian Mills, the Du Pont family home, now part of the Hagley Museum.

WILMINGTON, DELAWARE

The Montmorenci Stair Hall, one of the best-known and most impressive rooms in the Winterthur Museum and Gardens.

has been offering family vacations for over one hundred years. Founded in 1879 by three Methodist ministers named Lake, the town was, and is, dry, which may account for its attraction to families. The beach is 8 miles long, and the port is popular with yachtsmen for fishing, sailing, and sightseeing.

MARGATE CITY

Lucy the Margate Elephant
Atlantic Avenue
Margate City 08402
609–823–6473

Lucy the Margate Elephant is worth a trip to Margate. One of the four "Victorian follies" built by James V. Lafferty in the 1880s, Lucy stands six stories high. You can walk inside, climb up the stairs in her legs, and visit a museum. She was originally designed to lure buyers to the real-estate development run by Lafferty. In the 1960s it looked as if she might be cast aside as Atlantic City went into decline, but with the help of many children Lucy was preserved.

ATLANTIC CITY

The Atlantic City Expressway leads from the Garden State Parkway or Route 9 to Atlantic City.

"On the Boardwalk of Atlantic City"—the rollicking tune lured summer visitors to the pleasures of Atlantic City in past eras. Then a decline beginning in the 1930s ravished the town, and now, since the casino law of 1977, she seems to be recovering her old pizzazz.

In 1854, when the first railroad arrived, Atlantic City began to attract vacationers, and the first boardwalk was laid in 1870. The rolling chair, introduced in 1884 by a Philadelphia wheelchair manufacturer, is still a popular tourist vehicle for gliding along the boardwalk (you can also rent a bicycle). And yes, you can buy saltwater taffy in the shops along the boardwalk. Amusement piers house a variety of entertainments and frivolities. The beach itself is appealing: There is less undertow than usual because the configuration of the coastline somewhat shelters the beach; the Gulf Stream also makes both weather and water more temperate. Surfing is permitted, and lifeguards are on duty all summer. Fishermen haul in striped bass, flounder, kingfish, and snapper blues from the piers or the beach. You can also head out to sea in a charter boat to catch marlin, tuna, bonito, and albacore. Those interested in the less artificial aspects of the environment will want to visit **Absecon Lighthouse,** built in 1857, which now houses a marine environmental museum.

The revival of Atlantic City has less to do with its benign climate and setting than with money. Visitors who are interested in gambling will find one place after another—all eager to take their money. Perhaps even more fun than gambling is watching the intent faces of those bound and determined to break the bank in a casino. You will see row after row of clanging machines in a glittering warehouse of illusions, each one with a strained but hopeful face before it. Or you can watch hands: At the gaming tables people extend their hands full of bills, which pass through the croupier's hands directly into a slot from which they can never be retrieved. Chips are thrown both by hands with sparkling diamonds and those with work-worn fingers. Roulette wheels turn; chips are scooped up, stacked, sold, distributed; and card games continue hand after hand. The rooms themselves are a mirage of glass, gold, mirrors, and bright lights. When you tire of gambling, you can watch a show, often with big-name performers; if you want to be sure to get into a particular performance, get your tickets in advance.

**Absecon Lighthouse
Rhode Island &
Pacific avenues
Atlantic City 08404**

Just across the Absecon Inlet from Atlantic City lie the Brigantine barrier beach and, behind it, within sight of high-rise casinos, one of the most extensive protected salt marshes in the state. The Edwin B. Forsythe National Wildlife Refuge (609–652–1665) contains over 34,000

**EDWIN B. FORSYTHE
NATIONAL WILDLIFE
REFUGE**

acres of wetlands that attract flocks of migrating birds. You can walk on nature trails or drive through the refuge, which is reached by taking Route 9 north from Atlantic City through Absecon to Oceanville.

SMITHVILLE

**Town of Historic
Smithville
Route 9
Smithville 08201
609–652–3111**

Twelve miles north of Atlantic City, also on Route 9, you will find the **Town of Historic Smithville,** a restored village of thirty-three homes and shops collected from various locations in southern New Jersey. Each one dates from the 1800s and has been renovated for use in the village. The village is attractive, with winding streets, a lake, and many shops for you to explore. The **Towne Book Shoppe** (609–652–1999) has a well-chosen assortment of books. When you're ready for lunch, stop in the **Historic Smithville Inn** (609–652–7777). The original inn was built in 1787 by James Baremore; it was abandoned for many years and finally restored and reopened in 1952. The rest of the village grew around it.

PINE BARRENS

**Batsto Historic Site
Route 542
Hammonton 08037
609–561–3262**

From Smithville take Route 9 and the Garden State Parkway to New Gretna, then Route 542 west to **Batsto,** a jumping-off point for the Pine Barrens. Once the bottom of an ocean, the Pine Barrens are composed of hundreds of square miles of scrub oak and pine, blueberries and cranberries, and, believe it or not, wild orchids. It is also hard to believe that this wilderness of a million acres is located right in the middle of a megalopolis, just a few miles east of the Boston-Washington corridor. The Lenape Indians were probably the first to live there, but any traces of their existence have been swallowed up by the forest. Loggers probably moved in next, but again, not much remains of their existence. The discovery of bog iron inspired the construction of furnaces like the Batsto Furnace, built by Charles Read in

1766. Batsto Furnace was necessary as a supplier of munitions during the Revolutionary War. Glassworks also appeared on the scene for a short time but failed to be successful.

Joseph Wharton, from Philadelphia, bought many tracts of land in the barrens, totaling 99,672 acres around the Batsto River. The Batsto area of the Wharton State Forest is part of his estate. The village of Batsto (from the Swedish word *baatstoo,* meaning "steam bath") was founded by Swedish explorer Erik Mullica. The village has been renovated, and you can visit workers' cottages, post office, general store, gristmill, sawmill, ironmaster's mansion, and farm exhibits. When you get to the horse barn, look at the vertical slots in the walls, which were designed to prevent hay inside from molding. You may wonder about the workers' black homes, which are typical of the area. They were built of Jersey cedar clapboards that blacken with age and the weather.

Legends abound about the "Pine Robbers" who fled into the forest to safety. Some are based on historical fact; others are embellished fiction—believe what you will. Some say that Joe Mulliner, who was hanged in 1781, was the "Robin Hood" of the Pine Barrens. Apparently he was finally captured because he could not resist coming out of hiding to dance in a local tavern. Many stories have been told about a local "wizard" named Jerry Munyhon, who could make an ax chop wood without a hand to guide it, "catch" a bullet fired at him without being wounded, and inspire a rooster to pull a loaded wagon up a hill. "Pineys," the people who live deep in the forest, have tales to tell about the "Witch of the Pine," Peggy Clevenger. They say that she could turn herself into a rabbit and that she had a treasure of gold. Residents also tell about various monsters who inhabit the forest, including the Jersey Devil, who carried off farm and domestic animals, leaving cloven tracks behind.

If you've read John McPhee's *The Pine Barrens,* you will have some understanding about this part of New Jersey, which is so near megalopolis and yet so isolated and desolate.

Although you can drive through the Pine Barrens, you will probably get a better feel for this enchanted land if you choose to paddle along the network of rivers in the forest. the **Oswego, Wading, Batsto,** and **Mullica rivers** are all popular canoe routes. Canoes can be rented from **Atsion Recreation Area.** We rented a canoe from **Adams Canoe Rental** (694 Atsion Road, Vincentown; 609–268–0189) and were taken by truck to the beginning of our trip on the Batsto. Although we did not see another person during the five hours we were on the river, we did see lots of turkey buzzards, herons, Canada geese, mallards, woodpeckers, and water bugs. The winding river housed beaver dams, but we didn't spot a beaver. Cedars along the shore interspersed with sandbars and sandy banks were just right for a lunch stop.

**Atsion Recreation
 Area Ranger Station
Route 206
Atsion
609–268–0444**

**LONG BEACH
ISLAND**

Retrace your way through the Pine Barrens back to the Garden State Parkway or Route 9. Head north to exit 63 or the town of Manahawkin, and take Route 72 across a long causeway to **Ship Bottom.** Long Beach Island is an 18-mile barrier isle ranging in width from several blocks to a mile. During the eighteenth century fishermen, sea captains, and pilots lived on the island. Shipwrecks are concentrated along this sandspit, which was lethal to those caught in a storm, misled by lights on shore, or hugging the coast to make a fast passage into New York. The beach at **Holgate,** at the southern end, has been inundated with coins. Those who have made a study of the effects of wind and weather patterns on the beach know that after a northeast storm, which scoops up sand and brings new sand to the top, the west winds of the following high pressure system blow the top layers of sand away. Then the coins that are surfacing hold down a bit of sand as the surrounding loose sand blows away. This is the time to search for little mounds of sand—and—a coin on top!

Years ago there was an island named Tucker's Island at the south end of Long Beach Island; Tucker's has now been entirely reclaimed by the sea. In the 1800s, according to legend, a chest of Spanish coins was taken from Tucker's Island. Two men rowed in from a waiting sloop, inquired about the location of two cedar trees in relation to a lighthouse, dug up a chest, tossed the coins into sacks, and sailed away in their sloop. The empty chest was found by the crew at the Life Saving Station . . . as well as a rusty cutlass.

Captain Kidd
Stephen Vincent Bénet

This person in the gaudy clothes
Is worthy Captain Kidd.
They say he never buried gold,
I think, perhaps, he did.

They say it's all a story that
His favorite little song
Was "Make these lubbers walk the plank!"
I think, perhaps, they're wrong.

They say he never pirated
Beneath the Skull-and-Bones.
He merely traveled for his health
And spoke in soothing tones.

In fact, you'll read in nearly all
The newer history books

That he was mild as cottage cheese
—But I don't like his looks!

It is likely that pirates (Captain Kidd included) were in and out of the sheltered waters behind the island, Little Egg Harbor, and Barnegat Bay, plundering when they could and stashing their treasure against a precarious future. In addition to pirates, the island attracted a particularly noxious breed of scavengers known as "wreckers" or "mooncussers." They walked their horses carrying lights at night to simulate a vessel sailing close to shore. Wishing to cut their time going into New York, many captains veered closer to shore. The wreckers then reaped the benefits of their deception. One legend relates the story of the ghost who still walks the length of the island, sobbing. The girl who moans was forced to accompany her father, the leader of a wrecking group, as he removed rings and valuables from the corpses washed up on shore. When she came upon the still body of her lover, who had joined the crew of that ill fated-ship, she went mad and still walks the beach in ethereal form on dark nights.

Barnegat Lighthouse
Barnegat Lighthouse
  State Park
Long Beach Island
08008

Marking the inlet at the northern tip of the island, **Barnegat Lighthouse,** affectionately known as "Old Barney," was built in 1857 when an earlier lighthouse dating from 1834 had collapsed into the sea. You can climb up 217 steps for a sweeping seascape of bay, barrier beach, and ocean.

Patroling Barnegat
Walt Whitman

Wild, wild the storm, and the sea high running,
Steady the roar of the gale, with incessant undertone muttering,

Shouts of demoniac laughter fitfully piercing and pealing,
Waves, air, midnight, their savagest trinity lashing,
Out in the shadows there milk-white combs careering,
On beachy slush and sand spirts of snow fierce slanting,
Where through the murk the eastern death-wind breasting,
Through cutting swirl and spray watchful and firm advancing,
(That in the distance! is that a wreck? is the red signal flaring?)
Slush and sand of the beach tireless till daylight wending,
Steadily slowly, through hoarse roar never remitting,
Along the midnight edge by those milk-white combs careering,
A group of dim, weird forms, struggling, the night confronting,
That savage trinity warily watching.

ISLAND BEACH STATE PARK

Retrace your way to the Garden State Parkway and head north to exit 82 at **Toms River.** If you have not yet had your fill of barrier beaches and would like to enjoy one that is undeveloped, take Route 37 to Island Beach State Park. This 10-mile strip of land offers nature trails, picnicking, fishing, and swimming without the commercialism of beach towns or the clutter of real-estate developments.

From this point you can head north through the older exurban beach and river towns on the way to New York City—Mantoloking, Point Pleasant Beach, Spring Lake, Ocean Grove, Asbury Park, Long Branch, Shrewsbury, Red Bank. Or take the Garden State Parkway to I–195 to Route 571 for a scenic trip through the countryside to Princeton.

PRINCETON

Princeton has a rural charm that fits the image of a small, Ivy League university town and survives the astounding growth of high-tech research institutions and corporate headquarters in the surrounding countryside. As you drive into town from the north, west, or south, you will see one mansion after another, all beautifully landscaped with lush groundcover, gigantic old trees, and seasonal flowers. **Princeton**

Princeton University
Princeton 08540

University, like its counterpart in England (Cambridge), has a campus with a sense of space and tranquillity that seems forever immune from the bustle of the town or the highway just 1 mile east. Many of its buildings also imitate those of Cambridge colleges like King's or Trinity—in the collegiate Gothic style with gray stone—or the red brick of the newer parts of St. John's, interspersed with a few Victorian brownstones and Greek Revival buildings. Nostalgia for the nineteenth-century sense of "college days" sometimes overwhelms a visitor who wanders through the campus on a warm spring afternoon or evening, while a visit during reunions in June immerses you in the world of F. Scott Fitzgerald. The highlight of that celebration, the P-rade, is a visual celebration of the generations marching by, the young following the old, class by class, behind banners and in costume; we recall one in which Jimmy Stewart stood out because he was a head taller than anyone else in the Class of 1932.

The town was founded in 1696 by Quakers, who named it "Prince's Town." The university began as a college in 1746 in Elizabeth; then it moved to Newark and finally to Princeton in 1756. Nassau Hall served as barracks and a hospital for American and British troops one after the other during the Revolutionary War. Washington was victorious in the Battle of Princeton on January 3, 1777; a monument at Mercer, Nassau, and Stockton streets commemorates this battle. After the Revolution the Continental Congress met in Nassau Hall for six months in 1783.

Orange Key Guide
Service
Maclean House
Princeton University
Princeton 08540
609–452–3603; or
609–258–3676

You can take a free guided tour of the Princeton University campus by calling three days in advance to the **Orange Key Guide Service.** The oldest building on the campus, **Nassau Hall,** was named for the House of Orange that reigned in England when the college was founded; silencing its bell by climbing to the belfry and stealing the clapper was, for many years, an obligation of the new freshman class. The **Gothic Chapel** was built in 1928 and contains lovely stained-glass windows, which mountaineering students sometimes scale to worry their elders. The **Harvey S. Firestone Library,** built in the late forties, contains individual study carrels for students working on senior theses, rare books, and a superb collection of books and manuscripts made accessible by an open-stack system. The **James Forrestal Research Campus** was opened in 1951 to provide research facilities in the disciplines of applied mathematics, physics, and chemistry. It is located just beyond **Lake Carnegie,** east of the campus, and contains a cyclotron and other instruments for advanced research in atomic physics.

Morven, built in 1751 by one of the signers of the Declaration of Independence, Richard Stockton, hosted heads of state and presidents for years. When the Continental Congress convened in 1783, Washington, Madison, Hamilton, and others met in the house. At this writing the rooms have not been furnished, but there are plans for period rooms to chronicle three generations of Stockton family life. In 1987 a team of archaeologists began digging for artifacts to shed more light on the past history of Morven. It reopened in the summer of 1992.

Morven
55 Stockton Street
Princeton 08540
609-292-6300

Drumthwacket, a Greek Revival mansion built in 1834, is now the official residence of the governor of New Jersey. *Drumthwacket* means "Wooded Hill" in Gaelic. The house is open to the public on Wednesdays from noon to 2:00 p.m.

Drumthwacket
Stockton Street
Princeton 08540
609-924-3044

The **Historical Society of Princeton** has restored the **Bainbridge House,** which was built in 1766. It was the birthplace of William Bainbridge, who commanded the USS

Bainbridge House
158 Nassau Street
Princeton 08540
609-921-6748

Constitution during the War of 1812. Two period rooms have been restored, and a special museum room has been developed for children. Visitors can also receive information on self-guided tours on eighteenth-century houses in town, the university campus, and a Revolutionary War route in the Princeton-Trenton area.

Battlefield State Park is located 1½ miles southwest on Mercer Street. The **Thomas Clark House** (609–921–0074) was built by Thomas Clark, a Quaker farmer, in 1770. The tree marked **Mercer Oak** is where General Mercer fell mortally wounded before he was carried into the Clark farmhouse. **Rockingham,** also known as the Berrien Mansion, is 5 miles north of town on Route 518. Martha and George Washington lived there in 1783 while the Continental Congress was convening in Nassau Hall. His "Farewell Address to the Armies" was written in Rockingham, which has been restored with period furnishings.

Rockingham
Route 518
Princeton 08540
609–921–8835

If you're ready for lunch, head for the **Nassau Inn** in Palmer Square (609–921–7500). There are three restaurants in the inn to choose from: The Greenhouse, Palmer's, and the Yankee Doodle Tap Room. **J. B. Winberie** (609–921–0700) is also on Palmer Square. **Scanticon** (609–452–7800) contains several restaurants, including Tivoli Gardens, The Copenhagen Room, and the very elegant Black Swan. **Lahiere's** (609–921–2798) is another traditional restaurant in Princeton noted for its fine French cuisine.

From Princeton you can head to **Washington Crossing** on Route 206 and scenic Route 546 for exploration of the Delaware Canal area and Bucks County (see Itinerary G).

ITINERARY J:

Maryland

St. Michaels

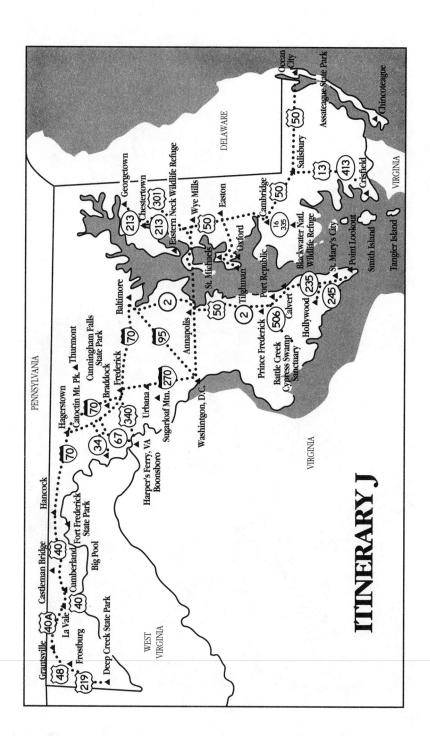

ITINERARY J

Maryland

This itinerary begins in historic Annapolis, a fine geographic center for explorations out in every direction. Chesapeake Bay divides southern Maryland (or the Western Shore) from the Eastern Shore, also called the Delmarva peninsula because Delaware, Maryland, and Virginia share the land between Chesapeake Bay and the Atlantic shore. Ocean City and Assateague Island National Seashore, at the most easterly point of Maryland, represent the extremes of beach hotels and wild seashore. Villages and towns along the Eastern Shore of Chesapeake Bay, from Crisfield in the south through Salisbury, Cambridge, Oxford, Easton, St. Michael's, and Chestertown, provide a full range of bayside communities, from those filled with working watermen to yachting centers. Touring south from Annapolis takes you to Prince Frederick, the harbors and shellfish of Solomons, the settlement at St. Mary's City, and Point Lookout. Heading north from Annapolis brings you to a rejuvenated Baltimore; then turning west toward the mountains takes you to the historic district in Frederick, Hagerstown, Cumberland, and Grantsville. Thus, in the span of 200 miles, you can move from Atlantic beaches through quiet bay villages and large cities to the Cumberland Mountains. In small compass, Maryland has it all.

⇜ *Annapolis* ⇝

Annapolis is a waterfront city with salt water washing right up into the town dock. This narrow slip of water juts in to meet the bottom of Main and Cornhill streets. Almost everyone gravitates at one time or another to the dock area—a busy place with fishing and pleasure boats going in and out. Annapolis has all the lure of an active port, as well as a rich historical heritage stretching back to its founding in the seventeenth century.

Annapolis was first established under the name of Providence, chosen by its Puritan settlers. Then a ship's captain was honored by the choice of his name, Proctor, for the town. Later it was called City by the Severn, where it is located. Some records refer to it as Anne Arundel Town, Arrundell Towne, or Arundelton. In 1694 it became the capital of Maryland, when Governor Francis Nicholson moved the center of government from St. Mary's to this centrally located site. He directed his commissioners "to survey and lay out in the most comodius and convenient parte and place of the said Towne six Acres of Land intire for the erecting a Court House and other buildings as shall be thought necessary and convenient." In 1694 Annapolis was chosen as the city's name to honor Queen Anne.

The city became an important and strategically located seaport, in addition to serving as the administrative center of Maryland during the Revolution. Ships sailed in and out of the harbor right past the blockade of English vessels. The Continental Congress met in the State House in 1783 and again in 1784 to ratify the Treaty of Paris ending the Revolution. During the Civil War Annapolis was important as a shipping center, partial to the Union side in spite of the mixed sentiments that plagued all of Maryland during that internecine conflict. Later in the century the infant Naval Academy—which had been founded in 1845, at least partly in response to the uproar over the mutiny on the brig *Somers,* in which a midshipman had been hanged—began to grow toward its present stature as a rival of West Point.

Annapolis was laid out in terms of the best urban planning of its day; you can easily walk anywhere you need to go along a series of streets that are spokes radiating from two sister circles, State and Church, at the center. (Car-less, we did this for a year and know it works.) No one could have imagined the impact of the automobile on this plan when it was established in 1694. You may be lucky enough to find a parking place on one of the streets not restricted to those with a resident's permit, but beware of the time limit, which is two hours on Maryland Avenue and State Circle. Prince George Street, King George Street, and College Avenue are also zoned for two-hour free parking, and that may not give you enough time to complete your tour. Traffic police are active, and they do tow. There is a parking ramp between Main Street and Duke of Gloucester Street, near the foot of the hill. If you are touring in season, you may find it easier to park in the Navy–Marine Corps Stadium, just off Route 50/301, and take a shuttle bus into town; it runs every fifteen minutes and charges a nominal fee. The bus looks like a trolley car from the past.

You can begin to know Annapolis by visiting **Three Centuries Tours of Annapolis** (48 Maryland Avenue; 410–263–5401) and taking a walking tour. This is the best way to see the city. Your family may enjoy being directed by a guide in colonial costume, who will pull relevant objects out of her basket as she reaches each new location. Our guide had a great deal of precise information, interspersed with anecdotes and stories, to make the history of Annapolis come alive. **Historic Annapolis** (410–267–8149), located in the **Old Treasury Building,** also offers walking tours. The

ANNAPOLIS

Old Treasury Building
State Circle
Annapolis 21404

Treasury, built in 1735, has the distinction of being the oldest building in Maryland.

Annapolis will captivate architecture buffs, and it could serve as a useful school for students of the evolution of architecture in America. As you walk around Annapolis, you'll notice buildings marked with historic district plaques that are color-coded according to date and style. Colors signify time periods as follows: provincial green (seventeenth century), terra cotta (eighteenth century), blue (Federal), verdigris (Greek Revival), aubergine (Victorian), and ochre (twentieth century). The earliest structure begins with plain seventeenth-century houses like the one at **130 Prince George Street.** This house was patterned after wooden-frame houses with little decoration, which were common in English villages. The gambrel roof is topped by the very large central chimney typical of colonial homes.

The Georgian period, from 1700 to 1780, presents carved classical motifs on a two-and-one-half-story building with tall chimneys at the ends, a center doorway, and all windows and dormers symmetrical. Some of them, like **186 Prince George Street,** have a center block and an attached building on either end.

The Federal period, from 1780 to 1840, is typified by either brick or frame structures that are simple in design, two and one-half or three stories high, with steeply pitched roofs and tall chimneys usually placed at the ends. An example of this period may be seen at **223–225 Duke of Gloucester Street.**

The Greek Revival period, from 1825 to 1850, was derived from the Greek temple with columns or pilasters on the facade below a triangular roof line, illustrated by the **Franklin Law Office** at 17 State Circle. The Gothic Revival style, from 1830 to 1880, used a pointed arch, buttresses, and rose windows; see **St. Mary's Church** on Duke of Gloucester Street.

The Romanesque Revival style features heavy round arches and plain walls copied from northern Italian buildings, exemplified by **St. Anne's** on Church Circle. The Italianate or Bracketed style of 1850–1900 is a popular Victorian Revival design, which was used in Annapolis at **132 Charles Street.** Flat facades and roofs with a carved wooden bracket under the cornice resemble the features of Italian palaces. Some Italianate houses have a peaked roof and a tower on one side and perhaps a bay window, as does the example at **243 Prince George Street.**

The French Second Empire period from 1865 to 1890 is known for the mansard roof, sometimes covered with multicolored slates. The house at **195 Duke of Gloucester Street** is typical of this period. The Queen Anne period of 1875–1890 may include gables, turrets, half-timbering, carved wood trim, and the use of several colors. Go to **138 Conduit Street** and **86–88 State Circle** for good examples of this style. Colonial Revival and Neo-Georgian styles date from 1895 to 1930, taking design features from the seventeenth century, Georgian, and Federal periods, as does the home at **59 Franklin Street.**

The **Maryland State House** was built in 1772 and has the honor of being the oldest state house in use in the United States. It also served as the U.S. Capitol from November 1783 to August 1784. George Washington resigned his commission as commander in chief of the Continental armies in the Old Senate Chamber. Patriotic fervor for this admired leader was expressed during a celebration the day before the resignation, given by Governor William Paca. Supplies for the evening were furnished by Mann's Hotel as follows: "ninety-eight bottles of wine, two and one-half gallons of spirits, nine pounds of sugar, a lot of limes, music and

Maryland State House
State Circle
Annapolis 21404
410–974–3400

waiters, and a dozen packs of cards." A hogshead of rum (116 gallons) was provided by James Makubbin. Food included "15 pounds of loaf sugar, 176 pounds of bacon, 284 pounds of salt beef, 52 pounds of shoat, 126 pounds of mutton, 272 pounds of veal, 183 pounds of beef, 7 lambs and 12 fowls."

The official end of the Revolutionary War came with the signing of the Treaty of Paris in the State House in 1784. Charles Willson Peale painted a number of portraits for the State House, including one of George Washington with Tench Tilghman, his aide-de-camp, that hangs over the fireplace in the **Old Senate Chamber.** There's a bronze plaque on the floor marking the spot where George Washington stood when he resigned. An audiovisual program, guided tour, and exhibits are available. Don't miss the pitted iron cannon displayed on the lawn. Governor Calvert had a number of these cannons—which had been brought from England in 1634 by the first settlers—mounted on the fort at St. Mary's. Used to defend the settlers against Indians, Spaniards, Frenchmen, or pirates, the cannons eventually fell into the water, where they lay for 200 years, becoming pitted in the process. A sister to this cannon can be seen at St. Mary's.

Governor Calvert House
58 State Circle
Annapolis 21404

If you are fascinated by "digs" of archaeological interest, walk into **Governor Calvert House.** From the entrance go straight back to a little room on the right, where you can walk on a glassed-in exhibition area that exposes the brick foundation of the heating system from the 1720s. This "hypocaust" probably heated a greenhouse and is one of the earliest heating systems in America. When the system was discarded, the brick outline was filled in with trash, such as bones, pins, buttons, hair, paper, lace, cloth, seeds, and fish scales. An earlier excavation of a lower level revealed bits of plates, cups, and bottles dating from the 1690s. (See Inns appendix.)

Walk up School Street to **St. Anne's Church.** An earlier Anglican church on the site dated from the 1690s; King William III contributed the communion silver with his coat of arms on it in 1695. In 1858 a fire destroyed the whole church except for the bell tower, the doorway, and the front wall. The church was rebuilt, and in 1866 a new bell was installed in the tower. In 1893 the **Sands Memorial Window** won first prize for ecclesiastical art at the Chicago World's Fair. The oldest grave in the cemetery is that of Amos Garrett, the first mayor of Annapolis, who died in 1727. You will see several gravestones there that were moved in from other parishes for preservation.

St. Anne's Church
Church Circle
Annapolis

Reynold's Tavern was built in 1735 on Church Circle. It has been used as a shop for hatmaking, a stocking factory, the home of a bank cashier, and a library and has now been restored as an inn. The **Maryland Inn** fits into a small segment of the circle, extending pie-shaped out from the apex. It was built in the 1770s by Thomas Hyde. (See Inns appendix.)

From Church Circle walk along College Avenue to **St. John's College,** which was called King William's School when it was founded in 1696. There is a legend that the treaty of peace with the Susquehannock Indians was signed under the large, 400-year-old tulip poplar tree called the **Liberty Tree.** Later this tree was a popular place for the Sons of Liberty to meet when they wanted to consider separation from England. Because it was in the open, they could easily spot an outsider approaching in time to conclude their conversation. After the Revolution, when the Marquis de Lafayette returned to America in 1824, he reviewed the Maryland Militia under the tree. Francis Scott Key attended the school, and so did two

St. John's College
60 College Avenue
Annapolis 21404
410–263–2371

nephews of George Washington, who graduated in 1796. It became a military school in 1884, a liberal arts college in 1923, and developed its noted "Great Books" syllabus in 1937.

Chase-Lloyd House
22 Maryland Avenue
Annapolis 21404
410–263–2723

Turn right onto King George Street to reach the **Chase-Lloyd House,** which was partially built by Samuel Chase, a signer of the Declaration of Independence. In 1771 Chase sold his unfinished house to Edward Lloyd IV, who finished the building. Francis Scott Key married Mary Taylor Lloyd there in 1802. The house is now a home for elderly ladies, "where they may find a retreat from the vicissitudes of life." You can visit the museum on the first floor. You can't miss seeing the cantilevered stairway and the magnificent Palladian window. The Chase coat of arms decorates some of the family china on display. Look at the Italian marble mantel, which depicts Shakespeare receiving keys from the Goddess of Wisdom in the parlor.

Hammond-Hardwood
House
19 Maryland Avenue
Annapolis 21404
410–269–1714

Across the street is the **Hammond-Harwood House,** which was designed by William Buckland for Mathias Hammond in 1774. Although Buckland died during construction, the house was completed by his junior partner, John Randall. Hammond reportedly was having the house built for an unknown bride-to-be, who then eloped with someone else, so he resolved not to live in the house and left Annapolis abruptly in 1776. He died at the young age of thirty-eight; the mystery of his forlorn love has never been solved.

While the house was in the process of construction, a change was made to reduce the height so that Hammond's neighbor, Edward Lloyd, would have a view of the harbor and city dock. This Georgian house displays semioctagonal pavilions at each end of the facade, an arched doorway, and recessed windows. Hammond had instructed the architect to design a house large enough for entertaining and yet cozy enough for family life during the cold winters. Hester Ann Harwood was the last person to live in the house, and when she died the house and its contents were sold at auction. The house was purchased for restoration, and, fortunately, some of the original pieces of furniture were recovered and other period furnishings were found, including some pieces made by John Shaw, a respected cabinetmaker who lived nearby. Ask about the false doors, which were installed to provide symmetry. And you might like to find out more about the tunnel under the house that may have led to the water. Two ancient keys were also found under the floor, one labeled "To the Secret Chamber" and the other "To the Secret Burying Place." Doesn't that stir your imagination?

The house contains a number of portraits by Charles Willson Peale. In the dining room look for the "gib door" located below the window on the right; the window becomes a door leading into the garden. Look for the griffin heads and leaf arabesques over the doors, windows, and fireplace in this room. Upstairs in one of the bedrooms are portraits of Ann and Mary Proctor that were painted in 1789. Ann is holding her doll, and, in fact, the same doll sits in a high chair in front of the painting today.

The **William Paca House** is built in the Palladian style popular in English country houses. Palladian houses have wings spreading out from a central house. This house was designed to serve as a home and as an office for Paca, an active legislator. During the nineteenth century the house was occupied as a boardinghouse, and in the next century it was used as an elegant hotel, **Carvel Hall.** In 1966 the Carvel Hall addition was demolished, leaving the original Paca House intact. After a great deal of study, the house was restored to its appearance of the period Paca lived there, between 1765 and

William Paca House
186 Prince George
Street
Annapolis 21404
410–263–5530;
410–263–5553

1780. Because of the muddy streets during that time, this house did not have carpets, but the bright blue walls draw the eye upward. The house is furnished with period pieces, some of them owned by Paca. Pieces of the family silver were recovered, including George II silver salts and an ornate sugar bowl. Original oriental porcelain of the Nanking pattern is on display.

Carvel Hall once stood on the present site of the garden. During restoration some of Paca's original garden was discovered, and now the two-acre eighteenth-century garden has been completely restored. Look for the unusual Chinese trellis bridge that matches the staircase in the house.

U.S. Naval Academy
King George Street
Annapolis 21404
410–263–6933

The **U.S. Naval Academy** should be entered at Gate 1 at the corner of Randall Street. You may take a guided tour or stroll through on your own with the help of a map (ask for one at the gate). Since there is more for you to see than is reasonably possible in a short time, we will suggest a few highlights. Perhaps the most remarkable building is the **Chapel,** which dates from 1904 and is filled with stained-glass windows dedicated as memorials to naval heroes. Look for the Votive Ship, a fifteenth-century Flemish carrack, which hangs from the ceiling in the rear of the nave; the tradition of hanging a ship in church symbolizes the devotion of sailors to God. Walk downstairs to the crypt to see the sarcophagus of John Paul Jones, his commission, and his sword. Another building to visit is the **U.S.N.A. Museum,** located in Preble Hall. It houses collections of ship models, paintings, uniforms, swords, and relics from the career of John Paul Jones. On your way between the Chapel and the museum, don't miss the **Statue of Tecumseh,** known by midshipmen as the "God of the C," the grade every cadet needs to pass courses. Pennies are tossed at him; he also receives good-luck left-handed salutes. Before any athletic contest with arch rival, Army, Tecumseh undergoes a makeup session and puts on war paint. Tecumseh is a copy of the figurehead on the wooden battleship *Delaware,* built in 1819.

Before you leave the grounds, stroll around the sea walls for views of harbor activity. Much of this land was reclaimed from the water for use as playing fields. The **Santee Basin** on the Severn River moors various fleets of sailboats used in training all midshipmen. The sailing team has 225 midshipmen and is the largest varsity team at the Naval Academy, one that has been very successful in intercollegiate competition. Boats moored in the basin include Naval Academy knockabouts, Shields sloops, International 420s, Lasers, and Windsurfers. Beyond the **Sailing Center** on the Annapolis Harbor side are a dozen 44-foot Luders yawls and a variety of larger ocean-racing boats that are actively campaigned in Chesapeake Bay and in the biennial Bermuda Race and other major worldwide ocean races. The Naval Academy feels that competitive sailing is one sport that presents most of the challenges the men will face as naval officers. From it they learn boat handling in relation to wind, waves, and current, other skills of seamanship, navigation, and the necessity of working together as a team.

The Annapolis harbor area is one of our favorite places to gaze at boats. Sailboats and powerboats are moored everywhere—along every inch of the town dock as well as up the back creeks. It is a haven for some of the finest sailing yachts in the country as well as for historic sailing craft. During the 1950s we became familiar with the lines of the working skipjacks, the last type of working sailing vessel used on Chesapeake Bay. The skipjack, a hard-chinned sloop with a mast raked sharply back that was developed during the 1860s, once numbered over 1,000 on the bay; now only a handful still go out for oysters. Two days a week oystermen may use motorboats, but they must use sails the rest of the week. The state of Maryland decreed this law in 1865 to protect the oyster industry from depletion. Skipjacks are now designated as the "state boat of Maryland"; you are likely to see some of them, or their larger two-masted cousins, the bugeyes, moored in the town dock. If you are eager to go out on the water, you will also find a number of charter companies and excursion boats along the dock. On the weekend in early October when the **Annapolis Boat Show** fills the town dock is the time to see more sailboats than you can imagine; power boats take over during another weekend show.

Stop for lunch in **Middleton Tavern** (City Dock; 410–263–3323), **Harbour House** (87 Prince George Street; 410–268–0771), **King of France Tavern** (Maryland Inn; 410–263–2641), **Reynold's Tavern** (7 Church Circle; 410–263–6599), **O'Leary's** (310 Third Street; 410–263–0884), or **Chart House** (300 Second Street; 410–268–7166). The **Market House** also offers seafood to eat in or take out; if soft-shell crabs are available, don't miss this delicacy of the bay.

~ *Southern Maryland* ~

You can take a tour of St. Mary's and Calvert counties by following this interesting itinerary.

PRINCE FREDERICK

To begin a tour of Southern Maryland from Annapolis, take Route 50 west to the junction with Route 2 at the edge of the city; then head south. Route 2 will join with Route 4 and lead into Prince Frederick, which was named for a son of King George II. Stop for a good meal at **The Old Field Inn** (Main Street; 410–535–5303). Friends also recommend **Rustic Farms** (Route 4; 410–586–1220), **Penwick House** (Route 4 at Ferry Landing Road, Dunkirk; 410–257–7077), **Surry Inn** (Route 4, Huntingtown; 410–535–0989), and **Shorter's Place** (Benedict; 410–274–3284).

Battle Creek Cypress Swamp Sanctuary (follow Route 2 and Route 506 4 miles southwest of town) contains bald cypress trees that are 50 to 125 feet tall. This stand of trees is the northernmost location of this species in North America. An elevated boardwalk trail leads through the swamp. Look for the 1- to 4-foot "knees" on the cypress trees that stick out; they are part of the root system. Stop in the nature center for films, exhibits, and demonstrations.

Battle Creek Cypress Swamp Sanctuary Gray's Road Prince Frederick 20678 410–535–5327

Jefferson Patterson Park and Museum (located on Route 265 near Port Republic) contains fifty-two archaeological sites dating back to 7500 B.C., nature trails, a museum, and a visitors' center. The Battle of St. Leonard's Creek was fought there during the War of 1812.

Jefferson Patterson Park and Museum Route 265 Prince Frederick 20678 410–586–0050

Head south again on Route 2/4 to the **Calvert Cliffs Nuclear Power Plant,** where a converted tobacco farm has displays on fossils found in the area as well information on nuclear power. There you can trace the geologic history of Chesapeake Bay from its formation to the present. Video games based on energy are available.

CALVERT

Calvert Cliffs Nuclear Power Plant Route 2/4 Calvert 21202 410–234–7484; 410–586–2200, Visitors' Center

Calvert Cliffs State Park provides public access to Calvert Cliffs, well known for Miocene fossils going back twenty million years. As animals died, they descended to the bottom of the sea and were preserved in layers of sediment. Fossils found on the beach include shark teeth, coral, whalebones, crocodile plates, and seashells. In 1968 a twenty-million-year-old whale skull was found that was about 5 feet

Calvert Cliffs State Park Calvert 21202 410–888–1622

long. You may keep any fossils found lying loose on the beach or in the mud, but you may not dig into the cliff, because that would accelerate erosion. The cliffs rise 100 feet above Chesapeake Bay, almost straight up, and trees at the top with exposed roots lean over. During storms the wave action tends to wash away part of the cliff, and rockslides are particularly threatening to would-be beach collectors. Look up the cliffs to see the many layers of deposited and solidified sediments, each containing different kinds of fossils.

This is also a good place to learn more about the geologic history of Chesapeake Bay. During the Pleistocene epoch, glaciers were developing and causing the sea level to lower and expose sandy sediment. Later, as they melted, the various streams merged into a river, the Susquehanna, which carved a path through the sedimentary layers to the sea. Ocean levels rose again and flooded the mouth of the river. Thus what we know now as Chesapeake Bay is the drowned valley of the Susquehanna River. Calvert Cliffs reveal that history in a particularly dramatic way.

Middleham Chapel
Route 4
Cove Point
410–326–3106

A mile north of the park, **Middleham Chapel** was founded in 1684 and is one of the oldest cruciform churches in Maryland. Many gravestones in the cemetery date from the 1700s. **Cove Point Light Station** at the end of Cove Point Road is the oldest tower lighthouse on Chesapeake Bay. Bring along your camera to photograph the view of Calvert Cliffs and other stretches of the Chesapeake shore.

Cove Point Light
 Station
Route 497
Cove Point
410–326–3254

SOLOMONS ISLAND

Nine miles down Route 2/4 lies Solomons Island, where the Patuxent River empties into Chesapeake Bay. The harbor, one of the deepest natural ports in the bay, is a mecca for boatbuilding, sailing, and fishing. Many bugeyes were built there during the nineteenth century, and it is loaded with boatyards and marinas today.

Calvert Marine Museum offers a three-part emphasis on paleontology, estuarine biology, and maritime history. The Calvert Cliffs are right next door, so to speak, providing a wealth of opportunity for exploration and collection of fossils. Exhibits on fossils of Calvert Cliffs in the Paleontology Room include a reconstructed ocean floor with fossil remains scattered about. Don't crack your head on the bird flying low—it is just an extinct, pelicanlike, false-toothed marine bird. You're lucky that this one is only half-size, because the wingspan was up to 22 feet in real life. You can also see the jaws from a prehistoric crocodile there. In the Hall of Estuarine Biology, tidewater birds, fish, crabs, oysters, and other marine life are displayed as models. You can touch some of the species displayed on the "touch table" and look through a microscope to see minute creatures. Maritime Hall accents local maritime history and has a real log canoe on display. The M. M. Davis & Sons Shipyard collection was taken intact from a working shipyard; with everything in process it looks as though the men had just left their work for lunch.

An 1883 lighthouse that was moved from nearby Drum Point in 1975 is now poised on the dock at the entrance to the museum's basin. The **Drum Point Lighthouse** is called a "screwpile" cottage light and is one of only three that served Chesapeake Bay at the turn of the century left intact. The lighthouse was fully restored from the original architectural plans with the help of Anna Weems Ewalt, who was born in that very lighthouse. The doctor assisting her mother came by dory to the lighthouse, then located ⅛ mile offshore, the day before Anna's birth. Anna lived there until she was one year old and then returned every weekend to

Calvert Marine Museum
Solomons Island
20688
410–326–3719

visit her grandparents in the lighthouse. She described watching her grandfather clean the lenses on the lighthouse lamp daily at dawn; it was quite a job because the kerosene flame smoked up the lenses. During a fog the bell had to be rung, which must have been earsplitting for the family to hear time after time after time. The mechanism for ringing it had to be wound by hand every two hours. Her grandfather used to tell the story of the time John Paul Jones's body was being transported back to Annapolis from France. He attributed the wild storm, which had all of the lighthouse windows leaking, to the fact that JPJ should not have been moved at all. During the cold winters the family lived in the kitchen, where the wood-burning range kept them warm. Anna's grandmother decorated the lighthouse for Christmas with holly, pyracantha, boxwood, and lots of hand-made ornaments. Anna enjoyed decorating the lighthouse for the museum each year at Christmas. If you are at the museum when the lighthouse is open, you can climb up through the trap door into the rooms of the house itself, then up a narrow spiral staircase to the lenses.

The museum offers a cruise on the *William B. Tennison,* a historic Chesapeake Bay bugeye, during the season. She was built in 1899 at Crabb Island, Maryland, and her hull is "chunk built" of nine logs. Originally she sailed, but in 1907 she was converted to power. She worked as an "oyster buy-boat," going from one oyster bar to the next, loading on shellfish from the dredgers, and delivering them to the oyster house. The cruise takes you around the Solomons Inner Harbor, by the Chesapeake Biological Laboratory and the U.S. Naval Recreation Center at Point Patience, and under the Thomas Johnson Memorial Bridge.

The Ballad of the Oysterman

It was a tall young oysterman lived by the river-side,
His shop was just upon the bank, his boat was on the tide;
The daughter of a fisherman, that was so straight and slim,
Lived over on the other bank, right opposite to him.

It was the pensive oysterman that saw a lovely maid,
Upon a moonlight evening, a sitting in the shade;
He saw her wave her handkerchief, as much as if to say,
"I'm wide awake, young oysterman, and all the folks away."

Then up arose the oysterman, and to himself said he,
"I guess I'll leave the skiff at home, for fear that folks should see;
I read it in the story-book, that, for a kiss his dear,
Leander swam the Hellespont,—and I will swim this here."

And he has leaped into the waves, and crossed the shining stream.
And he has clambered up the bank, all in the moonlight gleam;
O there were kisses sweet as dew, and words as soft as rain,—
But they have heard her father's step, and in he leaps again!

Out spoke the ancient fisherman,—"O what was that, my daughter?"
"'Twas nothing but a pebble, sir, I threw into the water."
Down fell that pretty innocent, as falls a snow-white lamb,
Her hair drooped round her pallid cheeks, like seaweed on a clam.

Alas for those two loving ones! she waked not from her swound,
And he was taken with the cramp, and in the waves was drowned;
But Fate has metamorphosed them, in pity of their woe,
And now they keep an oyster-shop for mermaids down below.

There are a number of places to enjoy
seafood in Solomons, including **Solomons Pier
Restaurant** (410–326–2424) and **The Dry Dock**
(410–325–4817).

From Solomons take the **Thomas
Johnson Memorial Bridge** across the Patuxent
River into St. Mary's County. This bridge was
built in 1977 for $34 million and was named for

the first governor of Maryland, who was born in Calvert County. Before the bridge was built, beginning in 1941, passengers were ferried to and from the Patuxent River Naval Air Station twice a day by Captain Leon Langley in *Miss Solomons*. After you have crossed the bridge, turn right on Route 235 to Hollywood and Route 245, where you turn right again to visit a remarkable plantation.

HOLLYWOOD

Sotterley on the Patuxent
Off Route 245
Hollywood 20636
410–373–2280

Sotterley on the Patuxent has a long low profile, tall chimneys, steep roofs, and cupola. Set high on the ridge, the house commands a superb view of the Patuxent River. Inside it is famous for a Chinese Chippendale staircase and pine paneling with shell alcoves in the drawing room. Look for the set of four cut-crystal wall fixtures complete with prisms. In the dining room the Chinese lattice-back mahogany chairs match the Chinese trellis stair. The great hall has shell-topped alcoves on both sides of the fireplace. In the bright red small parlor, check for the secret staircase that leads to an upstairs bedroom. Sotterley is a working plantation, and you can visit the outbuildings, including tenant houses, smokehouse, and tobacco shed. Look for the "rolling road" where slaves rolled hogsheads of tobacco down to the dock. If you would like to return to appreciate the full ambience of the house, inquire about the dinners that are planned for special occasions during the year.

ST. MARY'S CITY

St. Mary's City
Visitors' Center
St. Mary's City 20686
410–862–0990

Take Route 235 south to Route 489 and Route 5 to St. Mary's City, which was settled in 1634 under the royal charter of Lord Baltimore. Did you know that St. Mary's was Maryland's first capital?

On November 22, 1633, 140 settlers had boarded two ships, the *Ark* and the *Dove,* bound for Maryland. Seventeen were gentlemen who wanted to invest in the New World, and the rest worked after they arrived to pay for their passage. The ships originally had sailed from London in mid-October but were halted at the mouth of the Thames because they had not taken an oath of allegiance to the king. After all who were visible on board had taken the oath, the ships were allowed to sail. They landed in Cowes on the Isle of Wight to await departure on their four-month voyage across the Atlantic. Although the gentlemen investors may have had cabins, the rest of the contingent lived in a space about 100 feet by 30 feet, night and day, for those four months. They encountered a gale during their first days out, so they anchored in a harbor. Another vessel came down upon the *Dove,* however, which forced her to cut her anchor and sail out to sea. The *Ark* followed, and for a time they had fair winds. Another storm struck, and the ships were separated, each thinking the other had been lost, until they reached Barbados and were miraculously reunited. On March 25, 1634, the two ships landed on St. Clement's Island in the Potomac River. (A 40-foot cross stands there today as a memorial for those brave souls.) Within a few days the settlers had chosen the site that became Maryland's first capital, St. Mary's City. Governor Leonard Calvert sent a letter to England stating, "We have seated ourselves within one-half mile of the river within a pallizado of one-hundred twenty yards square." This group was firm in its resolve to guarantee religious and civil liberty for the settlers.

Unquestionably, the lives of those settlers were full of risks. To begin with, they had to survive four months in a tossing ship with poor food and rampant disease. When they landed, they were exposed to new disease such as malaria. Then most of them had to work for a number of years to pay for their passage before they could finally begin creating their own lives in the new land. These must have been hardy souls.

Today local people still bear the names of the early settlers, and some of them raise "sotweed," or tobacco, or "tong" for oysters as their forebears did long ago.

Archaeologists have been finding remnants of the past (in the form of bits and pieces of porcelain, earthenware, bones, and other items thrown out as trash more than three centuries ago) that help them to piece together the lives of these settlers. **St. Mary's Museum** has reconstructed a village from the records of the settlement. You can look over workers' shoulders as they continue their archaeological quest. As you walk around the State House, Farthing's Ordinary, and the Godiah Spray Tobacco Plantation, you can witness reenactments of Dan Clocker as he comes to town to drink, smoke, and tell his stories; Mrs. Nuthead loves to gossip as she runs the printing press; Chancellor Phillip Calvert tries Captain Fendall for treason in the State House; Captain Miles Cook sells indentured servants from the transom of the *Dove;* and the Spray family continues cultivating its tobacco. A replica of the *Dove* is moored on the river. She was reconstructed in time for the Bicentennial and commissioned in October 1978. Check with the visitors' center for information on the weekly schedule of events. If you are there during the summer season, you can enjoy the **Maryland Shakespeare Festival** right on the grounds.

POINT LOOKOUT

Route 5 will take you to the southernmost tip of Maryland, Point Lookout (410–872–5688). A visitors' center focuses on the Civil War, when a fort of earth was built there by Confederate prisoners of war. **Point Lookout State Park** (410–872–5688) offers fishing, hiking, beachcombing, swimming, and camping.

This is the conclusion of your tour of Southern Maryland. Return to Annapolis to continue on to Maryland's Eastern Shore or take Route 235 to Route 5 to I–95 to Washington, D.C.

❧ *Eastern Shore* ❧

Before the Chesapeake Bay Bridge north of Annapolis and the Chesapeake Bay Bridge and Tunnel from Norfolk to Cape Charles were built, the Eastern Shore was almost inaccessible to the major population centers nearby. Now that has changed, but the region still retains its aura of remoteness and timeless stability—almost as if the events and technologies across the bay in Washington and Baltimore were irrelevant to the relationships between men, boats, creeks, wildfowl, and fertile land. To get there from Annapolis, take Route 50 across the Chesapeake Bay Bridge.

From Route 50 take Route 213 to Route 662 to **Wye Oak State Park.** The Wye Oak is 400 years old; it reaches 95 feet high, has a trunk 21 feet in circumference, and stretches to a horizontal spread of 165 feet. This white oak is Maryland's state tree.

WYE MILLS

Wye Oak State Park
Wye Mills 21679

Route 50 south will take you to Easton, which was settled in the late seventeenth century. The **Third Haven Meeting House,** dating from 1682, is the oldest frame church still standing in America. It was built at the headwaters of the Tred Avon, and people arrived by boat for the meeting. Monthly meetings lasted all day long. William Penn preached there, and Lord Baltimore attended services there.

EASTON

Third Haven Meeting House
South Washington Street
Easton 21601

The **Historic Society Complex** contains an 1810, Federal-period town house; a Quaker cabinetmaker's cottage from the 1700s; period gardens; and a museum. You can get information on the other colonial homes to see in town there.

Historical Society Complex
29 South Washington Street
Easton 21601
410–822–0773

November is the month of the annual **Waterfowl Festival** at the Tidewater Inn in

Easton. Paintings, carvings, rare books, duck stamps, old decoys, guns, and hunting gear are on display, and you can learn about goose calling or attend a carving seminar, various workshops, and auctions.

ST. MICHAEL'S

Route 33 will take you to St. Michael's, which was known as Shipping Creek during the Revolution. There is a legend that the people who lived in town foiled a British attack by snuffing out all lights at ground level and hanging lanterns in the tops of trees. This caused the British ships to aim their guns high and shoot over the town. The **Miles River** is very popular with sailors and fishermen, and St. Michael's offers extensive facilities for mooring, repairing, and storing boats. It is a favorite spot for those who want to refit or rebuild their boats, combining the availability of supplies and gear with the pleasures of a quiet, beautiful town.

St. Mary's Square Museum
St. Mary's Square
St. Michael's 21663
410–745–9561

St. Mary's Square is an attractive green that also serves as the center of many town activities. **St. Mary's Square Museum** has local historical displays; behind the museum is another building, called the "Teetotal" building, that looks like a top and contains more exhibits.

Chesapeake Bay Maritime Museum
Mill Street
St. Michael's 21663
410–745–2916

The **Chesapeake Bay Maritime Museum** is an eighteenth-century complex focusing on the maritime history of the area and the bay. As you enter the museum, you'll see an overview of the "drowned river," beginning with the Indians who made their canoes by burning and then scraping a log with oyster shells—a sample is on display, partly finished. Colonists arrived and planted tobacco, with sassafras as a secondary crop during poor tobacco-crop years. You can learn about the log canoes; unlike the Indians' canoes, these were racing machines, such as *Flying Cloud* or the 1892 *Island Blossom,* that look beautiful with their sails trimmed. More exhibits on the Chesapeake Bay skipjacks offer a look at a dying world as they dwindle in number. Watermen have worked long and hard for years, some families going back to the 1600s, and they live only in the Chesapeake Bay area. Among their superstitions are the belief that bad luck will come to a boat containing anything blue; a hatch cover upside-down; a red brick used as ballast; a leaf, nut, or twig from a walnut tree on board; a woman on board; changing the name of a boat; or watching three crows flying across the bow. These men must also work only under sail except two days a week when a yawl boat may push with its motor.

The Waterfowl building displays decoys, guns, and a collection of stuffed birds. You'll learn how watermen went out in a white boat, wearing white clothing so the birds couldn't differentiate them from the light. Sandbags were placed behind some of the heavy guns so the kickback wouldn't damage the boat. Don't miss the 1910 guns that were really anywhere from three to eight barrels. Men went out in sinkboxes—boats with a hole in the middle to keep them more on a level with the top of the water. Some of the decoys are very old and valuable.

A large portion of the museum floats, including the sloop *J. T. Leonard,* a log-bottom bugeye, a skipjack, and a racing log canoe. The boat shed contains a variety of craft, including a Hampton-class loop, a Smith Island crabbing skiff, and a Pocomoke log canoe named *Lillian R.* There is no better or more pleasant place to study fine examples of major types of watercraft distinctive to the bay. The 1879 **Hooper Straight Lighthouse** is also on display.

Don't miss the **Cannonball House,** which achieved notoriety during the War of 1812. It seems that Mrs. Merchant was carrying her baby daughter down the stairs when a cannonball crashed through the roof, rolled across the attic floor, and careened down the stairs after her.

James Michener lived in the village while writing *Chesapeake* and still owns a house there. We enjoyed reading his account of the perfect crab cake in a local newspaper article.

We can recommend **Long Fellow's** (125 Mulberry Street; 410–745–2624) or **The Crab Claw** (Navy Point; 410–745–2900) for a seafood meal. If you are willing to work at it, order steamed crabs; you will learn how to pry off the apron, top shell, and legs and eventually expose succulent crab meat. (A small mallet is handy for the claws.)

Take a cruise on *The Patriot* (410–745–3100) or a nature expedition on the *Odyssey* (410–745–3255). You'll learn about wildlife in the Chesapeake Bay area.

TILGHMAN

From St. Michael's Route 33 leads to Tilghman Island, home port of many vessels in the skipjack fleet. The watermen there harvest oysters in the fall and winter, catch eels for crab bait in the spring, and spend the summer crabbing, fishing, and clamming. The island was originally known as Great Choptank Island, but its name was changed when Matthew Tilghman became the owner. A local carpenter purposely built hexagonal houses there so that no one side would be fully exposed to the force of the wind. In the fall the southern tip of the island is loaded with birds migrating south.

OXFORD

Oxford, situated at the mouth of the Tred Avon River where it joins the Choptank, has long been favored by yachtsmen because it's a sheltered place to anchor and good expertise is available on boat repairs. If you are returning from Tilghman's or St. Michael's, you can take the **Oxford-Bellevue Ferry,** which crosses to Oxford every twenty minutes (410–745–9023), or you can retrace your way along Route 33 to Route 50 and take Route 333 to Oxford.

Oxford was once a stamping ground for pirates, including Stede Bonner and Blackbeard Teach, when they needed repairs on their ships at Skillington's Shipyard. The town was second in size only to Annapolis during the early days of Chesapeake Bay civilization. Because of its location and sheltered anchorage, it was popular as a port of entry for the colony. London and Liverpool stores started branch stores in town where they exchanged goods for tobacco. Although Baltimore surpassed Oxford as a commercial port during the Revolution, Oxford bounced back after the Civil War with steady business in shipbuilding, oystering, and fish-packing.

One of the town fathers, Robert Morris, for whom the main street is named, was killed unexpectedly by the wadding from a ceremonial cannonball; his son was a signer of the Declaration of Independence. The **Robert Morris Inn** (410–226–5111), located right on the river, has a fine reputation for dining and overnight stays. Apart from the food, you will enjoy looking at its architectural features. It was built in 1710 by ships' carpenters and has wooden-pegged paneling and hand-hewn beams. (See Inns appendix.)

Tench Tilghman, another Oxford resident, rode from Yorktown to Philadelphia on October 17, 1781, to tell the Continental Congress that Cornwallis had surrendered. As Washington's aide-de-camp he was well known for his bravery. He is buried in the Oxford Cemetery; a monument stands by his grave as a memorial. Look across the cove to see **Plimhimmon,** which was the home of his widow, Anna Maria Tilghman.

The Ride of Tench Tilghman
Clinton Scollard

They've marched them out of old Yorktown, the vanquished red-coat host—
The grenadiers and fusiliers, Great Britain's pride and boast;
They've left my Lord Cornwallis sitting gnawing at his nails,
With pale chagrin from brow to chin that grim defeat prevails.
Their banners cased, in sullen haste their pathway they pursue
Between the lilied lines of France, the boys in Buff and Blue,
At least their arms away are cast, with muttering and frown,
The while the drums roll out the tune *The World Turned Upside Down!*

It's up, Tench Tilghman, you must ride,
 Yea, you must ride straightway,
And bear to all the countryside
 The glory of this day,
Crying amain the glad refrain,
 This world by field and town—
"Cornwallis' ta'en! Cornwallis' ta'en!
 The World Turned Upside Down!"

Roused Williamsburgh to hear the hoofs
 That loud a tattoo played,
While back from doorways, windows, roofs,
 Rang cheers from man and maid.
His voice, a twilight clarion, spoke
 By slow Pamunkey's ford;
In Fredericksburg to all the folk
 'Twas like a singing sword.

It thrilled while Alexandria slept
 By broad Potomac's shore,
And, like a forest-fire, it swept
 The streets of Baltimore.
With it Elk Tavern's rafters shook
 As though the thunder rolled;
It stirred the brigs off Marcus Hook
 From lookout to the hold.

When midnight held the autumn sky,

Again and yet again
It echoed through the way called High
Within the burg of Penn.
The city watch adjured in vain,—
"Cease! cease! you tipsy clown!"
Flung Tilghman out—"Cornwallis' ta'en!
The World Turned Upside Down!"

Where wrapt in virtuous repose
The head of Congress lay,
A clamor welled as though there rose
The Trump of Judgment Day.
"What madness this?" fierce called McKean,
In white nightcap and gown;
The answer came—"Cornwallis' ta'en!
The World Turned Upside Down!"

Then forth into the highways poured
A wild, exultant rout,
And till the dawn there swelled and soared
Tench Tilghman's victory shout;
Then bells took up the joyous strain,
And cannon roared to drown
The triumph cry—"Cornwallis' ta'en!
The World Turned Upside Down!"

In dreams, Tench Tilghman, still you ride,
As in the days of old,
And with your horse's swinging stride
Your patriot tale is told;
It rings by river, hill, and plain,
Your memory to crown—
"Cornwallis' ta'en! Cornwallis' ta'en!
The World Turned Upside Down!"

CAMBRIDGE

From Oxford return to Route 50, first on Route 333 and then on an unnumbered road heading due east where Route 333 swings north; then continue south to Cambridge. (Oxford and Cambridge are far closer here, and perhaps

**Dorchester County
Historical Society
Maryland Avenue
Cambridge 21613**

· **Blackwater National
Wildlife Refuge
Off Route 335
Cambridge 21613
410–228–2677**

more compatible, than they are in England.) The town was founded in 1684, mostly for the purpose of collecting customs fees. High Street is brick paved and lined with houses from the eighteenth and nineteenth centuries. Stop in the **Dorchester County Historical Society** for a map of the walking tour. You may also want to drive along the Choptank waterfront on a marked tourist route.

Twelve miles south of Cambridge off Route 335, you will find the **Blackwater National Wildlife Refuge,** which was developed for migrating waterfowl in 1932. Blackwater is used by ducks and Canada geese, snow geese, eagles, ospreys, towhees, woodpeckers, brown-headed nuthatches, bobwhite, woodcock, warblers, vireos, orioles, and flycatchers. Some of the endangered species have also been spotted there, including the bald eagle, Delmarva fox squirrel, peregrine falcon, and red-cockaded woodpecker. The visitors' center has exhibits and films. You can drive along a 5-mile road, hike on one of the walking trails, cycle, and watch birds from an observation tower.

SALISBURY

**North American
Wildfowl Art
Museum
Salisbury State
College
Salisbury 21801
410–749–6104**

Route 50 continues inland to Salisbury, which, unfortunately, suffered fires in 1860 and 1886; the historic district is now Victorian rather than colonial. The **North American Wildfowl Art Museum** highlights carvings of songbirds. The development of decoy carving is illustrated by the prolific work of Lem and Steve Ward; each decoy is a little different from the others. Their workshop has also been re-created. Visitors come into the museum through what looks like a rush-covered duck blind and are immediately enveloped in the sights and tape-recorded sounds of a marsh just before dawn. The sounds of wild Canada geese and the sunrise lead to flights of wildfowl. The museum displays some Indian rush decoys from the year 1000.

Newtown was the first residential area built after the fire of 1886. The oldest house in the city, **Poplar Hill Mansion,** which survived the fire, is located there. This Georgian house dates from 1805 and is furnished with period pieces. Bull's-eye windows, a Palladian window on the second floor, dentil molding, and a fan-shaped window at the doorway are special features of this home. A walking tour of the Newtown Historic District includes twenty-six houses. (Ask for walking-tour information at the chamber of commerce.)

From Salisbury you can go south for a side trip to Crisfield or east to Ocean City.

Salisbury Chamber of Commerce
300 East Main Street
Salisbury 21801
410–749–0144

Routes 13 and 413 lead to Crisfield, a town built on oyster shells. On the piers you can sample oysters barely out of the water. Crisfield is also the center of the crabbing industry of Chesapeake Bay; there is even a crab on the water tower.

CRISFIELD

Passenger ferries are available from Crisfield to **Smith Island** and to **Tangier Island;** cars are not allowed on either ferry. When you visit one of these remnants of the old life of Chesapeake Bay, you will be captivated by the absence of noise (apart from the motor scooters that have enabled children to re-create the noise of the modern world). Captain John Smith sailed to Smith Island in 1608 and named it. The people who live there now are descendants of the original settlers who left Cornwall in 1657; all of them still make a living from the sea, as they might have in southwestern England. Crab shanties on the docks and fishing boats portray an essential way of life there.

Captain John Smith reportedly named Tangier Island for the pirates of Tangiers. Then Joshua Thomas arrived on Tangier from Potato Neck on the mainland and converted everyone to Methodism. When 12,000 British troops camped on the island prior to the assault on Baltimore during the War of 1812, Thomas told them that they would not succeed—in fact, that God had told him they would fail. They returned in poor spirits following their defeat and admitted he was right. Today about 950 people live on the island, and all of them are involved in the fisheries.

If you visit either island by private boat, you will be treated to an extremely pleasant time warp as you enter harbors lined with fish shacks and houses on piles—but beware of the strong currents on the canals if you are docking across the stream; we spent half a day scraping off creosote from pilings at Tangier that left a memento on our topsides.

OCEAN CITY

Route 50 east from Salisbury will take you to Ocean City, where you can tickle your toes in the Atlantic. This resort town offers a boardwalk, swimming, fishing, shopping, and entertainment. At the south end of the boardwalk is the **Ocean City Lifesaving Station Museum,** which records the history of lifesaving efforts in town since 1891. Look for the artifacts brought up from shipwrecks off the Delmarva coast, including some dishes from the "China Wreck"; you can investigate shipwrecks further with the staff. The museum has a display of dollhouse models of the buildings once situated in Ocean City, and it has an aquarium.

Ocean City Lifesaving Station Museum
Ocean City 21842
410-289-4991

Assateague State Park and National Seashore

You can reach Assateague by following Route 50, Route 611, and the **Assateague Island Bridge.** The Indian name *Assateague* means "place across"; the island was once inhabited by a peaceful Indian tribe. It is a part of the barrier beach that runs along the coast from Florida to Massachusetts. The island is 37 miles long and varies from ⅕ mile to 1½ miles in width. Some of the sand dunes are 30 feet high. The mystery of shifting sands applies here, because there are many hulks from shipwrecks buried underneath. The beach has only a slight undertow, making it relatively safe for children in normal surf conditions.

There is much speculation about the origin of the wild ponies that live on the island. In 1947 Marguerite Henry wrote *Misty of Chincoteague,* a book that brought a great deal of attention to this interesting species. One explanation is a legend that the first ponies came ashore from a shipwrecked Spanish galleon. It is thought that they adapted themselves to the hardships of exposure during the winter, with limited food and water, and gradually evolved into hardy, small animals. There is a spot known as Spanish Bar, located in Pope Bay, where some say the vessel met her end. Other historians have a less romantic explanation: Horses belonging to Eastern Shore planters in the seventeenth century were allowed to graze on the island, and those that were not recovered developed into the breed that exists today.

The Assateague Island National Seashore was created by an Act of Congress and presidential signature on September 21, 1965. Assateague State Park (410–641–2120 state phone; 641–1441 national phone) contains 680 acres, and federal and state agencies share responsibility for wildlife. The **Chincoteague National Wildlife Refuge** is at the southern end of this barrier beach. In July each year some ponies are rounded up for a swim to Chincoteague Island, Virginia, where they are put up for auction. The National Park Service maintains a visitors' center at the north end of the island. Naturalists conduct canoe trips, guided nature walks, and clamming and fishing demonstrations daily during the season. The

Chincoteague National Wildlife Refuge Assateague Island

park offers picnicking, swimming, fishing, surfing, and camping. You can also reach the Chincoteague refuge at the southern end of the island by road from Chincoteague, Virginia.

From Assateague you can drive north along the coast into Delaware to join Itinerary H or continue on this itinerary by retracing your route on Route 50 west to Cambridge and north until it meets Route 213 to Chestertown.

CHESTERTOWN

If you want to see more Canada geese than you've ever seen in your life, go to Chestertown in the fall. We saw one "safe" pond, which was a city of geese that had spread its suburbs into the surrounding fields. Migrating geese must be grateful for this safe haven, where they can eat corn left in the fields and honk to each other. (Incongruously, another safe haven farther north is found in the corporate ponds and lawns of industrial New Jersey.) The noise they make is more like a symphony than cacophony to the initiated, with movements separated by pauses when the sounds completely stop for a fraction of a minute and then resume. Much of the Eastern Shore is charmed by these lovely birds, and you will see the motif on needlepoint pillows, decoys, lamps, writing paper, paintings, postcards, books, windsocks, wallets, purses, and jewelry.

Chestertown was founded in 1706 on the banks of the Chester River, although it had been designated as a town as early as 1668. Many waterfront homes were built during the 1700s, and a number of them are identified on a walking tour. (Other homes elsewhere in town are also on the tour.) Stop in the **Kent County Chamber of Commerce** for a brochure. The **Hynson-Ringgold House** dates from 1743 and is now the home of the Washington College president. At the end of that block and across the street is the **Customs House,** which has

Kent County Chamber of Commerce
118 North Cross Street
Chestertown 21620
410–778–0416

Flemish bond brick construction. Chestertown had its own version of the Boston Tea Party: On May 23, 1774, angry citizens boarded the brig *William Geddes* moored in front of the Customs House and threw the cargo of tea into the Chester River. The house across the street is called **Wide Hall;** this Georgian house was the scene of much action during the Revolution because the owner, Thomas Smythe, was the head of Maryland's provincial government from 1774 until the state's first constitution emerged in 1776. An unusual freestanding staircase was built in the house. The house at **107 Water Street** was built by Richard Smythe between 1784 and 1787. Woodwork from one of the second-floor rooms now resides in the Winterthur Museum near Wilmington, Delaware, in what is known as the "Chestertown Room."

Hynson-Ringgold House
Cannon & Water Streets
Chestertown 21620

    Washington College was founded in Chestertown in 1782 and is now the tenth-oldest institution of higher learning in America. George Washington was instrumental in the founding of the college and in 1789 received a doctor of laws degree there.

Washington College
College Avenue
Chestertown 21620

    If you're hungry, take a side trip west on Route 20 to the town of **Rock Hall,** which has been called the "Seafood Capital of Kent County." Over 1,000 skipjacks and bugeyes sailed out of Rock Hall during the early 1900s. **Waterman's Crab House,** overlooking the harbor on Sharp Street Wharf (410–639–2261), offers fresh seafood for lunch or dinner. Earlier Tench Tilghman landed in Rock Hall on his way from Virginia to Philadelphia with the news that the Revolutionary War had ended. He was given a horse in Rock Hall and rode to Philadelphia calling, "Cornwallis is taken! A fresh horse for the Congress!"

    ' Continue south on Route 445 to **Eastern Neck Island Wildlife Refuge,** a refuge for migrating birds during the spring and fall. The

Eastern Neck Island Wildlife Refuge
Route 445
Rock Hall 21661
410–639–7056

refuge was established in 1962 on 2,285 acres of marsh, ponds, and coves. This island was also one of the first places to be settled in the New World when, in 1650, Major Joseph Wickes built his home, "Wickliffe," there. Packet vessels sailed back and forth from the mainland to Bogle's Wharf on the east side of the island. Today the refuge offers environmental-education programs, and the observation tower, wildlife trail, and boardwalk are open to the public.

GEORGETOWN

From Chestertown head north on Route 213 to Georgetown, the site of an episode involving a courageous young woman during the War of 1812. British troops were in the process of burning all of the homes in town on May 6, 1813, when they ran up against the determination of Miss Kitty Knight, a beautiful and accomplished woman. Many of the towns-people salvaged what they could from their homes and fled, but she replied to the command to leave, "I shall not leave; if you burn this house, you burn me with it." Although the torch ignited her house twice, she managed to extinguish the flames. The officer in charge at last deferred to her courage and spared her home as well as the one next door.

Because of its accessibility to Wilmington and Philadelphia, Georgetown and the whole Sassafras River have developed into a major boating center. If you're ready for lunch, stop to enjoy the view and the food in **The Granary** (George Street; 410–275–8177).

At this point you can head north for Wilmington or Philadelphia to join Itineraries H or G or continue on this itinerary by returning to Annapolis and then going on to Baltimore. The reconstruction of interstate highways surrounding Baltimore is now nearly complete, so the easiest route to the inner-harbor area from Annapolis is via Route 2 to its intersection with

Route 100. Then go west and north on Route 100 to I–695; west on I–695 to I–295; north on I–295 to the intersection with I–95 and I–395; and finally north on I–395 until it dumps you off at the inner harbor. If this sounds like a complicated way to cover 30 miles, the interstate-highway designers must answer for it—all we can say is that it does work (at this writing!) as long as you stick by the numbers.

∼ *Baltimore* ∼

Baltimore evolved from early settlements at Jones Falls, now downtown, and Fells Point, an eighteenth-century shipbuilding center. Baltimore was an important port that produced many ships for the Continental navy during the Revolution. Privateers (privately owned armed warships) also used Baltimore for a base as they sailed out to demolish the British. During the War of 1812, the privateers again harassed the British and, in fact, seized 500 British merchant ships. The British were furious at these losses and became determined to destroy Baltimore.

During the summer of 1814, the British began to campaign in the Chesapeake. A fleet under Admiral Alexander Cochrane sailed up the bay, into the Patuxent River, then proceeded with infantry to Bladensburg, where they defeated American troops. They marched to Washington, burned the Capitol, the President's House, and other buildings. Back again on their ships, they sailed north in Chesapeake Bay, looking forward to getting rid of the "nest of pirates" in Baltimore. The citizens were aware of impending danger, however, and so dug trenches on Hampstead Hill, reinforced Fort McHenry, and made other preparations for defense. Church bells in town alerted the citizens, who took their positions as the British landed at North Point and started to march up Patapsco Neck. Colonel John Stricker and his men met the British on September 12 and fought the Battle of North Point. Although the Americans had to retreat, the British realized that a victory would not be so easy against such determined resistance. Also, their commander, General Robert Ross, was killed during that battle.

On the water the British began bombarding Fort McHenry for a period of twenty-five hours. Their 1,500 exploding shells did no essential damage to the fort, and eventually the British withdrew back to North Point.

They sailed away in defeat, and Baltimore was saved. Francis Scott Key was on board a small ship just out of range of action but in full view of the fireworks. He wrote "The Star-Spangled Banner" on the back of a letter he had in his pocket, and it was published the next day. It became our national anthem in 1931.

Defense of Fort M'Henry
Francis Scott Key

O! say can you see, by the dawn's early light,
  What so proudly we hail'd at the twilight's last gleaming,
Whose broad stripes and bright stars through the perilous fight,
  O'er the ramparts we watch'd, were so gallantly streaming?
  And the rockets' red glare, the bombs bursting in air,
  Gave proof through the night that our flag was still there . . .
    O! say, does that star-spangled banner yet wave
    O'er the land of the free, and the home of the brave?

On the shore, dimly seen through the mists of the deep,
  Where the foe's haughty host in dread silence reposes,
What is that which the breeze o'er the towering steep,
  As it fitfully blows, half conceals, half discloses?
  Now it catches the gleam of the morning's first beam,
  In fully glory reflected now shines on the stream—
    'Tis the star-spangled banner, O! long may it wave
    O'er the land of the free, and the home of the brave.

And where is that band who so vaultingly swore
  That the havoc of war and the battle's confusion
A home and a country should leave us no more?
  Their blood has wash'd out their foul foot-steps' pollution.
  No refuge could save the hireling and slave,
  From the terror of flight or the gloom of the grave;
    And the star-spangled banner in triumph doth wave
    O'er the land of the free, and the home of the brave.

O! thus be it ever when freemen shall stand
  Between their lov'd home, and the war's desolation,
Blest with vict'ry and peace, may the heav'n rescued land
  Praise the power that hath made and preserv'd us a nation!
  Then conquer we must, when our cause it is just,

And this be our motto—"In God is our trust!"
And the star-spangled banner in triumph shall wave
O'er the land of the free, and the home of the brave.

You can visit Fort McHenry, which is designed in the French star shape, with five bastions to produce crossfire against attackers. **Fort McHenry Visitors' Center** contains exhibits and brochures on the history of the fort and has an interesting taped slide show reenacting the battle.

FORT McHENRY

**Fort McHenry
Visitors' Center
Fort Avenue
Baltimore 21202
410–962–4290**

Baltimore's recent renaissance has transformed the inner harbor into a real showplace. By the 1950s Baltimore realized that urban decay and decline were destroying the once-thriving inner city. One hundred businessmen formed the Greater Baltimore Committee and created a redevelopment plan to raise the city from the ashes of its past. More than seventy-five new or reconstructed buildings now line the attractive waterfront. You can start at one end of the inner harbor and spend all day learning about science or history and enjoying the sights, with plenty left over to see on another visit.

INNER HARBOR

We suggest beginning your tour on **Federal Hill** in South Baltimore, where you can look across at the skyline of the inner harbor and the city beyond. This site was an observation point during the Civil War. For many years of Baltimore's maritime history, the lookout on the hill performed a useful service by keeping track of approaching ships that he could see but those in town could not. Then he would run up the appropriate flag on his pole to let shipowners know which vessel to expect.

**Federal Hill
Key Highway &
Battery
Baltimore**

Move around the harbor to the **Maryland Science Center and Davis Planetarium,** which houses a hands-on science experience on three floors. "Chesapeake Bay" is one of the per-

**Maryland Science
Center and Davis
Planetarium
601 Light Street
Baltimore 21202
410–685–5225**

Harborplace
301 Light Street
Baltimore 21202
410–332–4191

Constellation
Pier One
Pratt Street
Baltimore
410–539–1797

manent exhibits that appeals to all ages, with its 2,000-gallon tank teeming with estuarian life.

Harborplace is next, and we've found that if you wander through it before the rest of the tour you may spend more time than you had planned. (But be sure to see it sometime.) Two glass-enclosed pavilions that look like steamship-pier headquarters house many shops and restaurants. Don't miss the Sam Smith Market, on the second level of the Light Street Pavilion, where you will see a changing group of artists, collectors, and crafts people. The Colonnade Market and Trading Hall offers spices, flowers, coffee, wine, prime meats, baked goods, cheese, seafood, and fresh produce.

Next you'll come to the U.S. frigate **Constellation**, which was launched in 1797 as the first commissioned ship of the American navy. She developed the reputation of a "Yankee Racehorse" after her first encounter with an enemy man-of-war, the frigate **L'Insurgente**, which she captured easily. She served as a training ship for midshipmen and finally saw active duty as a flagship of the Atlantic Fleet during World War II.

You can explore the various decks of our first warship to see the actual living space for the men, storage areas for munitions and gear, and various exhibits. The spar deck is the top deck, where the running rigging that controls yards and sails is belayed ready for use. From this deck men would clamber up the ratlines to lookout stations on the tops (platforms where sections of masts join), which were also used by marines firing rifles during combat. Or they would climb onto the yards to set, furl, reef, or change sails while balancing with their feet on a single footrope below the yard, using both hands for the sail as they leaned against the yard. Starting from the bow, the masts on this vessel are fore, main, and mizzen; moving upward from the deck on each mast, the sails are the course, topsail, topgallant, and royal.

Climb down from the spar deck to the gun deck, where the guns stand ready to poke out of gun-ports. Again starting from the forward end of the deck, you will see the galley, bilge pump, and captain's quarters in the aft section. The captain of the *Constellation* was lucky enough to have his own private, if primitive, toilet protruding over one side of the hull and his bathtub over the other. Go down one more level to the berthing deck, where the crew slept forward and the officers aft. The orlop deck is next, with the hospital in the forward section. Below that is the hold with barrels of fish and dried, smoked, and salted meats, the powder magazine, and the sail loft. As you can imagine, space was at a premium, and rubbing elbows with your neighbor was more than a metaphor.

Life on board was sure to be crowded and might be boring after repeating the same routine day after day. Each sailor had duties to perform that were listed on a "station bill," so that he would know where to go when orders were given to get under way; bring the ship to anchor; tack, set, and furl sails; reef; and perform many other tasks of seamanship. Each man also had a station with a gun crew, where they trained every day so their teamwork would be perfect. Hours were divided into five four-hour watches and two two-hour dogwatches between 4:00 and 8:00 p.m. This schedule, still in use, allowed the watches to rotate so that a man would not stand the same watch on any two days.

Every morning the boatswain piped "up all hammocks," which was answered by "rise and shine." At the order "lash and stow," each man lashed up his hammock and went above decks to stow it in the spar-deck nettings for the day.

Next the men scoured the deck with "holystones and sand" until the deck was pronounced clean. When the ship was at anchor, some men cleaned the sides of the hull from platforms alongside the hull. At seven bells (7:30 a.m.) they cleaned up and fell into line for inspection. Next, sails were changed or trimmed, as needed, and the short pennant flown at night was changed for the 40-foot-long commission pennant flown during the day. At eight bells, after two or three hours of work, they were ready for breakfast. After breakfast the deck was swept, they all went to their battle stations for drill and then to their work stations as carpenter, sailmaker, rigger, cooper, or tailor. On Thursday mornings they scrubbed their hammocks, and on Fridays they washed their clothes. On Wednesdays and Saturdays the barber was available for shaves and haircuts. Below decks the cooks scrubbed their pots for inspection. At 11:30 a.m. the sweepers were called again; then at noon grog and dinner were served. During the next few hours, some of the men had free time and others worked. After supper the entire crew gathered on deck to watch the sunset, spin yarns, and talk. At "stand by your hammocks," each man was ready to receive his hammock as numbers were called. Hammocks were slung on hooks below, the older crew retired, and the younger ones got out their accordions and banjos and gathered to sing and tell stories. The colors were hauled down at 8:00 p.m., and at 9:00 p.m. everyone not on watch turned in. On Sundays church services were held, and only necessary work was done on board.

You are sure to come away from your tour with a respect for the disciplined life these men shared. Life at sea never matched the romantic imaginings that brought farm boys down from the hills to enlist.

As you continue your circuit of the inner

The United States Naval Academy, designated a U.S. National Historic Landmark in 1963.

ANNAPOLIS

Like many cities, Baltimore has restored its waterfront—called the Inner Harbor—and here visitors can learn about history and science as well as sightsee.

BALTIMORE

The famous Chincoteague ponies.

ASSATEAGUE ISLAND

World Trade Center
110 West Baltimore
  Street
Baltimore 21202
410–837–4515

harbor, the top of the **World Trade Center** is a great place to go for a view of the entire area. Ride up the elevator to the **Top of the World,** where you can look out of large picture windows onto the city and harbor. Exhibits trace the major historical events of Baltimore, and some of the famous people who have been involved in the history are represented in photographic displays.

National Aquarium in
  Baltimore
Pier 3
501 East Pratt Street
Baltimore 21202
410–576–3800

Next on your walking circuit is the **National Aquarium in Baltimore,** which provides visitors with a series of trips up escalators and moving ramps through five levels to view many varieties of marine life. When we were there, two beluga whales had just been placed in their tank and were only partly exposed to view so that they could get used to their new environment. These whales have a rounded, prominent forehead and a ridge on the back in place of the dorsal fin. They have forty teeth that are sharp in youth and become flattened as they age. Females grow to be about 13 or 14 feet in length; males grow to 18 feet. When born the calf is brown, then bluish gray, and finally white. Their eyes are brown, and we're convinced that the lips have a smile on them.

The story of their acquisition is a long one, leading to Churchill River in Manitoba, Canada. On this particular trip a group from the National Aquarium joined one from Connecticut's Mystic Marinelife Aquarium. Each person had a specific assignment as they set out in 14-foot aluminum catch boats. When a whale was spotted, the first man jumped onto the whale, and then the second man tied up the other end of the whale— either the tail or the pectoral fins. As you can imagine, it was not easy to hang onto a slippery whale, and many tries were necessary. When the whales were captured, they were lifted, all 850 pounds of them, onto a stretcher lined with water-soaked foam rubber to provide support and buoyancy. The four captured whales were placed in a holding tank for a few days and then flown to New York in mahogany boxes. They were accompanied by aquarium staff, who rubbed them with lanolin-based cream, sprayed them with water, and used icepacks to keep them cool and moist. When the two whales bound for Baltimore were ready to leave the aquarium in New York, they were lifted by crane to a truck that had been specially designed to take them to Baltimore. These 9-foot-long whales, named Anore and Illamar, adjusted to their new home and were soon involved in feeding and behavior demonstrations for the public.

As you move up through the aquarium, you will see "Maryland: Mountains to the Sea" on Level 2, illustrated by living exhibits from the mountains, tidal marsh, Eastern Shore, and Atlantic Beach. Level 3 contains a gallery of animals who survive through changing their body shape, color, methods of feeding, or movement. Level 4 presents the different coastal environments from the Atlantic to the Pacific. Look for the special "children's cove," where children can touch a variety of sea creatures. The South American Rain Forest on Level 5 is a moist, warm home to many crawling and flying creatures living in a green profusion of tropical plants. As you descend from it, you will have the chance to stare eyeball to eyeball at sharks and all sorts of fish in extensive tanks that surround your walkway down. This is an aquarium you'll want to visit and revisit; its exhibits are dramatically presented, and it is designed both to make you see the species and to understand its role in the ecological systems that surround it and us. Both in architecture and exhibit design, it is the most interesting aquarium we have ever visited.

At the end of the inner-harbor circuit, the

Baltimore Maritime Museum
Pier 4
Baltimore 21202
410–396–3854

Baltimore Maritime Museum exhibits the lightship *Chesapeake,* built in Charleston, South Carolina, in 1930. With her bright red hull, she once marked major shipping channels in Delaware, Chesapeake Bay, and Massachusetts. Now large buoys have taken over the job from most lightships. The USS *Torsk* is a submarine built in Portsmouth, New Hampshire, in 1944; the submarine saw action in Pearl Harbor, Guam, and the Sea of Japan in 1945. She was later used for training in New London, Connecticut, all along our Atlantic Coast, and in the Mediterranean and Norfolk, Virginia. She also participated in NATO exercises. She is 311 feet long, and her name came from the gadoid fish, which is like a codfish and found in the North Atlantic.

FELLS POINT

This early Baltimore community on the inner harbor, which was founded in 1732, is now being brought back to life with renovated and reconstructed buildings along the waterfront and surrounding blocks. Apartments, studios, and lofts are appearing, as are shops and restaurants. As a seaport Fells Point once had twenty shipyards, including some that built the famous Baltimore clippers in the last quarter of the eighteenth century and the first quarter of the nineteenth. These fast schooners had the distinctive clipper bow and are the forerunners of the later, larger, square-rigged clipper ships developed for the California trade in the middle of the nineteenth century. Their fame rests on their success as blockade runners and privateers during the War of 1812—the success that led to the unsuccessful British attack on Baltimore in 1814. A replica of one of these beautiful ships, the *Pride of Baltimore,* was commissioned October 23, 1988, after an earlier vessel with the same name was lost at sea several years before. When the ship is not on extended cruises to Europe, she is moored in the inner harbor, where she receives visitors.

Baltimore developed a series of ethnic neighborhoods, each quite distinct from the others. Waves of immigrants populated an Italian section, then Greek and Polish sections. Germans had arrived earlier, and one of their descendants was H. L. Mencken, a brilliant journalist and writer, who lived most of his life in a nineteenth-century row house overlooking Union Square. Sometimes called "The Sage of Baltimore," Mencken was a shrewd cynic who could turn the American public on its ear. You can visit the **Mencken House,** which has been restored and provided with an audiovisual presentation about his life. The Italian, Greek, and Polish sections still exist in areas to the east and north of Fells Point. There is an abundance of good ethnic restaurants in each of them.

Mencken House
1524 Hollins Street
Baltimore
410–396–7997

Mount Vernon Place is an elegant residential neighborhood with nineteenth-century mansions lining the square around the **Washington Monument.** You can't miss seeing this monument, which soars 160 feet into the air. Designed by Robert Mills, this monument was one of many dedicated to George Washington. The scene at the top depicts Washington resigning his commission as commander in chief of the Revolutionary army. What was then a rural setting at the edge of the city was chosen as the site for the monument, because the city fathers were worried about such a tall monument falling over. You can climb the 228 steps to the top for a fine view of the city.

MOUNT VERNON
PLACE

Washington
 Monument
Mount Vernon Place
Baltimore

From the monument cross to the west side of the square to the marble balustrade, where you will see two of a set of four bronzes by Antoine Louis Barye. The seated lion is also by Barye. To the left of the park is 1 West Mount Vernon Place, the **Thomas-Jencks-Gladding House.** This Classical Revival mansion has

Italian Renaissance details. Along the same side of the square, Number 3 has heavy, carved wooden doors decorated with lions. Number 5 once housed the Walters collection of art, which has now been transferred to the larger Walters Art Gallery. Number 7 is actually four houses in one, owned originally by Mrs. Henry Barton Jacobs and now by the **Engineering Society of Baltimore.** Number 13 was where the Reverend Billy Sunday lived when he was trying to save Baltimore from perdition in 1916; it was then owned by Henri Pratt James.

As you turn right and cross the street, look for the **Boy and Turtle** fountain by Henri Grenier. Across Cathedral Street and to the north you will find **704 Cathedral Street,** the home of H. L. Mencken and his wife for the five years she lived. The **Marburg House,** the home of Theodore Marburg, who was involved in drafting the covenants of the League of Nations, is at 14 West Mount Vernon Place. Number 8 was once owned by William Tiffany and is now the **Mount Vernon Club.**

Turn left at the corner to 700 North Charles Street, the Washington Apartments, which were originally designed to be eight stories high. A neighbor petitioned and won an ordnance prohibiting any building from rising higher than the Washington Monument. **Mount Vernon Place United Methodist Church** stands on the site of the house where Francis Scott Key died. The green serpentine stone has oxidized over the years. You can see that the spires are not as high as the monument. Number 14 East Mount Vernon Place was the home of William Patterson, whose daughter married Jerome Bonaparte, younger brother of Emperor Napoleon. Napoleon had the marriage annulled by the pope. Jerome went back to Europe in 1804, and Betsy stayed behind in Baltimore to have her baby; they never saw each other again.

Numbers 33, 31, and 21 were owned by three Baltimore sisters, the granddaughters of Charles Carroll, a signer of the Declaration of Independence. The **Peabody Institute** owns the southeast corner of Mount Vernon Place.

The **Walters Art Gallery** is housed in a reproduction of the sixteenth-century Palazzo Bianco in Genoa. The collection includes over 25,000 works of art dating back as much as 6,000 years. You can see Etruscan, Byzantine, Medieval, and Renaissance sculpture and painting, and the Chinese porcelain collection is extensive.

Walters Art Gallery
600 North Charles
Street
Baltimore
410–547–9000

Also on Charles Street you will find a number of shops and restaurants; it has been called "Culinary Corridor." Another good spot for lunch is nearby: **Society Hill** (58 West Biddle; 410–837–3630).

There is much more to see and do in Baltimore if you have some time to spend in this interesting city. Let us list a few additional sites: **Charles Center, Lexington Market, Peale Museum, Carroll Mansion, Edgar Allan Poe House, Baltimore & Ohio Railroad Museum, Babe Ruth Birthplace, Baltimore Museum of Art, Johns Hopkins Archaeological Museum, Baltimore Zoo,** and the **Star-spangled Banner Flag House.** For further information contact the **Baltimore Convention and Visitors' Bureau,** Pratt Street, Baltimore 21202; 410–837–4636.

☙ *Western Maryland* ☙

Route 70 will take you from Baltimore to Frederick, the town remembered for its "clustered spires" in John Greenleaf Whittier's poem. From Frederick there are a number of pleasant trips you can take in any direction in the surrounding countryside.

Originally called Fredericktown by the first   **FREDERICK**

English and German settlers in 1745, the town became a stop for wagon trains making their way through the Cumberland Gap and across the mountains to the west. Perhaps fortunately, because the settlers did not have the water transportation that was so easily available in eastern Maryland, they farmed their land instead of growing tobacco. Other communities found that tobacco soon depleted the soil, but the area around Frederick still has fertile soil.

Barbara Fritchie
John Greenleaf Whittier

Up from the meadows rich with corn,
Clear in the cool September morn,
The clustered spires of Frederick stand
Green-walled by the hills of Maryland.
Round about them orchards sweep,
Apple and peach tree fruited deep,
Fair as a garden of the Lord
To the eyes of the famished rebel horde.
On that pleasant morn of the early fall
When Lee marched over the mountain-wall
Over the mountains winding down,
Horse and foot, into Frederick-town.
Forty flags with their silver stars,
Forty flags with their crimson bars,
Flapped in the morning wind: the sun
Of noon looked down, and saw not one.
Up rose old Barbara Fritchie then,
Bowed with her four score years and ten
Bravest of all in Frederick-town
She took up the flag the men hauled down
In her attic window the staff she set,
To show that one heart was loyal yet.
Up the street came the rebel tread,
Stonewall Jackson riding ahead.
Under his slouched hat left and right
He glanced: the old flag met his sight.

"Halt"—the dust-brown ranks stood fast,
"Fire"—out blazed the rifle blast.
It shivered the window, pane and sash:
It rent the banner with seam and gash.
Quick as it fell, from the broken staff
Dame Barbara snatched the silken scarf.
She leaned far out on the window-sill,
And shook it forth with a royal will.
"Shoot if you must, this old gray head,
But spare your country's flag," she said.
A shade of sadness, a blush of shame,
Over the face of the leader came.
The nobler nature within him stirred
To life at that woman's deed and word,
"Who touches a hair on yon gray head
Dies like a dog! March on!" he said.
All day long through Frederick street
Sounded the tread of marching feet.
All day long that free flag tost
Over the heads of the rebels host.
Ever its torn folds rose and fell
On the loyal winds that loved it well,
And through the hill gaps sunset light
Shown over it with a warm good night,
Barbara Fritchie's work is o'er,
And the rebel rides on his raids no more.
Honor to her! and let a tear
Fall, for her sake, on Stonewall's bier,
Over Barbara Fritche's grave,
Flag of freedom and Union, wave!
Peace and order and beauty draw
Round the symbol of light and law
And ever the stars above look down
On thy stars below in Frederick-town.

During the early 1970s the town was in a
state of severe decline, with businesses moving
out and buildings deteriorating. Ronald Young
was elected mayor in 1974 and soon spearheaded a campaign to make Frederick a thriving

community again. Operation Town Action was formed and went to work, drawing up plans for renovation and revitalization of the historic district in conjunction with Frederick Preservation Advisers. Volunteers got involved with the physical labor needed to remove tacky facades and reveal or restore the original beauty of Frederick architecture. Telephone and power lines were buried underground to further enhance the appearance of the area. As business began to return, the group made plans for building parking ramps, so that shops in town could compete effectively with suburban malls without ruining the historic district for walking. Within a two-year period many volunteers had restored buildings, landscaped grounds, added new lighting, brought in new businesses, and designed the new courthouse complex. In 1976 Frederick won the All-American City Award, but it is not resting on its well-deserved laurels. A $10-million courthouse project has been finished, and the group is working on a $40-million park-and-building plant that will provide hotels, offices, and shops on one side of the creek and cycling and jogging paths on the other side.

The early settlers were just as tenacious when they repudiated the Stamp Act in 1765. And during the Civil War, the citizens paid a ransom of $200,000 to Confederate General Jubal Early so that he would not destroy their city. Although they had hoped the federal government would reimburse them, nothing has been done yet. The Frederick Reimbursement Bill is presented year after year after year.

Tourism Council of Frederick County
19 East Church Street
Frederick 21701
301–663–8687

Stop in the tourism council office for information on a walking tour of the historic district and on other sights in town. You can see the **City Hall,** where the ransom was paid to Early in 1864; the **Historical Society and Museum,** dating from 1830; the law offices of Roger B. Taney and Francis Scott Key; the **William Tyler**

Page Home (the author of the American Creed); several interesting churches; and the **Court Square** area, dating from 1756.

Don't miss the **Barbara Fritchie Museum.** Whittier's version of the brief encounter between Confederate General Stonewall Jackson and Barbara Fritchie is the one we remember because it symbolizes a remnant of civility in a brutal and bloody war.

Inside Barbara's small house you can see a quilt made from flax she had spun on her spinning wheel, as well as her petticoat and jacket. Look for the large roller that looks like a rolling pin; it was used to roll the lumps out of a straw mattress. The famous window, with flag flying, is still there. The flag contains thirty-five stars, the last added for West Virginia. A silk dress belonging to Barbara is on display, as well as a doll dress she made for a young relative. The china teapot that she used to serve tea to George Washington in 1791 is there. Don't miss the knotted cane with which she shooed Confederate soldiers away from her porch after they had insulted her beloved Union flag.

One-way streets in Frederick can be frustrating, but work your way north past Governor Thomas Johnson High School to **Rose Hill Manor,** which dates from the 1790s. This Georgian mansion was the home of Thomas Jefferson—who nominated George Washington as commander in chief of the Continental army—from 1794 until 1819. Now the house has been developed into a museum for children, where they can touch and play with nineteenth-century toys, try their hands at weaving, help make a quilt, and do a little colonial cooking. The guides are in costume and will help each child enjoy his or her experience there. The focus is on living history, so that you can "touch" your heritage and "see" the past.

Stroll around the grounds to the black-

Barbara Fritchie Museum
154 West Patrick Street
Frederick 21701
301–663–0630

Rose Hill Manor
1611 North Market Street
Frederick 21701
301–694–1648

smith shop, carriage museum, log cabin, and farm museum. When you walk through the gardens, you are welcome to touch, smell, or taste mint, lavender, basil, oregano, and other medicinal and culinary herbs. The vegetable section provides produce to be used in the kitchen. Come to visit and experience a quilting bee, soap making, candle dipping, and cooking various dishes. Special events are held during the year, including an Easter egg hunt, fall festival, Halloween tour, needlework show, and Christmas open house. Children can register for such workshops as birdhouse building, blacksmithing, holiday cooking, and crafts.

If you're ready for lunch, head for **The Province** (131 North Market Street; 301–663–1441) or **The Deli** (57 East Patrick Street; 301–663–8122). Next to the Deli is one of the largest antiques stores anywhere. **The Craftworks** (55 East Patrick Street; 301–662–3111) houses antiques on two full floors—whatever you're looking for has got to be there! (This concentration of antiques rivals **New Market,** located 8 miles east, which is another antiques center worth a visit.)

From Frederick you can take several excursions in different directions to see more of Western Maryland. A short excursion to the south leads to Sugarloaf Mountain (or you can go see it on your way to Washington, D.C.). To the north is Cunningham Falls State Park; to the west is Antietam Battlefield; and to the northwest are Hagerstown and Cumberland.

EXCURSION SOUTH OF FREDERICK

Sugarloaf Mountain
Sugarloaf Road
Mt. Ephraim

Heading south on Route 355 toward Urbana and Sugarloaf Mountain will take you to **The Blue Fox Inn** (4424-A Urban Pike; 301–831–4878) for lunch or dinner. Opened in 1985, it has attractive paneled rooms enlarged by the use of mirrors and a skylight. On the walls the blown-up photos of vegetables, fruits, and nuts look good enough to eat.

Continue on another mile to **The Turning Point Inn** (3406 Urbana Pike; 301–874–2421) for dinner (or lunch by prior reservation). You can even spend the night here. (See Inns appendix.)

To reach the base of Sugarloaf Mountain, take Route 80 west from Urbana and turn south on Thurston Road shortly after crossing I–270. Then go west on Sugarloaf Road toward the village of Mt. Ephraim. Sugarloaf Mountain, 1,282 feet high, is a great place to hike because you can see much of Frederick and Montgomery counties as well as parts of Virginia and West Virginia from the top. French trader and explorer Martin Chartier guided a Swiss nobleman, Baron Graffenried, over Sugarloaf Mountain in search of silver mines. "There is no more beautiful sight in the world," concluded Chartier. George Washington surveyed the area prior to 1769, and General Braddock passed through on his way to Fort Duquesne during the French and Indian War in 1769.

EXCURSION NORTH OF FREDERICK

Route 15 north leads to Cunningham Falls State Park and the Grotto of Lourdes. On the way you can take a brief side trip to see one or two covered bridges. The one near Lewistown at Utica is the largest in Frederick County and has the original bowstring and Howe trusses still intact. To get to it leave Route 15 on the Old Frederick Road south of Lewistown and turn left when you reach Utica Road. The other covered bridge, called Loys Station Bridge, is north of Creagerstown; take Old Frederick Road through Creagerstown and continue another 2 miles.

Catoctin Furnace, located in **Cunningham Falls State Park,** was built by the James Johnson Company in 1774. It played an important role during the Revolution by producing

**Cunningham Falls
State Park
14039 Catoctin
Hollow Road
Thurmont 21788**

**Catoctin Mountain
Park
Thurmont 21788
301–663–8330**

**Grotto of Lourdes
Grotto Road
Thurmont 21788
301–447–6122**

**St. Elizabeth Seton
Shrine
St. Joseph Provincial
House
Thurmont 21788**

**EXCURSION WEST OF
FREDERICK**

**Braddock Monument
Braddock Mountain
Frederick**

weaponry for the Continental army. The iron plates for the *Monitor* were cast there during the Civil War period. The workers at the furnace lived in a stone-cottaged village, which is open as a National Register historic district. **Cunningham Falls,** a 78-foot cascading waterfall in a deep gorge, is located on the other side of the park. Cunningham Falls State Park offers picnicking, swimming, boating, fishing, and camping.

Catoctin Mountain Park, adjacent to Cunningham, is a national park. Check in at the visitors' center for information on hiking trails and other recreational activities. You can also drive 14 miles on the back roads of the Catoctin ridge; be sure to stop at the scenic overlook on the east side of Hunting Creek Lake. The National Park Service displays the **Blue Blazes Still,** a real still used during Prohibition, as part of an interpretive program. The presidential retreat **Camp David** is located within the park but is not open to the public.

Continue on Route 15 8 miles north of Thurmont and follow signs to the **Grotto of Lourdes.** It is the first National Catholic Shrine in the United States and the oldest replica of Lourdes, France, in the Western Hemisphere. It is located on the side of the mountain above the campus of Mount St. Mary's College. A few miles farther on Route 15 will bring you to the **St. Elizabeth Seton Shrine** on the grounds of the **St. Joseph Provincial House.** She was the first native-born American to be canonized by the Catholic Church.

Head west from Frederick on Route 40, stay in the left lane, and bear left onto alternate Route 40. Continue up the mountain for 2 miles to the **Braddock Monument,** honoring General Edward Braddock, who did not survive his mission to liberate Fort Duquesne. The **Braddock**

Mountain scenic overlook provides a panoramic view of the valley below. Continue on through **Middletown,** the home of Revolutionary War hero Sergeant Lawrence Everhart. During the Battle of Brandywine, Everhart was one of two soldiers who carried the wounded General Lafayette more than 2 miles for help.

A little farther along Route 40A you will come to **Old South Mountain Inn** (301–432–6155), which has served as a hotel, tavern, restaurant, stagecoach station, and private home. Across the street from the inn are four historical markers detailing the emplacement of troops there during the Civil War.

From Route 40A take Monument Road for 1 mile to **Washington Monument State Park** to see the monument that was one of the first memorials to George Washington. The citizens of Boonsboro built the monument in this park in one day on July 4, 1827.

The monument is quite close to **Greenbrier State Park,** which was developed by the state in the early 1960s. (Access to the park, however, is from Route 40, not Route 40A.) You can hike through a section of the Appalachian Trail or go picnicking, swimming, boating, fishing, or camping in the park.

Head back to Boonsboro and take Route 34 to Sharpsburg and follow signs to **Antietam,** where the bloodiest day of the Civil War took place during the Battle of Antietam (or Sharpsburg) on September 17, 1862. Clara Barton, after helping the wounded during that battle, exclaimed, "War is a dreadful thing. . . . Oh, my God, can't this civil strife be brought to an end?" In the battle 41,000 soldiers under Confederate General Robert E. Lee clashed with 87,000 soldiers of the Federal Army of the Potomac led by General George B. McClellan, who reputedly said, "If I cannot whip Bobbie

Washington Monument State Park Monument Road Boonsboro

Lee, I will be willing to go home." Bloody Lane was the area of greatest fatalities. At the end of that day, Federal losses were 12,410 and Confederate losses 10,700. Stop in the **Antietam Visitors' Center** to see a film on the action of that day.

Antietam Visitors' Center
Antietam
301–432–5124

HARPER'S FERRY, WEST VIRGINIA

Route 67 will take you south to **Harper's Ferry, West Virginia.** In 1733 Peter Stephens set up a ferry service crossing the Potomac and Shenandoah rivers. Fourteen years later Robert Harper took over Stephens's ferry service and added a mill. During the 1790s President George Washington promoted the establishment of an armory in Harper's Ferry. The town's growth followed the construction of the Chesapeake and Ohio Canal and the Baltimore and Ohio Railroad in the 1830s.

In October 1859 John Brown's raid took place during the dead of night as twenty-two men took control of the armory, ending only when Robert E. Lee and Jeb Stuart took possession of the building. Brown was hanged at Charles Town on December 2, 1859. In 1861 the armory was burned so that it would not be available to the Confederates. As it happened, both the Union and Confederate sides occupied the town one after the other. In 1862 Stonewall Jackson captured the town; by then many of the townspeople had moved away because of the continued anguish of war in their area.

Harper's Ferry
National Historical
Park
Harper's Ferry, West
Virginia 25851

Harper's Ferry National Historic Park has been involved in a great deal of restoration, including more work after the floods in 1985. Stop in the visitors' center for information on historical sites to visit. The site of both the park and the town, on the steep hillsides of a peninsula overlooking the roaring rapids of two powerful rivers, is worth a visit in itself. Thomas Jefferson wrote that "the scene is worth a voyage across the Atlantic," and Carl Sandburg wrote, "Harper's Ferry is a meeting place of winds and water, rocks and ranges."

If you are interested in white-water trips, consider contacting one of these outfitters: **River & Trail Outfitters** (Route 2, Valley Road, Knoxville, Maryland 21758; 301–695–5177), **Blue Ridge Outfitters** (Box 750, Harper's Ferry, West Virginia; 304–725–3444), or **Harper's Ferry Riders** (Box 267, Knoxville, Maryland 21758; 301–834–8051). You can also canoe-camp along the Potomac and Shenandoah rivers· and the adjacent C&O Canal from Spring Gap Campground to Harper's Ferry, a distance of 115 miles. Most of this trip is flat-water. Or you can cycle and hike along the canal.

HAGERSTOWN

The excursion northwest from Frederick begins with Hagerstown, reached by I–70 west. The town was founded in 1762 as Elizabeth Town to honor the wife of settler Jonathan Hager. Visit the **Hager House and Museum.** Sometimes called "Hager's Fancy," the house was built over a spring to ensure a source of water during an Indian attack. This stone house has eighteenth-century period furnishings.

Hager House and Museum ·
19 Key Street
Hagerstown 21740
301–739–8393

FORT FREDERICK STATE PARK

Continue on I–70 to Big Pool and Route 56 to **Fort Frederick State Park** (301–842–2155), which is the only remaining British stone fort in the country. It was begun in 1756 during the French and Indian War. Barracks have been reconstructed and historical events are reenacted by military units in eighteenth-century costume. An orientation film and museum describe the historical development of the fort. The park offers cycling, camping, nature and hiking trails, boating, and fishing.

HANCOCK

Continue on I–70 to Hancock. The town has the distinction of being on the narrowest bit of Maryland in the western part of the state across the Mason-Dixon line from Pennsylvania.

In fact, during the 1760s a seventy-three–year boundary dispute between the Penns of Pennsylvania and the Calverts of Maryland finally came to a head. It was finally resolved by the surveying of the Mason-Dixon line, which left only a 2-mile strip of land for Maryland between Pennsylvania and West Virginia. In 1839 the C&O Canal was completed to Hancock, bringing prosperity to the area. The next section, to Cumberland, was finished in 1850. You can visit the **C&O Visitors' Center** to see models of canal boats and locks. A slide show and exhibits present the story of canal development over the years.

**C&O Visitors'
Center
Main Street
Hancock 21750**

The **Tonoloway Aqueduct** carried canal water over Tonoloway Creek; it is one of eleven aqueducts along the canal. You can hike along the towpath that runs from Georgetown to Cumberland. This 12-foot-wide path is overgrown in some places and may wash out after a heavy rain. Much of the path is built of the earth and crushed stone that made a good surface for the mules. Tent campsites are spaced every 5 miles along the 165-mile section from Carderock to Cumberland, and one is located midway between Seneca and Georgetown. Drive-in campgrounds are located at McCoys Ferry, Fifteen Mile Creek, and Spring Gap. Canoeing is available with portages around the locks. Canoes may be rented at **Swains Lock** and **Fletcher's Boat House.** For more information contact the superintendent of the **C&O Canal National Historical Park.**

**C&O Canal National
Historical Park
Box 4
Sharpsburg 21782
301–739–4200**

If you visit Hancock in the fall, the air will be perfumed with the fragrance from apple and peach orchards around the town. In September there is a Canal Apple Festival to attend.

CUMBERLAND

Six miles east of Cumberland on Route 40 is **Rocky Gap State Park,** located in a natural saddle between Evitts Mountain and Martin Mountain. The park offers fishing, boating, nature trails, hiking, picnicking, and camping.

Route 40 will bring you to Cumberland, which has a National Historic District composed of Federal and Georgian Revival homes. **History House** displays a primitive kitchen, a music room, and a library with a collection of genealogical materials. You can get information on a walking tour from **Allegheny County Tourism.**

George Washington's Headquarters was his first military headquarters. He began as an aide-de-camp to General Braddock and during the French and Indian War used the cabin as his headquarters. A taped narration is available while you view the exhibit from the outside.

Cumberland was the eastern end of the historic Cumberland Trail—our country's first road built with federal funds. It brought prosperity to Cumberland, which was a supply terminus for overland transportation. The B&O Railroad arrived in Cumberland in 1842, and the C&O Canal was completed in 1850. Take a stroll along the Fort Cumberland Trail around the site of Fort Cumberland.

The **Cumberland Narrows,** just west of town on Route 40A, is a sheer break in the Allegheny Mountains, with a rocky cliff rising 800 feet above Wills Creek. There is a legend that Lover's Leap is the site of the tragic suicide of an Indian princess and English settler when they could not marry. Drive to the top of the eastern wall for a panoramic view of Cumberland and the Narrows.

A few miles west of the Narrows on Route 40A, the **LaVale Toll Gate House** (301–729–4938), dating from 1835, was the first tollgate on the National Road in Maryland. Read the plaque to see how much was charged for

Rocky Gap State Park
Route 40
Cumberland 21502
301–777–2138

History House
218 Washington Street
Cumberland 21502
301–777–8678

Allegheny County
 Tourism
Baltimore & Green
 Streets
301–777–5905

George Washington's
 Headquarters
Riverside Park
Cumberland 21502

wagons, animals, and pedestrians to pass through. The **Clarysville Bridge,** built in 1807, is the only remaining original bridge from the National Road in Allegany County.

GRANTSVILLE

**Casselman Bridge
Route 40A
Granstville**

Farther along Route 40A **Stanton's Mill,** just east of Grantsville, is the oldest gristmill in Garrett County that is still operating. Its original grinding stones are on display. **Casselman Bridge,** ½ mile east of Grantsville, was the longest single-span stone arch bridge in the country when it was built in 1813. Local people were sure that the bridge would collapse when the supporting logs were removed. The contractor loosened them the night before the opening ceremony and then stood under the bridge to prove his faith in its strength.

**Penn Alps
Route 40A
Grantsville 21536**

Continue west on Route 40A. **Penn Alps** is a Mennonite crafts center and restaurant in an 1820 log house. You can watch pottery being made, spinning, and clock making. During the summer more than 200 quilts are on display at the **Summerfest and Quilt Show. Casselman Inn** (Main Street; 301–895–5055) was built in the mid-nineteenth century. You can stop for lunch or to browse in the antiques shop.

This far-western part of Maryland is a fine place to come for outdoor living with mountains, waterfalls, and the largest freshwater lake in the state. You can come in the summer, spring, and fall for water sports and hiking, and again in the winter for skiing. Contact **Deep Creek–Garrett County Promotion Council** or **Maryland Forest and Park Services.**

**Deep Creek–Garrett
County Promotion
Council
Oakland 21550
301–334–1948**

**Maryland Forest and
Park Services
Tawes State Office
Building
580 Taylor Avenue
Annapolis 21401
301–269–3771**

This is the western end of Itinerary J, which now turns back east to Washington (Itinerary K) via Route 40, I–70, and I–270. It is also easy to connect with Itinerary F (South Central Pennsylvania) by taking I–81 north from Hagerstown to Gettysburg.

ITINERARY K:

Washington, D.C. and Virginia

WASHINGTON, D.C.

Washington, D.C. and Virginia

This last itinerary covers the Washington, D.C. area. The city itself is a museum of the history of our country. Most Americans, having been steeped in history as schoolchildren, want to visit Washington at some point. Years of watching historic events on television will make you feel you've been there before.

➳ *Washington, D.C. Area* ➳

The Washington, D.C., area may not be romantic to the government employees working there, but it certainly is to those who visit. Whether visiting for the first time or the fifteenth, visitors cannot help but be impressed by the beauty of the city's buildings, laid out according to a carefully articulated plan and meticulously landscaped with expanses of green lawn punctuated by flowering trees. The pervading sense of lives from the past that influenced our present well-being is ethereal yet real. Our founding fathers worked hard to provide a solid basis for the new, experimental nation and left us with a legacy to carry on, but they also lived hard, active lives and suffered defeats as well as successes. A visit to Washington should lead you backward into history, beyond the seeming permanence of the monuments to the struggles behind the achievements they memorialize.

In 1790 Congress was tied up with the thorny problem of where to situate our capital city. With diverse ideas ringing in his ears, George Washington settled the problem by choosing this site just 18 miles from his home at Mount Vernon. A 100-square-mile area was designated, and Major Pierre Charles L'Enfant, who had served on Washington's Continental army staff, was asked to design the city. Thinking of Paris, L'Enfant created scenic squares and circles with 160-foot-wide avenues spreading out like the spokes of a wheel.

George Washington died before he had a chance to live in the President's Mansion, but President John Adams moved into the unfinished house in 1800. In 1814 the British burned the President's Mansion, the Capitol, and the original Library of Congress. A thunderstorm fortunately put out the flames before the entire city went up in smoke. In 1815 rebuilding began. As the blackened planks of the President's mansion were repaired, they were also painted white, thus generating the name "The White House." Work progressed slowly, and in 1842 Charles Dickens could still write that the city had "spacious avenues that begin in nothing and lead nowhere, streets a mile long that only want houses, roads and inhabitants, public buildings that need but a public to be complete. . . ."

Because the site along the Potomac consisted of swampy, low ground with a canal running through it, floods were frequent. The Capitol was finished in 1863 as a symbol of unity (or perhaps tenacity) during difficult times. Abraham Lincoln commented, "If the people see the Capitol going on, it's a sign we intend the Union shall go on." After the Civil War the canal was filled and became Constitution Avenue. By 1874 Alexander Shepherd had improved sewers, sidewalks, and streets. Frederick Law Olmsted landscaped the Capitol grounds with thousands of trees. The Smithsonian Institution started to house exhibits from the 1876 Philadelphia Centennial in a Norman-Gothic castle in addition to the Arts and Industries Building.

The Washington Monument was in the process of construction for thirty-six years and was finally completed in 1884. A steam-driven elevator was available to take men to the top, but women and children had to walk up the 897 steps because of anxiety about the safety of the elevator. By the end of the nineteenth century, more buildings had been completed, including the Library of Congress, Union Station, Corcoran and Renwick Galleries of Art, the Bureau of Printing and Engraving, Post Office, Treasury Buildings, and the National Portrait Gallery. The design of the parks began in 1901, and Japan sent three thousand cherry trees as a gift in 1912.

The Botanic Gardens appeared in 1902, the Museum of Natural History in 1911, the Lincoln Memorial in 1922, and the Freer Gallery of Art in 1923. President Franklin Delano Roosevelt provided jobs in his WPA program during the Great Depression to build structures within the "Federal Triangle." In 1941 the National Gallery of Art was completed as a gift from Andrew Mellon. The Jefferson Memorial and the Pentagon were built in 1943, and the John F. Kennedy Center for the Performing Arts opened in 1971. The Smithsonian continued to make additions, including the Air and Space Museum, Hirshhorn Museum, and Sculpture Garden. The East Wing of the National Gallery of Art was designed by I. M. Pei and completed in 1979.

As in other cities, renovation of rundown areas has produced new parks, shops, and hotels. The Old Post Office has begun a new life as "The Pavilion," where a glass elevator whisks people up to an observation deck in the "clock tower." The Washington, D.C. Convention Center opened in 1982.

Before you leave home, contact the **Washington, D.C. Convention and Visitors Association** for information. Or you can stop at the **Visitor Information Center** (14th Street and Pennsylvania Avenue), which is in the

WASHINGTON, D.C.

**Washington, D.C.,
Convention and
Visitors Association
1212 New York
Avenue, N.W.
Washington, D.C.
20005
202–789–7038**

"Willard Collection" of shops. Handy phone numbers include **Dial-an-Event** (202–737–8866), **Dial-a-Park** (202–485–PARK), **Dial-a-Museum** (202–357–2020), and **National Archives Exhibits** (202–523–3000).

We have been lucky enough to find a place to park in the touring areas of Washington—sometimes—but if you are there in high season you may be wise to leave your car in a parking garage or in one of the suburbs and take the "Metro" into town. You can easily walk from one site to another, from the Capitol through the green Mall, parks, and gardens all the way to the Potomac. **Tourmobile Sightseeing** (1000 Ohio Street, S.W.; 202–554–7950) or the **Old Town Trolley** (3150 V Street; 202–269–3020) are also available for rides from one site to another, and the Metro or a cab will take you to outlying places of interest.

**Washington
Monument
Washington, D.C.
202–426–6841**

How about an eagle's-eye view of the area from the top of the **Washington Monument** to begin your tour? Get there early (it opens at 9:00 a.m.) to avoid waiting in line. An elevator will take you up to the 500-foot level, where you can look out in all directions. Look for the Capitol to the east, the White House to the north, the Jefferson Memorial to the south, and the Lincoln Memorial to the west. (As you might imagine, the view sparkles with lights at night, so try to return then.) Then look slowly outward in each direction to identify major buildings and landmarks lying in concentric circles around the monument and the Mall; when your eyes have had their fill, you have the choice of walking down 897 steps or returning to ground by the elevator.

From the monument, begin your explorations of the riches of the Mall. (But you don't need to be "rich" to explore. Most of the buildings on the Mall are museums of the Smithsonian Institution and have no admission fee.) On the north side the **National Museum of American History** is particularly appealing to children with its collection of vehicles, such as a 1913 Model T Ford, a Conestoga wagon, and a 280-ton steam locomotive. Don't miss Archie and Edith Bunker's chairs and end table from their TV series, which are displayed in a glass case on the second floor. On the third floor there's a model of the Capitol building entirely of glass rods by a fabrication process known as lamp work. The original Star-spangled Banner that flew over Fort McHenry in 1814 is in the museum, and don't miss George Washington's false teeth. Ball gowns worn by the First Ladies are on display. One of the most popular items, the Foucault Pendulum, is suspended from the ceiling of the fourth floor, illustrating the idea that the earth does rotate. Children can participate in the activities of several Discovery Corners.

By now you may be ready for lunch, so head out the Constitution Avenue side of the museum and turn onto 12th Street to **The Pavilion** in the **Old Post Office**. With specialty-food shops, restaurants (we like **Fitch, Fox, and Brown;** 202–289–1100), and food kiosks to choose from, you're sure to find a place for lunch, and you can watch entertainers or listen to music while you eat. While you're there, take a look at the 315-foot clock tower, which is the third-tallest building in the city.

Back on the north side of the Mall is the **National Museum of Natural History.** If you are fascinated by sixty-five-million-year-old dinosaurs, you have come to the right place. Don't miss "Uncle Beazley," a gigantic model of a Triceratops dinosaur that is stationed outside and loves to be climbed. Animals, fish, insects, birds, rocks, and minerals are displayed in this museum. The Hall of Gems contains, among other things, the 45.5-carat Hope Diamond and

National Museum of American History
Constitution Avenue & 14th Street, N.W.
Washington, D.C. 20560
202–357–2700

Pavilion in the Old Post Office
Pennsylvania Avenue & 12th Street, N.W.
Washington, D.C. 20560
202–289–4224

National Museum of Natural History
Constitution Avenue & 10th Street, N.W.
Washington, D.C. 20560
202–357–2700

a diamond tiara containing 950 gems worn by the Empress Marie Louise. Children will enjoy the Discovery Room, where they can feel a variety of specimens. Look for the 5.03-carat red diamond, which was put on display in 1988, and the fossil of Tanytrachelus, a 200-million-year-old reptile.

National Gallery of Art
Constitution Avenue & 4th Street, N.W.
Washington, D.C. 20560
202–737–4215

The **National Gallery of Art** contains countless famous masterpieces that will entice both infrequent and experienced gallery-goers. If your time is limited, you can rent an Acoustiguide, which takes you to a selected number of paintings that most visitors want to see. Children can pick up a treasure-hunt form at the information desk in the West Building. Twentieth-century art is displayed in the East Wing, reached by an underground concourse. If you've waited for lunch, you might like to have it in pleasant surroundings beside the underground waterfall here.

Capitol
Constitution & Independence Avenues
Washington, D.C.

Head up to the **Capitol,** past the **Reflecting Pool** and **Ulysses S. Grant Memorial,** which portrays the action of cavalry and artillery during the Civil War. The Capitol can be entered through the East Portico, where presidential inaugurations take place. Visitors can take a scheduled tour that begins every fifteen minutes or wander through on their own. Look at the frescoes high in the dome, with 15-foot-high statues that look life-size from the floor. John Trumbull, an aide to George Washington, painted four of the historical paintings on the Rotunda walls. Did you know that this is a whispering dome? There are a number of places where you can stand and hear people talking from across the Rotunda, which must be inconvenient at times for congressmen. Check to be sure that Congress is in session by observing the American flag flying over the south chamber for the House, or the north chamber for the Senate. If you would like to sit in the **Visitors'**

Gallery in the Senate or the House, pick up a pass in the office of your senator or congressman. (To get to the offices, you can use the subway that connects the Capitol with the federal office buildings.) If you are from abroad, you can show your passport to receive a pass. Nearby, a popular spot for lunch is **The Monocle** (107 D Street, N.E.; 202–546–4488).

Just below the Capitol, across Maryland Avenue from the Reflecting Pool, the **Botanic Gardens** are housed in a Victorian-style greenhouse. Where else can you see a waterfall in the midst of a busy city? Four seasonal shows include azaleas in February, spring flowers in March and April, chrysanthemums in November, and poinsettias in December.

Botanic Gardens
Maryland Avenue &
1st Street, S.W.
Washington, D.C.
20560
202–225–8333

More buildings of the Smithsonian Institution fill most of the south side of the Mall. First you will come to the **National Air and Space Museum,** which may be counted among the most popular sites anywhere. There you can see the Wright brothers' 1903 *Kitty Hawk;* Lindbergh's *Spirit of St. Louis;* Amelia Earhart's *Vega;* the Apollo 11 *Columbia,* which took Neil Armstrong, Edwin Aldrin, and Michael Collins to the moon; and much more. The *Voyager,* which flew around the world without refueling, is in the south lobby. Look for the U.S. flag and flight patch that were found in the cabin debris of the *Challenger.* The Albert Einstein Planetarium presents a voyage into the expanse beyond the solar system. There is a display on balloons and airships that traces the development from early flights. The Langley Theater presents a number of films that are related to air and space travel.

National Air and
Space Museum
Independence Avenue
& 7th Street, N.W.
Washington, D.C.
20560
202–357–2700

Several of the Smithsonian museums have cafeterias or restaurants, but the newest is very dramatic. On the east end of the Air and Space Museum, you can't miss a large glass addition, which is actually two restaurants in one—a cafeteria on the lower level and the **Wright Place**

**Hirshorn Museum and
Sculpture Garden
Independence Avenue
and 8th Street, S.W.
Washington, D.C.
20560
202–357–2700**

**Art and Industries
 Building
900 Jefferson Drive,
S.W.
Washington, D.C.
20560
202–357–2700**

**The Castle
1000 Jefferson Drive,
S.W.
Washington, D.C.
20560
202–357–2700**

(202–371–8777) above. You can dine with a
view of the Capitol.

The **Hirshhorn Museum** looks like a
doughnut because the design was planned to
minimize sun damage to the works of art. The
Sculpture Garden next to the museum features
Auguste Rodin's sculpture *Burghers of Calais,*
which dramatically portrays the town fathers
wearing nooses around their necks as they hand
over the keys of their city to British invaders.

The **Art and Industries Building** contains
the pieces displayed during the Philadelphia
Exposition of 1876. Victorian items of all kinds,
furniture, pistols, silverware, and horse-drawn
carriages are collected in this second-oldest
building of the Smithsonian Institution.

Next to the Art and Industries Building is
The Castle, which once was the only building
of the Smithsonian. Designed by James
Renwick, Jr., it was completed in 1855 and still
has charm with its peaks and turrets. Children
will love riding on the carousel located in front
of The Castle. A Wurlitzer organ provides music.
A visitors' center is there too.

The **Enid A. Haupt Garden,** behind The
Castle, is the place to sit down and relax amid
seasonal flowers. Then stroll into twin museums
on the grounds, both built in 1987.

The **National Museum of African Art**
devotes exhibits to the art of sub-Saharan Africa.
The collection includes the Royal Benin Art
exhibit of traditional court art. Look for the mask
from Angola of a woman made from wood,
fiber, and metal; a carved headdress from
Somalia; a headdress from Nigeria made of
wood, fiber, and red abrus seeds; a wooden figure of a Zairian Yombe woman holding her
child; a Lower Niger bronze industry vessel; and
a figure of an officer from the Cameroon grass-
fields.

Next door the **Arthur M. Sackler Gallery**

includes work from China, South and Southeast Asia, and the ancient Near East. The collection includes Persian manuscripts as well as Chinese bronzes, jades, and lacquerware. Look for a gilt-and-silver bowl from the seventh century, a sculpture of an Indian goddess from the tenth century, and a bronze wine holder from the tenth century B.C.

The final building in the Smithsonian complex on the south side of the Mall is the **Freer Gallery of Art,** based on the collection of Charles Lang Freer of Detroit. As you emerge from the wonders of the Smithsonian, pass the Washington Monument again and cross the Ellipse to the White House.

The **White House,** which celebrated its 200th anniversary in 1992, can be visited on a VIP tour if you contact your senator or congressman in advance for a ticket to go through earlier in the day than the more crowded regular tours. Friends also suggest getting in line at about 11:55 a.m. when the wait is usually shorter than earlier. As you are waiting in line to get in, be on the lookout for the president or one of his advisers driving in or out. (When we were last there, we were given the full treatment with a helicopter landing the president on the lawn.)

**White House
1600 Pennsylvania
Avenue, N.W.
Washington, D.C.
20500
202–456–2200**

The first room visitors see is the Library, which contains literally wall-to-wall books on American life. Portraits of American Indians meeting President Monroe in 1821 are displayed there. In the Vermeil Room you'll see gilded silver from Europe and America and a portrait of Eleanor Roosevelt.

Upstairs the tour takes you to the East Room, which you have seen on TV during performances and conferences. It is also the place where the body of John F. Kennedy lay in state. Cut-glass chandeliers from 1902 dazzle the eye in this white-and-gold room. Gilbert Stuart's painting of George Washington hangs on the east wall; Dolley Madison saved it during the great fire of 1814. Abigail Adams hung her laundry in this room, Theodore Roosevelt's children rollerskated on the parquet floors, and his guests watched wrestling and Japanese jujitsu performances.

The Green Room was the site of knitting and embroidery sessions by cabinet and diplomatic corps wives in ages past. Dolley Madison's silver candlesticks, a 1785 French clock on the mantel, the oldest portrait of Benjamin Franklin on public display (1767), and *The Last of the Mohicans* painting by Asher B. Durand enhance this 1810 Federal-style parlor.

Elliptically shaped, the Blue Room is often used by the president to receive heads of state and other guests. Gilded chairs covered with blue silk upholstery with an eagle on the back are eye-catching. The White House Christmas tree stands in this room every December.

The Red Room walls are covered by a red-satin fabric with an ornate gold border. Look for the musical clock given by the president of France in 1952. If you like intrigue, remember Rutherford B. Hayes's slim margin of one electoral vote in March 1877. Fearing that something might go wrong, President Grant encouraged Hayes to take the oath of office one day early; it was done in this room.

The State Dining Room is handsome, with floor-to-ceiling oak paneling dating from Theodore Roosevelt's tenure in 1902. Abraham Lincoln's portrait hangs above the mantel.

If you are there during the Christmas season, you may take the candlelit tour of the White House. On Easter Monday you can watch the famous Easter Egg Roll on the lawn. Children apparently gathered there as early as 1877 to roll eggs, and now they come every year. In 1981 each child received a wooden egg with the White House insignia on it as a prize. If you're ready for lunch after your tour, try the **Hay-Adams** (One Lafayette Square; 800-424-5054), the **Morrison-Clark** (Massachusetts Avenue and 11th Street, N.W.; 800-332-7898) or the **Old Ebbitt Grill** (675 15th Street, N.W.; 202-347-4801).

From the White House retrace your way across the Ellipse and turn right to stroll through the Constitution Gardens toward the **Vietnam Veterans Memorial,** the wall designed by Maya Ying Lin. Names of the 58,007 Americans who lost their lives in Vietnam are listed on the wall, in chronological order of death. The Reflecting Pool leads to the **Lincoln Memorial,** which looks like a Greek temple with its thirty-six Doric columns. Daniel Chester French designed the statue of Lincoln and then supervised the carving done by the Piccarilli Brothers during a four-year-period. Look carefully at Lincoln's hands, which stand for "A" and "L" in sign language. Did you know that there is a cave under the statue? This cavern is filled with stalactites and stalagmites created by the construction of the monument. You can explore it on a one-hour guided tour with the National Park Service if you bring your own flashlight and wear hiking boots. (Call 202-426-6841 for information.)

**Lincoln Memorial
West Potomac Park at
23rd Street, N.W.
Washington, D.C.**

Look across the Tidal Basin to see the rounded **Thomas Jefferson Memorial,** just a pleasant walk away from the Lincoln Memorial, as befits the intentions of Washington's original planners. Fifty-four Ionic columns march around the circular structure, and the portico facing the Mall is supported by additional columns. Inside the memorial you will see a statue of Jefferson that reaches the height of 19 feet; Rudolph Evans was the sculptor.

**Jefferson Memorial
Tidal Basin
Washington, D.C.**

A number of attractions are located within 1 or 2 blocks of the Mall area; those which are a little farther away are easily accessible by taxi or Metro.

Library of Congress
10 First Street
Washington, D.C.
20540
202–287–5458

The **Library of Congress,** across the street from the facade of the Capitol, contains priceless treasures of U.S. history. You can see an eighteen-minute slide show to become oriented before you take a tour of the stacks. Rare books include one of three remaining Gutenberg Bibles dating from 1455 and a fifteenth-century illuminated Bible manuscript from Mainz, Germany. The Main Reading Room is striking, with three colors of marble leading up to the dome. The Juilliard String Quartet sometimes performs there, playing one or more of the five Stradivarius violins in the collection.

On the other side of East Capitol Avenue, facing the Library of Congress, is the **U.S. Supreme Court.** As the highest tribunal in the country, the Supreme Court is made up of nine members who hear 170 cases selected as being significant from more than 5,000 petitions each year. The justices are robed in black, a contrast against the red draperies, and they are in session two weeks each month from October to June.

U.S. Supreme Court
First Street &
** Maryland Avenue,**
N.E.
Washington, D.C.
20543
202–252–3000

National Archives
Pennsylvania Avenue
& 7th Street, N.W.
Washington, D.C.
20408
202–523–3218

The **National Archives,** just a block off the north side of the Mall between the National Museum of Natural History and the National Gallery of Art, houses the Declaration of Independence, the Bill of Rights, and the U.S. Constitution, and twenty-one floors of other documents. The most significant documents are sealed in helium for protection and are placed in the Rotunda near the Constitution Avenue entrance. You can take a tour on weekdays, or, if you make arrangements in advance, a "Behind the Scenes" tour is available.

Federal Bureau of
** Investigation**
10th Street &
** Pennsylvania**
** Avenue, N.W.**
Washington, D.C.
202–324–3477

The **Federal Bureau of Investigation** reportedly has 164,756,933 sets of fingerprints, and none of them match. The "Ten Most Wanted Lists" that you have seen on bulletin boards in your local post office is made up there. If you take a tour, you will see exhibits on crime detection and fingerprinting, as well as memorabilia taken from notorious criminals. You can see John Dillinger's death mask, a display of hollowed-out items used to transport microfilm, and samples of drugs, pipes, and needles. The lab has a serology section to study blood and a document area to identify handwriting, printing, fraudulent checks, and stolen art. We saw boxes labeled "Evidence: Do Not Disturb" waiting to be gone through. The firearms collection includes 5,000 revolvers, a rifle similar to the one that killed John F. Kennedy, and a cane that is really a 28-gauge shotgun. An oversized bullet model illustrates how bullets differ in striations after they are fired from different guns. More labs conduct analysis on hairs, fibers, paint, rubber, and other materials. The indoor target range presents demonstrations on target shooting.

The **National Geographic Society** is a bit off the beaten path but is still within walking distance of the FBI and the Mall. The Society has a variety of treats to offer visitors. The Explorer's Hall offers displays of exploration of the earth, sea, and sky. Look for a gigantic globe to set the stage for your tour. Hands-on displays encourage the visitor to relate to tornadoes, sea exploration, and more. There are artifacts from both the Peary and the Byrd polar expeditions. The 100th anniversary of the National Geographic Society was celebrated in 1992.

The **John F. Kennedy Center,** located on the riverfront, includes the Eisenhower Theatre, the Opera House, the Concert Hall, the American Film Institute Theatre, and restaurants. A sculpture of President John F. Kennedy is done in bronze. Go up to the rooftop terrace for a panoramic view. The Hall of States displays the flag of each U.S. state, and the Hall of Nations contains the flag of every nation recognized by the United States.

National Geographic Society
17th & M Streets, N.W.
Washington, D.C.
20036
202–857–7588
weekdays;
857–7000 weekends

John F. Kennedy Center
New Hampshire Avenue & F Street, N. W.
Washington, D.C.
20566
202–254–3850

Union Station
Columbus Plaza
Washington, D.C.
202-289-1908

Don't miss the recently renovated **Union Station.** It had fallen into disrepair with leaking roofs and mushrooms growing on the floor, and its glory had faded. Restoration began in August 1986, and the building was opened with a gala celebration in September 1988. Union Station opened its doors for the first time in 1907, the largest train station in the world. Daniel Burnham designed this structure, which cost $4 million to build. Thirty-six Roman legionnaires stood guard over the main hall; although they were designed naked, officials demanded the addition of shields. Seven pounds of gold leaf now glimmer from the 320 octagons in the ceiling of the main hall. Marble from Greece and Italy now covers the floors. Eventually the building will house many shops and restaurants, as well as outdoor cafes for people-watching.

Washington Cathedral
Mount St. Alban at
Massachusetts &
Wisconsin Avenues,
S. W.
Washington, D.C.
202-537-6200

Washington Cathedral (the Cathedral Church of St. Peter and St. Paul) is now completed. As you approach it, you will pass the Bishop's Garden, colorful with seasonal flowers. The cathedral spires are magnificent as they reach skyward. Inside, the stained-glass windows are brilliant with sunlight illuminating their hues. The west rose window can be called the jewel of the cathedral, with its vivid colors radiating out from a diamondlike center. The creator, Rowlan LeCompte, wrote, "The west rose seeks to sing its own hymn to the universe." He also designed the Maryland window, which depicts religious toleration. Symbols of Maryland were carved into the Maryland Bay—a crab, starfish, oyster, terrapin, and a mother opossum with babies on her back. A statue of George Washington, by Lee Lawrie, stands 7 feet 6 inches tall in the Washington Bay. In the Baptistery stands the pink Tennessee-marble font. Two windows above the font depict the ceremony of baptism. Wood carvings on the choir stalls include Noah's Ark, St. George and the dragon, and Moses in the bullrushes. The Children's Chapel is like a miniature church for little ones. Needlepoint kneelers with a variety of animals, both wild and pets, appeal to children.

You may be lucky enough to be at the cathedral for a carillon or pipe organ concert. The **London Brass Rubbing Center** (202–364–0030) is adjacent to the gift shop. If you've always wanted to hang a rubbing in your home, here is the place to do it. The original brasses still reside in their respective churches in England, but the center has facsimile models, which you can't tell from the real thing. We have rubbed in English churches and also in a rubbing center and enjoy having all of our results hanging around our home. It is easy to rub—just a little elbow grease is required—and you can take home an unusual memento. Ask to rub the depiction of Margaret Peyton, with its delicate, ornate dress and pensive facial expression.

The **National Zoological Park,** also called the **Washington Zoo,** is housed on 176 acres located at the southern end of Rock Creek Park. Follow six large poles, marked with animal signs, to each of the animal areas (orange for Lion Trail, brown for Elephant, black for Zebra, green for Crowned Crane, blue for Polar Bear, and yellow for Raccoon Trail). Among the most famous of the zoo's inhabitants are Ling-Ling and Hsing-Hsing, the pandas sent from the People's Republic of China in 1972. They seem to sleep much of the day, but if you come at feeding time you're sure to see them awake. Smokey the Bear (the second one in the zoo) has been around since 1950 when a little cub, who had been burned, was presented to the zoo. The Great Flight Cage houses all sorts of birds, and you can join them in their cage. When you get to the beaver area, you will find portholes in the glass so you can see their homes underwater. Don't miss the Zoolab learn-

**National Zoological Park
3000 Connecticut Avenue
Washington, D.C. 20008
202–673–4800**

ing center, where children can touch and handle all sorts of exhibits.

There are other areas in Washington to visit, such as **Georgetown** and **Foggy Bottom.** Once a tobacco port, Georgetown is now a very fashionable place to live. Boutiques, restaurants, pubs, and jazz clubs keep the place active far into the night. Georgetown University is also in Georgetown. Foggy Bottom was once a fume-clogged industrial area in the mid-nineteenth century, but no longer. The Kennedy Center for the Performing Arts, Watergate, and the World Bank have replaced Christian Heurich's brewery, among other things.

Diners come from miles around to try **Clyde's** (3236 M Street, N.W.; 202–333–9180), **American Cafe** (1211 Wisconsin Avenue, N.W.; 202–944–9464), **Japan Inn** (1715 Wisconsin Avenue, N.W.; 202–337–3400), **1789 Restaurant** (1226 36th Street, N.W.; 202–965–1789), and **Le Caprice** (2348 Wisconsin Avenue, N.W.; 202–337–3394).

ARLINGTON, VIRGINIA

Arlington National Cemetery
Arlington, Virginia
703–697–2131

Arlington House and Arlington National Cemetery are located just across the bridge from the Lincoln Memorial. **Arlington National Cemetery** is best seen by Tourmobile because there is a vast amount of ground to cover, some of which is hilly. The **Tomb of the Unknowns** is a single block of white marble decorated with wreaths. Four U.S. servicemen from World Wars I and II and the Korean and Vietnam conflicts are interred there. The Changing of the Guard Ceremony is carried out every half hour in summer and every hour in winter. John F. Kennedy's grave is marked by the eternal flame and a slate headstone, and Robert F. Kennedy is also buried there.

Arlington House, also known as the **Custis-Lee House,** was the home of Robert E. Lee and his bride, Mary Custis, from 1831 to

1861. Martha Washington's son, John Custis, bought the land in 1778, and in 1802 his son, George Washington Parker Curtis, built the house. His daughter, Mary Anna Randolph Custis, inherited it and married Robert E. Lee. Lee wrote about Arlington House, "My affections and attachments are more strongly placed than at any other place in the world." The Lees went back and forth from army stations to Arlington. During the Civil War the Union army used the house as a headquarters. Property owners of homes occupied by Federal troops were still required to appear in person to pay their taxes; because the Lees could not appear, the house was confiscated in 1864. In February 1865 Robert E. Lee was named general in chief of the Armies of the Confederate States, and he surrendered to Ulysses S. Grant on April 9 of the same year.

In 1925 Congress approved restoration of the house. Some of the furnishings belonging to the Lee family were returned. Look to the right into the family parlor to see Lee's traveling desk, which he carried from post to post. The green chairs and the silver tea service in the parlor also belonged to the Lees. The ceiling lantern in the center hall is a copy of one that hangs at Mount Vernon. Robert E. Lee was accustomed to stroll through his rose garden each morning and pick a rose to lay beside the plate of each lady at breakfast in the family dining room. The dining room table, china, silver, and goblets all belonged to the Lees. Upstairs you will see the Lees' bedchamber, where he spent an agonizing night deciding whether he should support the Union his family had helped to build or follow the wishes of six generations of Lees in Virginia. A portrait painted by August Hervieu in 1831 of Mary Custis just before her marriage to Lee hangs in the house. Lafayette described the view from the front portico as the "finest view in the world."

Arlington House
Arlington, Virginia
22210
703–557–0613

MOUNT VERNON

Mount Vernon
Mount Vernon, or
Alexandria, Virginia
22121
703–780–2000

Outside of the Washington, D.C. area but definitely a part of a visit to our capital is historic Mount Vernon, located south of Alexandria, Virginia, and accessible from Route 1 south and Route 235 (703–780–2000). John Washington, George's great-grandfather, patented the Mount Vernon homesite in 1674. Augustine Washington, George's father, inherited the property in 1726, and in 1732 George was born. When Augustine Washington died in 1743, George's elder half-brother, Lawrence, inherited Mount Vernon. George Washington eventually inherited the plantation from Lawrence and then wrote, "No estate in United America is more pleasantly situated than this. It lies in a high, dry and healthy Country 300 miles by water from the Sea . . . on one of the finest Rivers in the world. . . ." In spite of this admiration for his own estate, he was not able to live there for years at a time while he was involved in fighting the French and Indian War and the Revolutionary War, as well as establishing the nation as its first president. When he was in residence, he studied the newest crop technology and was successful as a planter.

After George's marriage to Martha Dandridge Custis, widow of Daniel Parke Custis, he wrote, "I am now, I believe, fixed at this Seat with an agreeable Consort for Life and hope to find more happiness in retirement than I ever experienced amidst a wide and bustling World." Martha Washington spent eight winters with him during his northern encampments. He resigned his commission in 1783 and hoped to spend his remaining life at Mount Vernon. In 1789 he became president for the next eight years, which kept him away from Mount Vernon much of the time. When he finally did retire, he had only two and one-half years left at his beloved Mount Vernon before he died.

The mansion is a familiar sight to most

Americans because photographs of this large white colonial building with its long, columned piazza have appeared frequently. George Washington added onto the smaller house he had inherited before his marriage to Martha and made other additions in later years. The banquet hall is striking with a Palladian window, green decor, and an ornate fireplace. Because music played such an important role in the social life at Mount Vernon, you will see a number of musical instruments in the "little parlor." George Washington gave "one very good Spinit" to his stepdaughter, Patsy Custis, and her brother received a violin and "a fine German flute"; Nelly Custis was given a harpsichord in 1793, straight from London. The West Parlor has an ornate fireplace and mantel with the Washington coat of arms on the top, and James Sharples painted the portraits of George and Martha Washington hanging there. The dining room has a gallery of prints and a decorated ceiling. Upstairs George Washington's bedroom contains his unusually wide bed, in which he died in 1799; the Windsor armchair next to the bed was in that position when he died.

Outside visitors can explore the "dependencies." The kitchen, where a staff of two cooks and two waiters produced sumptuous meals, now houses a collection of utensils and cooking gear. According to one writer, "The dinner was very good, a small roasted pigg, boiled leg of lamb, roasted fowls, beef, peas, lettuce, cucumbers, artichokes, puddings, tarts. We were desired to call for what drinks we chose." Other buildings include the smokehouse, greenhouse, icehouse, storehouse, coach house, and slave quarters. A museum has been added to house the large collection of Washington artifacts.

George and Martha Washington are buried in the family vault. He directed that "the family

Vault at Mount Vernon requiring repairs, and being improperly situated besides, I desire that a new oné of Brick and upon a larger Scale, may be built at the foot of what is commonly called the Vineyard Inclosure—on the ground which is marked out—in which my remains, with those of my deceased relatives (now in the old Vault) and such others of my family as may chuse to be entombed there, may be deposited."

Because of the popularity of Mount Vernon with tourists, we suggest you arrive early in the morning, tour the mansion, and then stroll around the grounds in uncrowded leisure.

WILLIAMSBURG

Colonial Williamsburg
Box 1776
Williamsburg, Virginia
23187–1776
800–HISTORY

Another excursion from Washington takes travelers to **Colonial Williamsburg** via Routes 95, 295, and 64. You can also plan a circle tour from Washington, going south to Williamsburg, across the Chesapeake Bay Bridge-Tunnel, north through the Delmarva peninsula, and then back across the Chesapeake Bay Bridge to Annapolis, Baltimore, or Washington.

Step back in time two centuries as you walk on the streets of colonial days in the footsteps of those who helped develop our nation. We suggest that you head for the Visitor Center, which is well marked as you come into town. A film, *Williamsburg—the Story of a Patriot,* provides orientation for your visit. Leave your car in the parking lot, and take a shuttle bus to the Historic Area. Duke of Gloucester Street is the "Main Street" of Williamsburg, and it runs for a mile between the Capitol and the College of William and Mary. Visitors can immerse themselves in the eighteenth century by wandering into buildings along this and adjoining streets.

Stop to chat with interpreters in costume, who are eager to tell you about their crafts. Max, in the Milliner's Shop, told us about the fans that George Washington ordered there. The milliner had the latest styles in clothing and was considered a fashion consultant, as she stitched new gowns for balls, changed the trim with the times, and suggested wearing "heartbreakers" (corkscrew curls).

Across the street in the King's Arms Tavern visitors are encouraged to exchange eighteenth-century news and views with the proprietress, the widow Jane Vobe. She assured us that she doesn't gossip but just tells what she hears—after all, one has to watch one's tongue or be put in the pillory. Cocking her ear, she wondered who might be listening but added that as long as you can hear slaves you know they're working and not listening. She told Robert that he should really shave off his beard when he has time, as men with hair on their faces either have something to hide or are pirates. Men who want to stay in her fourteen-room inn pay 7½ pence for two-to-a-bed comfort. Meal costs can't exceed 1 shilling—dinner is served at two of the clock, and supper at nine of the clock, with the same food brought back redecorated. It pays to appear the first time food is served.

Having got into an eighteenth-century mood with two colorful characters, we headed for the **Capitol building.** As we stood by the green seats in the House of Burgess, we could hear "George Washington" explaining a bill that had to do with hogs. It seems that the hogs had been taking a bath in the drinking water, and he thought they should be fenced in so people could drink clean water. Legislation had to be sent to the King in England, and so an answer could be expected in a few years. More seriously, he explained the Virginia Resolves against the Townshend Acts in 1769. "Patrick Henry" delivered his "Caesar-Brutus" speech, which offered a solution against the Stamp Act.

The Council Chamber is colorful, with a turkey work carpet on the table. The portrait of Queen Anne reminds us that she had seventeen children, who all died in infancy except the Prince of Gloucester, who died at age 11. The General Court was the place where pirates were sentenced to be "turned off," or hanged. People could be pardoned the first time, but a T (theft) or M (murder) was burned into the palm of the hand near the thumb.

One of the favorite buildings is the **Governor's Palace,** which housed seven royal governors and also the first two governors of the Commonwealth of Virginia, Patrick Henry and Thomas Jefferson. In 1780 the residence of the governor was moved to Richmond. The building was used as a hospital after the battle of Yorktown. In 1781 it burned completely.

Today visitors enter through the hall decorated with guns, swords, pistols, and muskets arranged in patterns. From his office to the left of the door, the butler managed visits from those who wished to see the governor. By their clothing and posture, he was able to screen the less important visitors, who waited in the hall; the more important ones, who were escorted into the parlor on the right; and the most important ones, who walked upstairs. Upstairs visitors can walk through several bedrooms with period furnishings. Don't miss the set of fashion prints—one for each month of the year. The Ball Room is where the governor sits at the "preferred" end, along with portraits of King George III and Queen Charlotte; when visitors bow to him, they are also bowing to the King and Queen.

The **Public Hospital,** in operation from 1773 to 1885, displays conditions for the mentally ill, including a 1773 cell with a pallet on the floor over a lump of straw, a blanket, and a chamber pot—similar to a prison. The window was barred, and patients were chained to the wall. By 1845 each one lived in a small apartment with bed, table, chair, and a plaster wall.

During this age of "moral management," patients were encouraged to spend time doing something—playing the violin, spinning, or playing cards, for example. The "custodial care" era lasted from 1862 to 1885. Patients were subjected to physical restraints and entertained with picnics and tea parties.

The **DeWitt Wallace Decorative Arts Gallery** is accessible by walking through the hospital and downstairs. Collections include musical instruments, silver, pewter, ceramics, clocks, globes, furniture, paintings, costumes, and textiles. Favorites include an Aesop's fable candlestick, "The Tiger and the Fox," from 1765; a Greybeard face jug from 1645; a pair of lead-glazed earthenware rabbits from 1820; a turquoise tea urn from 1770; brass pipe tampers from 1650; crewel wool needlework from 1750; and more.

The **Abby Aldrich Rockefeller Folk Art Center** opened after renovation and expansion in May 1992. She began collecting folk art in the 1920s. Today the collection includes shop signs, weather vanes, a carousel figure, portraits, furniture, chests, quilts, sewing tools, mariner's tools, and toys. We enjoyed the clown tobacconist sign from 1868, a group of weather vanes, a lion carousel figure, a monkey inkwell, a calico cat from 1900–1920, a 1907–1915 mechanical pump on three levels, and a 1795 Pennsylvania Dutch Easter rabbit, to name a few.

There are many places to have lunch or dinner in Williamsburg. Try the **Williamsburg Inn** (804–229–2141); also at the same phone number are **King's Arms Tavern, Chowning's, Mrs. Campbell's Tavern, Shields Tavern,** and **Williamsburg Lodge.**

CARTER'S GROVE

Drive 8 miles east of Williamsburg to **Carter's Grove,** which is a plantation on the James River. The land was purchased by "King"

Carter for his daughter Elizabeth. The original house was completed in 1755, and two wings were added in 1930 to connect the house with a kitchen on one end and a laundry on the other. The McCrea family purchased the house in 1928, and Mrs. McCrea lived there until her death in 1960. It is now owned by the Colonial Williamsburg Foundation, which conducted an archaeological search to discover signs of an early seventeenth-century settlement called Martin's Hundred. The **Winthrop Rockefeller Archaeology Museum** is an underground museum displaying artifacts from the dig. Mockleyware cooking pots from A.D. 200–900 are there, as are lead from casement windows with the words "John . . . 1625," a 1613 farthing coin, a seventeenth-century helmet, and the story of a woman, "Granny," who was partly scalped, with photos of her bones. Wolstenholme Towne was once part of Martin's Hundred, and some houses, stores, and the fort are now marked. An eighteenth-century slave quarter has been reconstructed on the site. Interpreters tell the story of the African-Americans who lived there.

As we entered the mansion, we left our calling cards on the silver tray as people did 200 years ago. Portraits of the McCrea family hang on the dining room wall, including one of seventeen-year-old Molly McCrea in a yellow dress with flowers on the bodice. She died in 1960 at age eighty-four. The kitchen is a mixture of black iron pots in the large fireplace and an early Hotpoint electric stove. The Drawing Room is also called the "refusal" room because both Washington and Jefferson proposed to a lady there and both were refused.

JAMESTOWN

Jamestown is just off Route 31, 6 miles from Williamsburg; it can also be reached from the Colonial Parkway. Jamestown was the first permanent colony in the New World, established by England in 1607. Three ships, the *Susan Constant,* the *Godspeed,* and *Discovery* brought the colonists to Jamestown; it took them five months to reach the New World. Replicas of the ships are usually moored at the dock for visitors to see.

Thatched houses were built inside the James Fort, along with public buildings and the church. The settlers were not used to farming, and after Captain John Smith sailed back to England in 1609, a "starving time" took many lives. They had almost given up hope when more settlers arrived from England with supplies and the urge to become wealthy with tobacco cultivation. By 1619 government had been developed, and Jamestown was the center until the capital was moved to Williamsburg in 1699.

A re-created Powhatan Village offers the chance to see how the Indians lived, prepared food, made tools and weapons, and prepared for war. Some of their Tidewater Indian pipes and arrowheads are on display in the museum.

**Jamestown Settlement
Box JF
Williamsburg, Virginia
 23187
804-229-1607**

Visit **Yorktown Victory Center** for the sequence of events leading up to the victory of the American Revolution: from the 1763 Treaty of Paris (which increased British holdings in our country), the Boston Tea Party, the First Continental Congress, and the conflicts with Britain to the battle at Yorktown, when the British surrendered. A film, *The Road to Yorktown,* gives a picture of the events. Learn about life on board a ship from the artifacts taken from the *Betsy,* a British merchant ship sunk in the Siege of Yorktown, in the "Yorktown's Sunken Fleet" display.

"Witnesses to Revolution" includes portrayals of six persons—an African-American patriot, a loyalist, a Quaker pacifist, two Continental army soldiers, and the wife of a Virginia planta-

YORKTOWN

**Yorktown Victory
 Center
Box 1976
Yorktown, Virginia
23690
804-887-1776**

tion owner. Information was gathered from their personal diaries and correspondence.

Outside the Continental Army Camp offers interpreters who explain the life of those in the camp. Soldiers' tents, two officers' tents, a weapons tent, and a cooking center have been re-created. You may be there for a military drill, demonstration of musket loading and firing, or food preparation.

A typical farm is represented by the outline of a house and a separate kitchen. Herbs and vegetables are grown in the garden and corn and tobacco in a nearby field.

This concludes Itinerary K. You will probably find that you've only scratched the surface and will want to head off in another direction for more exploration. Happy traveling!

APPENDIX

Mount Joy

Inns, Hotels, and Bed & Breakfast Establishments in the Mid-Atlantic States

The following list of inns and bed-and-breakfast accommodations includes a selection ranging from those which are inexpensive to establishments worthy of a "big splurge" occasion. We have tried to include those with an interesting historical past or a beautiful setting.

On the whole, inns and B&Bs in the United States are more expensive than their counterparts in Europe, but they are more appealing than comparable motel accommodations. Some of them offer special rates during their off-peak times, such as weekends in cities and weekdays in the country, or at quiet times in their seasonal cycle through the year. Prices will vary, but all of them offer personal attention to make your stay pleasant; for once you will be something more than twenty to forty bytes on a computerized reservation list. Your host or hostess may offer you a glass of sherry, fresh fruit in your room, flowers, bath oil in the bathroom, or a foil-wrapped chocolate on your pillow. You may find that your hosts will offer you an hour of conversation during an evening, and you may become friends and return year after year. B&B hosts and guests share one quality that appeals more and more to most Americans: They like to talk and to meet new friends in each region they visit. So it is no wonder that those who have traveled widely prefer staying in someone's home rather than in an anonymous hotel owned by a corporate chain. Almost all of the inns and B&Bs serve complimentary breakfast, but only the inns serve lunch and dinner. Occasionally we have listed accommodations that do not fit the criteria for inns or B&Bs but are nevertheless the most appealing in the area.

In no case do we pretend or intend to be comprehensive. We recommend good places that we know something of without prejudice to equally good places that we are ignorant of, many of which we hope to discover in future travels. Our listings of accommodations are neither inclusive nor exclusive—but only an adjunct to the book's itineraries for the convenience of those who do not wish to spend much of their time finding a good place to sleep.

≋ *Accommodations by State* ≋

DELAWARE

New Castle

The Jefferson House, The Strand at the Wharf, New Castle, Delaware 19720. Phone: 302–323–0999 or 323–8944. Dating from colonial times, this 200-year-old landmark is located at the foot of the wharf.

Rehoboth Beach

The Corner Cupboard Inn, 50 Park Avenue, Rehoboth Beach, Delaware 19971. Phone: 302–227–8553. This B&B offers eighteen rooms and a solarium lined with plants.

MARYLAND

Annapolis

Prince George Inn, 232 Prince George Street, Annapolis, Maryland 21401. Phone: 410–263–6418. This centrally located inn offers four Victorian town-house rooms all decorated differently, from ornate armoires and carved headboards to white wicker furniture and brass beds.

Historic Inns of Annapolis, 16 Church Circle, Annapolis, Maryland 21401. Phone: 410–263–2641; from Maryland 800–638–8902; 800–847–8882 outside of Maryland. This company offers five historic inns located in the center of town, with restaurants and entertainment.

Baltimore

Admiral Fell Inn, 888 South Broadway (Fells Point), Baltimore, Maryland 21231. Phone: 800–BXB–INNS or 410–522–7377. Dating from the late 1800s, this thirty-seven–room inn has been completely refurbished with antiques and period pieces.

Society Hill is a company that operates three hotels in the city of Baltimore. Society Hill-Hopkins, 3404 St. Paul Street, Baltimore, Maryland 21218. Phone: 410–235–8600. Society Hill Hotel, 58 West Biddle Street, Baltimore,

Maryland 21201. Phone: 410–837–3630. Society Hill-Government House, 1125 North Calvert Street, Baltimore, Maryland 21202. Phone: 410–752–7722. Each hotel is in a renovated historic building, and all are decorated with antiques.

The Shirley Madison Inn, 205 West Madison Street, Baltimore, Maryland 21201. Phone: 410–728–6550. The 1880s-renovated building contains seventeen units with cooking facilities and private baths. The owner has collected antiques from England, including carved armoires and desks.

Berlin

Atlantic Hotel, 2 North Main Street, Berlin, Maryland 21811. Phone: 410–641–3589. This 1895 Victorian hotel is on the National Register of Historic Places. Antiques, oriental rugs, and Tiffany lamps add to the Victorian flavor.

Easton

The Tidewater Inn, Dover and Harrison streets, Easton, Maryland 21601. Phone: 410–822–1300. There are 119 rooms in this brick building, an elegant spiral staircase, and an outdoor pool.

Frederick

The Turning Point Inn, 3406 Urbana Pike (Route 355 near Urbana), Frederick, Maryland 21701. Phone: 301–874–2421. This is a lovely Victorian mansion built by Dr. Perry in 1910 on four acres of land, with flowering dogwood, beech trees, and a giant pear tree. Four large bedrooms have been renovated in different styles.

Oxford

Oxford Inn, Box 627, Oxford, Maryland 21654. Phone: 410–226–5220. Located at the head of Town Creek with views of the harbor as well, this inn offers a variety of accommodations, including suites.

Robert Morris Inn, P.O. Box 70, The Strand, Oxford, Maryland 21654. Phone: 410–226–5111. Dating from the early 1700s, the inn was once the home of Robert Morris, a friend of George

Washington. Some of the thirty-six rooms have fireplaces and antique furnishings.

The Inn at Perry Cabin, P.O. Box 247, Route 33, St. Michaels, Maryland 21663. Phone: 410–745–5178. Located on the Miles River, this inn used to be a riding academy whose resident thoroughbred, named "Spectacular Bid," once won the Kentucky Derby.

The Parsonage Inn, 210 North Talbot Street, St. Michaels, Maryland 21663. Phone: 410–745–5519. Once a parsonage, this 1883 building was built of bricks from the owner's brickyard. It is now a seven-room bed-and-breakfast inn with Victorian decor.

St. Michaels Harbour Inn and Marina, 101 North Harbor Road, St. Michaels, Maryland 21663. Phone: 800–955–9001. Located on the water with a spectacular view of the lighthouse and maritime museum across the harbor, this recently built inn is comfortable and ideally situated.

Wades Point Inn, Box 7, St. Michaels, Maryland 21663. Phone: 410–745–2500. This nineteenth-century home, built by a shipwright, is set on the water, with sights and sounds of birds and boats.

Chesapeake-House, Tilghman, Maryland 21671. Phone: 410–886–2123. This 1856 inn on the water attracts fishermen, who spend their days out with Captain Buddy Harrison.

Tilghman Island Inn, Tilghman Island, Maryland 21671. Phone: 410–886–2141. The inn is located on the water overlooking Knapps Narrows, which joins the Choptank and the Chesapeake. You'll see the skipjacks going by, as well as lots of birds.

The Abbey, Columbia Avenue and Gurney Street, Cape May, New Jersey 08204. Phone:

609–884–4506. This Gothic villa has a 60-foot tower and seven guest rooms and is furnished with Victorian antiques, including 12-foot mirrors and marble-topped dressers.

The Chalfonte, 301 Howard Street, Cape May, New Jersey 08204. Phone: 609–884–8409. This inn provides rocking chairs on the porch, 103 rooms, and traditional southern cooking served family-style. Entire families return year after year.

The Mainstay, 635 Columbia Avenue, Cape May, New Jersey 08204. Phone: 609–884–8690. A twelve-room Victorian inn that was once an elegant gentleman's club now has Victorian furnishings, 12-foot mirrors, marble-topped sideboards, loveseats, and crystal chandeliers.

Princeton

Marriott Residence Inn, 4225 Route 1, Princeton, New Jersey 08450. Phone: 201–329–9600. Residence Inns offer a place to fix a meal in your own kitchen after a day of sightseeing or business. Studio suites include a separate living room, some with fireplaces.

Nassau Inn, Palmer Square, Princeton, New Jersey 08540. Phone: 800–243–1166 or 609–921–7500. A tradition in Princeton, this inn is wonderful for a getaway weekend. Its location can't be beat.

Scanticon, 100 College Road East, Princeton, New Jersey 08540. Phone: 800–222–1131 or 609–452–7800. Located in a park, the building is architecturally exciting with brick and strategic glass windows. Walking and jogging trails are right there, as are tennis courts.

The Peacock Inn, 20 Bayard Lane, Princeton, New Jersey 08540. Phone: 609–924–1707. Dating from 1775, this three-story inn has housed F. Scott Fitzgerald, Albert Einstein, and Bertrand Russell, among others.

NEW YORK

The Desmond Americana, 660 Albany

Shaker Road, Albany, New York 12211. Phone: 800–448–3500 or 518–869–8100. The hotel looks like an eighteenth-century village with a variety of building styles. There's an interior courtyard that continues the village theme. Located near the airport.

Inn at the Century, 997 New Loudon Road, RD 1, Box 287, Cohoes, New York 12047. Phone: 518–785–0931. This inn has a colonial theme. It is located north of Albany on Route 9.

Sheraton Airport Inn, 200 Wolf Road, Albany, New York 12205. Phone: 518–458–1000. Located 2 miles from the airport, convenient for overnight before and after a flight.

Albany

Bonnie Castle Resort, Holland Street, P.O. Box 219, Alexandria Bay, New York 13607. Phone: 315–482–4511 or 800–521–5514. Built in 1877 as a mansion for Dr. Josiah Holland, the resort has been enlarged to include facilities for tennis and swimming, as well as a conference center.

The Ledges, P.O. Box 245, Alexandria Bay, New York 13607. Phone: 315–482–9334. Once an estate on nine acres, The Ledges provides a quiet atmosphere right on the shore of the St. Lawrence River. Free dockage is provided for guests with boats.

Alexandria Bay

Gansett Green Manor, Box 799, Main Street, Amagansett, New York 11930. Phone: 516–267–3133. Gardens and fountains add to the restful atmosphere here. Many rooms have kitchens and electric fireplaces.

The Mill Garth Inn, Box 700, Windmill Lane, Amagansett, New York 11930. Phone: 516–267–3757. This historic inn offers lawns and gardens for the pleasure of guests.

Amagansett

Springside Inn, Route 38, Auburn, New York. Phone: 315–252–7247. Originally a boarding school in the 1850s, then used as part of the

Auburn

Underground Railroad during the Civil War, the inn has been operating since 1919.

Aurora

Aurora Inn, Main Street, Aurora, New York 13026. Phone: 315–364–8842. Located on the eastern shore of Cayuga Lake, this inn has been in operation for more than 150 years. The rooms have been renovated and decorated with Stickley furniture.

Bear Mountain Park

Bear Mountain Inn, Route 9W, Bear Mountain Park, New York 10911. Phone: 914–786–2731. This lodge looks like a European chalet. Recreational facilities are nearby.

Blue Mountain Lake

The Hedges, Blue Mountain Lake, New York 12812. Phone: 518–352–7325. This rustic retreat features stone and log cottages furnished with oak and typical Adirondack pieces.

Hemlock Hall, Blue Mountain Lake, New York 12812. Phone: 518–352–7706. Cottages on the lake nestled in the forest setting of birch, balsam, and pine attract guests during the summer season.

Bolton Landing

Melody Manor Motel, P.O. Box 366, Bolton Landing, New York 12814. Phone: 518–644–9750. This is a pleasant resort on the west side of Lake George, offering pool and lake swimming, water-skiing, and tennis.

The Sagamore, Bolton Landing, New York 12814. Phone: 518–644–9400. This is just the place for a splurge or a getaway weekend on beautiful Lake George.

Buffalo

E.B.'s B&B, 781 Richmond Avenue, Buffalo, New York 14222. Phone: 716–882–1428. This family-run B&B is in a turn-of-the-century home right in downtown Buffalo.

Canandaigua

Oliver Phelps Country Inn, 252 North Main Street, Canandaigua, New York 14424. Phone: 716–396–1650. This Federal home was built by Nathaniel Norton near the historic Granger Homestead.

Thendara Inn & Restaurant, 4356 East Lake Road, Canandaigua, New York 14424. Phone: 716–493–4868. Built as a retirement home for Senator John Raines, the inn dates from 1900. It is right on the river.

Cazenovia

Brae Loch Inn, Route 20, Cazenovia, New York 13035. Phone: 800–722–0674 or 315–655–3431. Entering the Brae Loch is like stepping into a bit of Scotland, as you are greeted by bagpipe music in the vestibule. Nine guest rooms are decorated with antiques, and each one is different.

Lincklaen House, Box 36, 79 Albany Street, Cazenovia, New York 13035. Phone: 315–655–3461. Dating from 1835, this house features Williamsburg chandeliers, painted wood panels, delft tiles, chandeliers, and three fireplaces on the ground floor.

Chestertown

The Balsam House, Friend's Lake, Chestertown, New York 12817. Phone: 518–494–2828 or 494–4431. This nineteenth-century inn contains twenty recently redecorated rooms furnished with antiques and "Grandmother" spreads.

The Friend's Lake Inn, Chestertown, New York 12817. Phone: 518–494–4251. Built in the 1860s, the inn has been renovated with brass beds, Americana antiques, and quilts. Some of the rooms have a lake view.

Clarence Hollow

Asa Ransom House, 10529 Main Street, Clarence Hollow, New York 14031–1684. Phone: 706–759–2315. Dating from 1853, the building is on the grounds of an 1803 gristmill built by Asa Ransom. The dining room, library, and guest rooms reflect the charm of the old days.

Cold Spring Harbor

Hudson House, 2 Main Street, Cold Spring, New York 10516. Phone: 914–265–9355. This 1832 building contains fourteen guest rooms, antique furnishings, the Half Moon Bar reminiscent of Henry Hudson, and balconies off some of the rooms.

Cooperstown

Hickory Grove Inn, RD2, Box 898, Cooperstown, New York 13326. Phone: 607–547–8100. A popular stagecoach stop since the early 1800s, the inn also provided hospitality for steamboat travelers. Wide-board floors, print wallpaper, and oriental rugs are enhanced by antiques.

Inn at Cooperstown, 16 Chestnut Street, Cooperstown, New York 13326. Phone: 607–547–5756. Built as an annex to the Fenimore Hotel in 1874, the inn is in the center of the Historic District.

Corning

Rosewood Inn, 134 East First Street, Corning, New York 14830. Phone: 607–962–3253. Built in 1855 in Greek Revival style, this inn retains the charm of the past. The rooms are furnished in period pieces; two suites are available.

Diamond Point

Canoe Island Lodge, Lake Shore Drive, Diamond Point, New York 12824. Phone: 518–668–5592. This is a popular resort on Lake George that offers lake swimming, water-skiing, barbecues on an island, sailing, and tennis. It has a lodge and cottages, some with fireplaces.

Dolgeville

Adrianna Bed & Breakfast, 44 Stewart Street, Dolgeville, New York 13329. Phone: 315–429–3249. This home, attractively decorated with print wallpaper and a wildflower theme, is right in the foothills of the Adirondack Mountains.

Dundee

The Red Brick Inn, RD2, Box 57A, Dundee, New York 14837. Phone: 607–243–8844. The innkeeper also makes wine and champagne; you can visit his cellar to see the bottles quietly aging. Rooms are attractive.

East Hampton

Bassett House, P.O. Box 1426, East

Hampton, New York 11937. Phone: 516–324–6127. Built in 1830, this house has a charm all its own. The living room is a fascinating array of miscellaneous items, including a red-leather barber's chair, three stuffed bears, a stoplight, an oriental picture, and a wooden sea chest.

The Huntting Inn, 94 Main Street, East Hampton, New York 11937. Phone: 516–324–0410. Located in the center of town, the inn offers pleasant country gardens.

Fredonia

White Inn, 52 East Main Street, Fredonia, New York 14063. Phone: 716–672–2103. The twenty guest rooms have been redecorated with designer wallpapers and furnished with antiques and prints. The original owner's coat of arms hangs over the fireplace. There is a full restaurant.

Garrison

The Bird and Bottle Inn, Nelson's Corners, Old Albany Post Road, Garrison, New York 10524. Phone: 914–424–3000. Once a stagecoach stop before the Revolution, the inn maintains colonial charm with fireplaces, wide-plank floors, and antique furnishings.

Geneva

Geneva on the Lake, 1001 Lochland Road, Route 14S, Geneva, New York 14456. Phone: 315–789–7190 or 800–3GENEVA. This Italian Renaissance villa has recently been renovated; it offers elegance and peaceful surroundings on ten acres of landscaped gardens and woods.

The Inn at Belhurst Castle, Box 609, Geneva, New York 14456. Phone: 315–781–0201. Dating back to 1885, the castle was built with materials from Europe. It is decorated with stained-glass windows, antique porcelain figurines, and other antiques. The grounds are pleasant and extend to the shore of Seneca Lake.

Inlet

Holl's Inn, Inlet, New York 13360. Phone:

315–733–2848 or 357–2941. Holl's Inn is probably the last traditional Adirondack inn in the Fulton Lakes Chain. It has been run with warm hospitality by the Holl family since 1935. People come for vacations in the summer, year after year, often requesting the same room.

Ithaca

Buttermilk Falls Bed & Breakfast, 110 East Buttermilk Falls Road, Ithaca, New York 14850. Phone: 607–275–3947 or 272–6767. The Rumsey family has lived in this house for five generations. You can hike beside the falls up to Pinnacle Rock; it's all within hearing distance of the house.

Rose Inn, 813 Auburn Road, Route 34, P.O. Box 6576, Ithaca, New York 14851. Phone: 607–533–7905. In 1809 "The House with the Circular Staircase" was built as a home for Abraham Osmun. The staircase is made of Honduras mahogany. Nine guest rooms with period furniture welcome guests to elegance in a peaceful country setting.

Keene

The Bark Eater, Alstead Mill Road, Keene, New York 12942. Phone: 518–576–2221. At one time a stagecoach stop, the Bark Eater has been welcoming guests since the 1800s. The rooms are furnished with country antiques, and there is a cottage with a sleigh bed. Cross-country skiers and white-water-rafting enthusiasts gather around the fireplaces after a day of exercise.

Lake George

Cedarbrook Motel, Box 2387, Lake Shore Drive, Lake George, New York 12845. Phone: 518–668–2886. Located 1 mile north of Lake George Village, Cedarbrook is a quiet haven for a restful vacation.

Dunham's Bay Lodge, R.R. 1, Box 1179, Lake George, New York 12845. Phone: 518–656–9242. This lodge on the lake attracts swimmers, sailors, and those who want to relax.

Roaring Brook Ranch & Tennis Resort, Luzerne Road, Lake George, New York 12845.

Phone: 518–668–5767. This resort offers tennis, badminton, sauna baths, shuffleboard, pool swimming, riding, archery, basketball, volleyball, table tennis, and hiking.

Tall Pines Motel, P.O. Box 506, Route 9, Lake George, New York 12845. Phone: 518–668–5122. Located minutes from Lake George, the Tall Pines also features a pool on the grounds. The bike trail is across the road, and hiking is delightful in the area.

Lake Placid

Adirondack Loj, Box 867, Lake Placid, New York 12946. Phone: 518–523–3441. The Adirondack Mountain Club operates several lodges in the area, including Adirondack Loj, located 8 miles south of Lake Placid. It is accessible by car.

Interlaken Lodge, 15 Interlaken Avenue, Lake Placid, New York 12946. Phone: 518–523–3180. Eight rooms decorated with Victorian furnishings welcome guests.

Lake Placid Manor, Whiteface Inn Road, Lake Placid, New York 12946. Phone: 518–523–2573. Once an Adirondack camp dating to 1895, the manor is located on the shores of Lake Placid and has views of Whiteface Mountain. Rooms are decorated in typical Adirondack style with birchwood furniture, white spreads, and curtains.

Mirror Lake Inn, 5 Mirror Lake Drive, Lake Placid, New York 12946. Phone: 518–523–2544. In January 1988 a fire destroyed the entire 105-year-old main building, but we are happy to report that the reopening of the inn was held six months later. Some pieces, such as the 1895 grandfather clock and the grand piano, were saved from the fire to grace the new building.

Montauk

Gurney's Inn, Old Montauk Highway, Montauk, New York 11954. Phone: 516–668–2345. The inn dates from 1926, when Carl Fisher began as innkeeper.

Mumford

Genesee Country Inn, 948 George Street, Mumford, New York 14511. Phone: 716–538–2500. An 1880s plaster mill, which later manufactured hubs, handles for hammers, and wheel spokes, became a private residence after the turn of the century. A creek wanders through the property, and you can explore the woods for waterfalls.

New Paltz

The Mohonk Mountain House, Lake Mohonk, New Paltz, New York 12561. Phone: 914–255–1000 or 255–4500. Established in 1869 by the Smiley family, this place offers views of the mountains, cliffs, and crystal-clear lake that draw guests, who then return year after year.

New York

The Algonquin, 59 West 44th Street, New York, New York 10036. Phone: 212–840–6800. Just walk into the lobby and you will want to stay in this inn from the past. As you drink tea, have a cocktail, or eat dinner, you will know that the literary spirits of years ago were there before you. Even Hamlet the cat, who resides under one of the sofas, has style.

Embassy Suites Hotel, 1568 Broadway, New York, New York, 10036. Phone: 800–362–2779, 800–325–9033, or 212–719–1600. This new hotel is located in Times Square above the Palace Theater.

The Essex House, 160 Central Park S., New York, New York, 10019. Phone: 800–NIKKO–US or 212–247–0300. Renovated in 1991. The hotel is located across from Central Park.

Hotel Macklowe, 145 West 44th Street, New York, 10036. Phone: 800–MACKLOWE or 212–768–4400. The hotel is located close to Times Square in the theater district.

Hotel Salisbury, 123 W. 57th St., New York, New York, 10019. Phone: 800–223–0680 or in NY state 800–446–4560 or 212–246–1300. Located opposite Carnagie Hall and Central Park is not far away.

Rihga Royal Hotel, 151 West 54th Street, New York 10019. Phone: 800–937–5454 or 212–307–5000. Opened in 1990, the hotel is conveniently located in Manhattan's business center. The building is architecturally interesting, with its horizontal bay windows set into brick and granite.

Sheraton Manhattan, 52nd Street & Seventh Avenue, New York, New York, 10019. Phone: 212–581–3300. Newly renovated in 1992, the hotel was previously named the Sheraton City Squire.

The Warwick, 65 West 54th Street, New York, New York 10019. Phone: 800–223–4099 or 212–247–2700. This recently renovated building was built by William Randolph Hearst in 1927 for Marion Davies, who had a suite on the twenty-seventh floor. The location is perfect for business or pleasure.

The Wyndham, 42 W. 58th St., New York, New York, 10019. Phone: 212–753–3500. A family-run hotel located near Fifth Avenue and Central Park. It is popular with well-known theatrical performers.

North River

Garnet Hill Lodge, North River, New York 12856. Phone: 518–251–2821. Named for the garnet mine nearby, the lodge was built in 1936 as a residence for miners. Now it attracts skiers in the winter and vacationers who want to enjoy Thirteenth Lake in the summer.

Ogdensburg

Maple Hill Country Inn, Route 37, Riverside Drive, Box 21, Ogdensburg, New York 13669. Phone: 315–393–3961. This Cape Cod house is located in the midst of large maples on a hill overlooking the St. Lawrence River.

Pittsford

Oliver Loud's Inn, Bushnell's Basin, Pittsford, New York 14534. Phone: 716–248–5200. Dating from 1812, the building was moved to its present location on the Erie

Canal in 1986. Oliver Loud was the first innkeeper, beginning in 1813.

Poughkeepsie

Inn at the Falls, 50 Red Oaks Mill Road, Poughkeepsie, New York 12603. Phone: 914–462–5770. Opened in the fall of 1985, this B&B has elegant rooms and suites. There are four-poster beds, armoires, and roll-top desks in the English rooms; black-lacquer furniture in the contemporary rooms; and country-style furnishings in other rooms.

Rhinebeck

Beekman Arms, Route 9, Rhinebeck, New York 12572. Phone: 914–876–7077. Dating from 1766, this hotel claims to be the oldest in America. George Washington did sleep here, as did a number of other leaders from the past. Several other buildings have been added to the Beekman Arms, including the Delamater House just down the street and other rooms in the courtyard.

Rochester

East Avenue Inn, 384 East Avenue, Rochester, New York 14607. Phone: 716–325–5010. This inn is located on elegant East Avenue, where the first families of Rochester built mansions. The downtown area is within walking distance, as are many of the museums.

Strathallan, 550 East Avenue, Rochester, New York 14607. Phone: 716–461–5010. Once an apartment complex, the Strathallan contains suites, kitchens, and balconies.

Woodcliff the Lodge, Box 22850, Rochester, New York 14692. Phone: 800–365–3065 or 716–381–4000. Woodcliff is set on top of a hill with views of the Bristol Hills. The Sports and Golf Club offers tennis, fitness, swimming, and golf.

Round Top

Winter Clove Inn, Round Top, New York 12473. Phone: 518–622–3267. Five generations of the same family have been welcoming guests since 1850 to this peaceful mountain setting.

The American Hotel, Main Street, Sag Harbor, New York 11963. Phone: 516–725–3535. Built in 1846, the hotel is located in the middle of Sag Harbor, so you can walk wherever you want to explore.

Sag Harbor

The Point, Saranac Lake, New York 12983. Phone: 800–255–3530 or 518–891–5678. Once the camp of William Rockefeller, this inn has a 30-foot living room with stone fireplaces at each end. Nine guest rooms all have private baths, and some have fireplaces and terraces.

Saranac Lake

The Adelphi Hotel, 365 Broadway, Saratoga Springs, New York 12866. Phone: 518–587–4688. Built in 1877, the Adelphi was part of the social life of the summer season in Saratoga. Victorian furnishings enhance the rooms' high ceilings and windows.

Saratoga Springs

Ram's Head Inn, Box 638, Shelter Island Heights, New York 11965. Phone: 516–749–0811. Located on Coecles Harbor, the inn provides varied craft, including sailboats, a paddle boat, and a kayak. Guests can also arrive in their own boats.

Shelter Island Heights

The Sherwood Inn, 26 West Genesee Street, Skaneateles, New York 13152. Phone: 315–685–3405. Built in 1807 as a tavern, the building became an inn sometime later. The fifteen guest rooms are fitted with period furnishings from the early nineteenth century through the Victorian age.

Skaneateles

The Lakehouse, Shelley Hill Road, Stanfordville, New York 12581. Phone: 914–266–8093. This getaway retreat for special occasions is located in the woods on a lake. Each room is decorated with antiques, four-poster beds, and Jacuzzi tubs.

Stanfordville

Merrill Magee House, Warrensburg, New York 12885. Phone: 518–623–2449. This nine-

Warrensburg

teenth-century Greek Revival house has a new guest house composed of ten elegant rooms with fireplaces. Peek into the ladies' room for a surprise in the bathtub.

PENNSYLVANIA

Bethlehem

Hotel Bethlehem, 437 Main Street, Bethlehem, Pennsylvania 18018. Phone: 215–867–3711. Located right in the center of town, within walking distance of the Moravian historical sites.

Canadensis

The Overlook Inn, RD1, Box 680A, Dutch Hill Road, Canadensis, Pennsylvania 18325. Phone: 717–595–7519. The twelve guest rooms have been remodeled and decorated with prints, plants, and country crafts. More rooms are available in the Carriage House and the Lodge.

The Pine Knob, Box 295, Route 447, Canadensis, Pennsylvania 18325. Phone: 800–426–1460 or 717–595–2532. This pre–Civil War inn features antique furnishings, lots of books to read, and a grand piano in the living room.

Champion

Seven Springs Mountain Resort, Champion, Pennsylvania 15622. Phone: 814–352–7777. Helen and Adolph Dupre built their first home in 1932; it is now one of the restaurants on the property. The Dupres built many log cabins, and now the resort also includes a large hotel.

Cresco

Crescent Lodge Country Inn, Paradise Valley, Cresco, Pennsylvania 18326. Phone: 800–392–9400 or 717–595–7486. Family-run for forty years, the inn has a new building that has increased the estate into a circle of accommodations on the grounds.

Carbondale

Fern Hall, RD1, Box 1095, Crystal Lake, Carbondale, Pennsylvania 18407. Phone: 717–222–3676. The house was built in 1916 by one of the founders of Johnson & Johnson

Pharmaceutical Company. It is located on Crystal Lake and has gardens and a lawn.

Ephrata

Historic Smithton, a Bed & Breakfast Country Inn, 900 West Main Street, Ephrata, Pennsylvania 17522. Phone: 717–733–6094. Each bedroom in this inn has its own fireplace and a sitting area with comfortable chairs, reading lamps, and a writing desk.

Erwinna

The Golden Pheasant Inn, River Road, Erwinna, Pennsylvania 18920. Phone: 215–294–9595. Built in 1857 for bargemen on the canal, the inn now offers fourteen guest rooms. There are two Victorian dining rooms and a greenhouse dining area.

Greensburg

Mountain View Inn, 1001 Village Drive, Mountain View Village, Greensburg, Pennsylvania 15601. Phone: 412–834–5300. The Mountain View truly does have a wonderful view that guests can enjoy from the large windows in the dining rooms as well as from the porches. There are antiques around every corner, including a life-size little girl doll and a baby doll in a lovely old cradle.

Kennett Square

Longwood Inn, 815 East Baltimore Pike, Kennett Square, Pennsylvania 19348. Phone: 215–444–3515. The family-owned and -operated inn is located near Longwood Gardens.

Lewisburg

The Lewisburg Hotel, 136 Market Street, Lewisburg, Pennsylvania 17837. Phone: 717–523–1216. The hotel is 150 years old but has recently been renovated. Walt Whitman once stayed there.

The Pineapple Inn, 439 Market Street, Lewisburg, Pennsylvania 17837. Phone: 717–524–6200. This Federal-style house was built in 1857 by the architect Louis Palmer.

Lititz

General Sutter Inn, 14 East Main Street, Lititz, Pennsylvania 17543. Phone:

717–626–2115. The inn was founded in 1764 by the Moravian church. John Augustus Sutter arrived in Lititz to find a cure for his arthritis, and the inn was then named for him. Twelve bedrooms are furnished with country antiques and Victorian pieces.

Lumberville

Black Bass Hotel, Route 32, Lumberville, Pennsylvania 18933. Phone: 215–297–5815. The hotel was built in the 1740s for traders and traveling businessmen; in the 1830s it was popular with passengers on canal boats. Anglophiles will enjoy this chance to see the most extensive collection of royal commemorative pieces in the country. The hotel is right on the river, and some of the rooms have terraces overlooking the water.

Mercersburg

The Mercersburg Inn, 405 South Main Street, Mercersburg, Pennsylvania 17236. Phone: 717–328–5231. Built as a residence in 1910, this mansion contains a handsome marble stairway and mahogany paneling. Antiques include four-poster beds with canopies. A forty-three–bell carillon, on the grounds of Mercersburg Academy, is a treat to hear.

Mount Joy

Cameron Estate, RD1, Box 305, Mount Joy, Pennsylvania 17552. Phone: 717–653–1773. Built in 1805 by Dr. John Watson, this inn later became the home of Simon Cameron, Lincoln's first secretary of war. Bedrooms are filled with period furnishings, oriental rugs, and quilts, and some have fireplaces.

New Hope

Centre Bridge Inn, Box 74, New Hope, Pennsylvania 18938. Phone: 215–862–2048 or 862–9139. The nine guest rooms contain colonial furnishings, and some have four-poster beds. River views are abundant, and you can watch the ducks just a foot from the terrace.

Hotel du Village, corner of North River Road and Phillips Mill Road, New Hope, Pennsylvania 18938. Phone: 215–862–9911 or

862–5164. Located on part of a tract of land granted to the Ely family of William Penn in the seventeenth century, the inn has also been a country residence and a school.

The Inn at Phillips Mill, North River Road, New Hope, Pennsylvania 18938. Phone: 215–862–2984. Originally a stone barn built in 1750, the inn has been restored and now offers five bedrooms furnished with antiques, quilts on four-poster beds, and dried-flower bouquets.

Pineapple Hill, 1324 River Road, New Hope, Pennsylvania 18938. Phone: 215–862–9608. The pineapple motif represents hospitality, and this 1780 house certainly offers a welcome. Six bedrooms are furnished in country style with brass, spool, or rope beds, quilts, folk art, and antiques. The ruins of a stone barn have been preserved to frame the swimming pool.

The Wedgwood Inn, 111 West Bridge Street, New Hope, Pennsylvania 18938. Phone: 215–862–2570. Built in 1870 over the ruins of an earlier structure where General Alexander Lord Stirling encamped in December 1776, the inn offers rooms in the house and newly renovated rooms in an adjacent house. As you might imagine, Wedgwood pieces are displayed throughout the inn.

Newton Square

Fifer's Folly, 3561 North Providence Road, Newton Square, Pennsylvania 19073. Phone: 215–353–3366. A 1715 pre-Revolutionary Quaker farmhouse, located next to Ridley Creek State Park, is now a B&B. The house is filled with historical memorabilia.

Orrtanna

Hickory Bridge Farm, Orrtanna, Pennsylvania 17353. Phone: 717–642–5261. Located in the foothills of the Appalachian Mountains, the farm has rooms in the farmhouse and cottages in the woods on the bank of a stream. The farm is in a good location for touring Gettysburg.

Philadelphia

Society Hill Hotel, 301 Chestnut Street, Philadelphia, Pennsylvania 19106. Phone: 215-925-1394. Originally built as an oyster house in 1832 and then pressed into duty as a recruiting station during the Civil War, Society Hill became an inn in the early 1900s. Twelve rooms feature brass beds and fresh flowers. The hotel is located in the middle of the historic district.

The Independence Park Inn, 236 Chestnut Street, Philadelphia, Pennsylvania 19106. Phone: 800-624-2988. A mid-nineteenth century Victorian inn with beautiful cherry and rosewood lobby.

Penn's View Inn, Front & Market streets, Philadelphia, Pennsylvania 19106. Phone: 800-331-7634 or in Pennsylvania 215-922-7600. This inn is located in a restored warehouse right on Front Street.

Pittsburgh

Westin William Penn Hotel, William Penn Place, Pittsburgh, Pennsylvania 15230. Phone: 800-228-3000 or 412-281-7100. The lobby is positively dazzling; its arches, mirrors, crystal chandeliers, and ornate ceiling were copied from the Château of Fontainebleau.

Scranton

Royce Hotel–Lackawanna Station, 700 Lackawanna Avenue, Scranton, Pennsylvania 18503. Phone: 800-23-ROYCE or 717-342-8300. The hotel is inside the 1908 railroad station; it is on the National Register of Historic Places.

South Sterling

The Sterling Inn, Box 2, South Sterling, Pennsylvania 18460. Phone: 717-676-3311 or 800-523-8200 from Connecticut, New York, New Jersey, Maryland, Delaware, and Washington, D.C. The living room is filled with comfortable sofas, chairs, and lots of books, and the ambience encourages conversation with new friends before dinner.

Uniondale

Wiffy Bog Farm B&B, Box 83, West Clifford, RD1, Uniondale, Pennsylvania 18470.

Phone: 717–222–9865. This Victorian home is furnished with family heirlooms and antiques. There's also a pond for canoeing and fishing.

Adams Inn, 1744 Lanier Place, N.W., Washington, D.C. 20009. Phone: 202–745–3600. A turn-of-the-century town house offering bed-and-breakfast.

Guest Quarters Suite Hotel, 2500 Pennsylvania Avenue, N.W., Washington, D.C. 20037. Phone: 800–424–2900 or 202–333–8060. This hotel is within walking distance of the White House. Bring your family and cook your dinners in your own kitchen after days of sightseeing trips. A similar hotel is located at 801 New Hampshire Avenue, N.W., Washington, D.C. 20037; phone: 202–785–2000.

Hay-Adams Hotel, One Lafayette Square, N.W., Washington, D.C. 20006. Phone: 800–424–5054 or 202–638–6600. The hotel was built in 1927 in Italian Renaissance style. Beautiful antiques, gold leaf, and seventeenth-century Medici tapestry enhance the interior. The view of the White House from some of the rooms is magnificent.

Hotel Washington, Pennsylvania Avenue, N.W. at 15th Street, Washington, D.C. 20004. Phone: 202–638–5900. The White House is only a block away, and the mall is within easy reach. You can stroll through the Smithsonian and come home to put your feet up.

Kalorama Guest House, 1854 Mintwood Place, N.W., Washington, D.C. 20009. Phone: 202–667–6369. This is a Victorian house dating from 1880 and decorated with period furnishings and artwork. The six guest rooms have brass headboards, comforters, and oriental rugs.

Morrison-Clark, Massachusetts Avenue and Eleventh Street, N.W., Washington, D.C. 20001. Phone: 800–332–7898 or 202–898–1200. Within

WASHINGTON, D.C.

the hotel is an 1876 mansion; additions have taken place that keep the original feeling of a turn-of-the-century Victorian home.

Vista International Hotel, 1400 M Street, N.W., Washington, D.C. 20005. Phone: 202–420–1700. This new hotel contains a spectacular, fourteen-story, glass-canopied atrium lobby. You can meet friends under the clock here, as in New York.

VIRGINIA

Chincoteague

Driftwood Motor Lodge, Beach Road, Box 575, Chincoteague, Virginia 23336. Phone: 804–336–6557. Overlooks Chincoteague Wildlife Refuge.

Island Belle Motor Lodge, Beach Road, Box 585, Chincoteague, Virginia 23336. Phone: 804–336–3600. New in 1991, the lodge is not far from the Chincoteague Wildlife Refuge.

Refuge Motor Inn, Box 378, Chincoteague, Virginia 23336. Phone: 800–544–8469 or 804–336–5511. The motor inn is located just across the bridge from Chincoteague Wildlife Refuge.

Williamsburg

Colonial Williamsburg Hotels, Williamsburg, Virginia 23187–1776. Phone: 800–HISTORY. Colonial Williamsburg properties include The Williamsburg Inn, Providence Hall, Colonial Houses & Taverns, Williamsburg Lodge, Williamsburg Woodlands, and Governor's Inn. Guests will find great variety from which to choose. All are within the Historic Area, or just outside it, and some are right on Duke of Gloucester Street.

Kingsmill Resort, 1010 Kingsmill Road, Williamsburg, Virginia 23185. Phone: 800–832–5665 or 804–253–1703. Kingsmill is a community within itself, built on land owned by Richard Kingsmill in 1736. Deer can be seen in the woods, almost undisturbed by walkers and golfers.

Index to Attractions and Restaurants